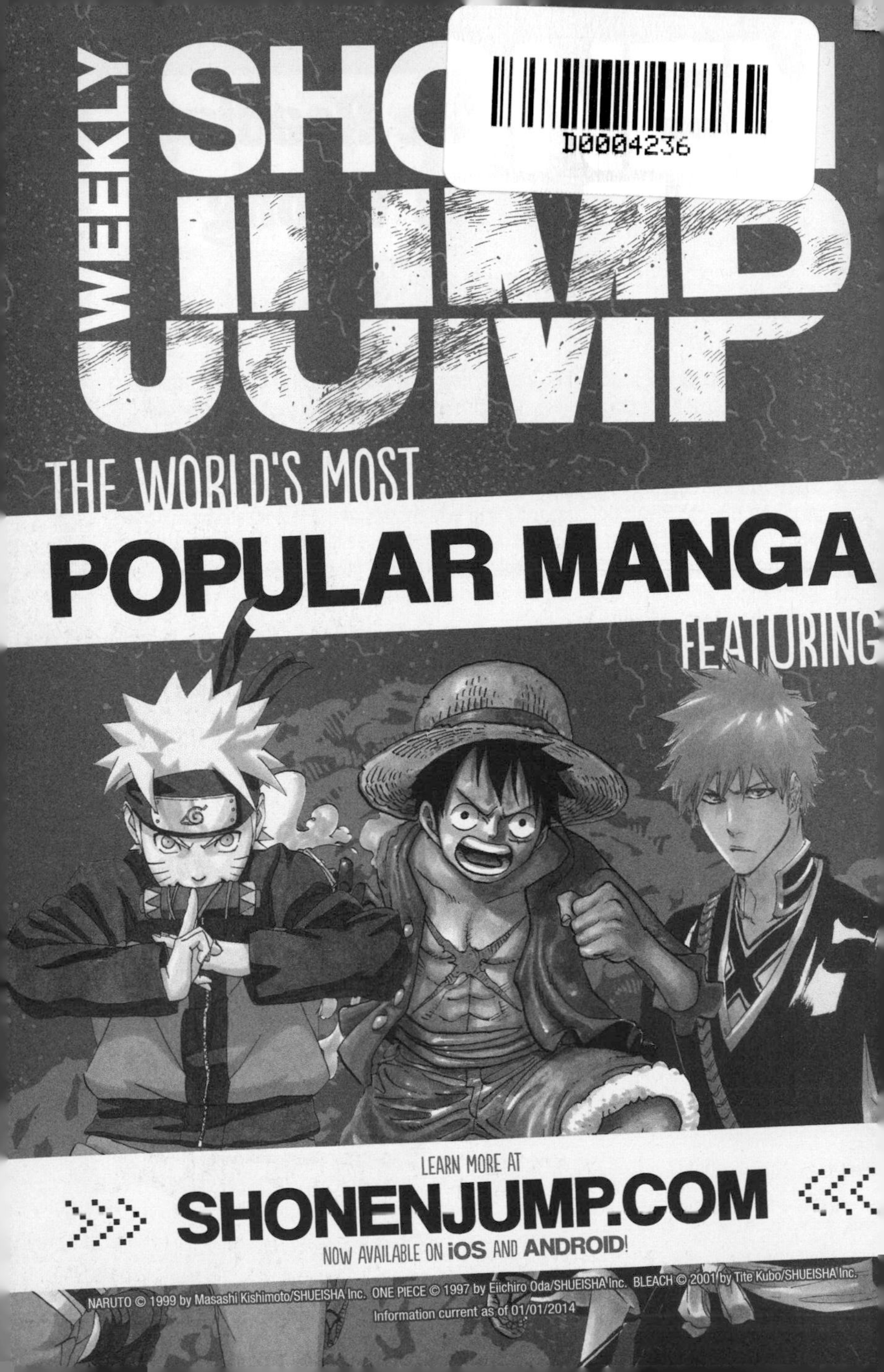
WEEKLY
JUMP
THE WORLD'S MOST
POPULAR MANGA
FEATURING
LEARN MORE AT
SHONENJUMP.COM
NOW AVAILABLE ON iOS AND ANDROID!
NARUTO © 1999 by Masashi Kishimoto/SHUEISHA Inc. ONE PIECE © 1997 by Eiichiro Oda/SHUEISHA Inc. BLEACH © 2001 by Tite Kubo/SHUEISHA Inc.
Information current as of 01/01/2014

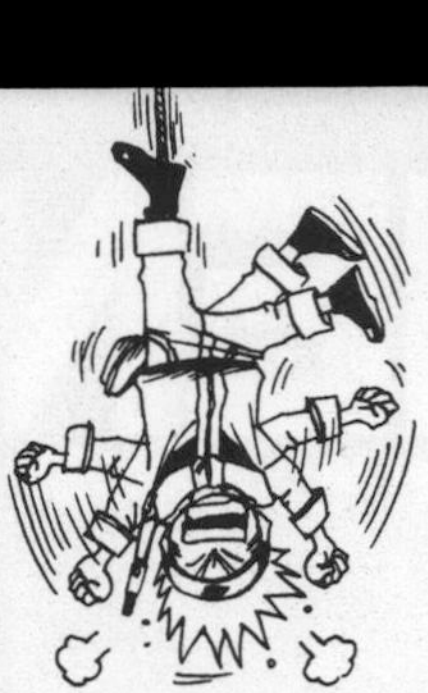

You'r
in the
Direction!!

Whoops! Guess what? You're starting at the wrong end of the comic!

...It's true! In keeping with the original Japanese format, **Naruto** is meant to be read from right to left, starting in the upper-right corner.

Unlike English, which is read from left to right, Japanese is read from right to left, meaning that action, sound effects and word-balloon order are completely reversed... something which can make readers unfamiliar with Japanese feel pretty backwards themselves. For this reason, manga or Japanese comics published in the U.S. in English have sometimes been published "flopped"—that is, printed in exact reverse order, as though seen from the other side of a mirror.

By flopping pages, U.S. publishers can avoid confusing readers, but the compromise is not without its downside. For one thing, a character in a flopped manga series who once wore in the original Japanese version a T-shirt emblazoned with "M A Y" (as in "the merry month of") now wears one which reads "Y A M"! Additionally, many manga creators in Japan are themselves unhappy with the process, as some feel the mirror-imaging of their art alters their original intentions.

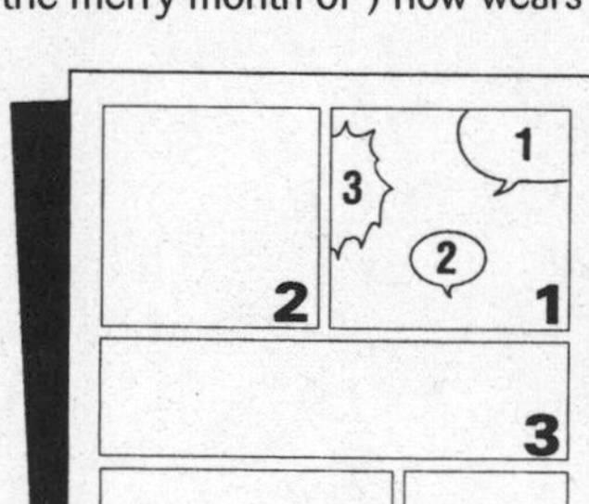
1
2
3
1
2
3
4
5
6

We are proud to bring you Masashi Kishimoto's **Naruto** in the original unflopped format. For now, though, turn to the other side of the book and let the ninjutsu begin...!

—Editor

SHONEN JUMP MANGA EDITION

NARUTO

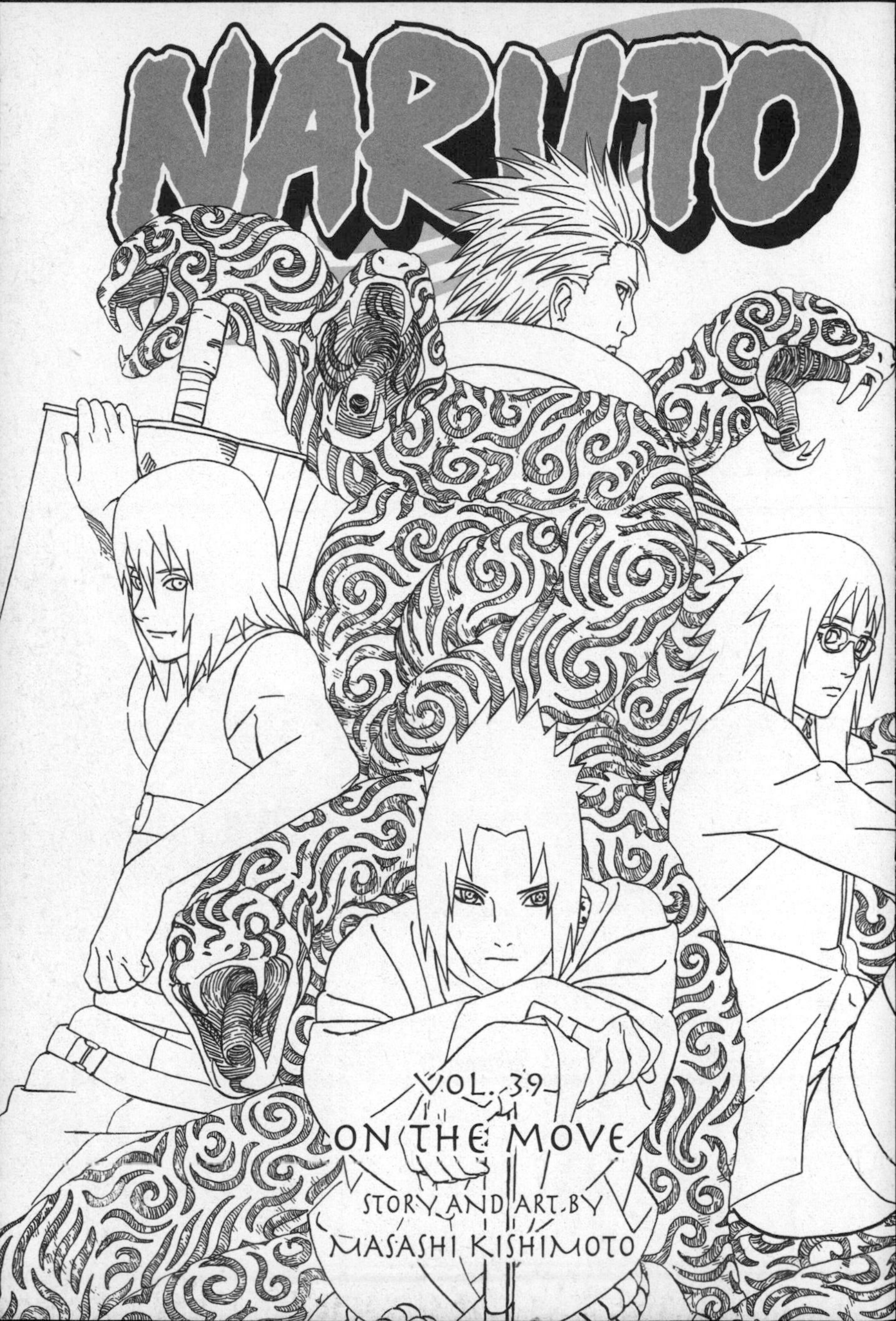

VOL. 39

ON THE MOVE

STORY AND ART BY
MASASHI KISHIMOTO

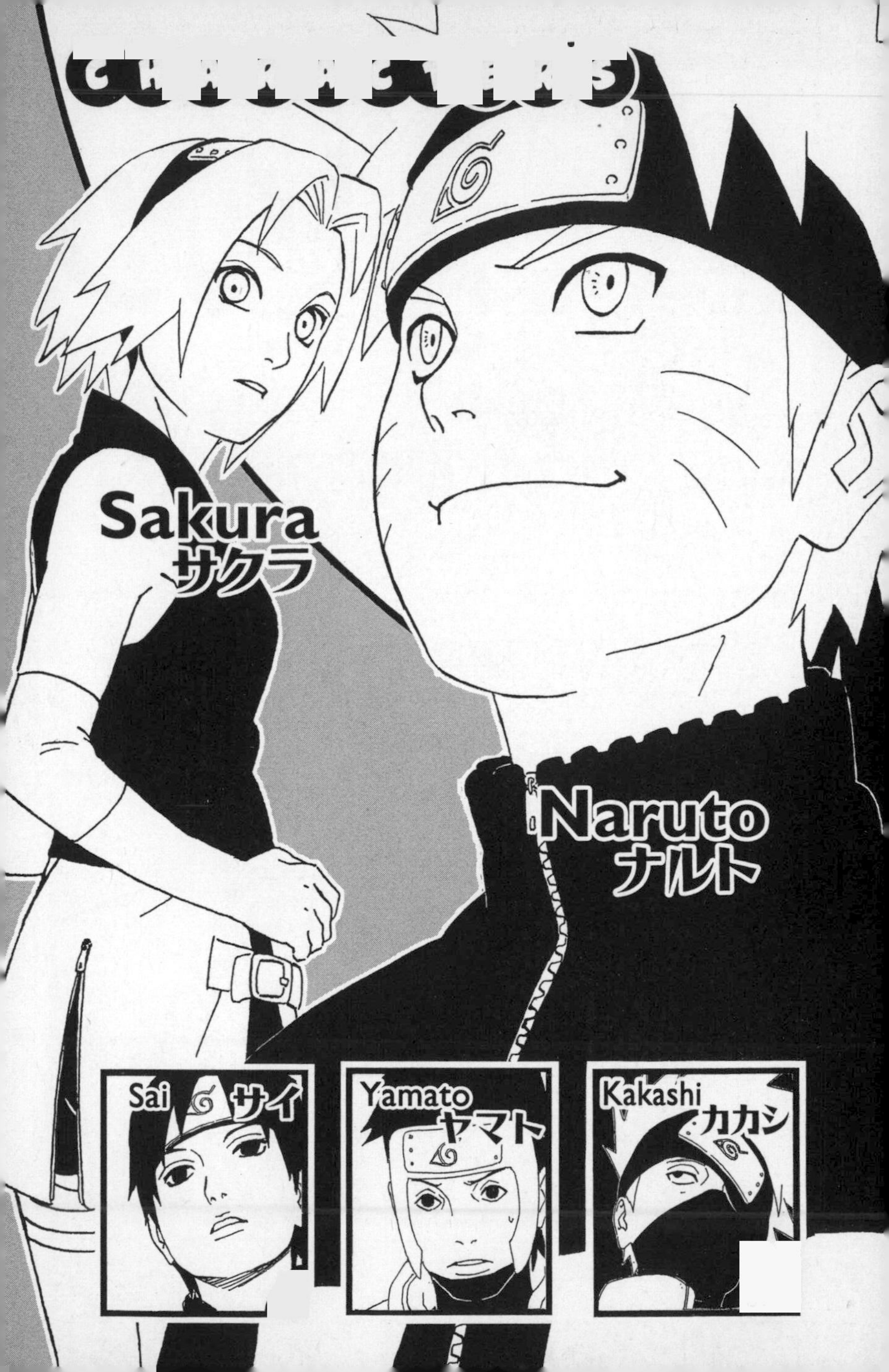
Naruto
ナルト
Sakura
サクラ
Kakashi
カカシ
Yamato
ヤマト
Sai
サイ

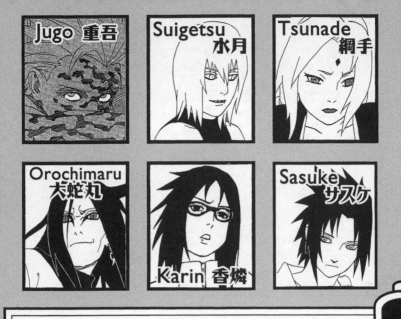

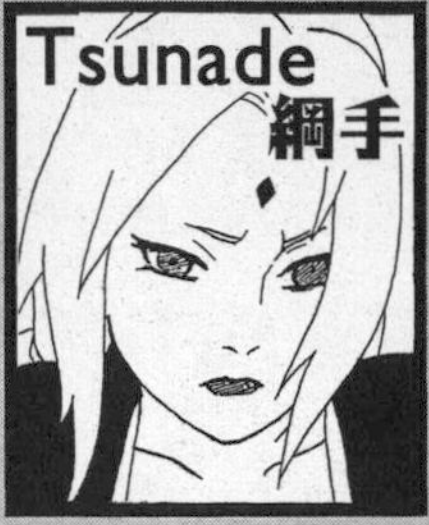
Tsunade
綱手
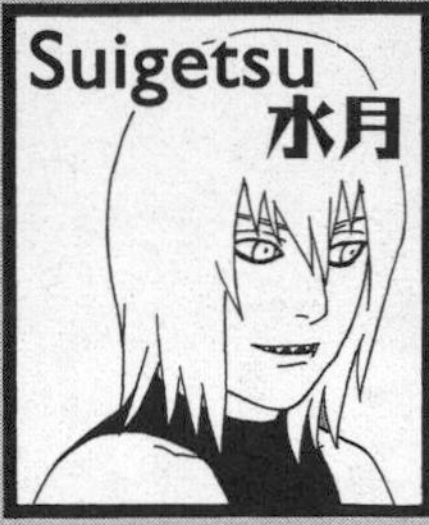
Suigetsu
水月
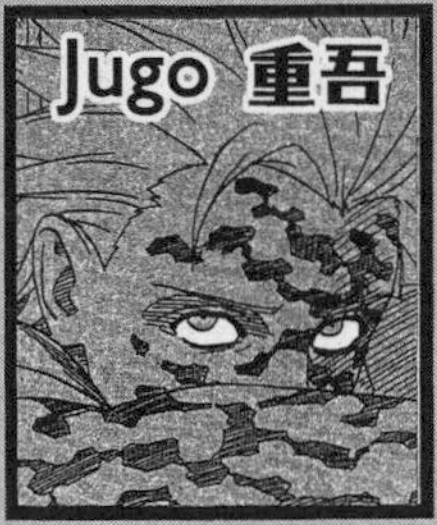
Jugo 重吾
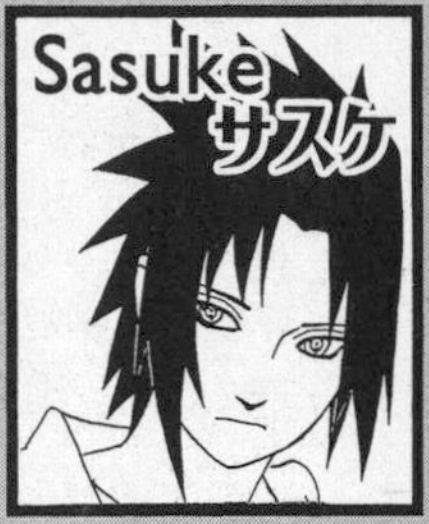
Sasuke
サスケ
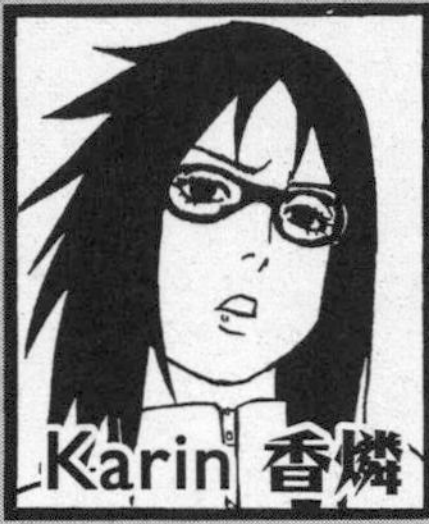
Karin 香燐
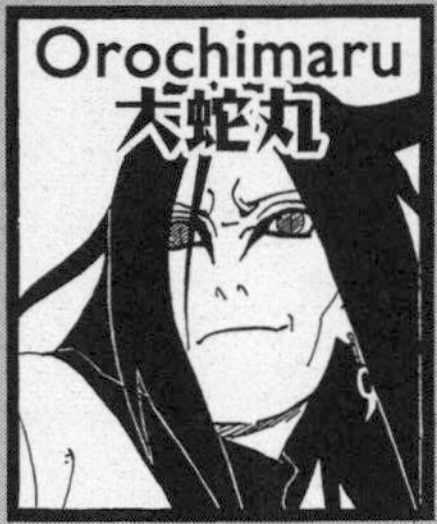
Orochimaru
大蛇丸

The Story So Far…

Once the bane of the Konohagakure Ninja Academy, Uzumaki Naruto now serves dutifully among the ranks of the Konoha shinobi—an illustrious group of ninja sworn to protect their village from the forces of evil seeking to destroy it from without and within…

While the threat of the criminal organization known as the Akatsuki looms ever-present, Naruto's former classmates—Shikamaru, Choji and Ino—embark on a mission to find Captain Asuma's killer. And when their quest brings them into conflict with Kakuzu—one of the Akatsuki's deadliest members—it's Naruto who takes the enemy down with a display of power that rivals even the Fourth Hokage himself!

Meanwhile, Uchiha Sasuke continues down the dark path he set out upon when he joined Lord Orochimaru, one of Konoha's greatest foes. Convinced he's learned all he can from his dark master, Sasuke betrays and kills Orochimaru. With one of his goals accomplished, he begins assembling a team of powerful allies in order to achieve his ultimate goal—the destruction of his brother, Uchiha Itachi! Having enlisted the swordsman Suigetsu and the tracker Karin, there remains but one last person for him to recruit…

NARUTO

VOL. 39
ON THE MOVE

CONTENTS

NARUTO

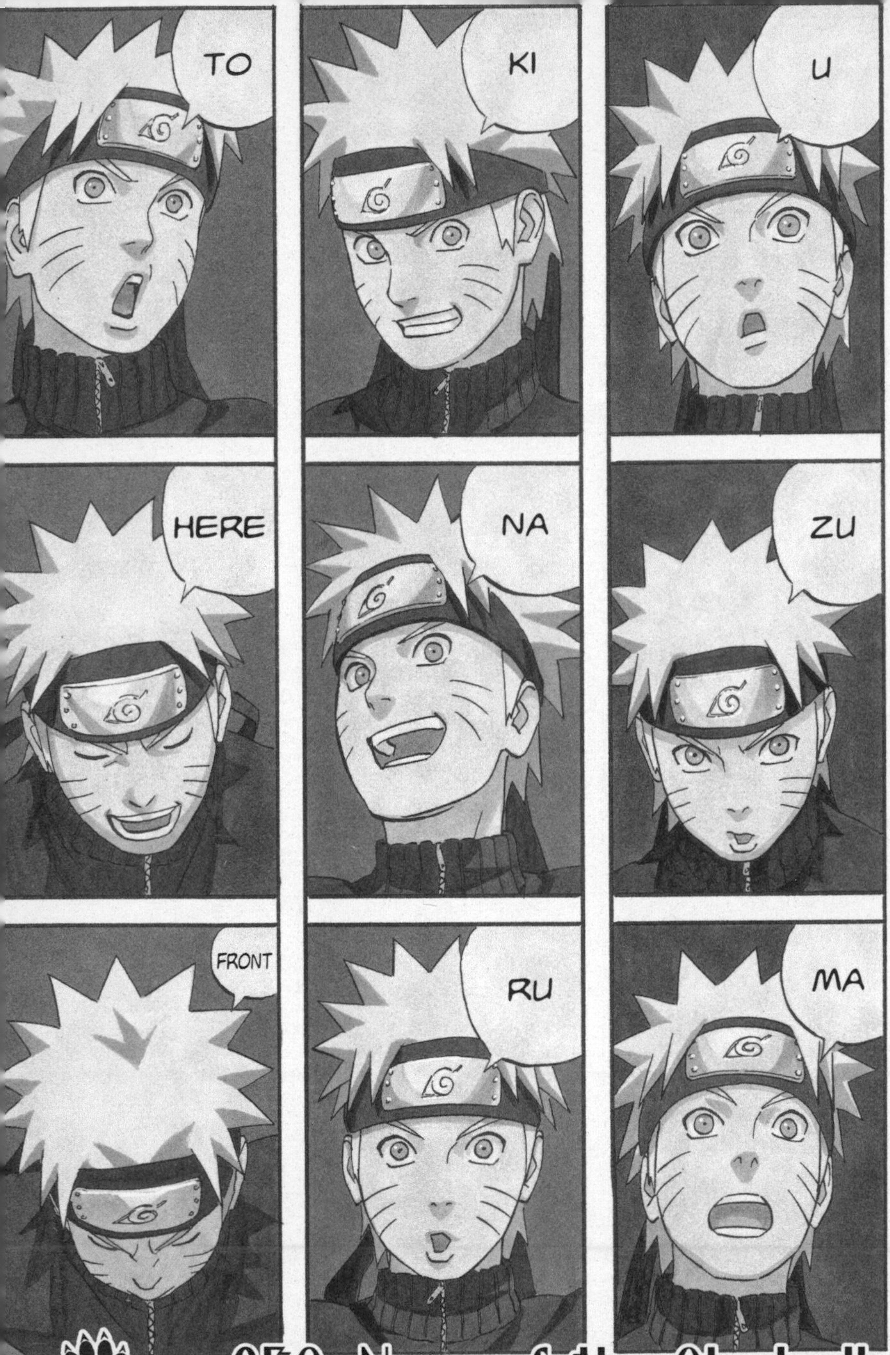
U
KI
TO
ZU
NA
HERE
MA
RU
FRONT

Number 350: News of the Clash...!!

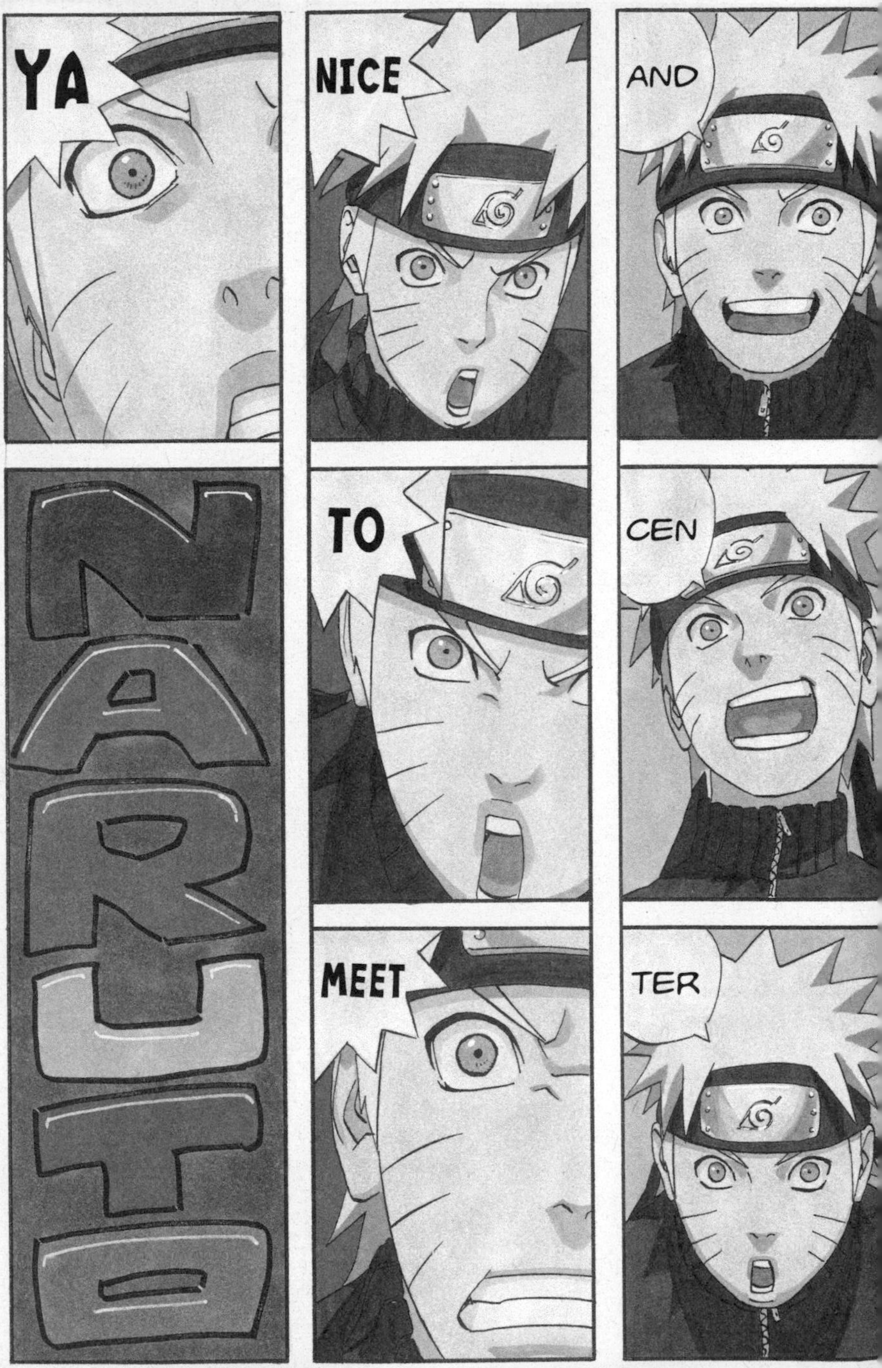
AND
CEN
TER
NICE
TO
MEET
YA
NARUTO

NARUTO

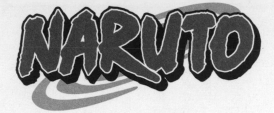

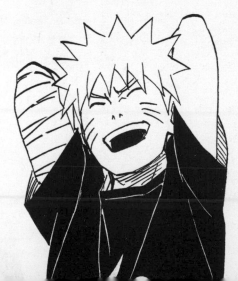

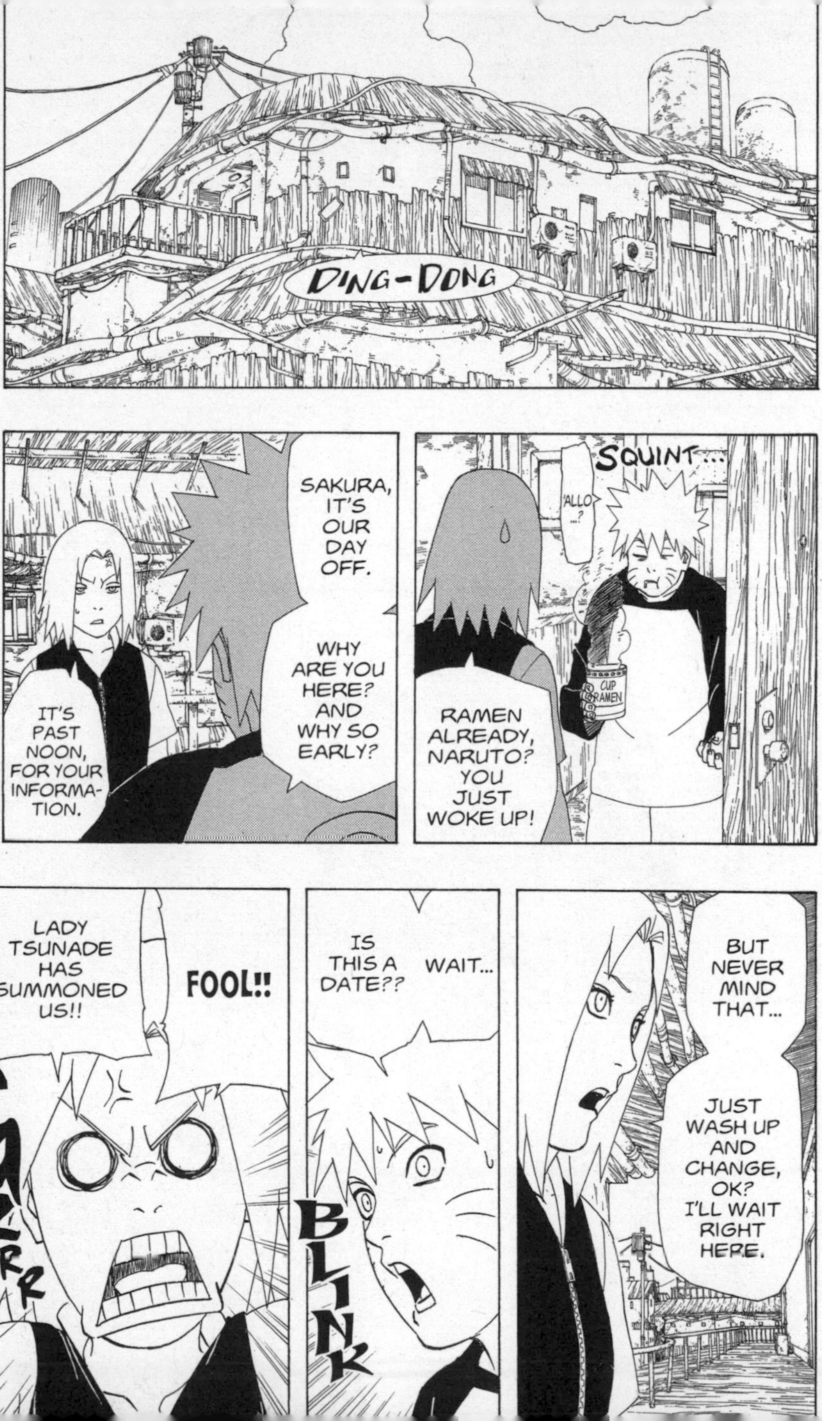
DING-DONG
SQUINT...
'ALLO ...?
RAMEN ALREADY, NARUTO? YOU JUST WOKE UP!
SAKURA, IT'S OUR DAY OFF.
WHY ARE YOU HERE? AND WHY SO EARLY?
IT'S PAST NOON, FOR YOUR INFORMATION.
BUT NEVER MIND THAT...
JUST WASH UP AND CHANGE, OK? I'LL WAIT RIGHT HERE.
WAIT...
IS THIS A DATE??
BLINK
FOOL!!
LADY TSUNADE HAS SUMMONED US!!
GRRR

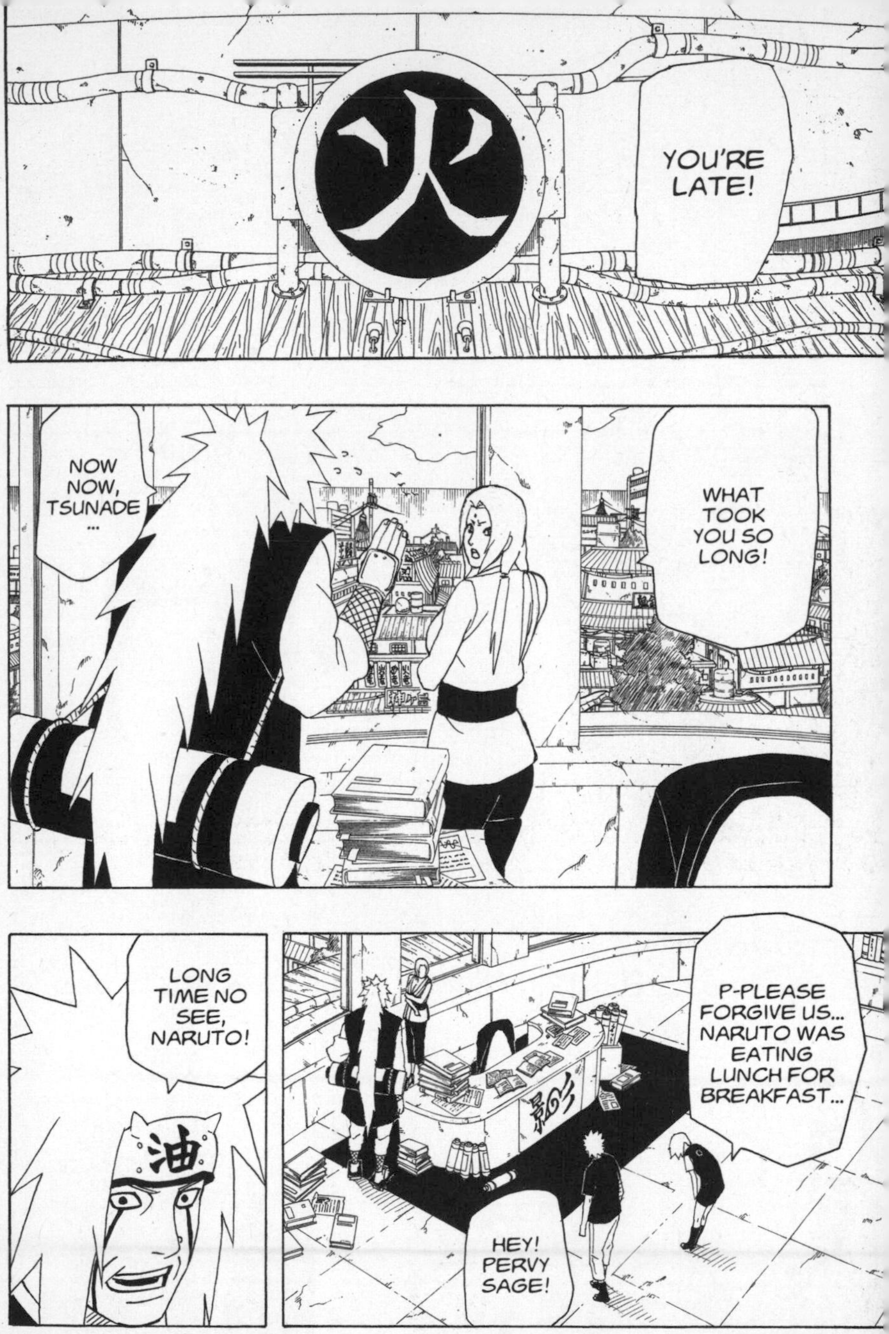
YOU'RE LATE!
WHAT TOOK YOU SO LONG!
NOW NOW, TSUNADE ...
P-PLEASE FORGIVE US... NARUTO WAS EATING LUNCH FOR BREAKFAST...
HEY! PERVY SAGE!
LONG TIME NO SEE, NARUTO!

READ THIS WAY

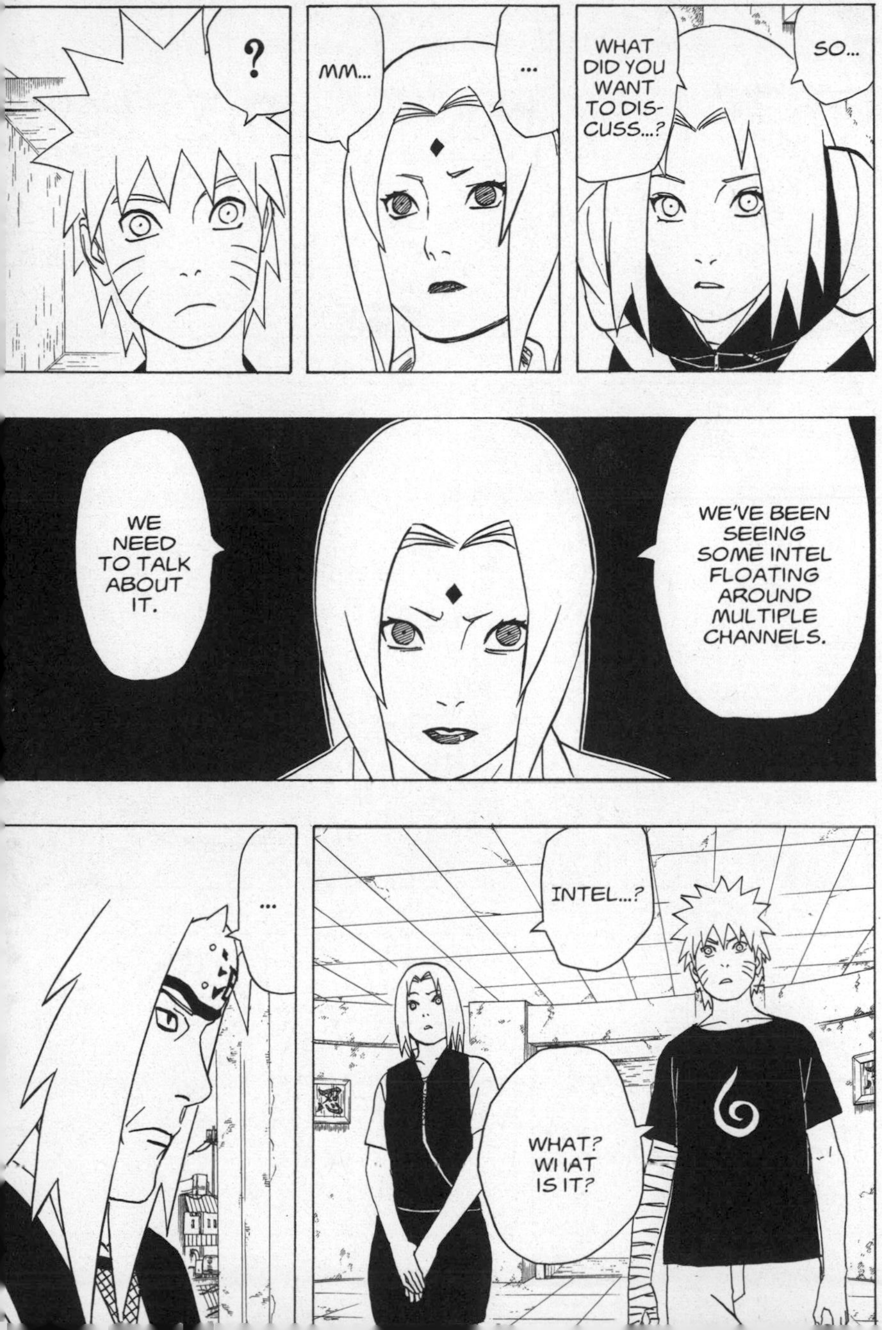
SO...
WHAT DID YOU WANT TO DISCUSS...?
...
MM...
?
WE'VE BEEN SEEING SOME INTEL FLOATING AROUND MULTIPLE CHANNELS.
WE NEED TO TALK ABOUT IT.
INTEL...?
WHAT? WHAT IS IT?
...

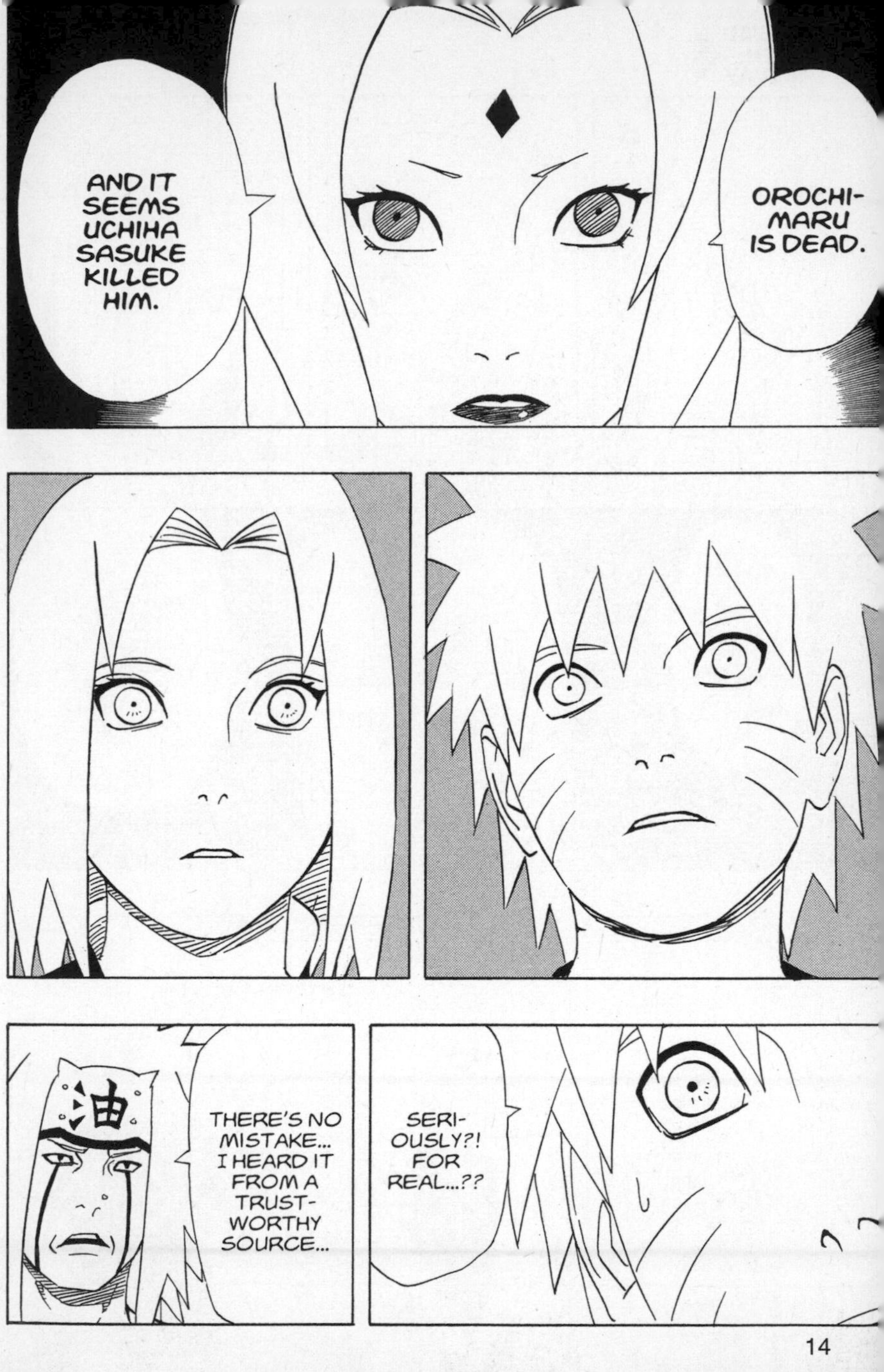
OROCHIMARU IS DEAD.
AND IT SEEMS UCHIHA SASUKE KILLED HIM.
SERIOUSLY?! FOR REAL...??
THERE'S NO MISTAKE... I HEARD IT FROM A TRUSTWORTHY SOURCE...
油

READ THIS WAY

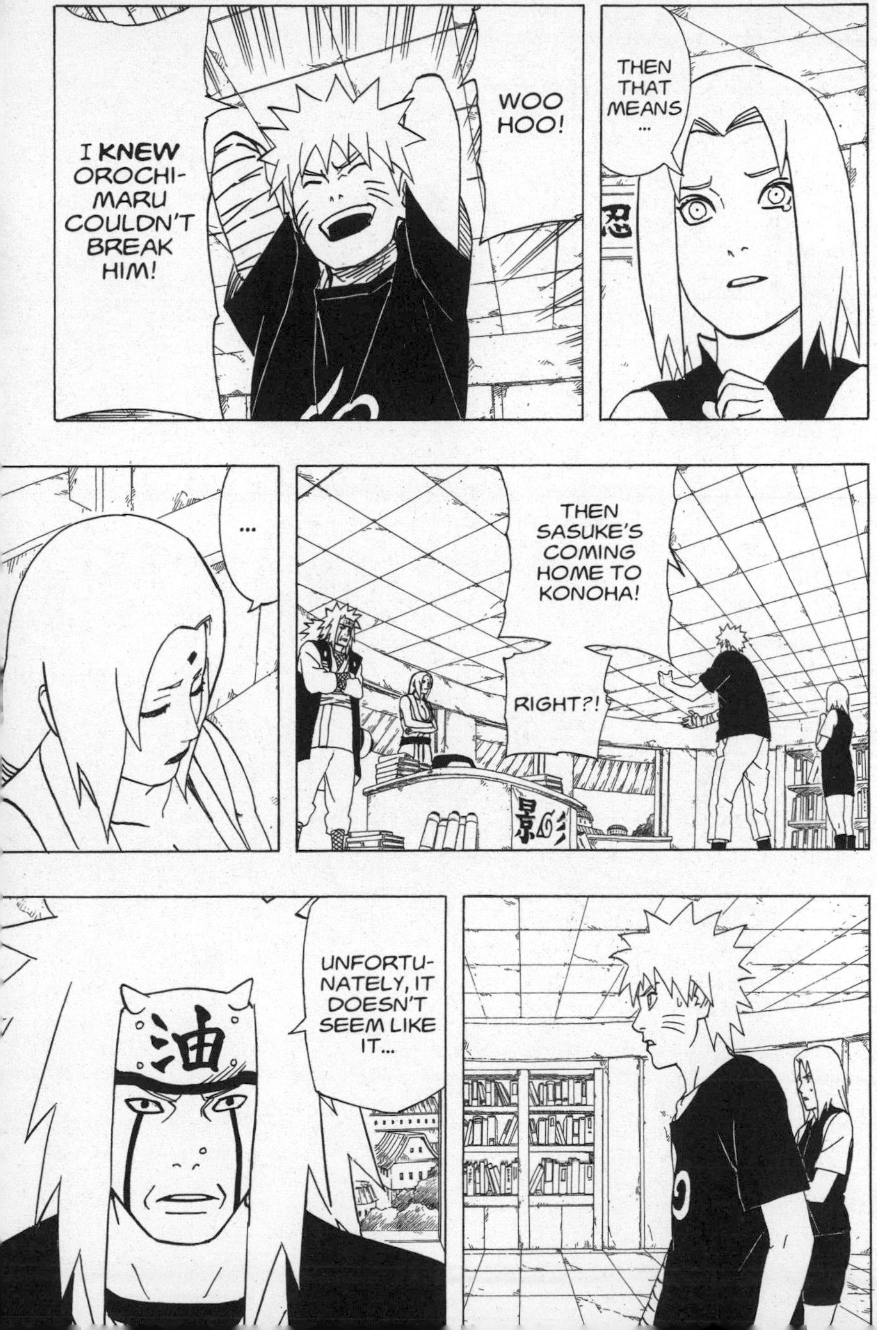
THEN THAT MEANS ...
忍
WOO HOO!
I KNEW OROCHIMARU COULDN'T BREAK HIM!
THEN SASUKE'S COMING HOME TO KONOHA!
RIGHT?!
影
...
UNFORTUNATELY, IT DOESN'T SEEM LIKE IT...
油

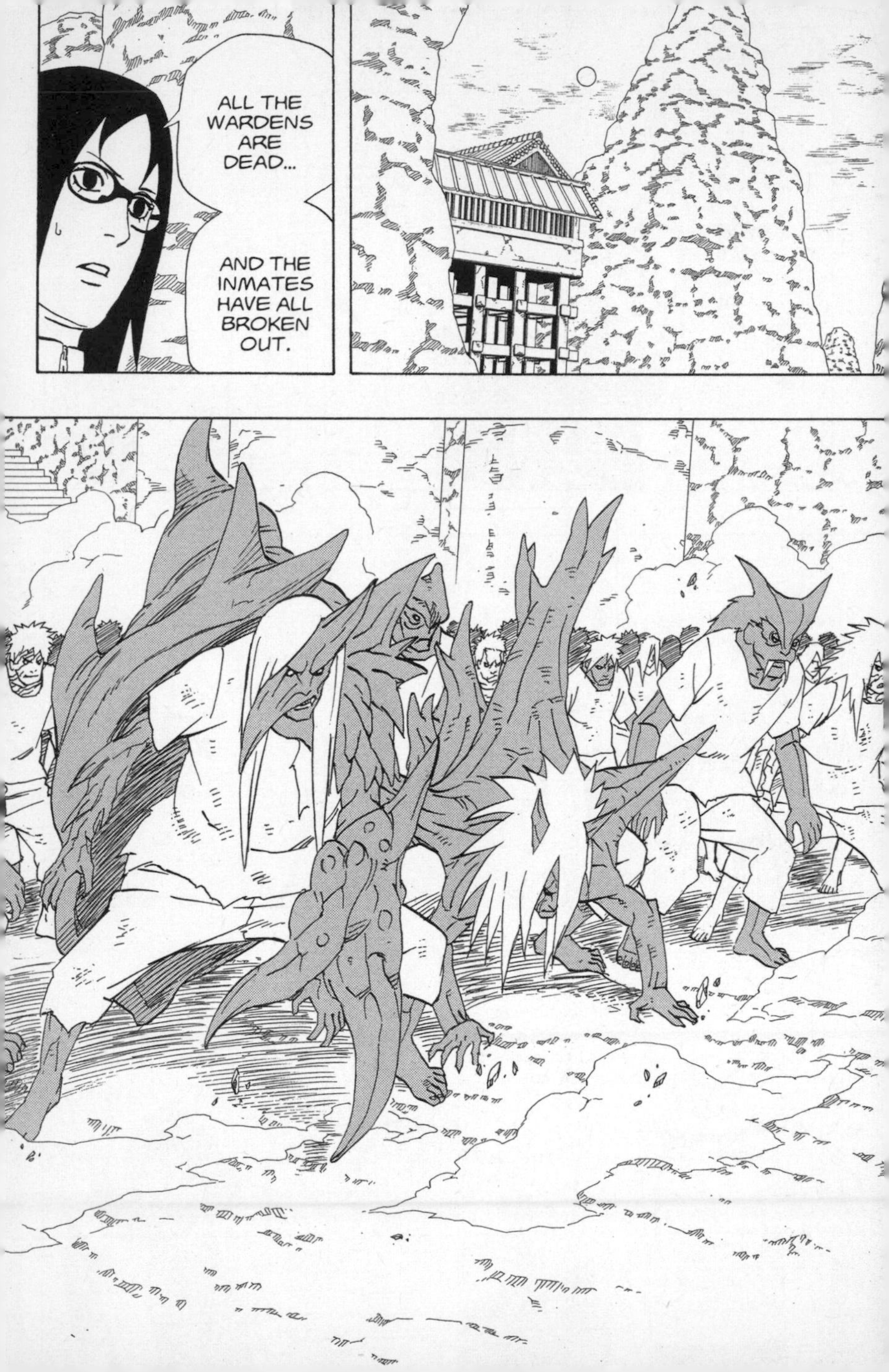
ALL THE WARDENS ARE DEAD...
AND THE INMATES HAVE ALL BROKEN OUT.

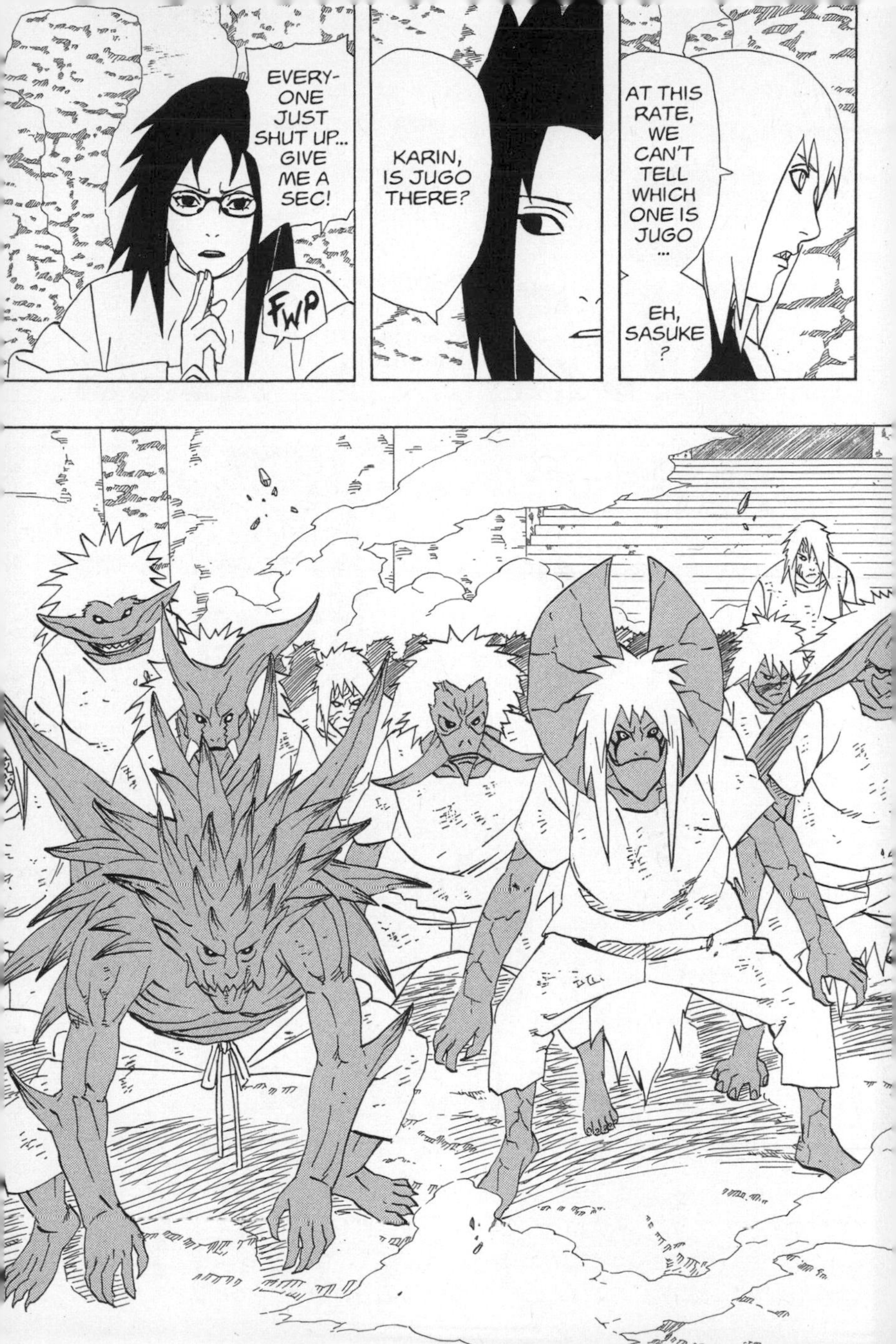
AT THIS RATE, WE CAN'T TELL WHICH ONE IS JUGO...
EH, SASUKE?
KARIN, IS JUGO THERE?
EVERY-ONE JUST SHUT UP... GIVE ME A SEC!
FWP

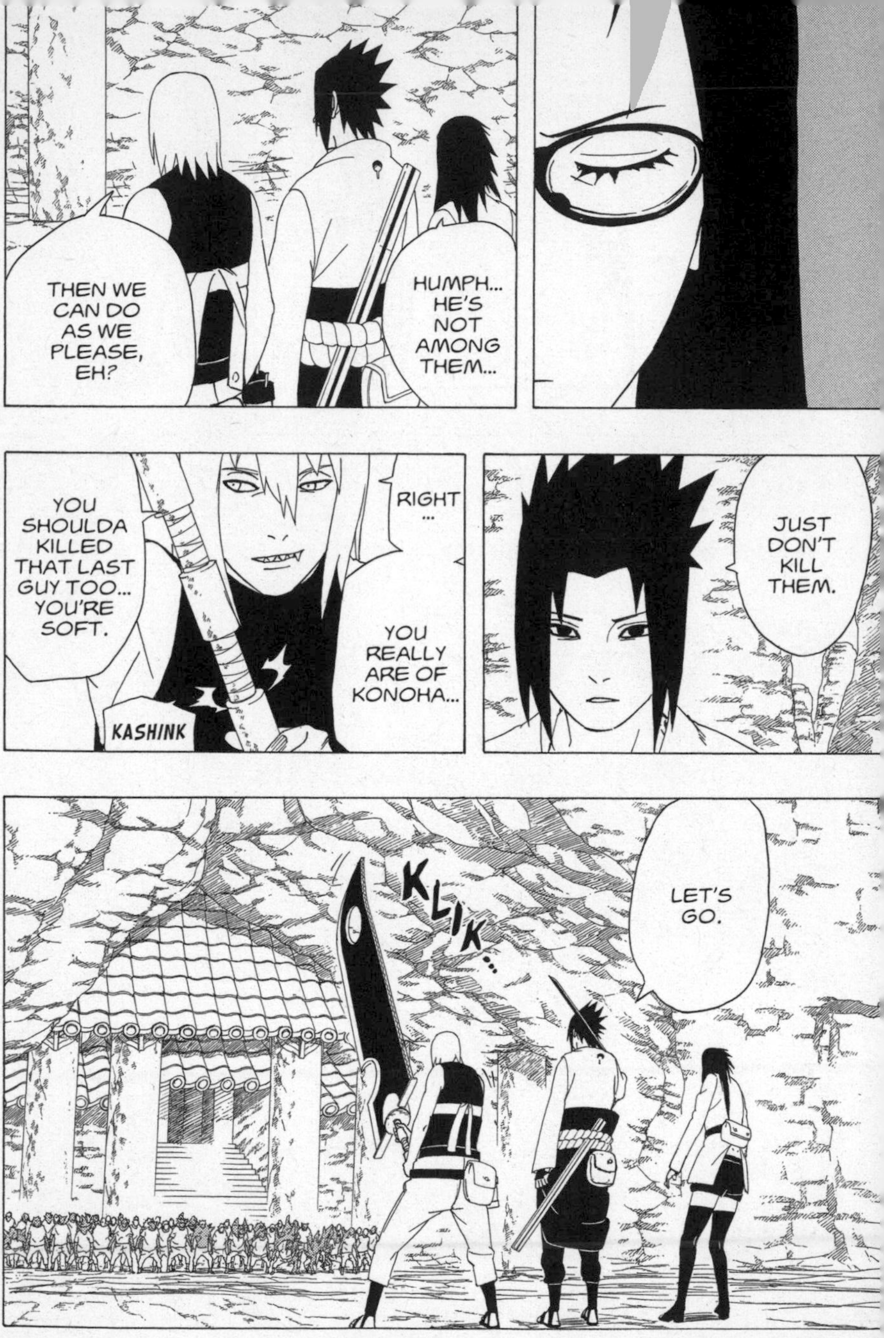
HUMPH... HE'S NOT AMONG THEM...
THEN WE CAN DO AS WE PLEASE, EH?
JUST DON'T KILL THEM.
RIGHT ...
YOU REALLY ARE OF KONOHA...
YOU SHOULDA KILLED THAT LAST GUY TOO... YOU'RE SOFT.
KASHINK
KLIK...
LET'S GO.

READ THIS WAY

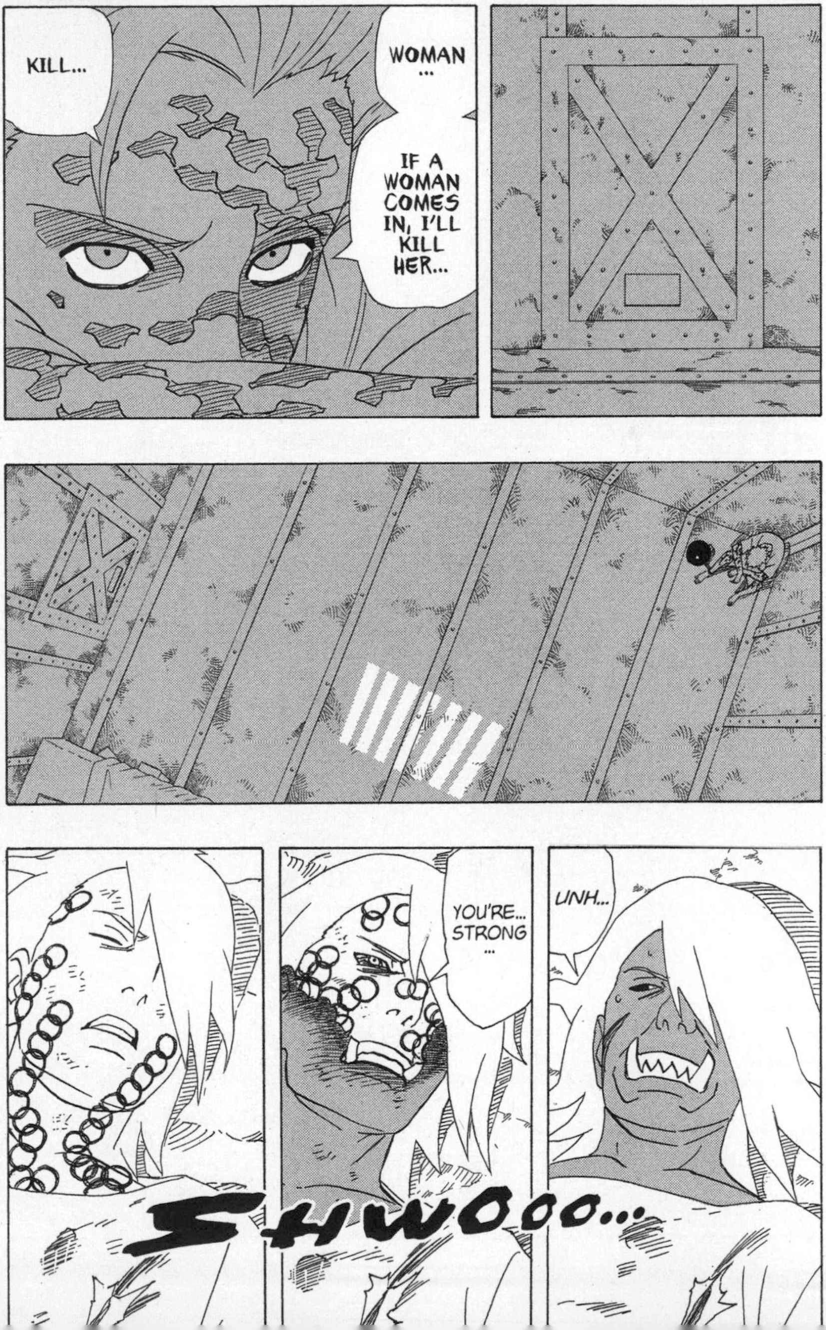
WOMAN ...
IF A WOMAN COMES IN, I'LL KILL HER...
KILL...
UNH...
YOU'RE... STRONG ...
SHWOOO...

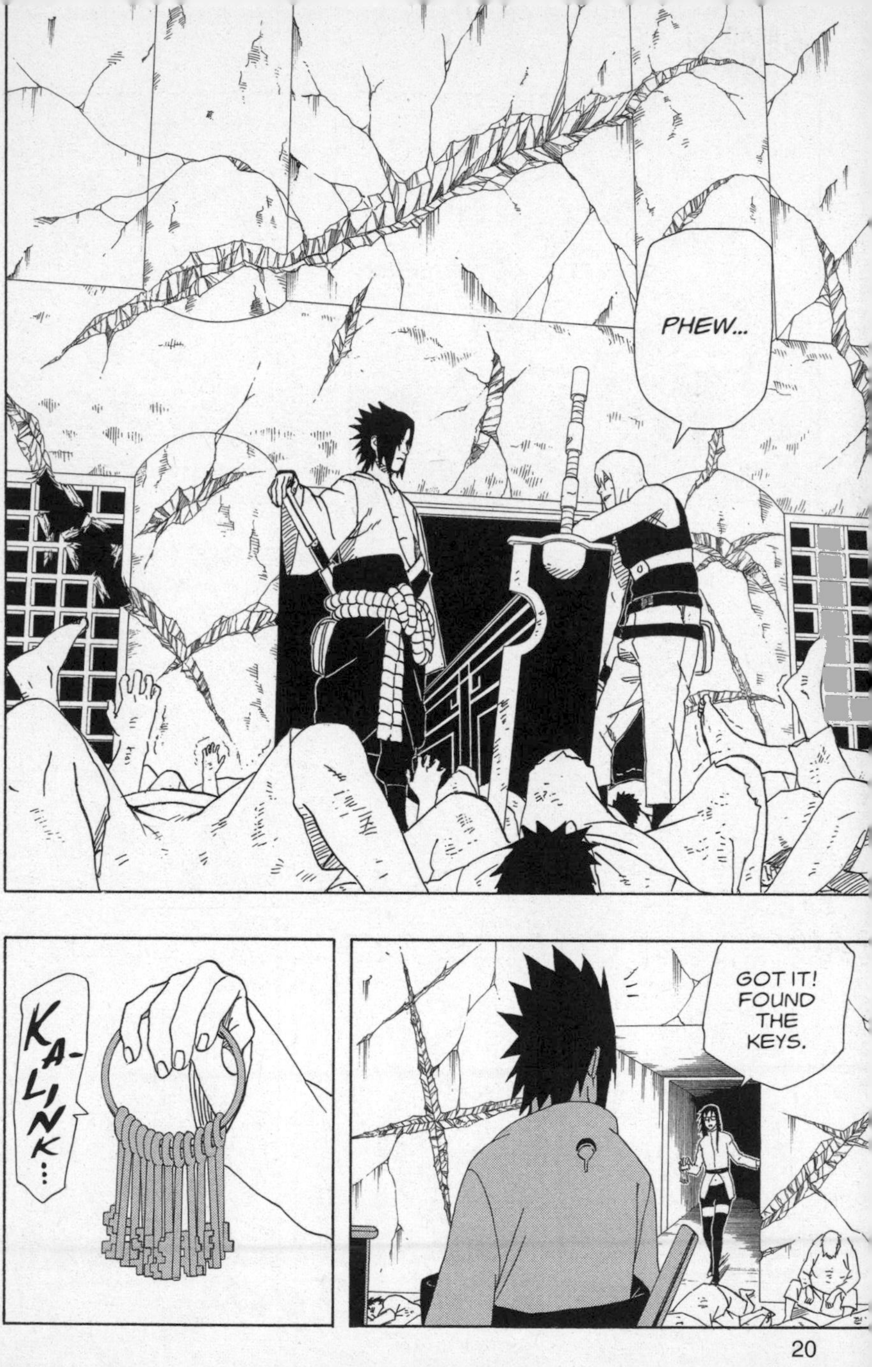
PHEW...
GOT IT! FOUND THE KEYS.
KA-LINK...

READ THIS WAY

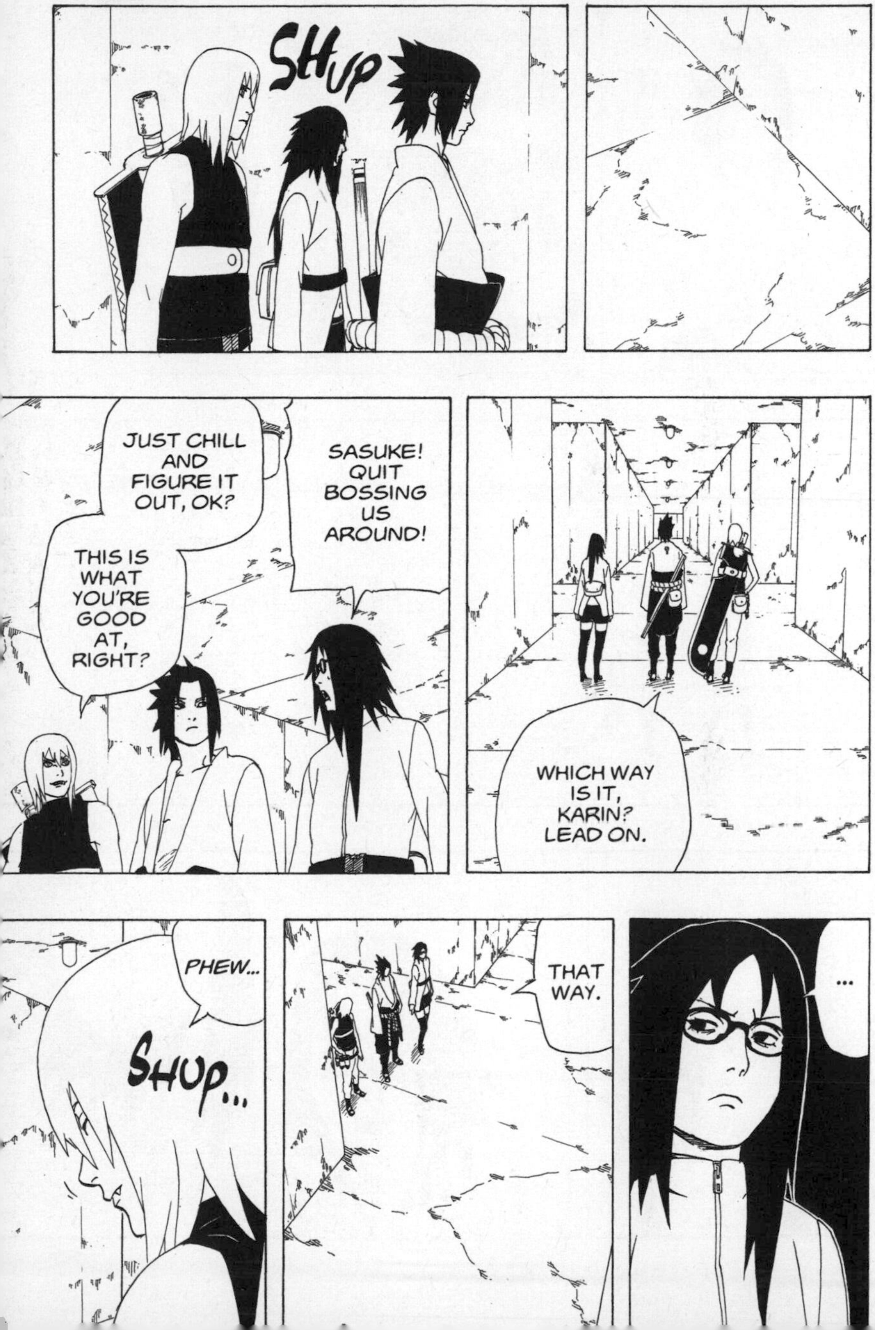
SHUP
WHICH WAY IS IT, KARIN? LEAD ON.
SASUKE! QUIT BOSSING US AROUND!
JUST CHILL AND FIGURE IT OUT, OK?
THIS IS WHAT YOU'RE GOOD AT, RIGHT?
...
THAT WAY.
PHEW...
SHUP...

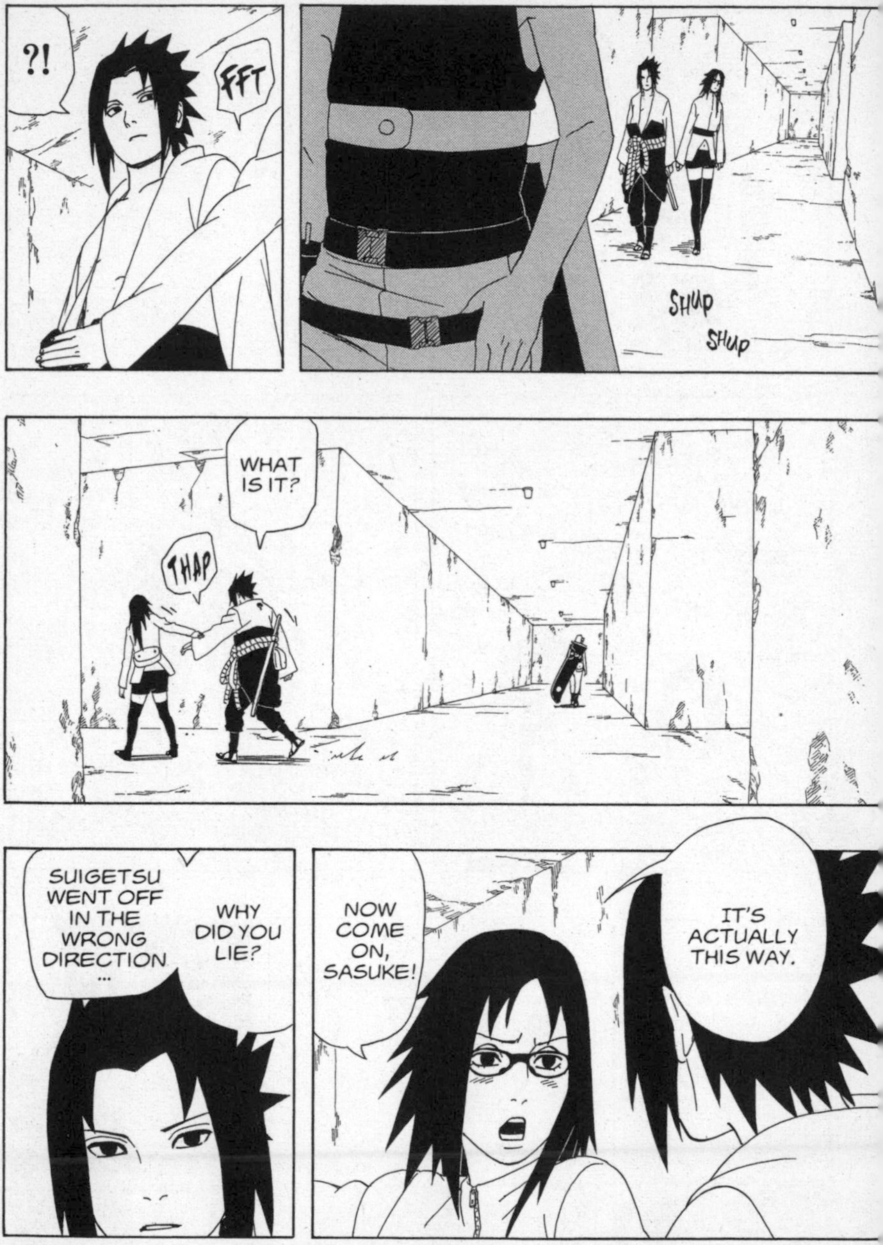
SHUP
SHUP
FFT
?!
WHAT IS IT?
THAP
IT'S ACTUALLY THIS WAY.
NOW COME ON, SASUKE!
SUIGETSU WENT OFF IN THE WRONG DIRECTION ... WHY DID YOU LIE?

READ THIS WAY

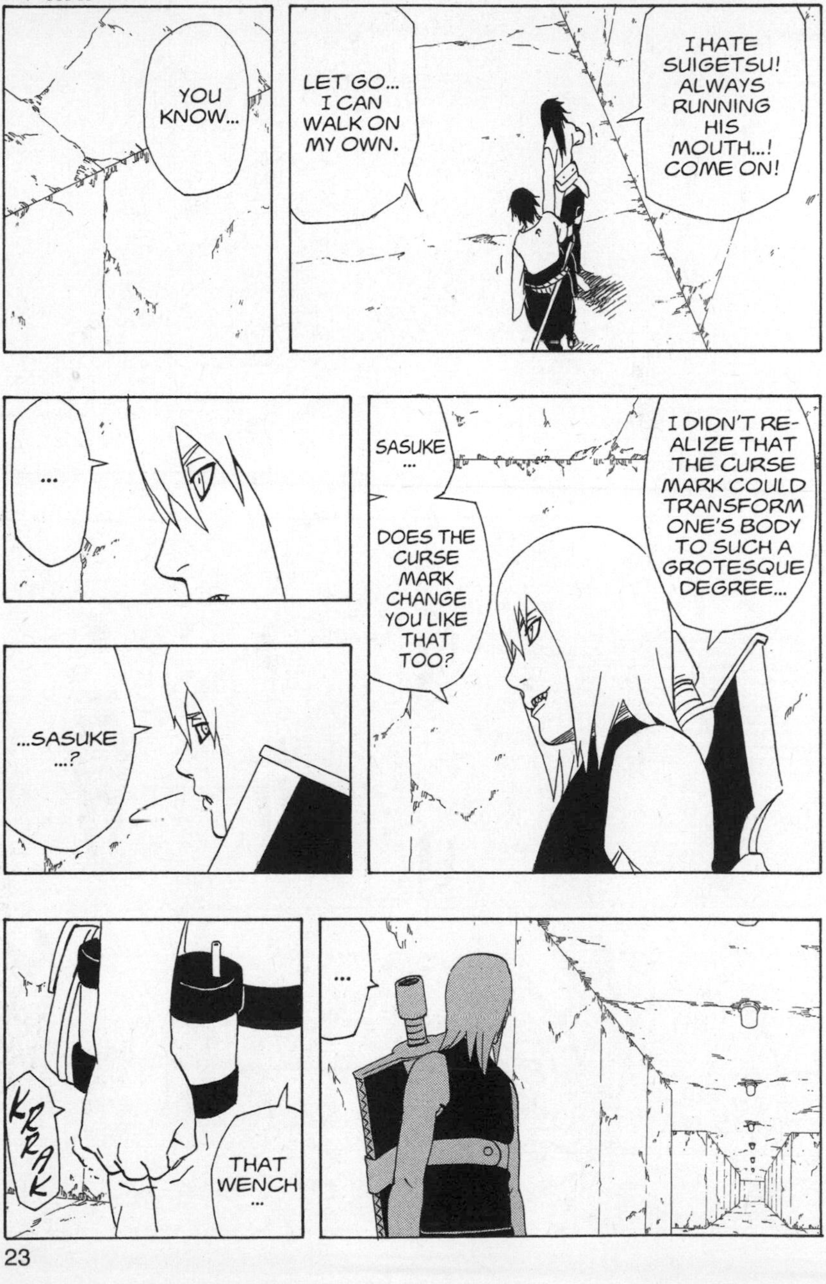

I HATE SUIGETSU! ALWAYS RUNNING HIS MOUTH...! COME ON!
LET GO... I CAN WALK ON MY OWN.
YOU KNOW...
I DIDN'T RE-ALIZE THAT THE CURSE MARK COULD TRANSFORM ONE'S BODY TO SUCH A GROTESQUE DEGREE...
SASUKE ...
DOES THE CURSE MARK CHANGE YOU LIKE THAT TOO?
...
...SASUKE ...?
...
THAT WENCH ...
KRRAK

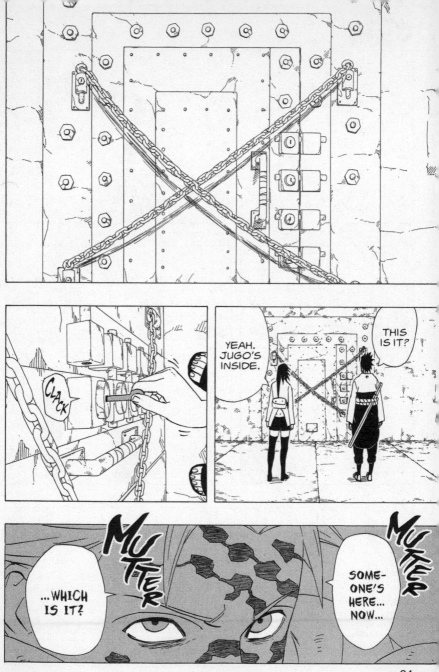

CLACK

YEAH. JUGO'S INSIDE.

THIS IS IT?

MUTTER

...WHICH IS IT?

MUTTER

SOMEONE'S HERE... NOW...

24

READ THIS WAY

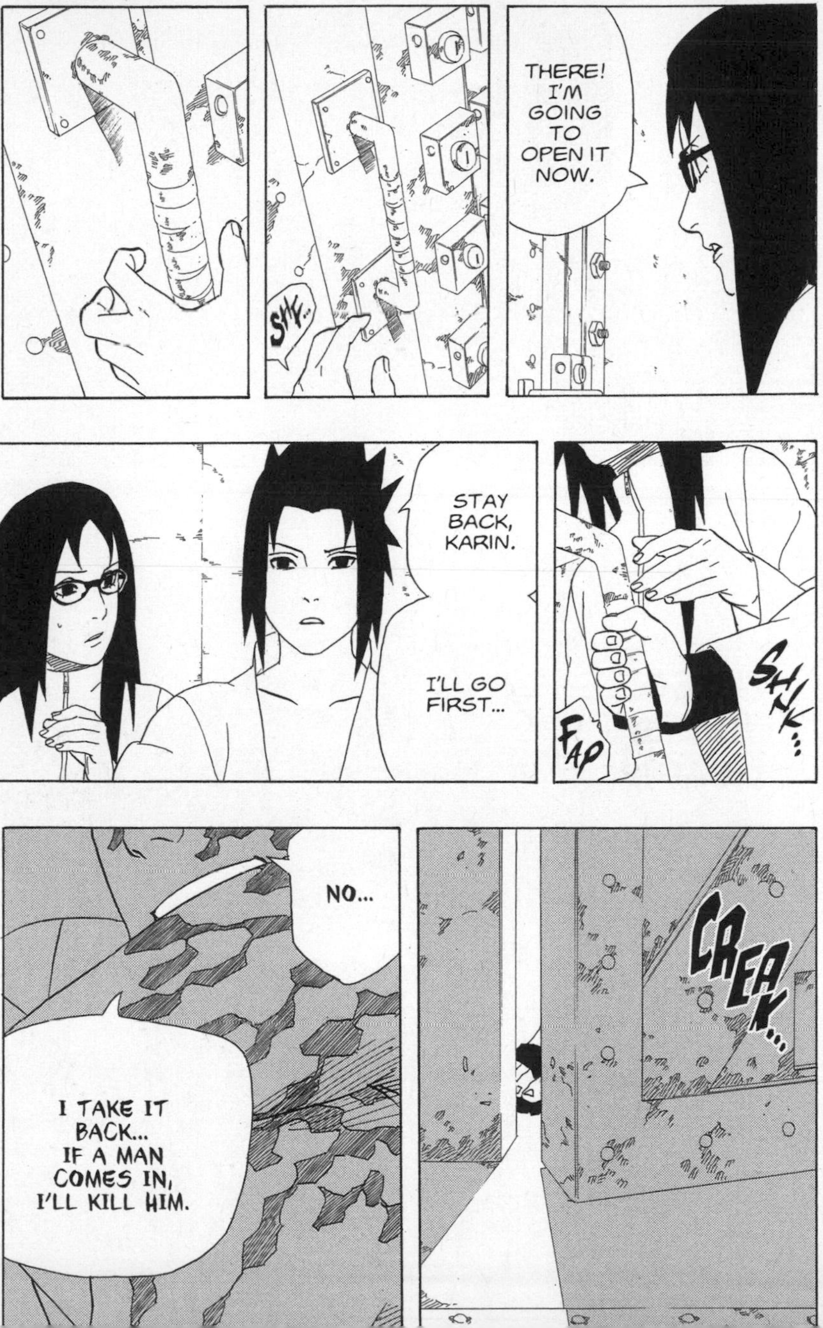
THERE! I'M GOING TO OPEN IT NOW.
SHF...
SHNK...
FAP
STAY BACK, KARIN.
I'LL GO FIRST...
CREAK...
NO...
I TAKE IT BACK... IF A MAN COMES IN, I'LL KILL HIM.

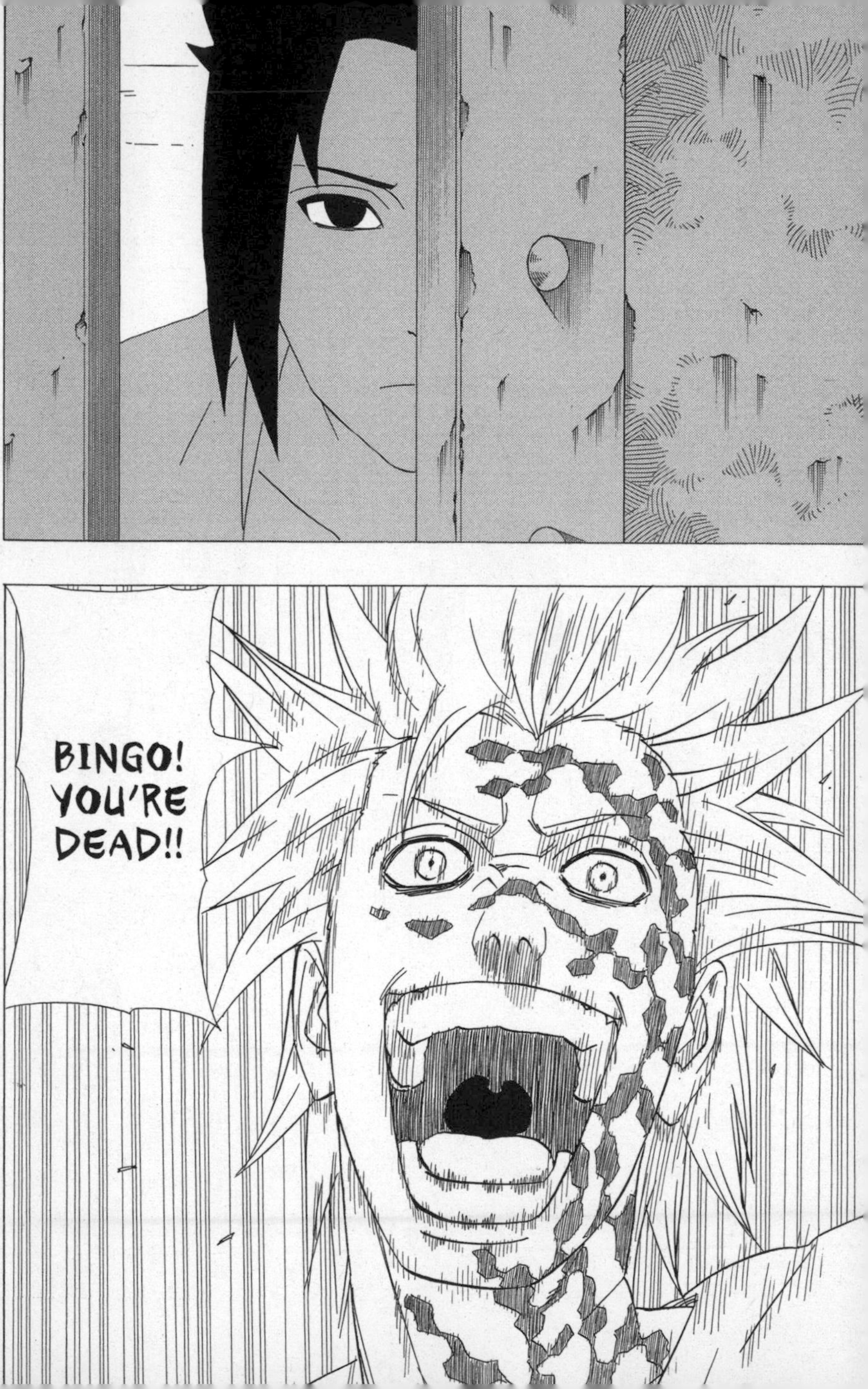
BINGO! YOU'RE DEAD!!

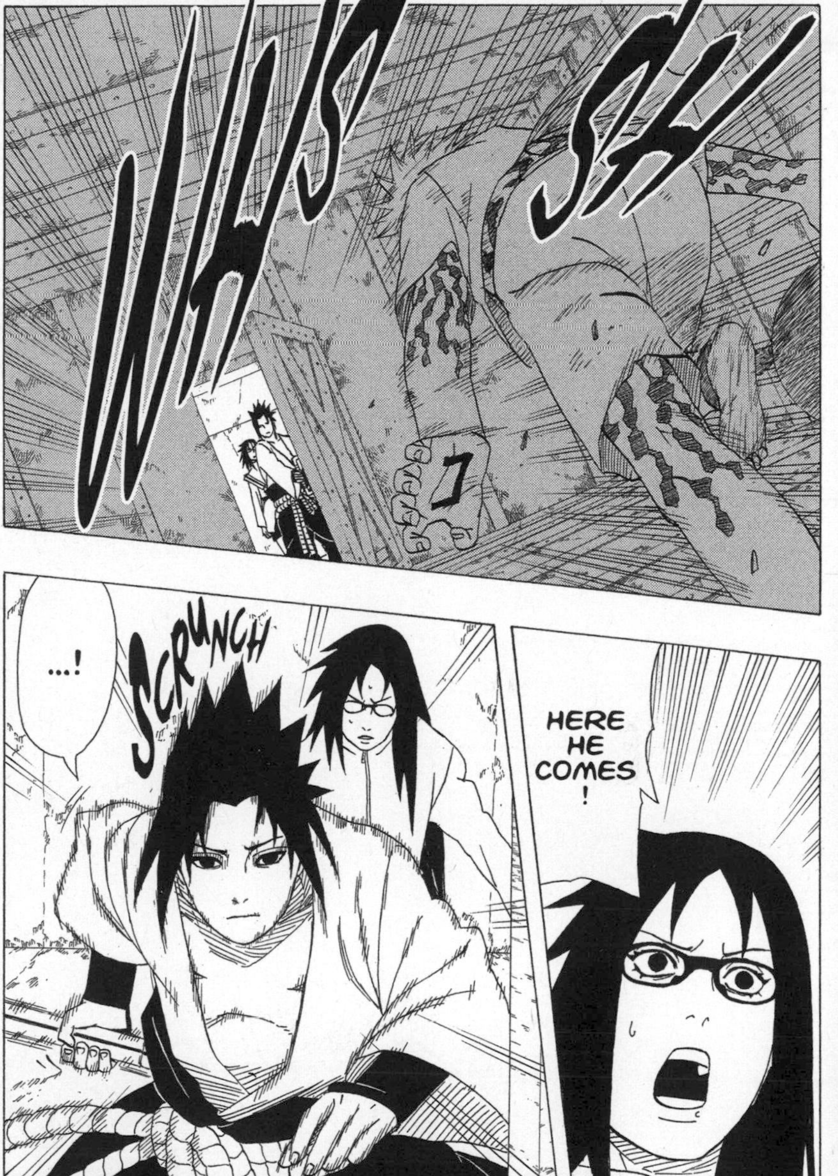
WHUS
SH
HERE HE COMES!
...!
SCRUNCH

NARUTO

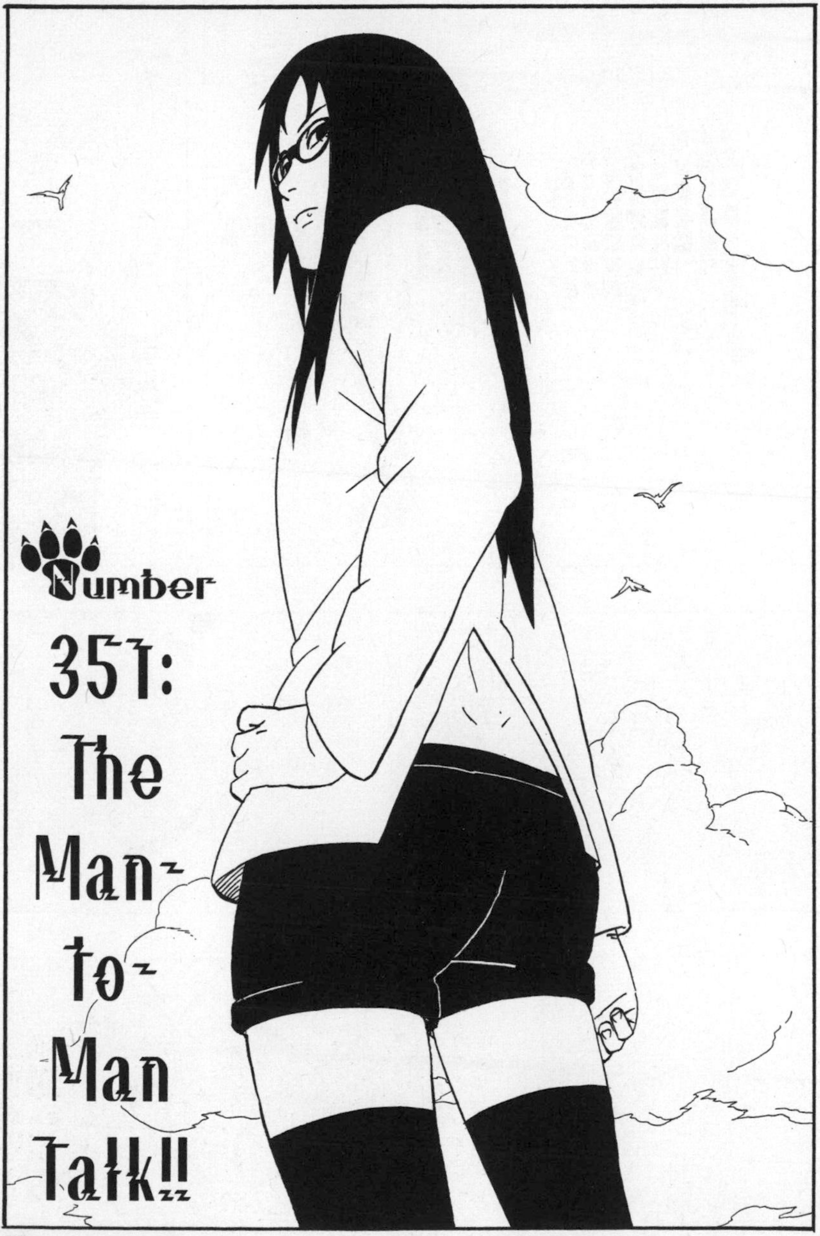
Number
351:
The Man-to-Man Talk!!

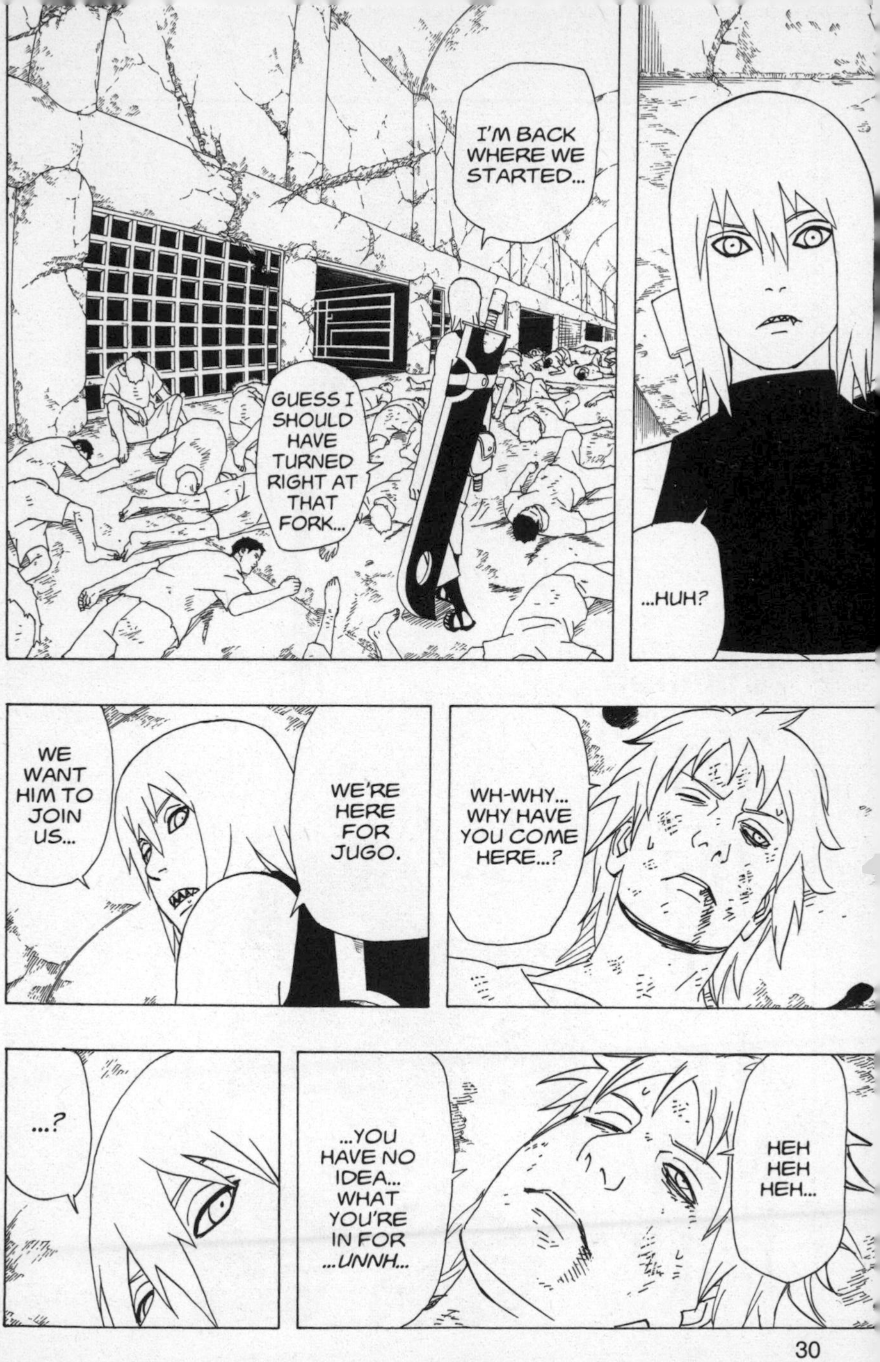
...HUH?
I'M BACK WHERE WE STARTED...
GUESS I SHOULD HAVE TURNED RIGHT AT THAT FORK...
WH-WHY... WHY HAVE YOU COME HERE...?
WE'RE HERE FOR JUGO.
WE WANT HIM TO JOIN US...
HEH HEH HEH...
...YOU HAVE NO IDEA... WHAT YOU'RE IN FOR *...UNNH...*
...?

READ THIS WAY

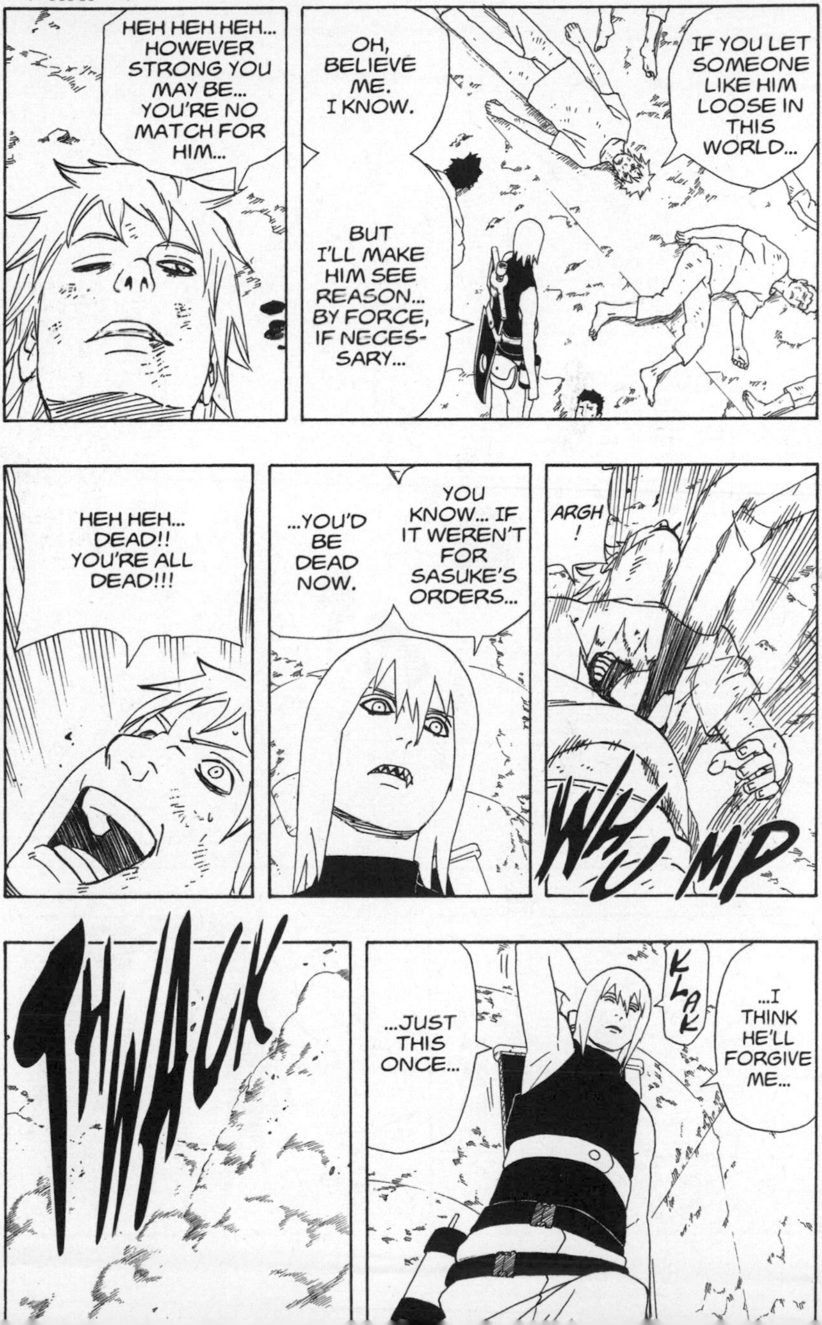

IF YOU LET SOMEONE LIKE HIM LOOSE IN THIS WORLD...
OH, BELIEVE ME. I KNOW.
BUT I'LL MAKE HIM SEE REASON... BY FORCE, IF NECES-SARY...
HEH HEH HEH... HOWEVER STRONG YOU MAY BE... YOU'RE NO MATCH FOR HIM...
ARGH!
WHUMP
YOU KNOW... IF IT WEREN'T FOR SASUKE'S ORDERS...
...YOU'D BE DEAD NOW.
HEH HEH... DEAD!! YOU'RE ALL DEAD!!!
KLAK
...I THINK HE'LL FORGIVE ME...
...JUST THIS ONCE...
THWACK

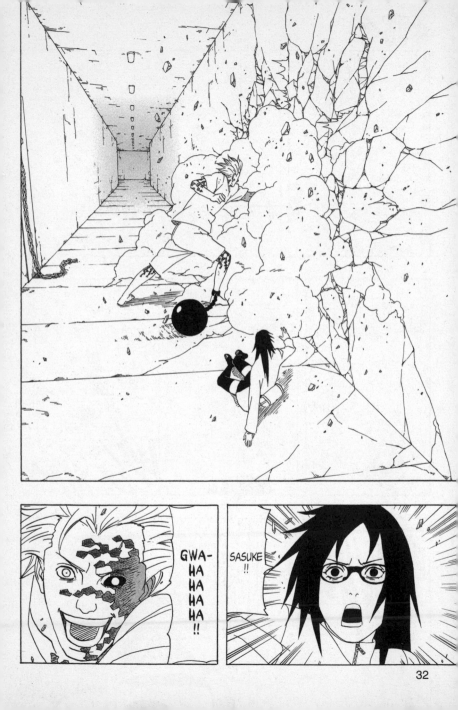

GWA-
HA
HA
HA
HA
!!

SASUKE
!!

READ THIS WAY

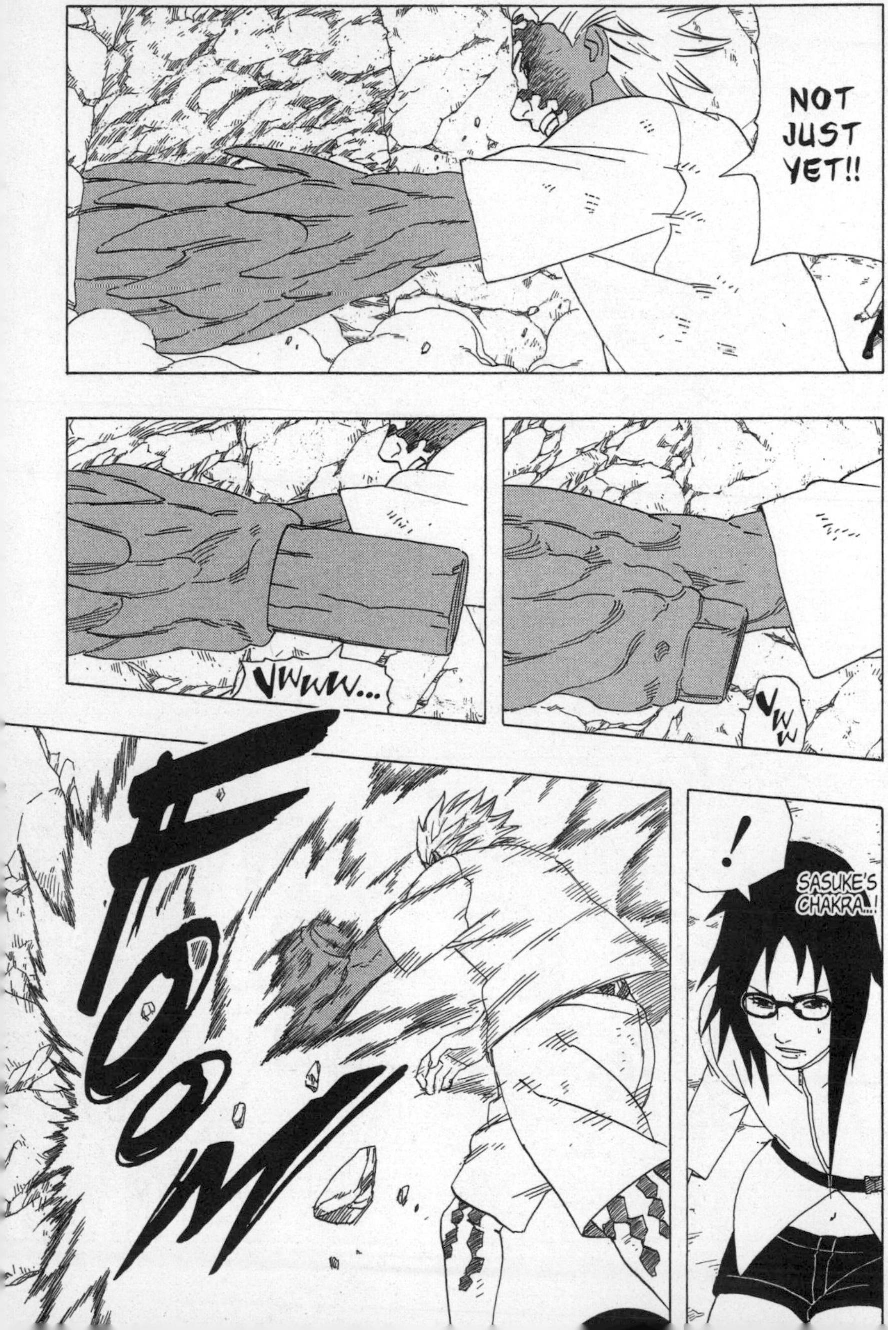
NOT JUST YET!!
VWW
VWWW...
!
SASUKE'S CHAKRA...!
FOOM

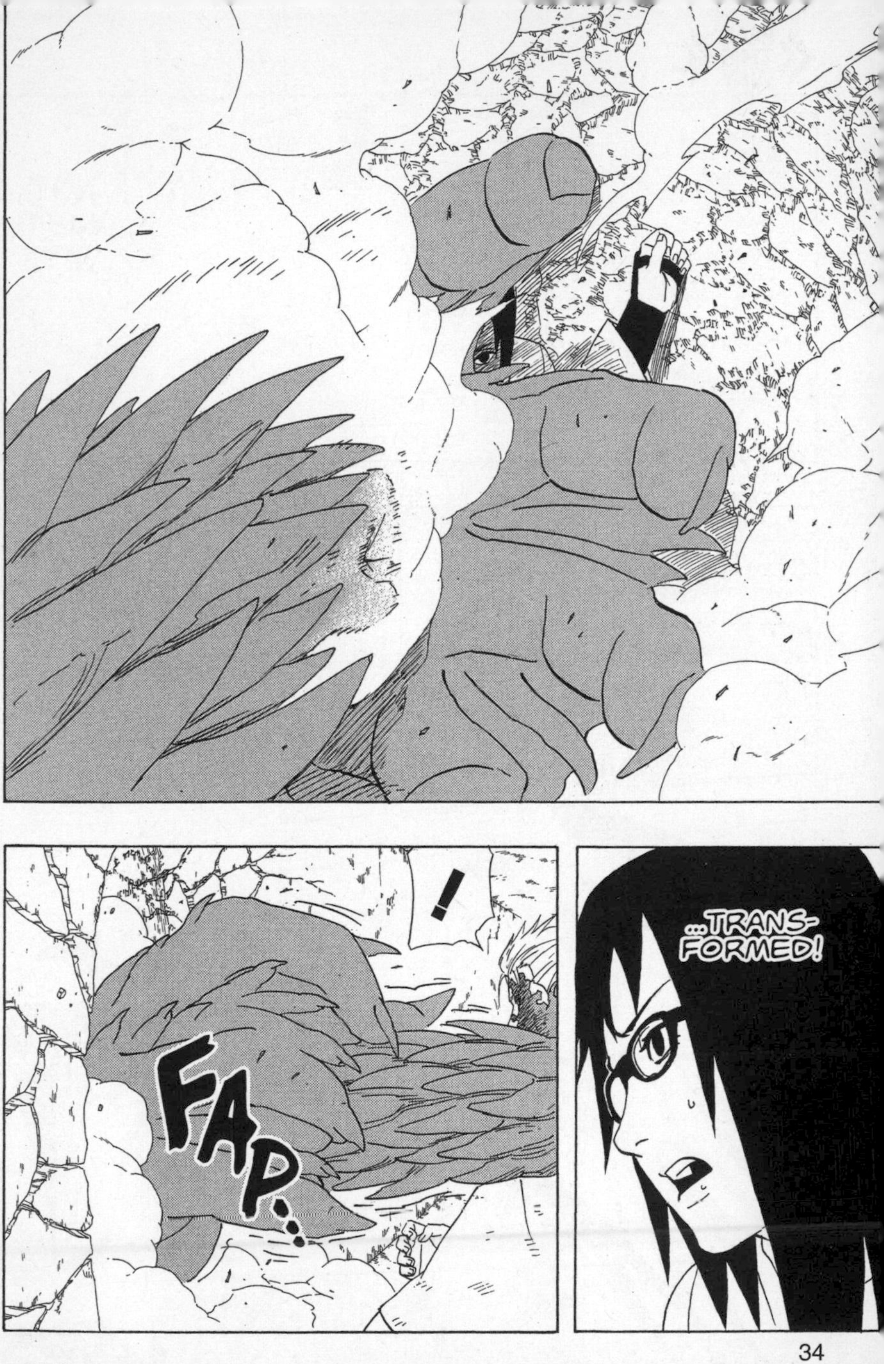
...TRANS-FORMED!
!
FAP...

READ THIS WAY

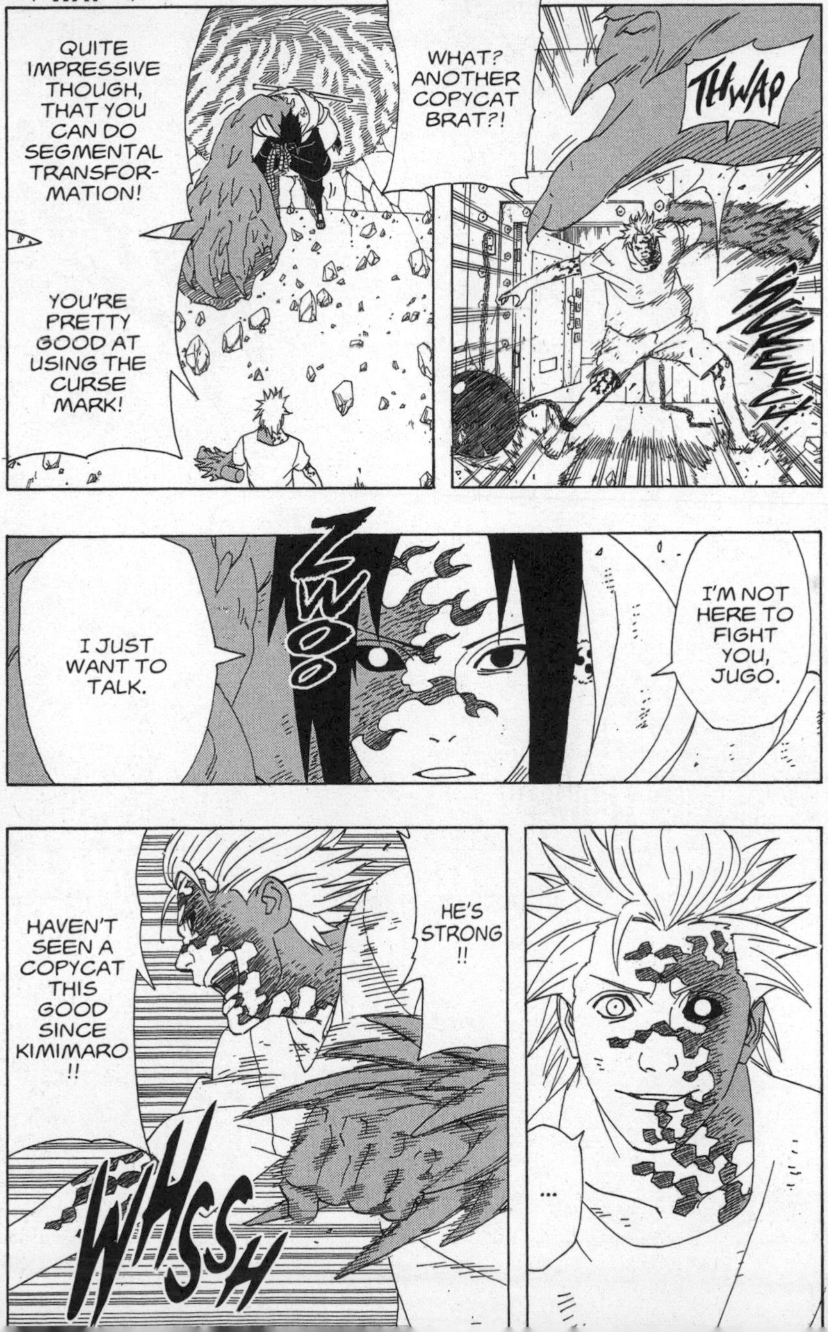
THWAP
WHAT? ANOTHER COPYCAT BRAT?!
QUITE IMPRESSIVE THOUGH, THAT YOU CAN DO SEGMENTAL TRANSFORMATION!
YOU'RE PRETTY GOOD AT USING THE CURSE MARK!
I'M NOT HERE TO FIGHT YOU, JUGO.
ZWOO
I JUST WANT TO TALK.
...
HE'S STRONG !!
HAVEN'T SEEN A COPYCAT THIS GOOD SINCE KIMIMARO !!
WHSSH

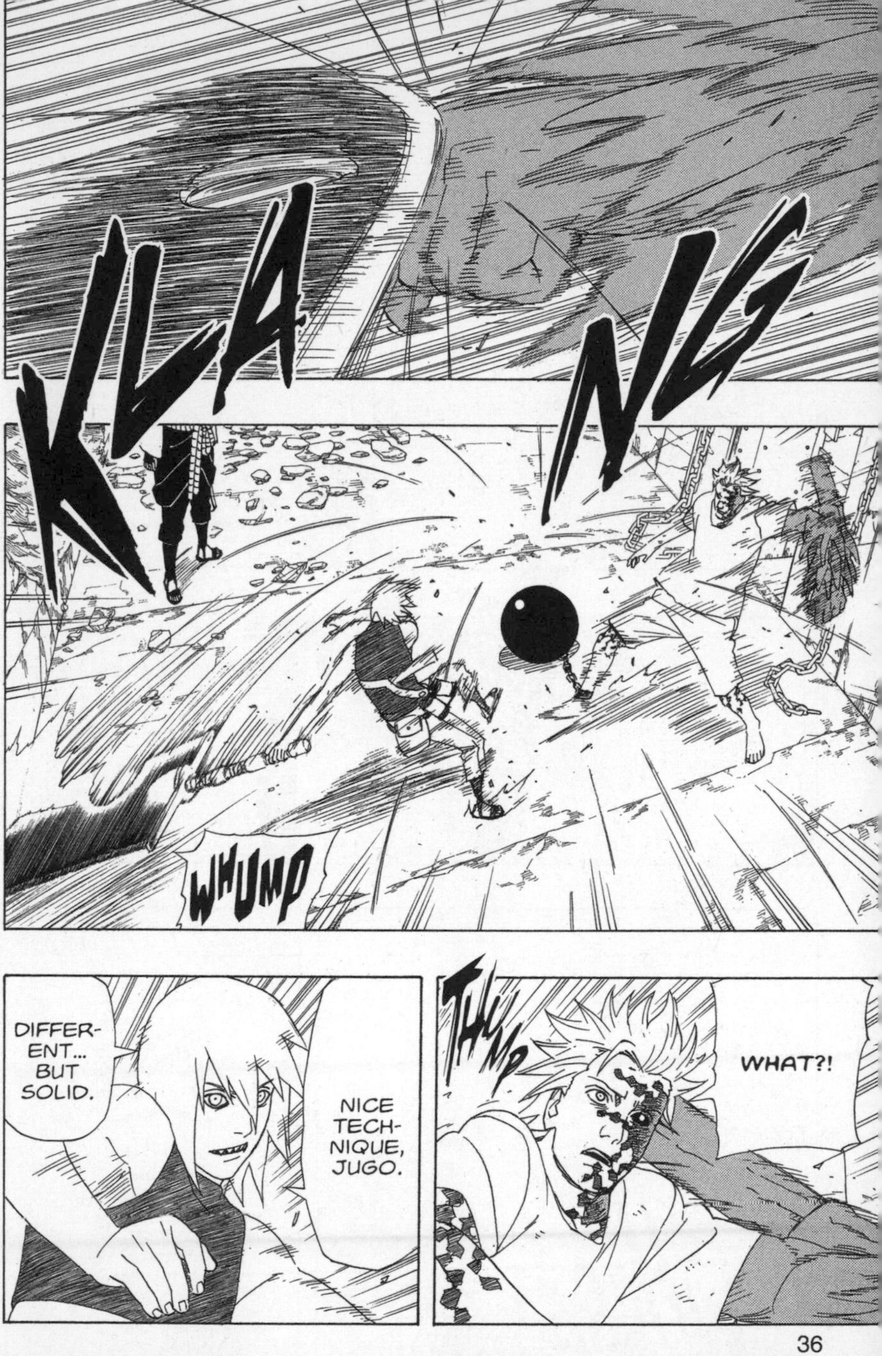
KLANG
WHUMP
THUMP
WHAT?!
NICE TECHNIQUE, JUGO.
DIFFERENT... BUT SOLID.

READ THIS WAY

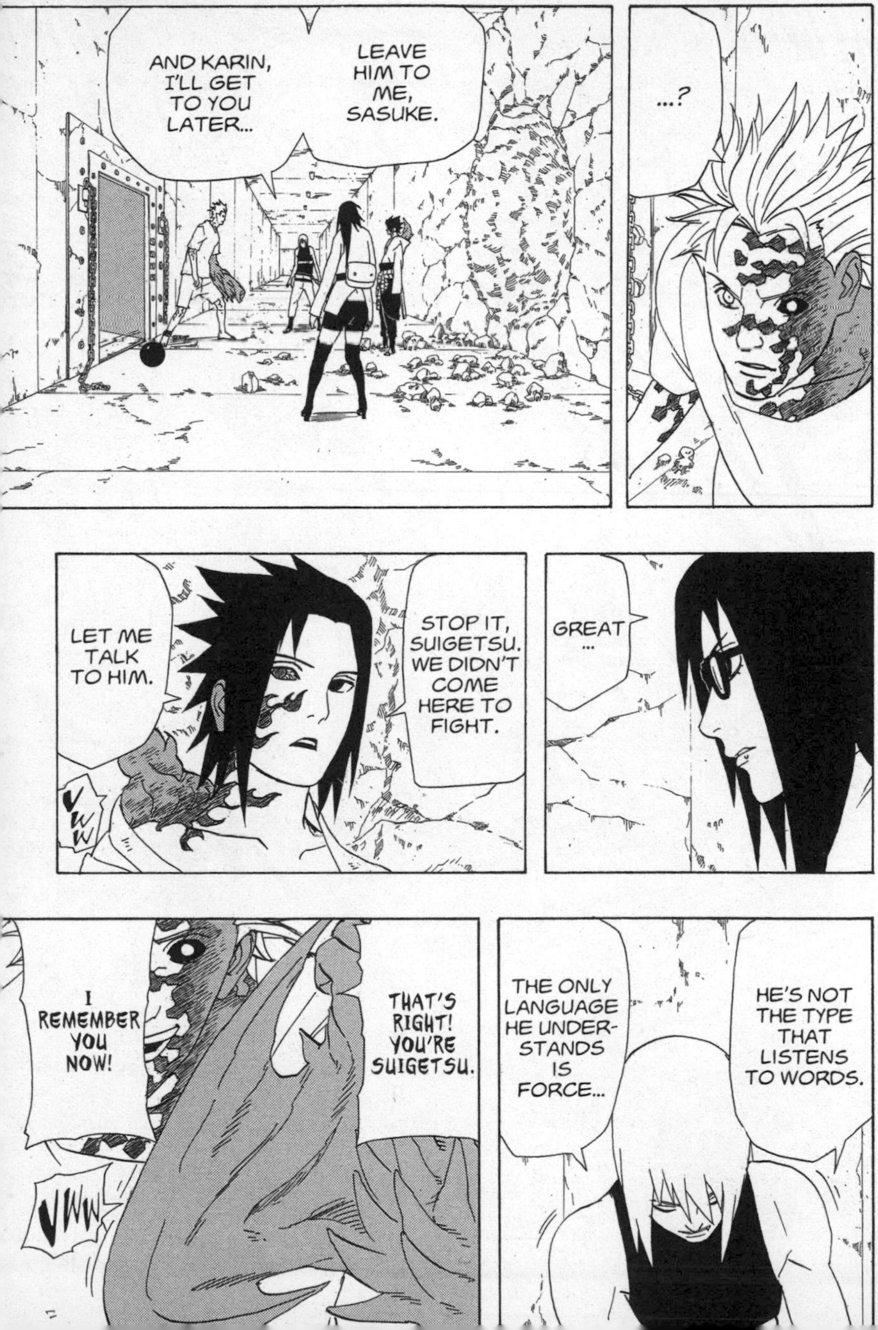
...?
LEAVE HIM TO ME, SASUKE.
AND KARIN, I'LL GET TO YOU LATER...
GREAT ...
STOP IT, SUIGETSU. WE DIDN'T COME HERE TO FIGHT.
LET ME TALK TO HIM.
VWW
HE'S NOT THE TYPE THAT LISTENS TO WORDS.
THE ONLY LANGUAGE HE UNDER-STANDS IS FORCE...
THAT'S RIGHT! YOU'RE SUIGETSU.
I REMEMBER YOU NOW!
VWW

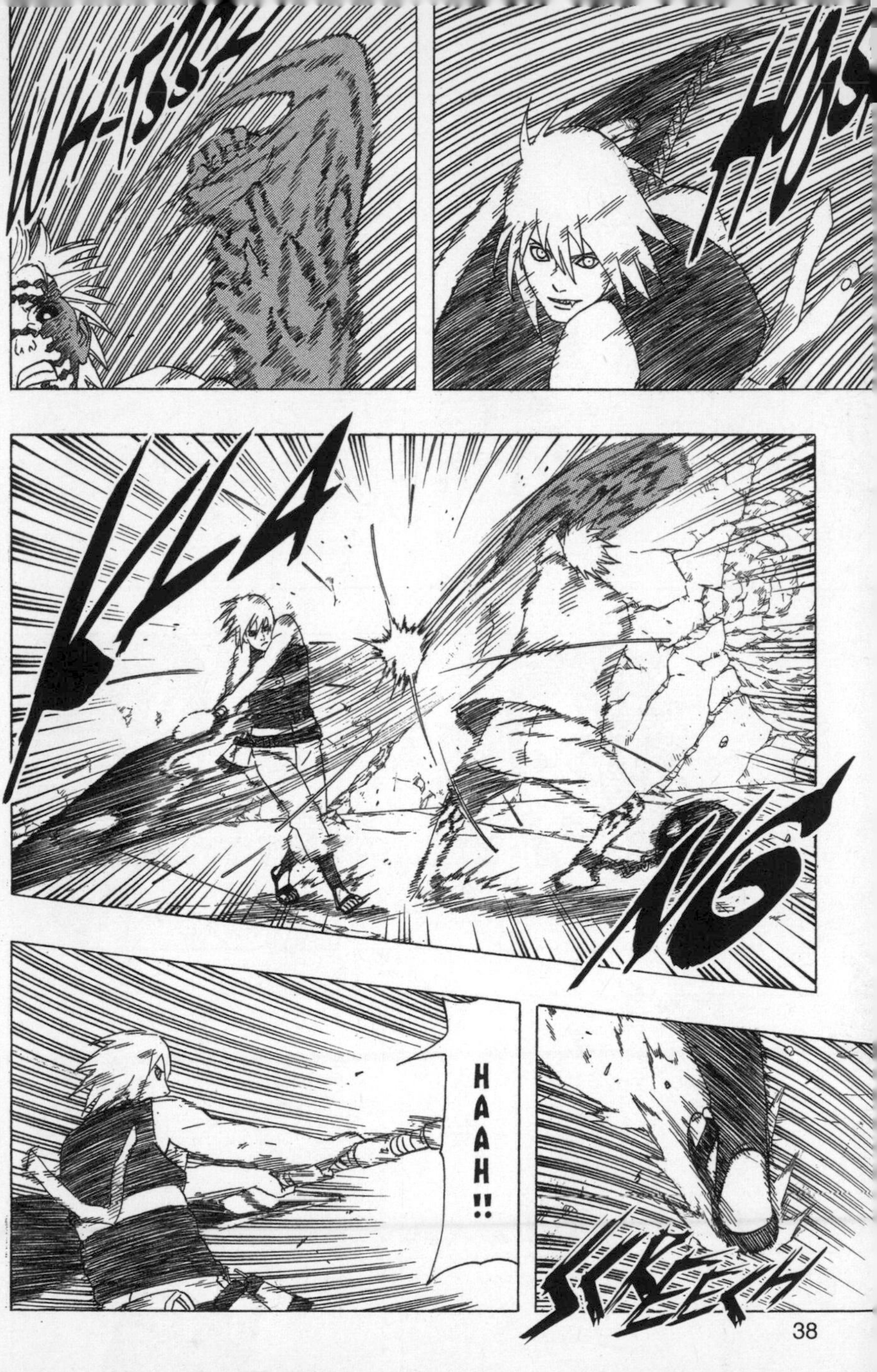
KLANG
HAAAH!!
SCREECH

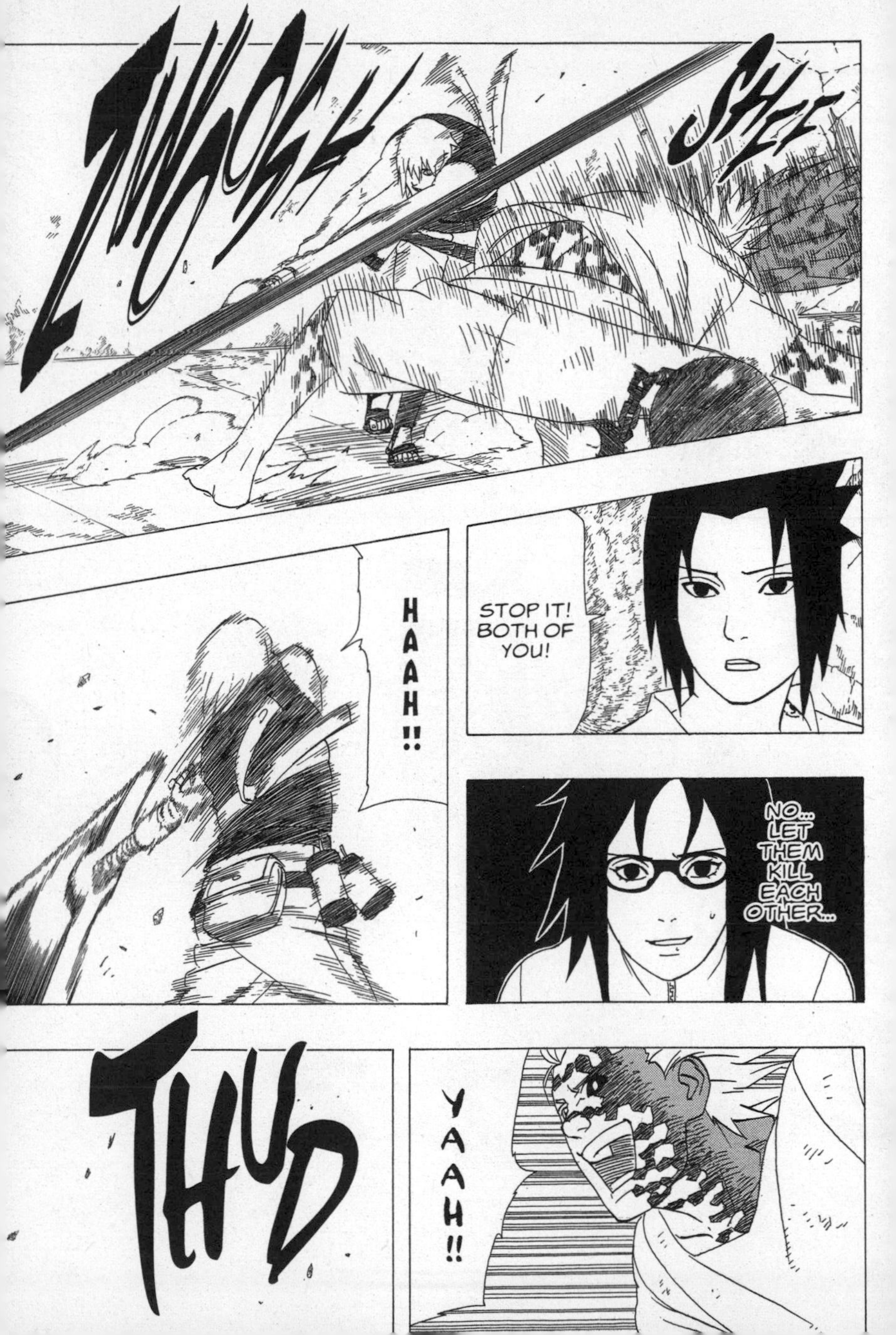
STOP IT! BOTH OF YOU!
NO... LET THEM KILL EACH OTHER...
HAAH!!
YAAH!!
THUD

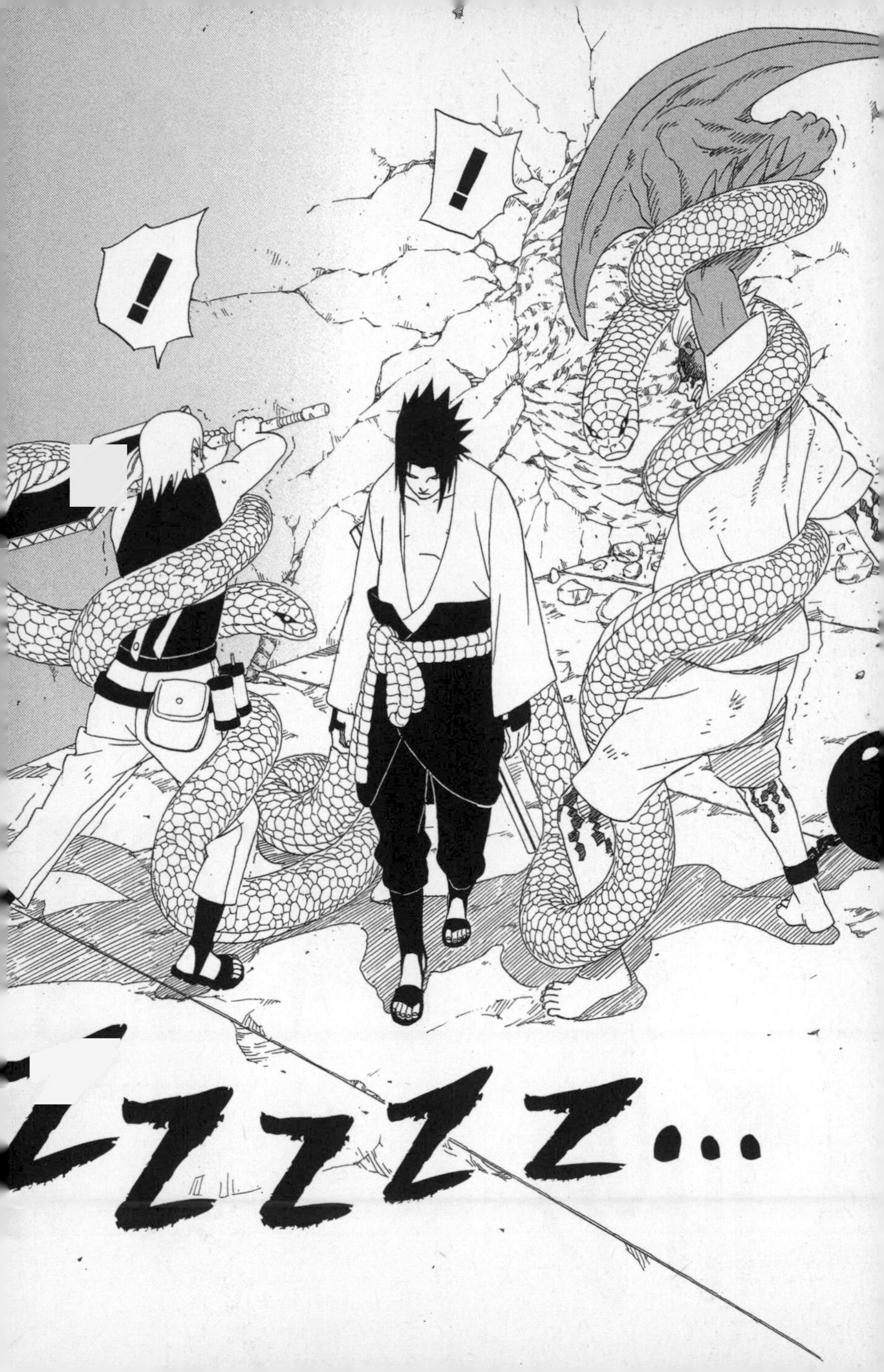
!
!
ZZZZ...

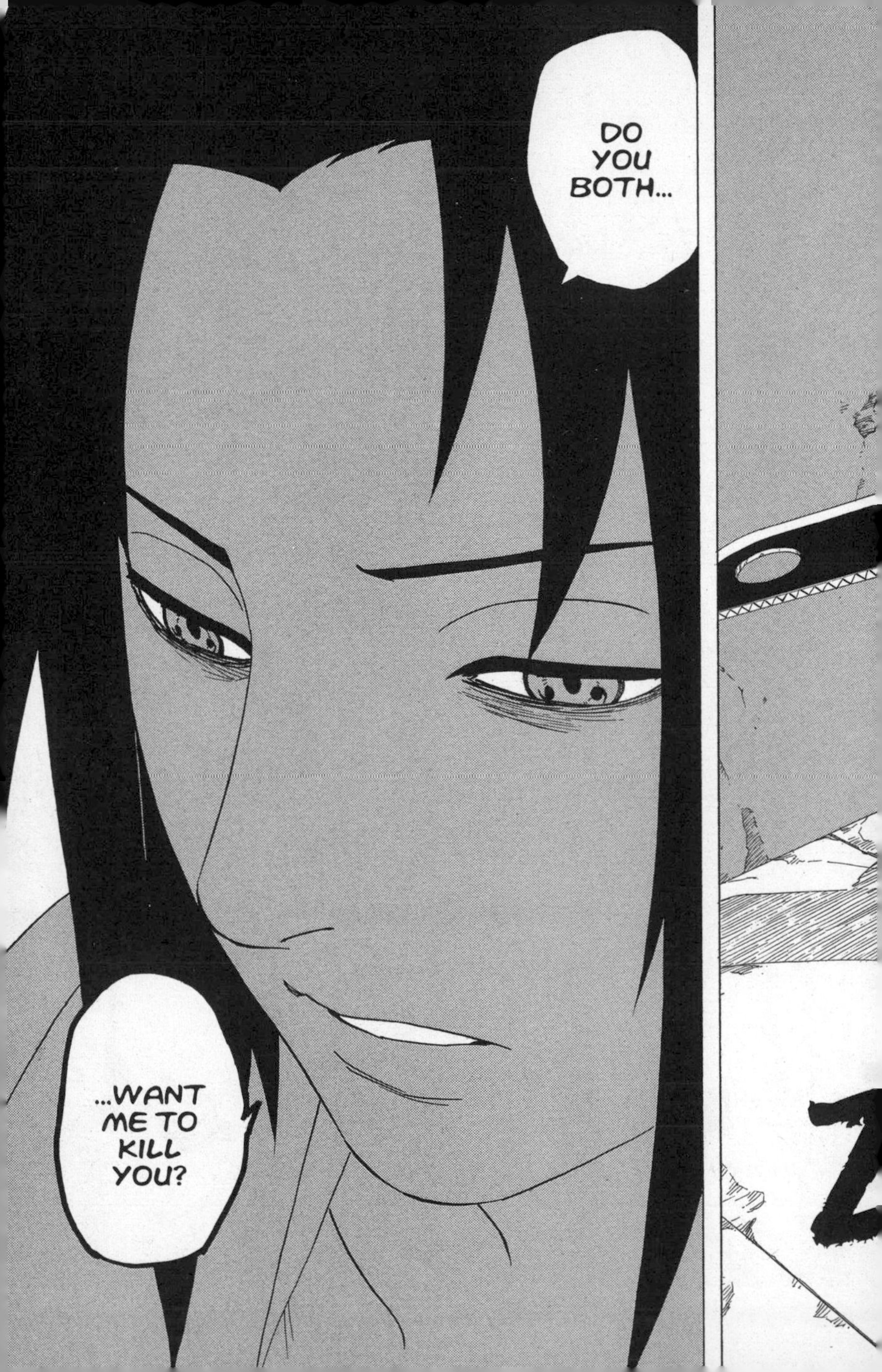
DO YOU BOTH...
...WANT ME TO KILL YOU?

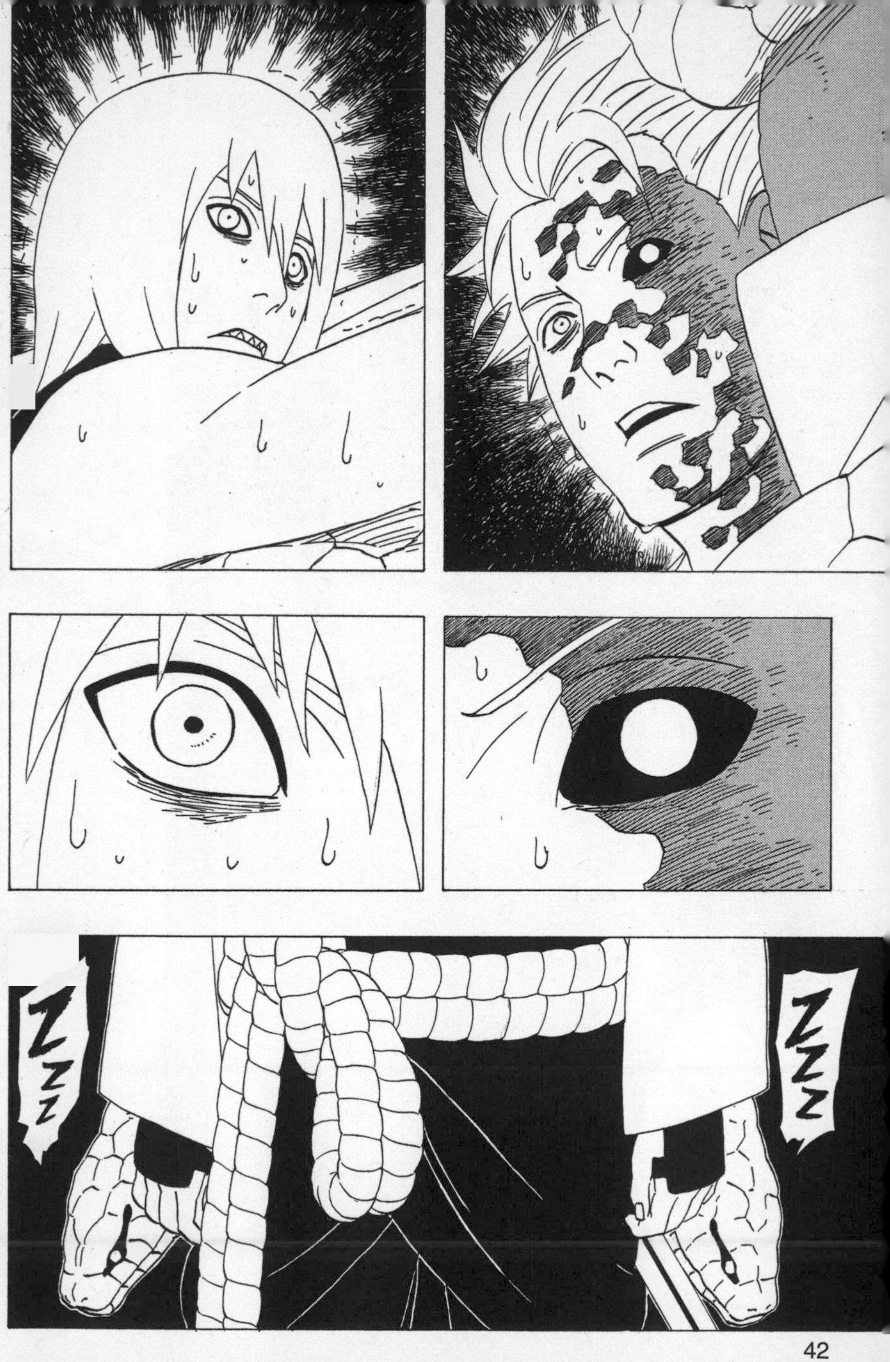
ZZZ
ZZZ

READ THIS WAY

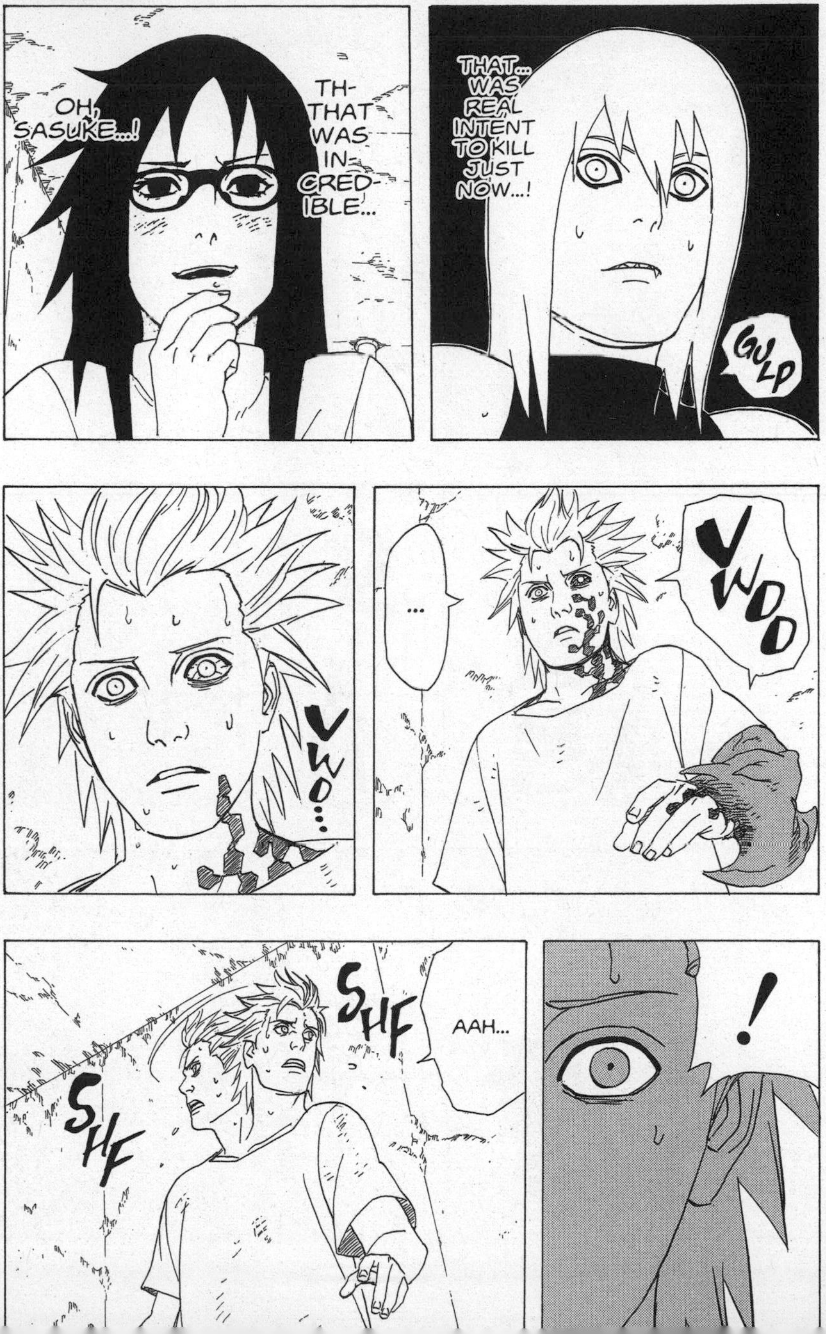
THAT... WAS REAL INTENT TO KILL JUST NOW...!
GULP
TH-THAT WAS IN-CRED-IBLE...
OH, SASUKE...!
VWOO
...
VWO...
!
AAH...
SHF
SHF

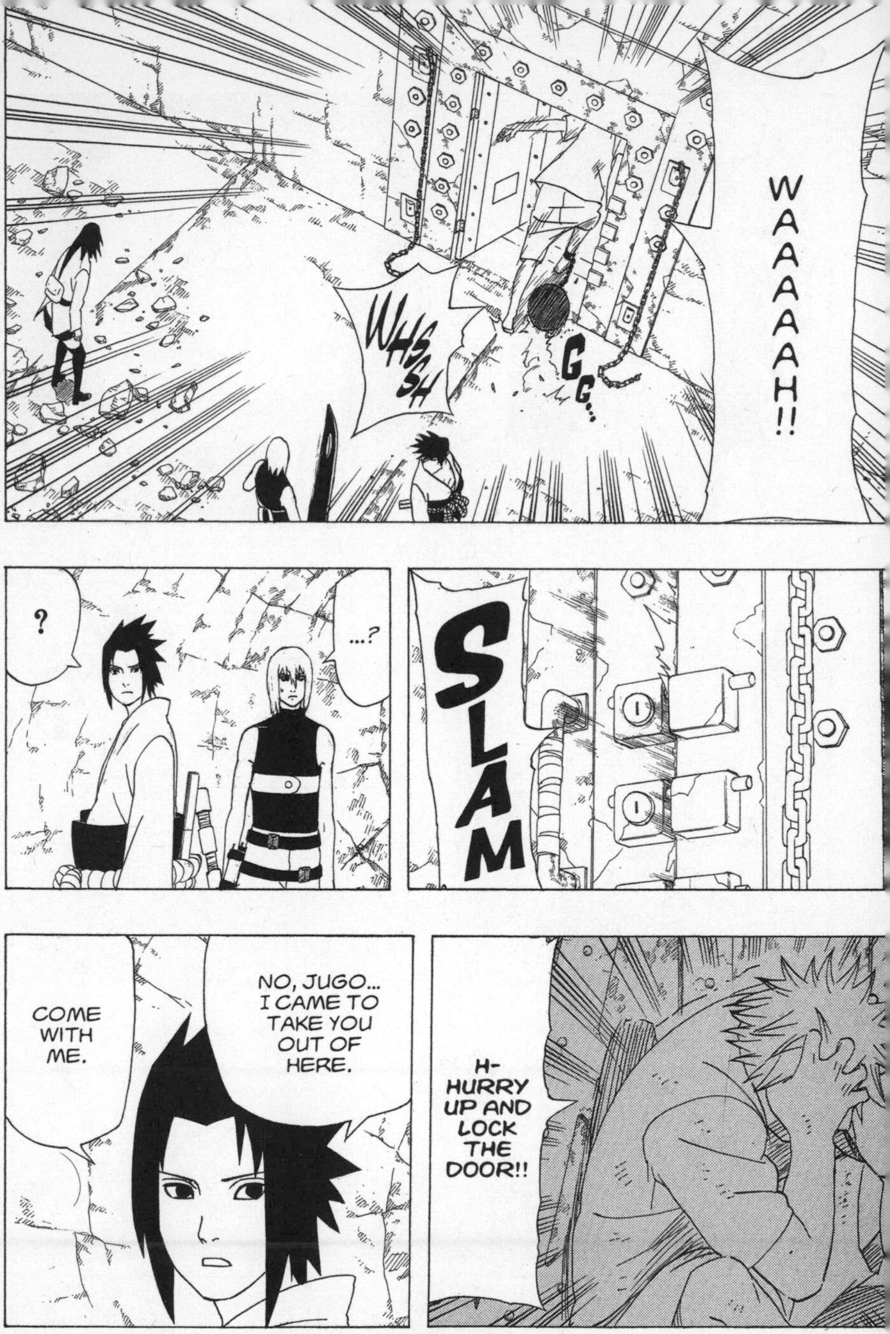
WAAAAAAH!!
GG...
WHSSH
SLAM
...?
?
H-HURRY UP AND LOCK THE DOOR!!
NO, JUGO... I CAME TO TAKE YOU OUT OF HERE.
COME WITH ME.

READ THIS WAY

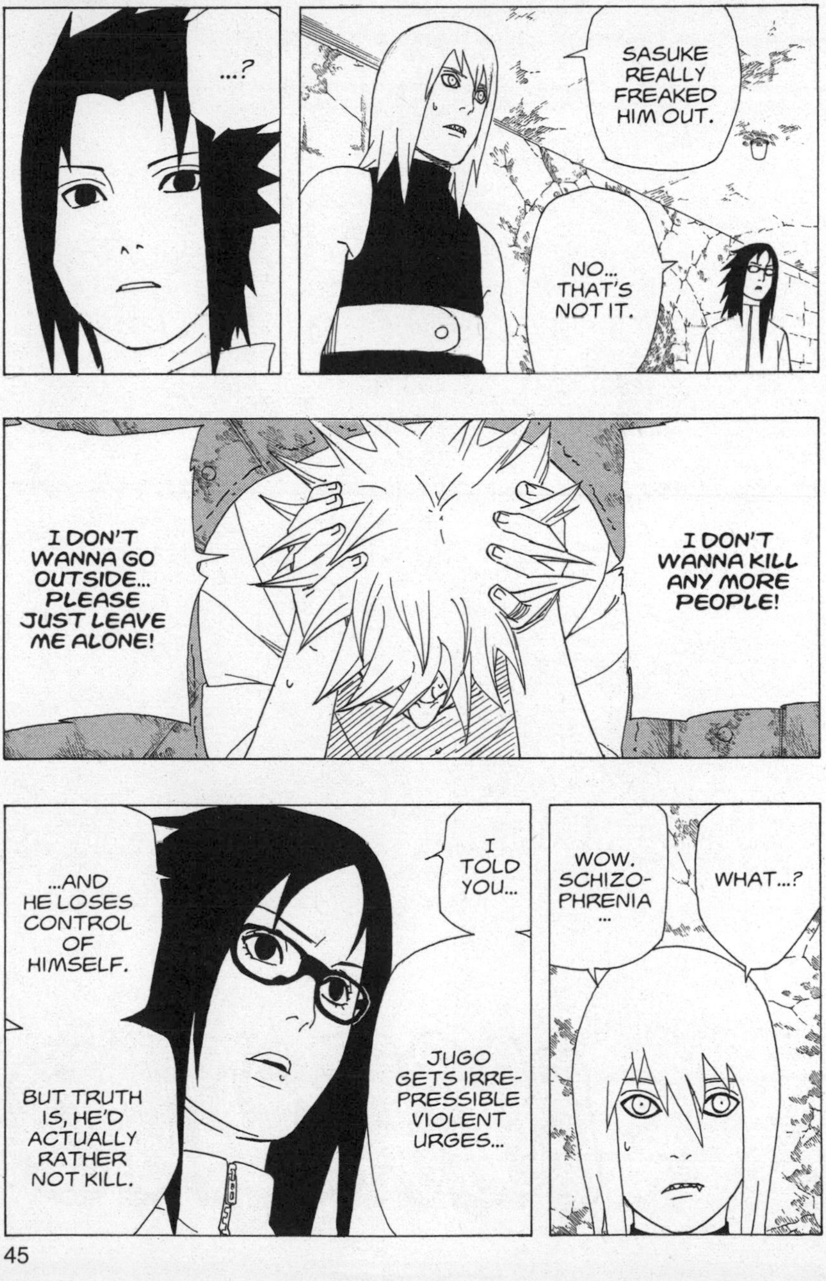
SASUKE REALLY FREAKED HIM OUT.
NO... THAT'S NOT IT.
...?
I DON'T WANNA KILL ANY MORE PEOPLE!
I DON'T WANNA GO OUTSIDE... PLEASE JUST LEAVE ME ALONE!
WHAT...?
WOW. SCHIZOPHRENIA...
I TOLD YOU...
JUGO GETS IRREPRESSIBLE VIOLENT URGES...
...AND HE LOSES CONTROL OF HIMSELF.
BUT TRUTH IS, HE'D ACTUALLY RATHER NOT KILL.

NARUTO

Number 352: His Plan...!!

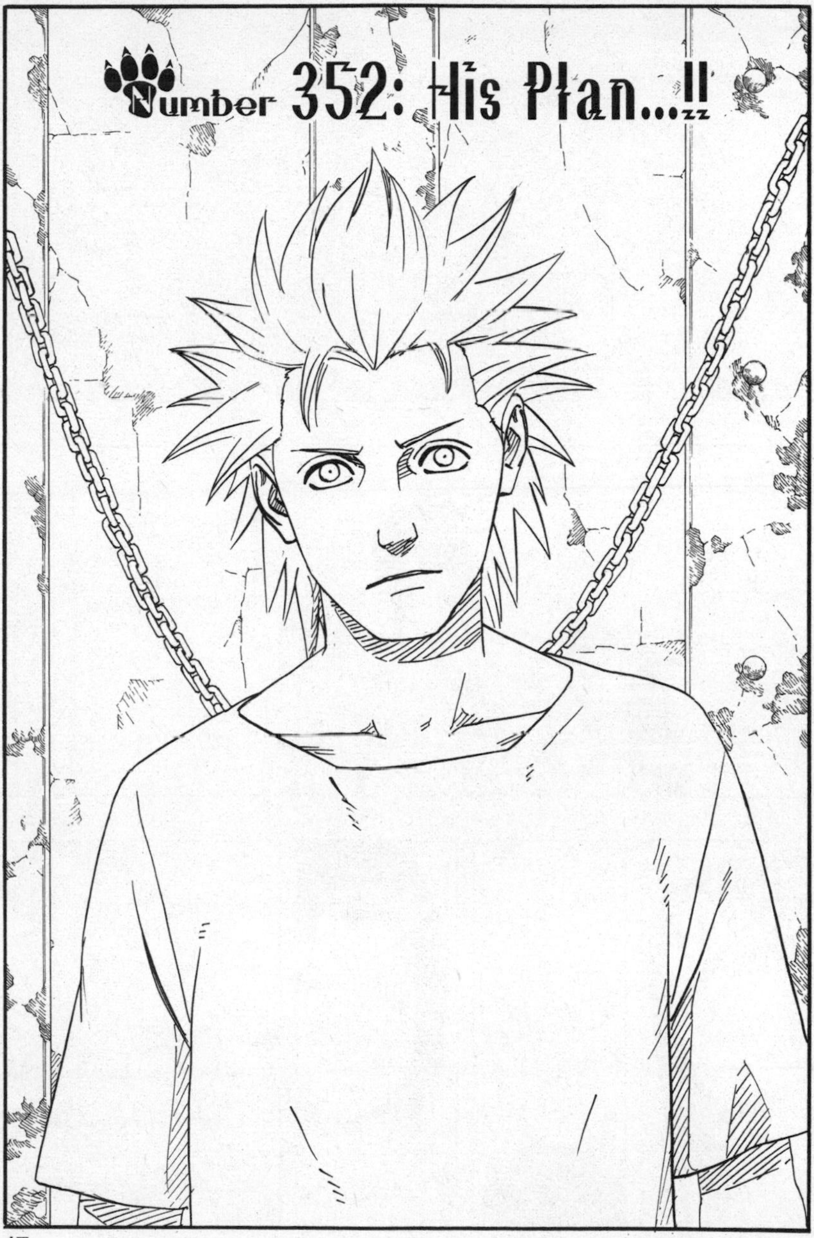

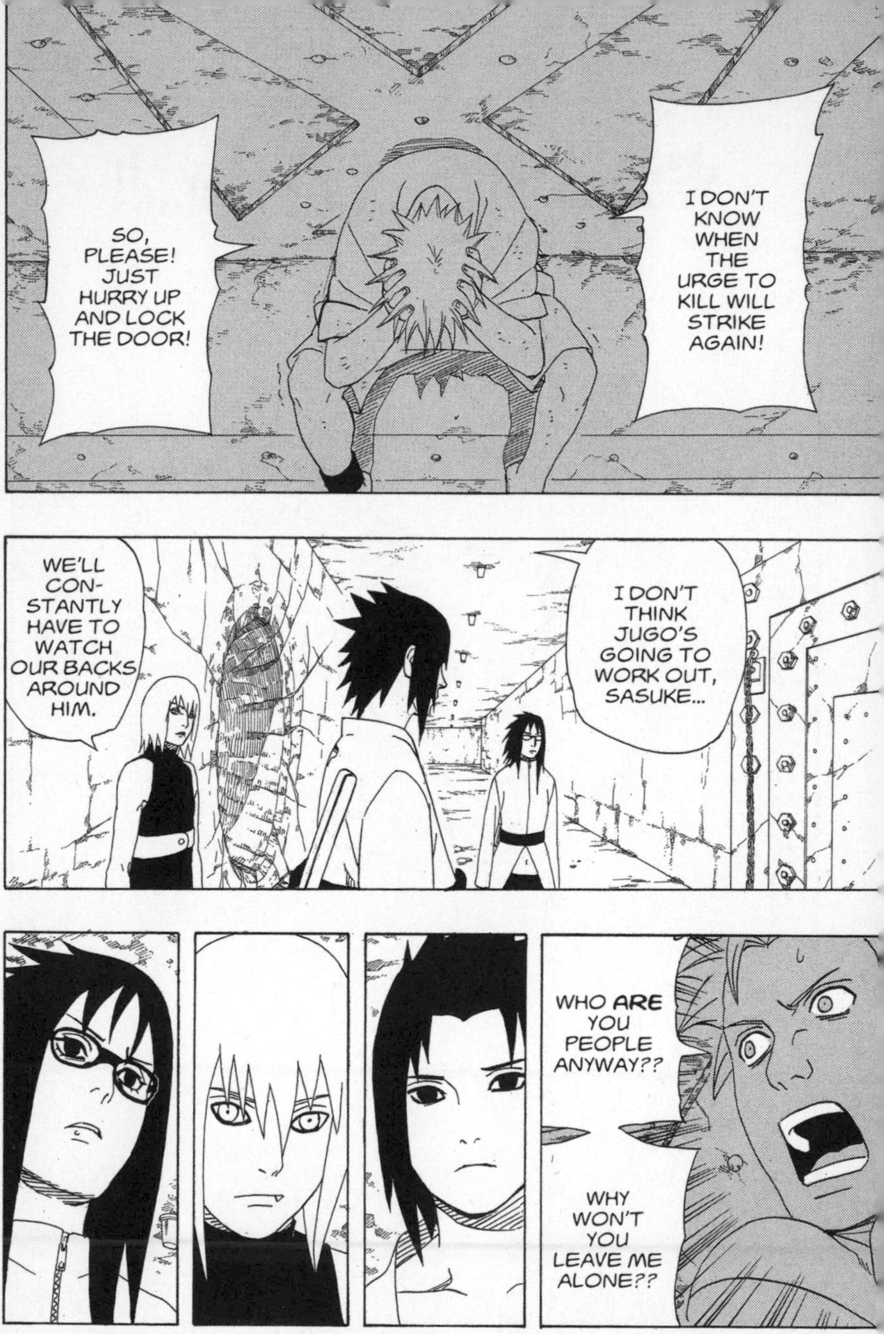
I DON'T KNOW WHEN THE URGE TO KILL WILL STRIKE AGAIN!
SO, PLEASE! JUST HURRY UP AND LOCK THE DOOR!
I DON'T THINK JUGO'S GOING TO WORK OUT, SASUKE...
WE'LL CON-STANTLY HAVE TO WATCH OUR BACKS AROUND HIM.
WHO **ARE** YOU PEOPLE ANYWAY??
WHY WON'T YOU LEAVE ME ALONE??

READ THIS WAY

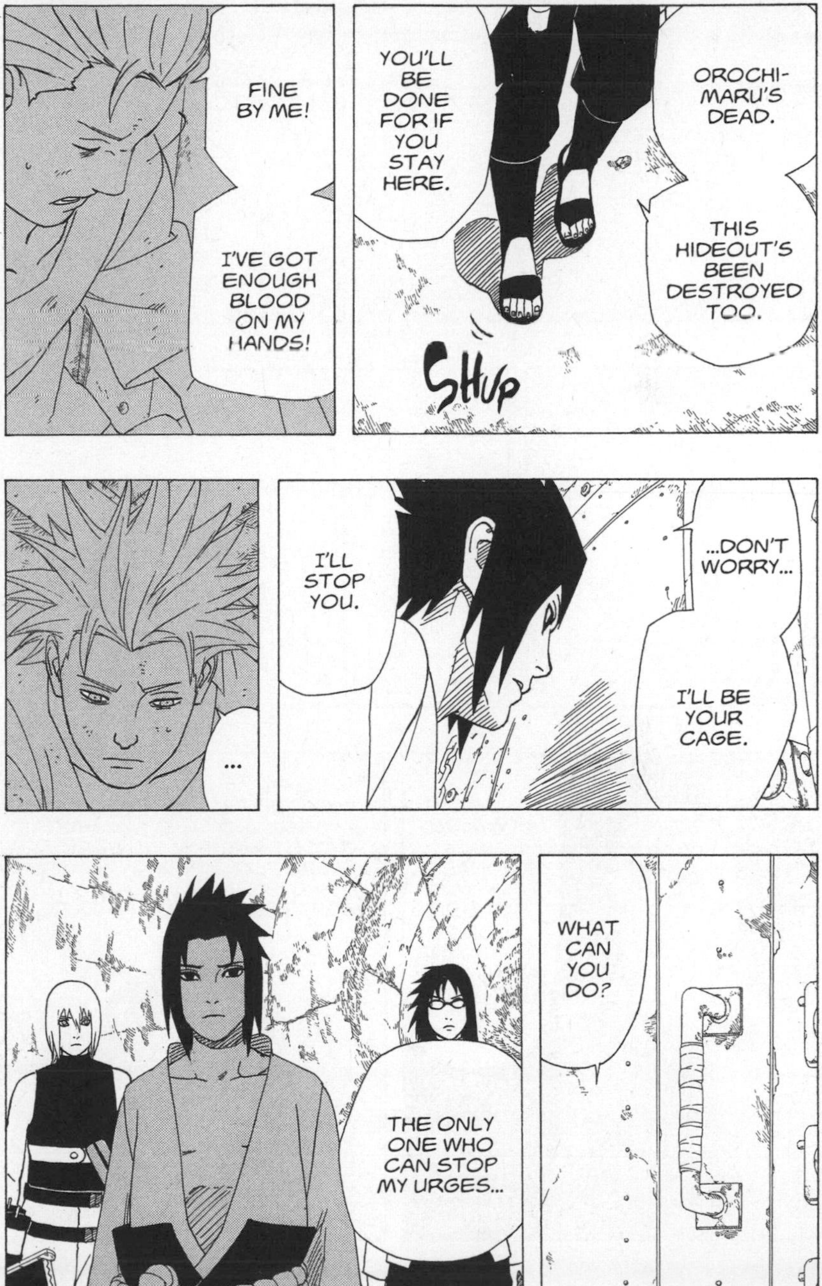
OROCHI-MARU'S DEAD.
THIS HIDEOUT'S BEEN DESTROYED TOO.
YOU'LL BE DONE FOR IF YOU STAY HERE.
SHUP
FINE BY ME!
I'VE GOT ENOUGH BLOOD ON MY HANDS!
...DON'T WORRY...
I'LL BE YOUR CAGE.
I'LL STOP YOU.
...
WHAT CAN YOU DO?
THE ONLY ONE WHO CAN STOP MY URGES...

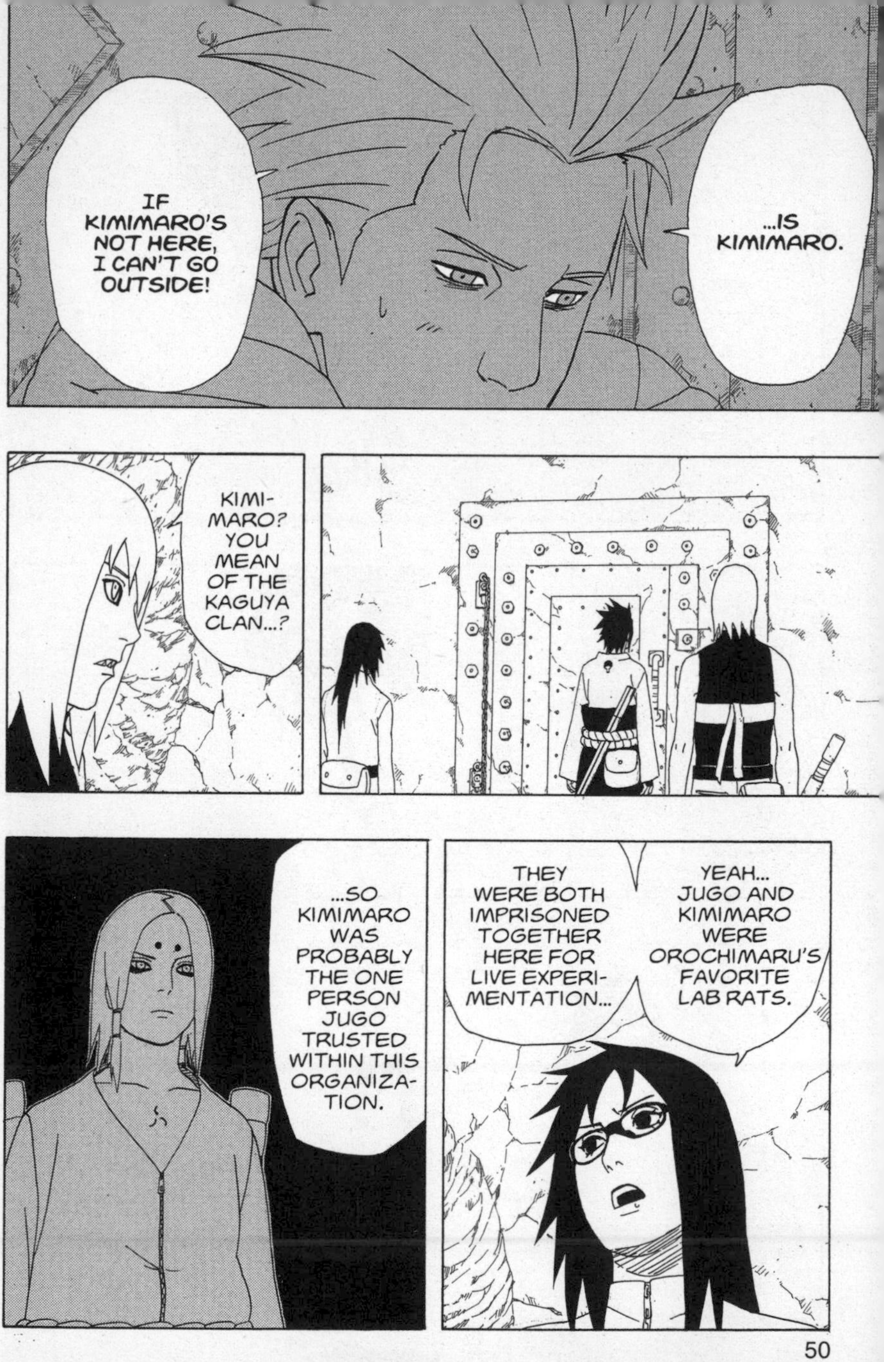
...IS KIMIMARO.
IF KIMIMARO'S NOT HERE, I CAN'T GO OUTSIDE!
KIMI-MARO? YOU MEAN OF THE KAGUYA CLAN...?
YEAH... JUGO AND KIMIMARO WERE OROCHIMARU'S FAVORITE LAB RATS.
THEY WERE BOTH IMPRISONED TOGETHER HERE FOR LIVE EXPERI-MENTATION...
...SO KIMIMARO WAS PROBABLY THE ONE PERSON JUGO TRUSTED WITHIN THIS ORGANIZA-TION.

READ THIS WAY

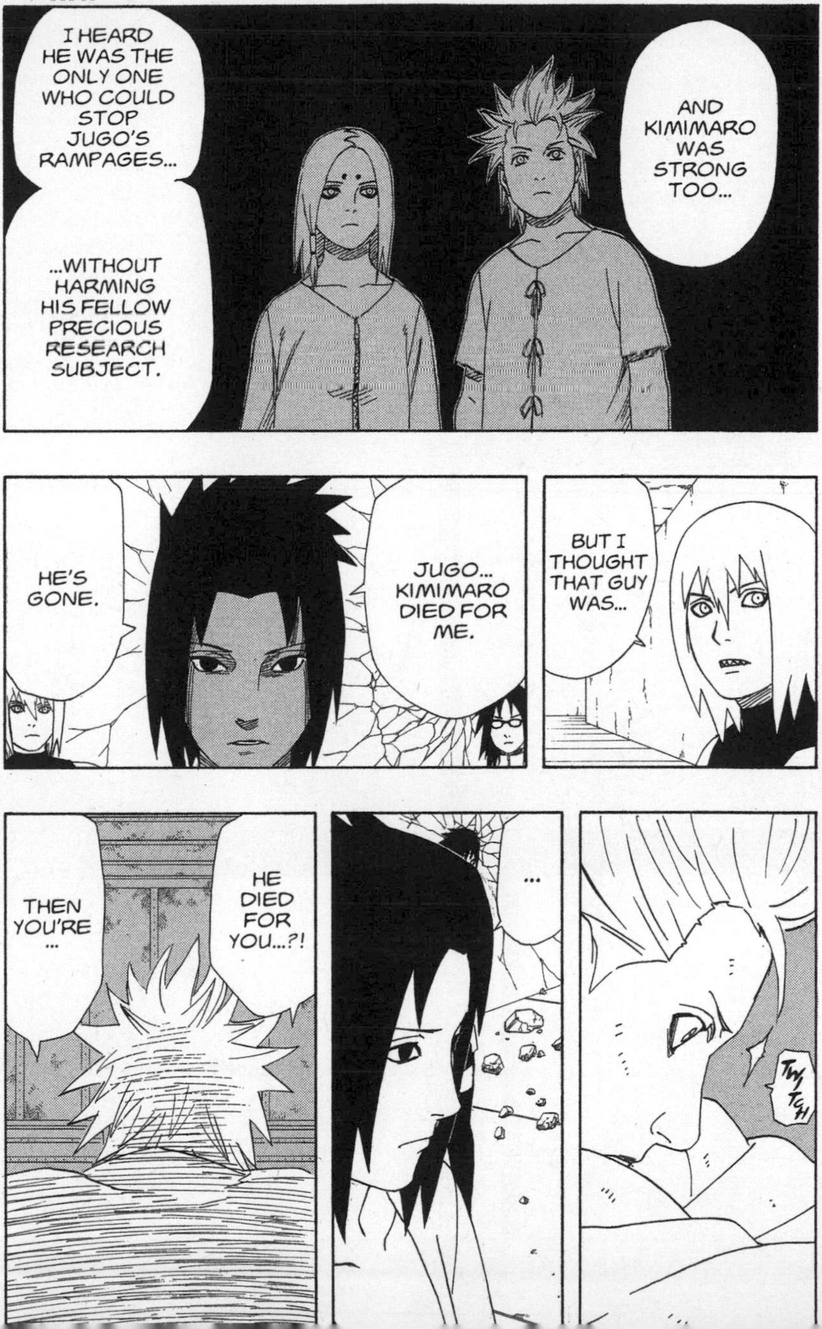
AND KIMIMARO WAS STRONG TOO...
I HEARD HE WAS THE ONLY ONE WHO COULD STOP JUGO'S RAMPAGES...
...WITHOUT HARMING HIS FELLOW PRECIOUS RESEARCH SUBJECT.
BUT I THOUGHT THAT GUY WAS...
JUGO... KIMIMARO DIED FOR ME.
HE'S GONE.
TWITCH
...
HE DIED FOR YOU...?!
THEN YOU'RE ...

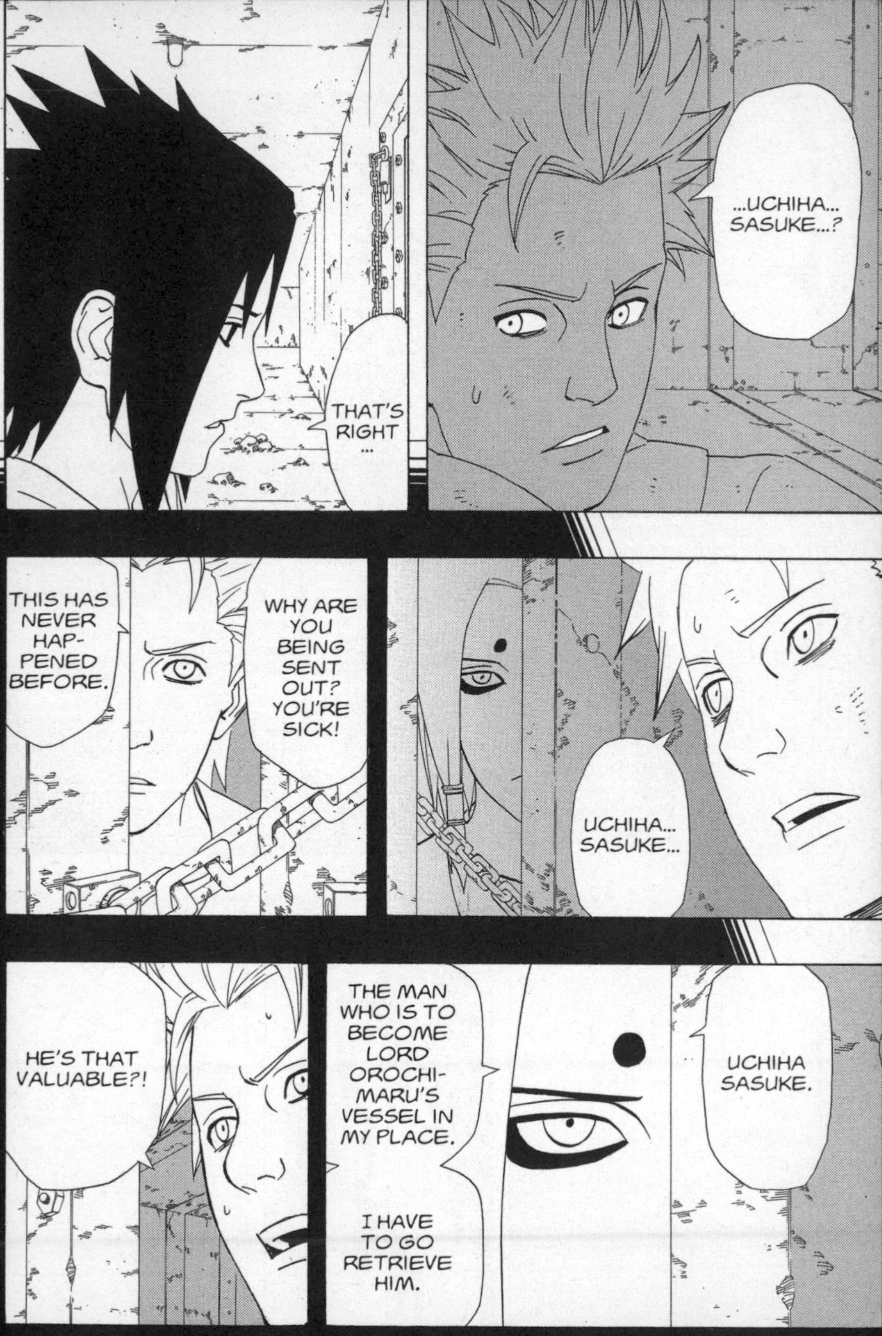
...UCHIHA... SASUKE...?
THAT'S RIGHT ...
UCHIHA... SASUKE...
WHY ARE YOU BEING SENT OUT? YOU'RE SICK!
THIS HAS NEVER HAP-PENED BEFORE.
UCHIHA SASUKE.
THE MAN WHO IS TO BECOME LORD OROCHI-MARU'S VESSEL IN MY PLACE.
I HAVE TO GO RETRIEVE HIM.
HE'S THAT VALUABLE?!

READ THIS WAY

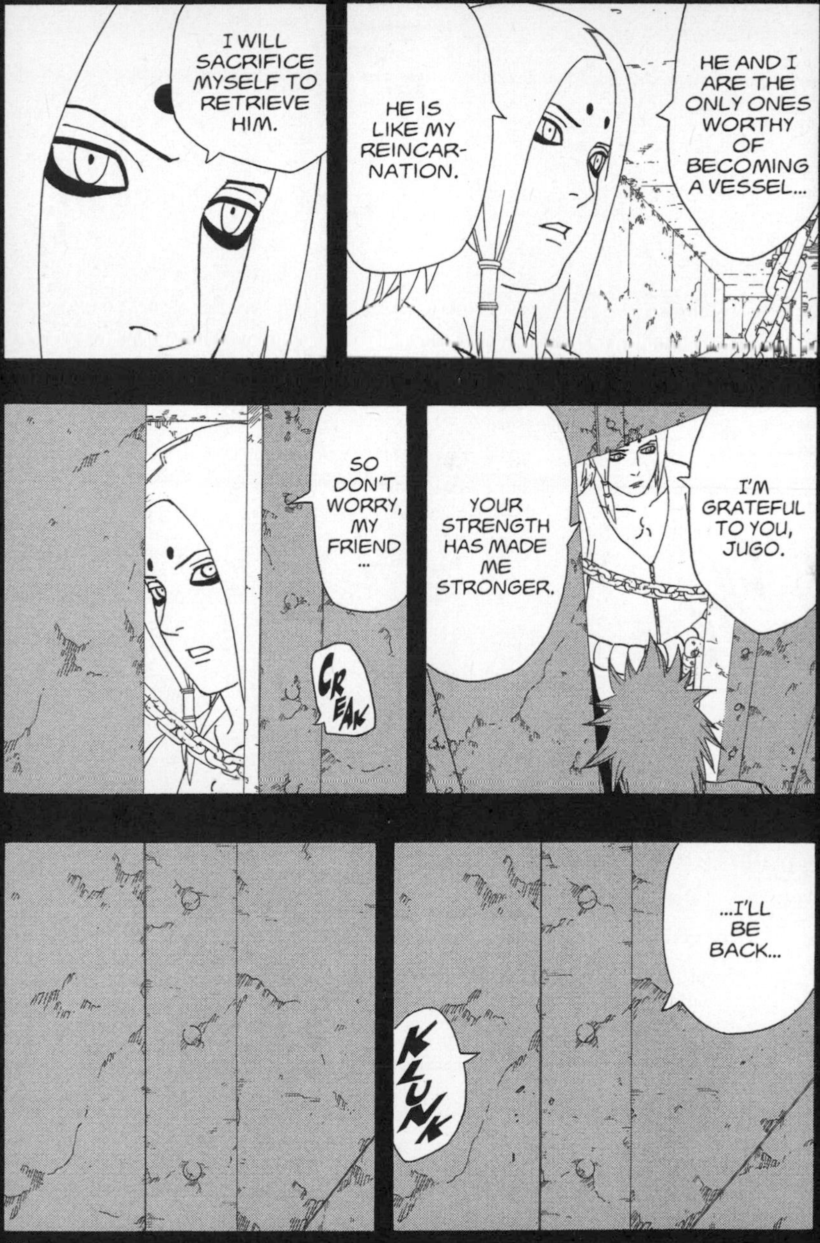
HE AND I ARE THE ONLY ONES WORTHY OF BECOMING A VESSEL...
HE IS LIKE MY REINCARNATION.
I WILL SACRIFICE MYSELF TO RETRIEVE HIM.
I'M GRATEFUL TO YOU, JUGO.
YOUR STRENGTH HAS MADE ME STRONGER.
SO DON'T WORRY, MY FRIEND ...
CREAK
...I'LL BE BACK...
KLUNK

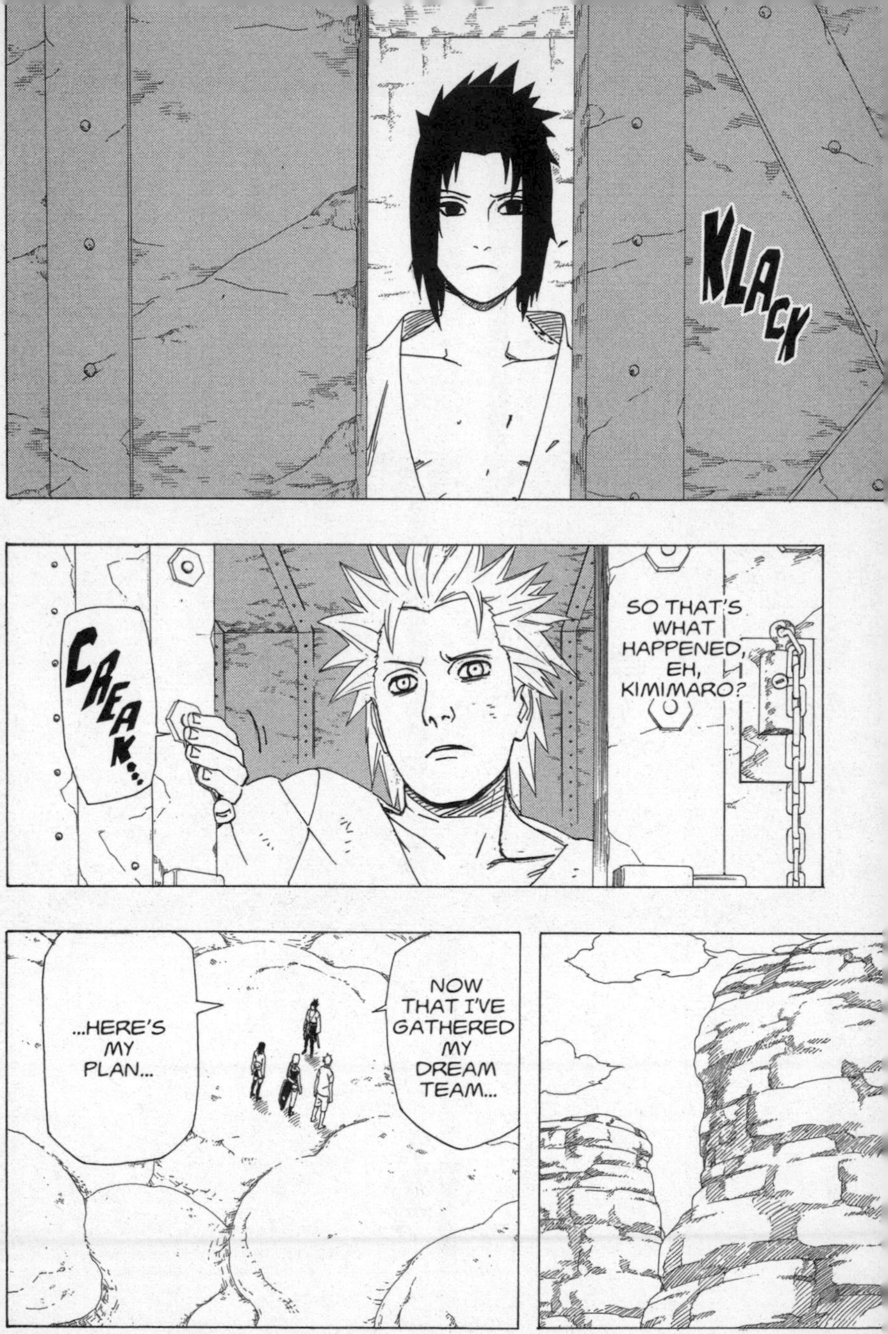
KLACK
SO THAT'S WHAT HAPPENED, EH, KIMIMARO?
CREAK...
NOW THAT I'VE GATHERED MY DREAM TEAM...
...HERE'S MY PLAN...

READ THIS WAY

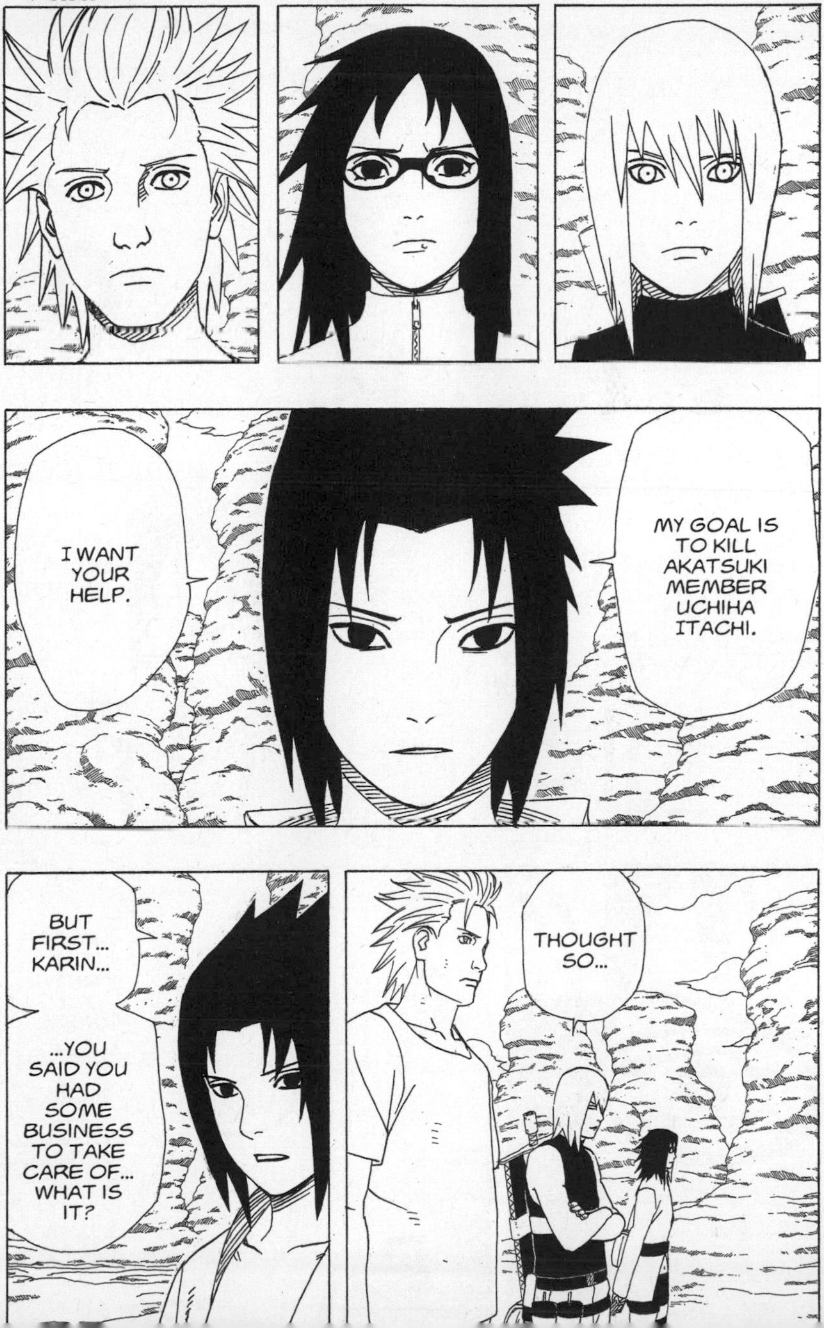
MY GOAL IS TO KILL AKATSUKI MEMBER UCHIHA ITACHI.
I WANT YOUR HELP.
THOUGHT SO...
BUT FIRST... KARIN...
...YOU SAID YOU HAD SOME BUSINESS TO TAKE CARE OF... WHAT IS IT?

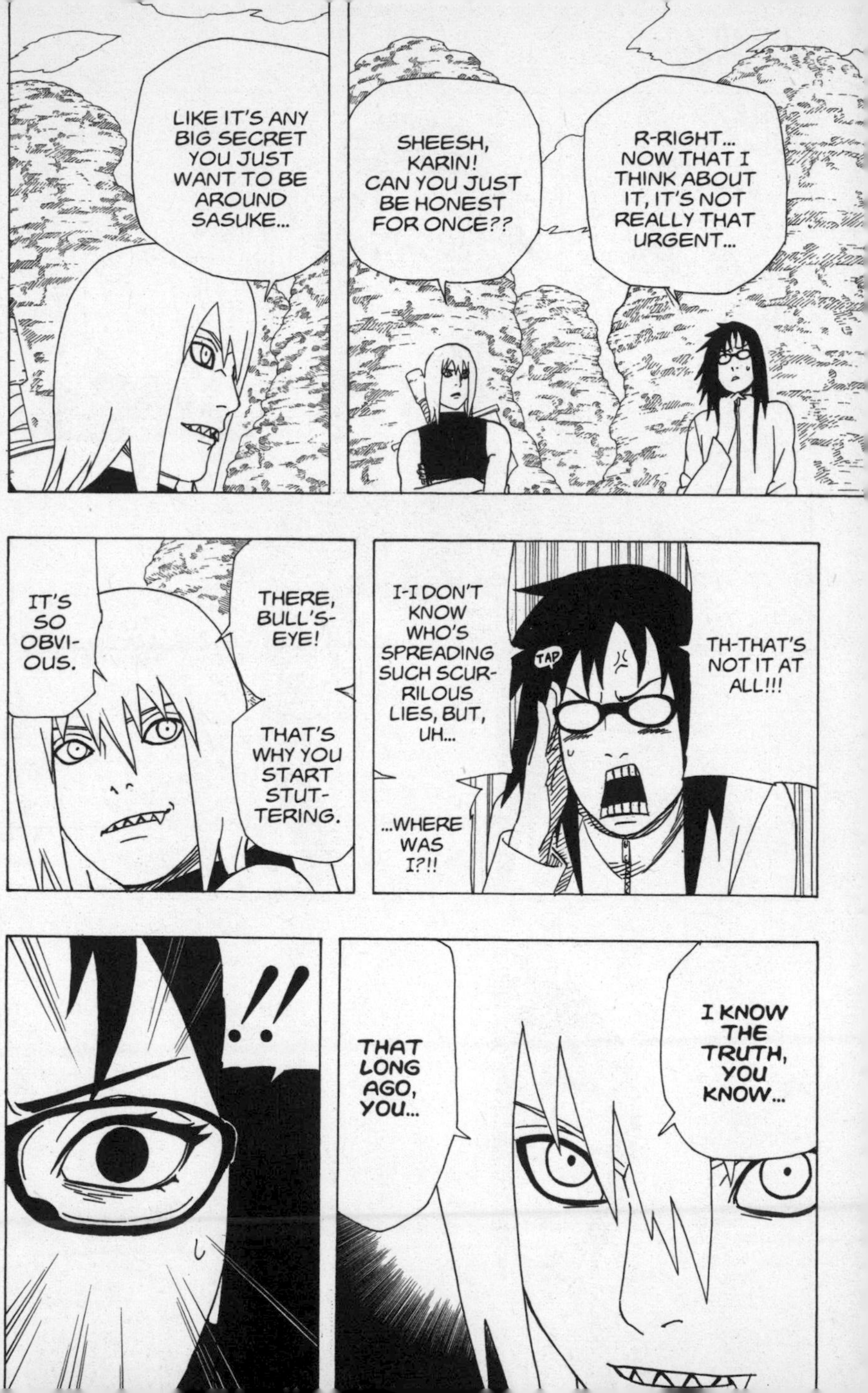
R-RIGHT... NOW THAT I THINK ABOUT IT, IT'S NOT REALLY THAT URGENT...
SHEESH, KARIN! CAN YOU JUST BE HONEST FOR ONCE??
LIKE IT'S ANY BIG SECRET YOU JUST WANT TO BE AROUND SASUKE...
TH-THAT'S NOT IT AT ALL!!!
TAP
I-I DON'T KNOW WHO'S SPREADING SUCH SCURRILOUS LIES, BUT, UH...
...WHERE WAS I?!!
THERE, BULL'S-EYE!
IT'S SO OBVIOUS.
THAT'S WHY YOU START STUTTERING.
I KNOW THE TRUTH, YOU KNOW...
THAT LONG AGO, YOU...
!!

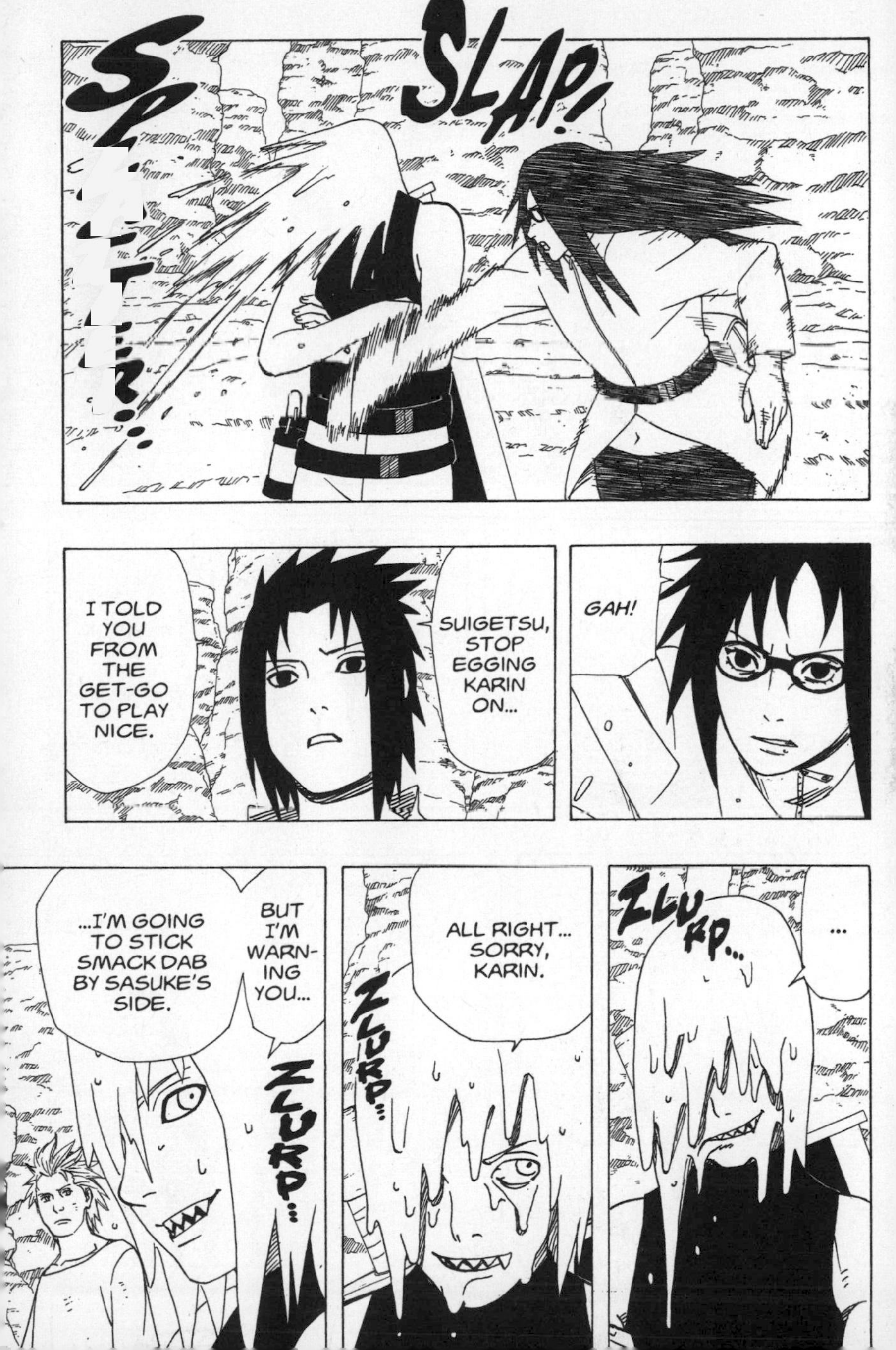
SLAP!
GAH!
SUIGETSU, STOP EGGING KARIN ON...
I TOLD YOU FROM THE GET-GO TO PLAY NICE.
ZLURP...
...
ALL RIGHT... SORRY, KARIN.
ZLURP...
BUT I'M WARNING YOU...
...I'M GOING TO STICK SMACK DAB BY SASUKE'S SIDE.
ZLURP...

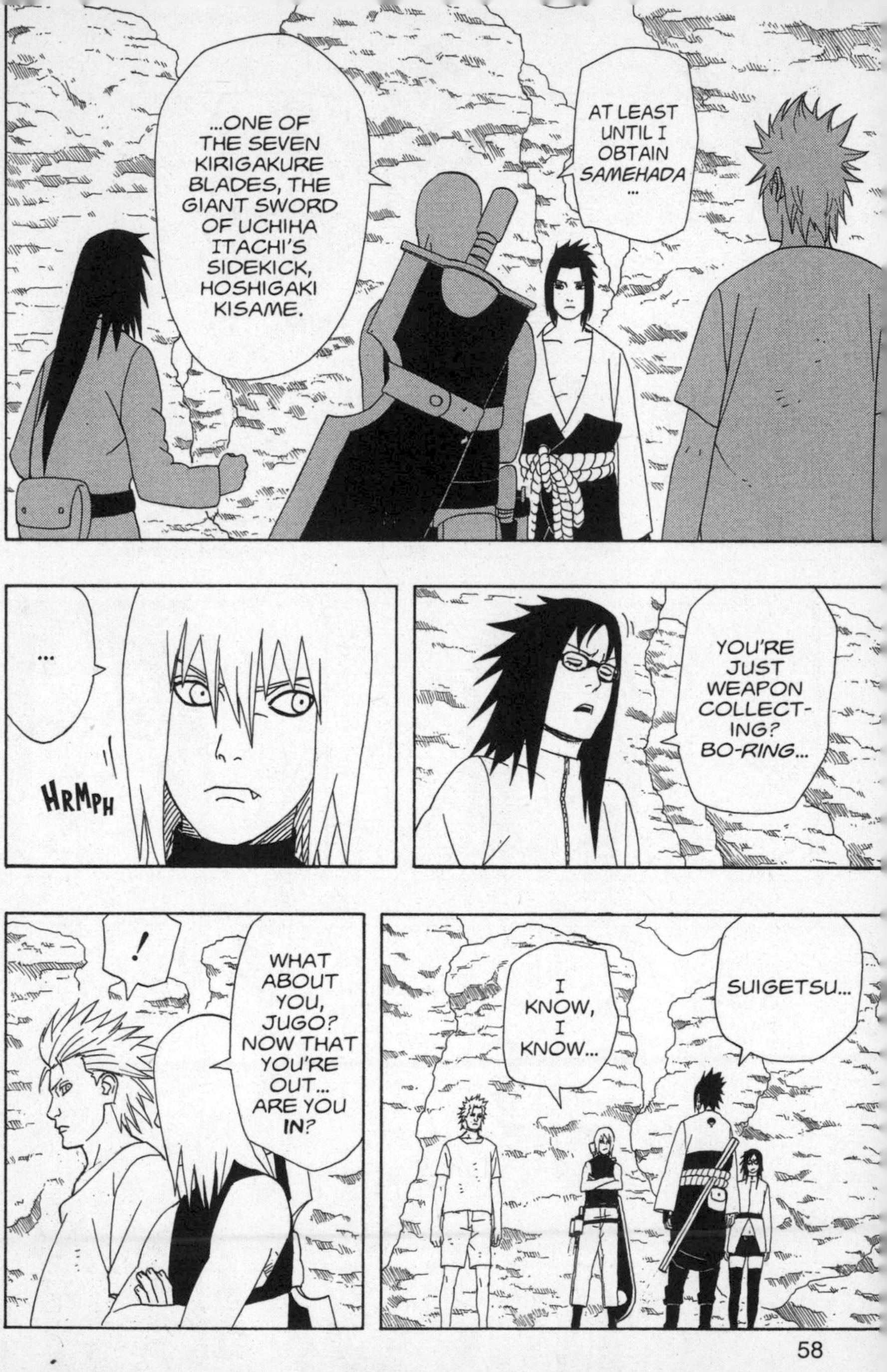
AT LEAST UNTIL I OBTAIN *SAMEHADA* ...
...ONE OF THE SEVEN KIRIGAKURE BLADES, THE GIANT SWORD OF UCHIHA ITACHI'S SIDEKICK, HOSHIGAKI KISAME.
YOU'RE JUST WEAPON COLLECTING? BO-*RING*...
...
HRMPH
SUIGETSU...
I KNOW, I KNOW...
WHAT ABOUT YOU, JUGO? NOW THAT YOU'RE OUT... ARE YOU **IN**?
!

READ THIS WAY

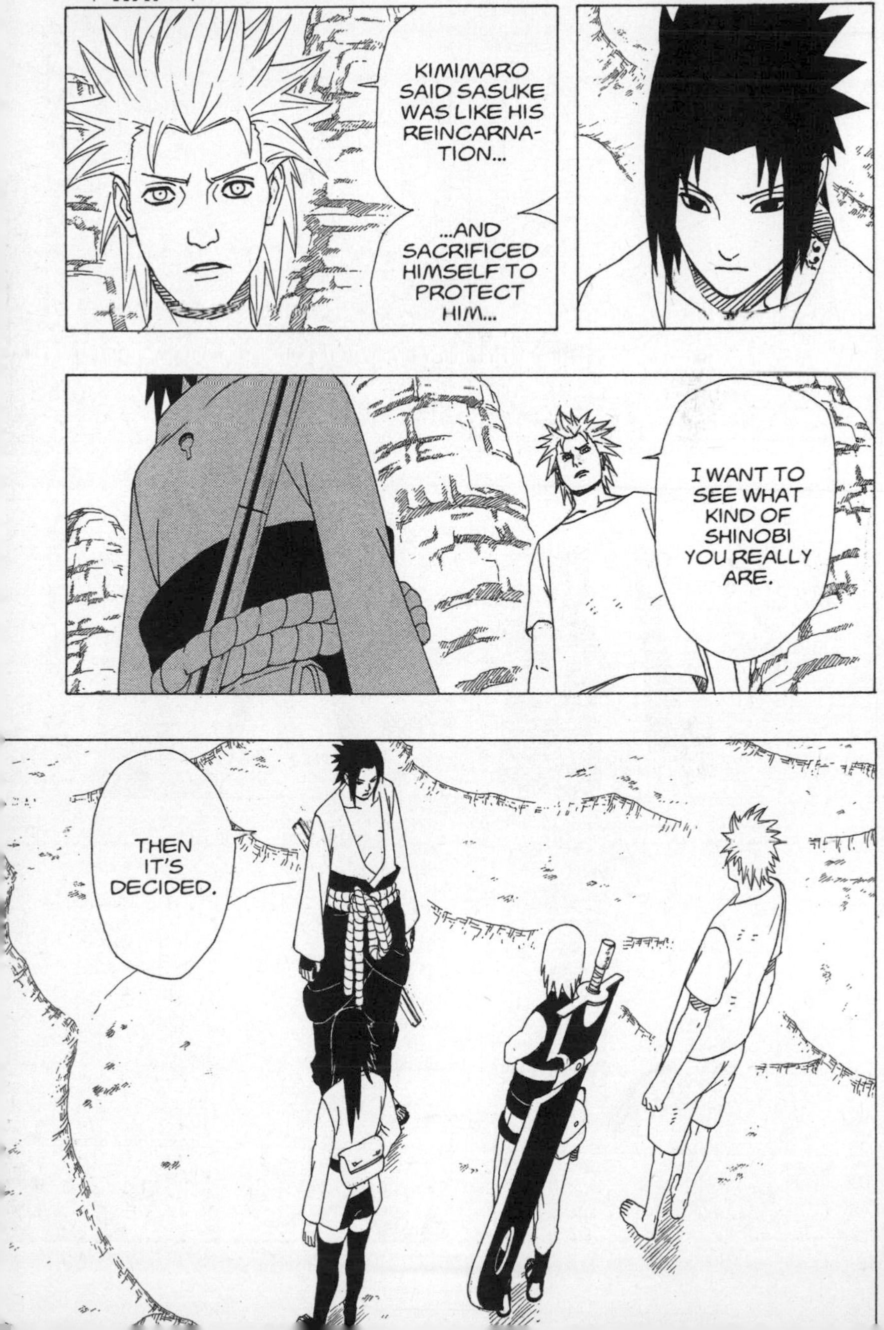
KIMIMARO SAID SASUKE WAS LIKE HIS REINCARNATION...
...AND SACRIFICED HIMSELF TO PROTECT HIM...
I WANT TO SEE WHAT KIND OF SHINOBI YOU REALLY ARE.
THEN IT'S DECIDED.

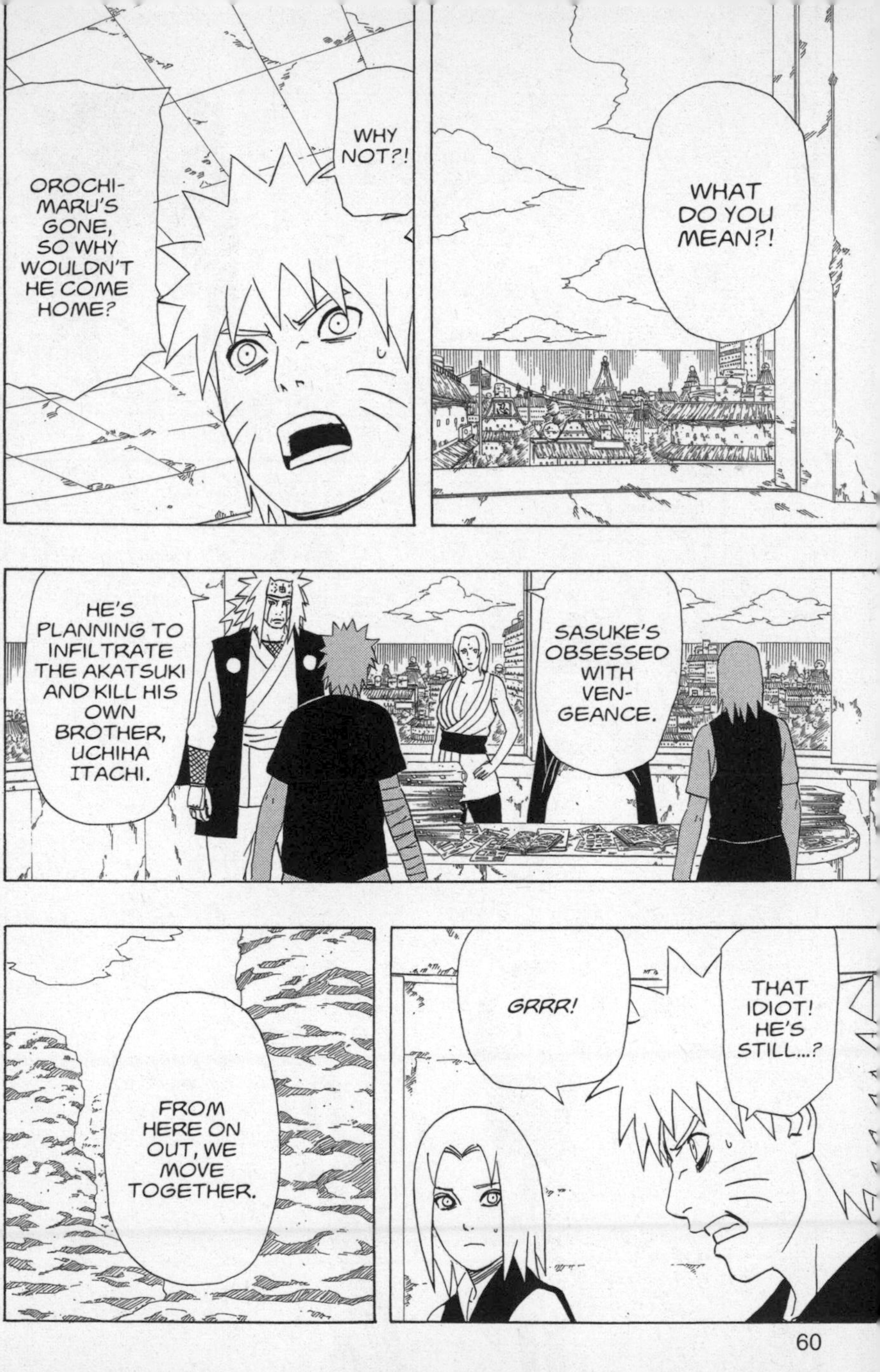
WHAT DO YOU MEAN?!
WHY NOT?!
OROCHI-MARU'S GONE, SO WHY WOULDN'T HE COME HOME?
SASUKE'S OBSESSED WITH VEN-GEANCE.
HE'S PLANNING TO INFILTRATE THE AKATSUKI AND KILL HIS OWN BROTHER, UCHIHA ITACHI.
THAT IDIOT! HE'S STILL...?
GRRR!
FROM HERE ON OUT, WE MOVE TOGETHER.

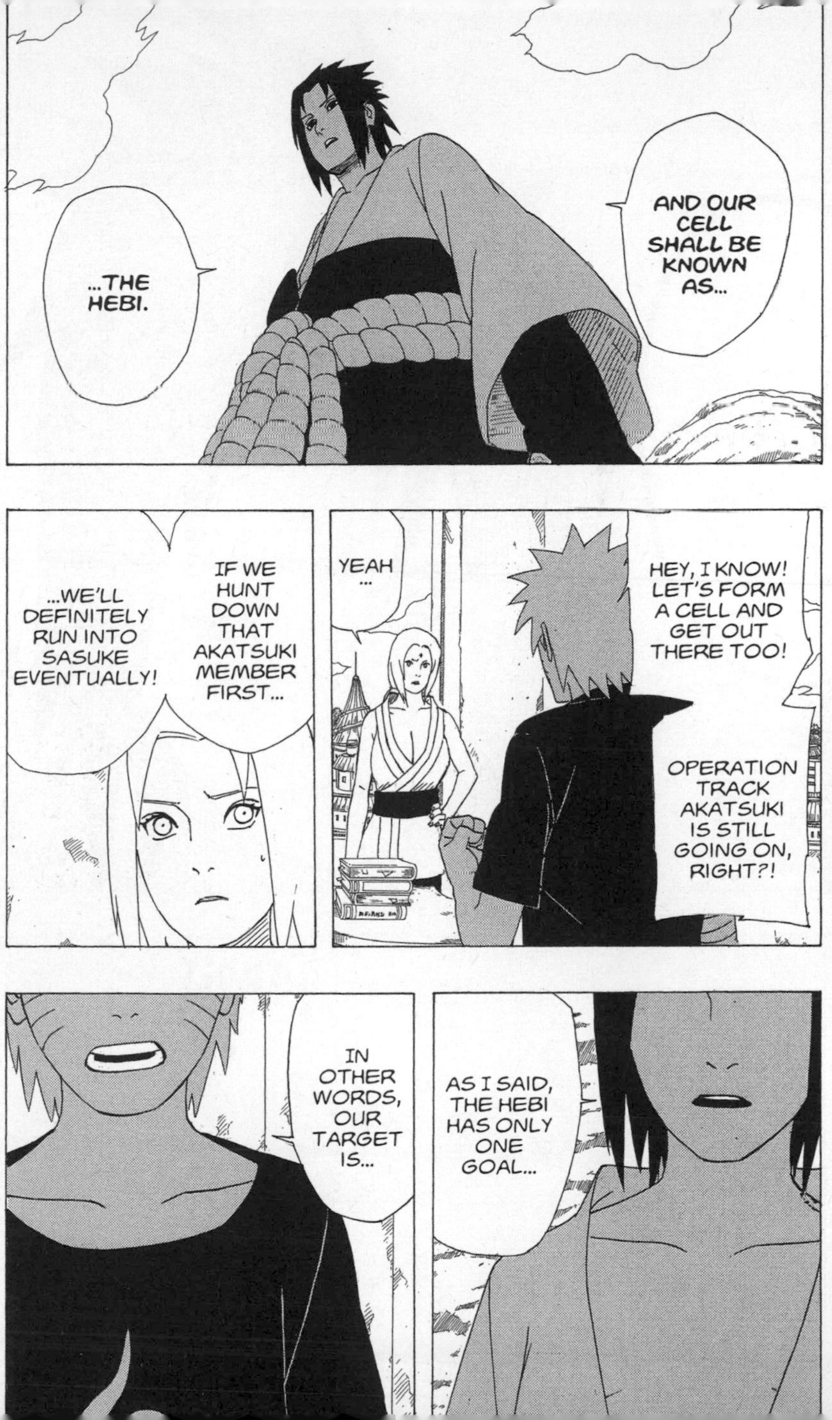
AND OUR CELL SHALL BE KNOWN AS...
...THE HEBI.
HEY, I KNOW! LET'S FORM A CELL AND GET OUT THERE TOO!
OPERATION TRACK AKATSUKI IS STILL GOING ON, RIGHT?!
YEAH ...
IF WE HUNT DOWN THAT AKATSUKI MEMBER FIRST...
...WE'LL DEFINITELY RUN INTO SASUKE EVENTUALLY!
AS I SAID, THE HEBI HAS ONLY ONE GOAL...
IN OTHER WORDS, OUR TARGET IS...

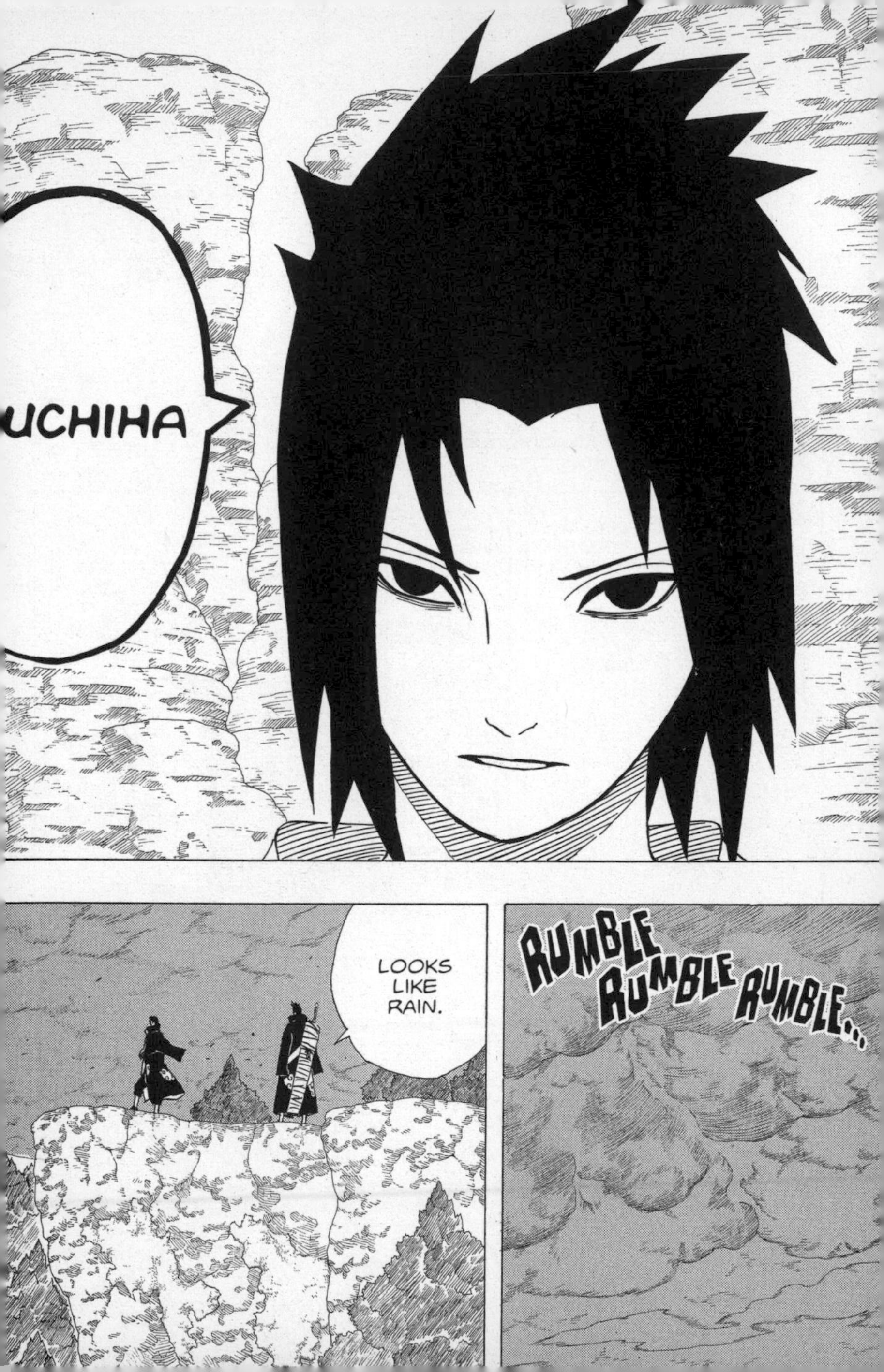
UCHIHA
RUMBLE RUMBLE RUMBLE...
LOOKS LIKE RAIN.

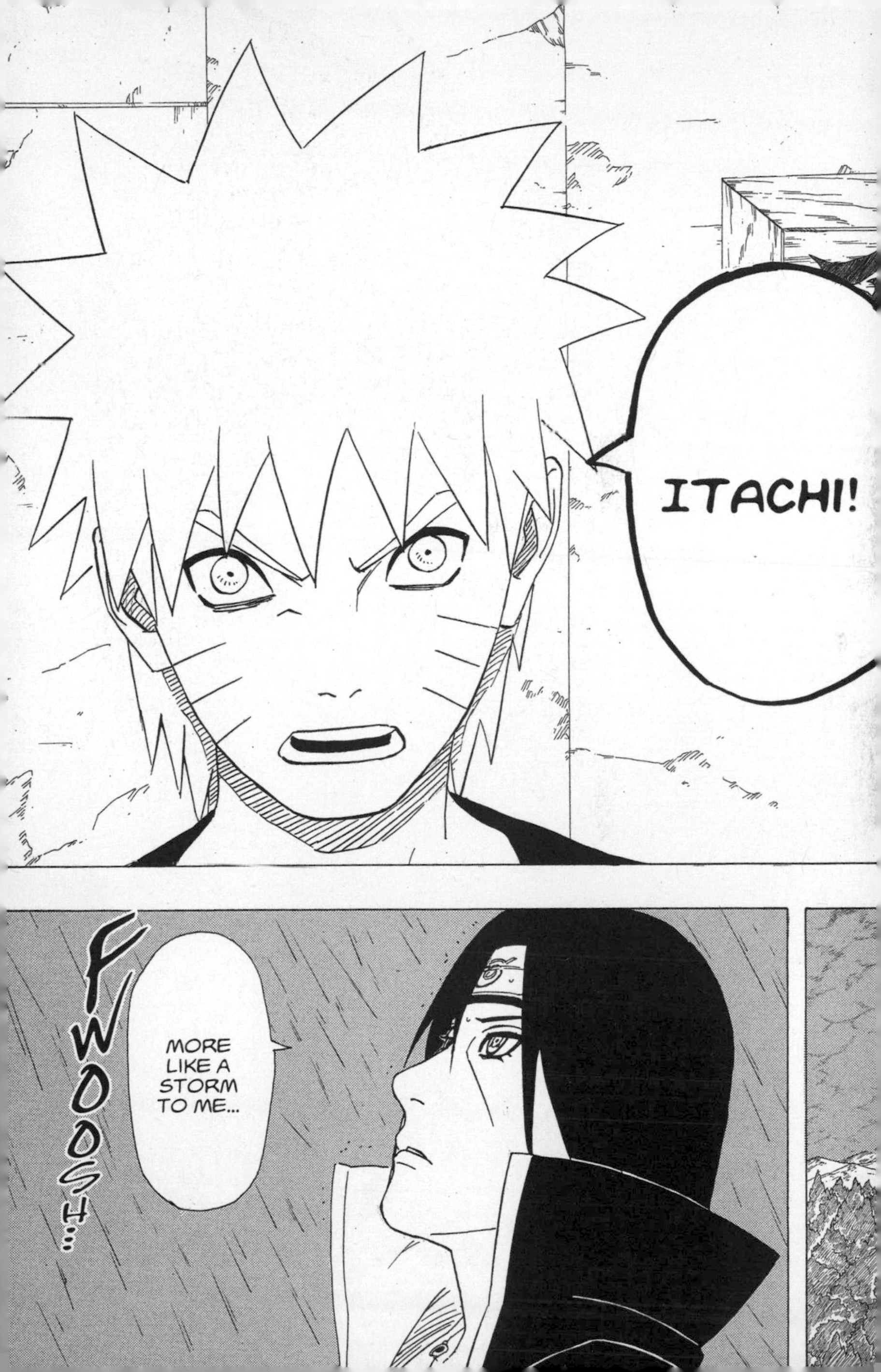
ITACHI!
MORE LIKE A STORM TO ME...
FWOOSH...

NARUTO

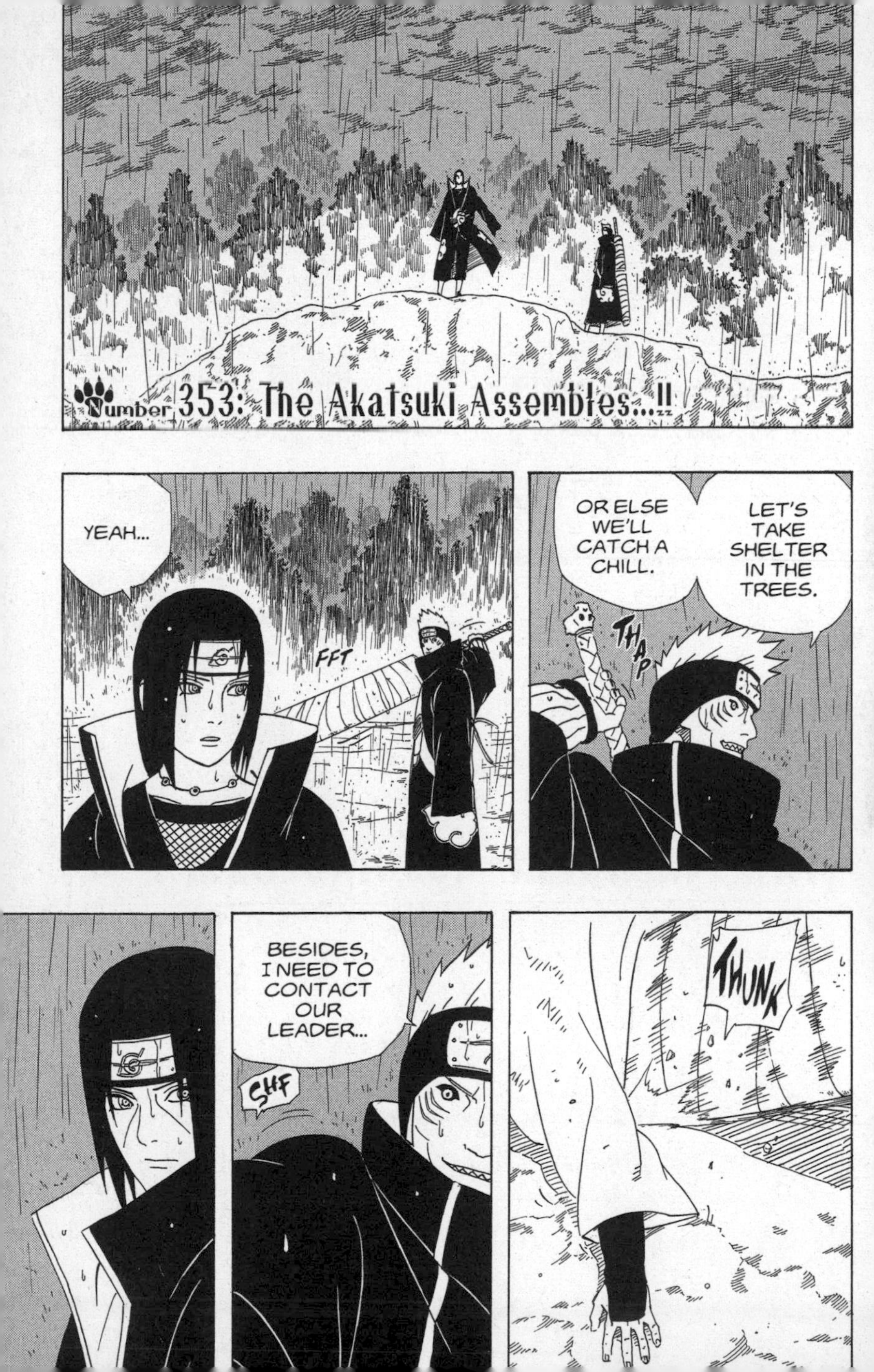
Number 353: The Akatsuki Assembles...!!
LET'S TAKE SHELTER IN THE TREES.
OR ELSE WE'LL CATCH A CHILL.
THAP
YEAH...
FFT
THUNK
BESIDES, I NEED TO CONTACT OUR LEADER...
SHF

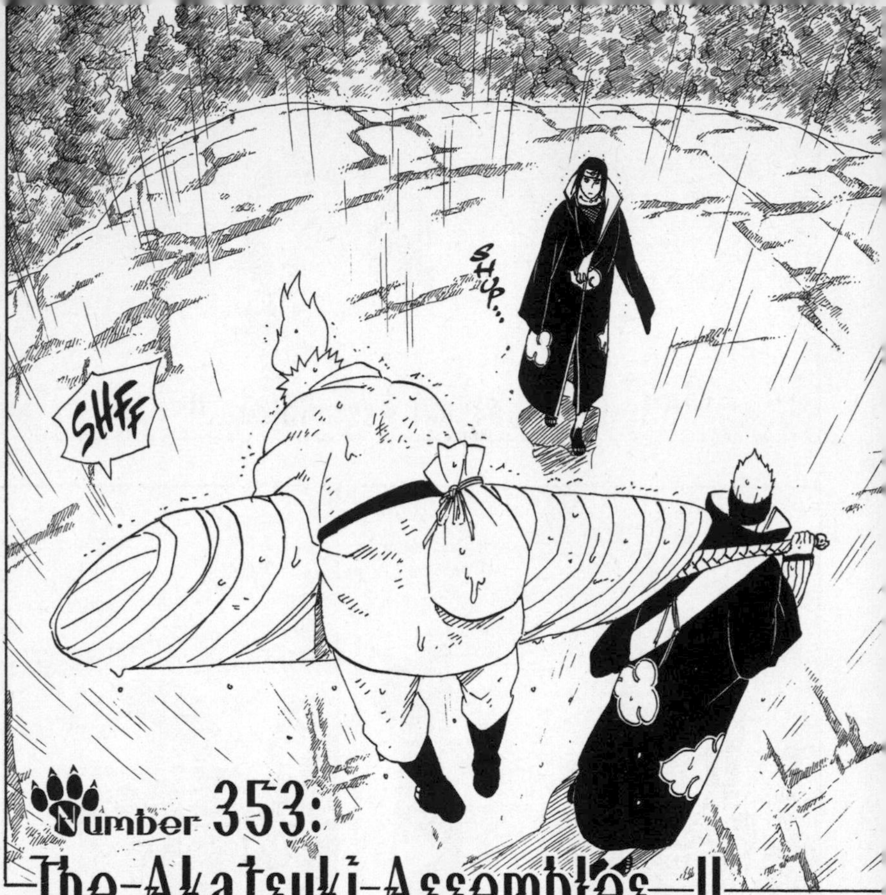
SHUP...
SHFF

Number 353: The Akatsuki Assembles...!!

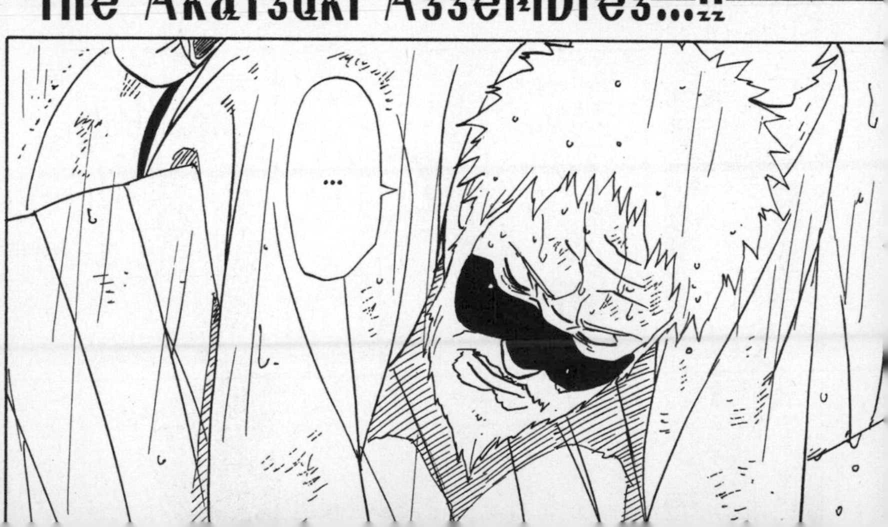
...

READ THIS WAY

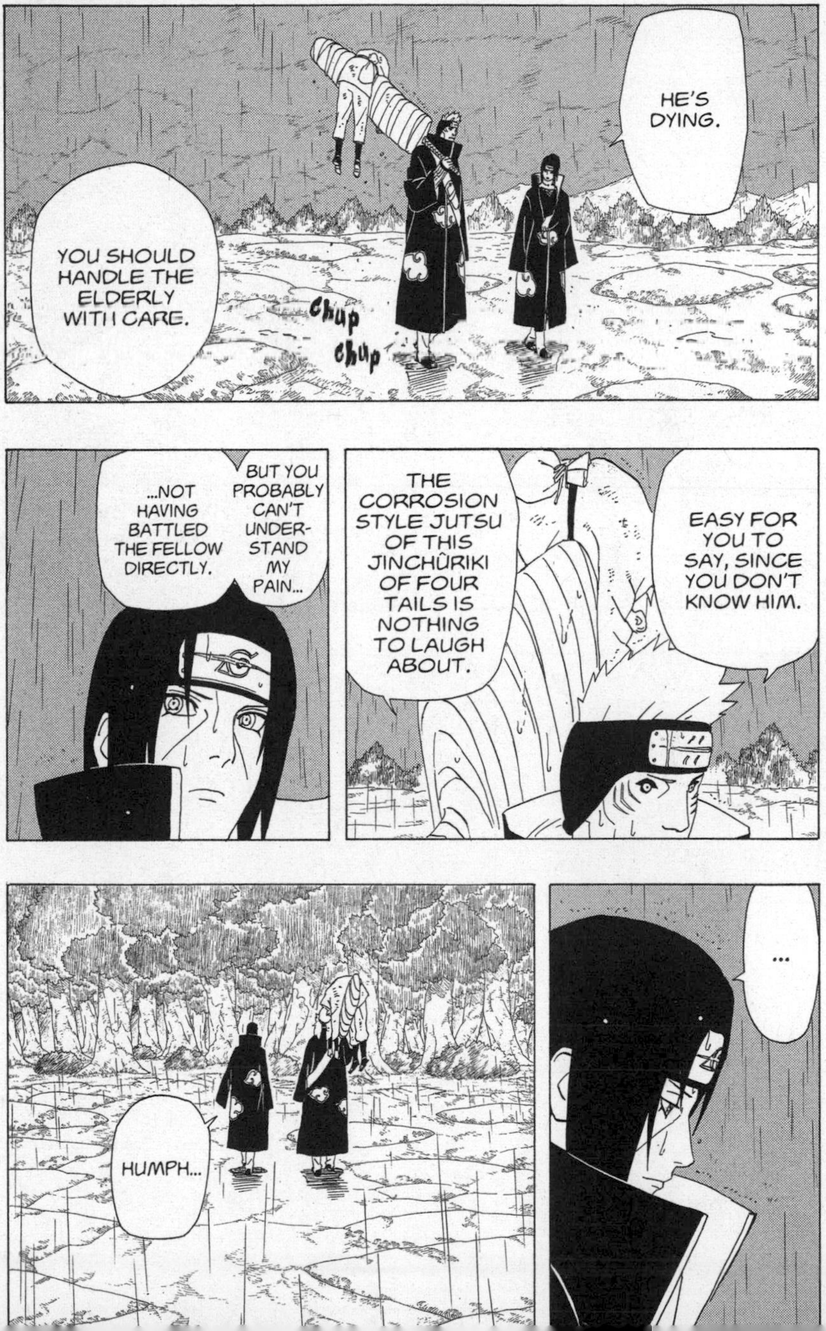
HE'S DYING.
YOU SHOULD HANDLE THE ELDERLY WITH CARE.
CHUP
CHUP
EASY FOR YOU TO SAY, SINCE YOU DON'T KNOW HIM.
THE CORROSION STYLE JUTSU OF THIS JINCHŪRIKI OF FOUR TAILS IS NOTHING TO LAUGH ABOUT.
BUT YOU PROBABLY CAN'T UNDERSTAND MY PAIN...
...NOT HAVING BATTLED THE FELLOW DIRECTLY.
...
HUMPH...

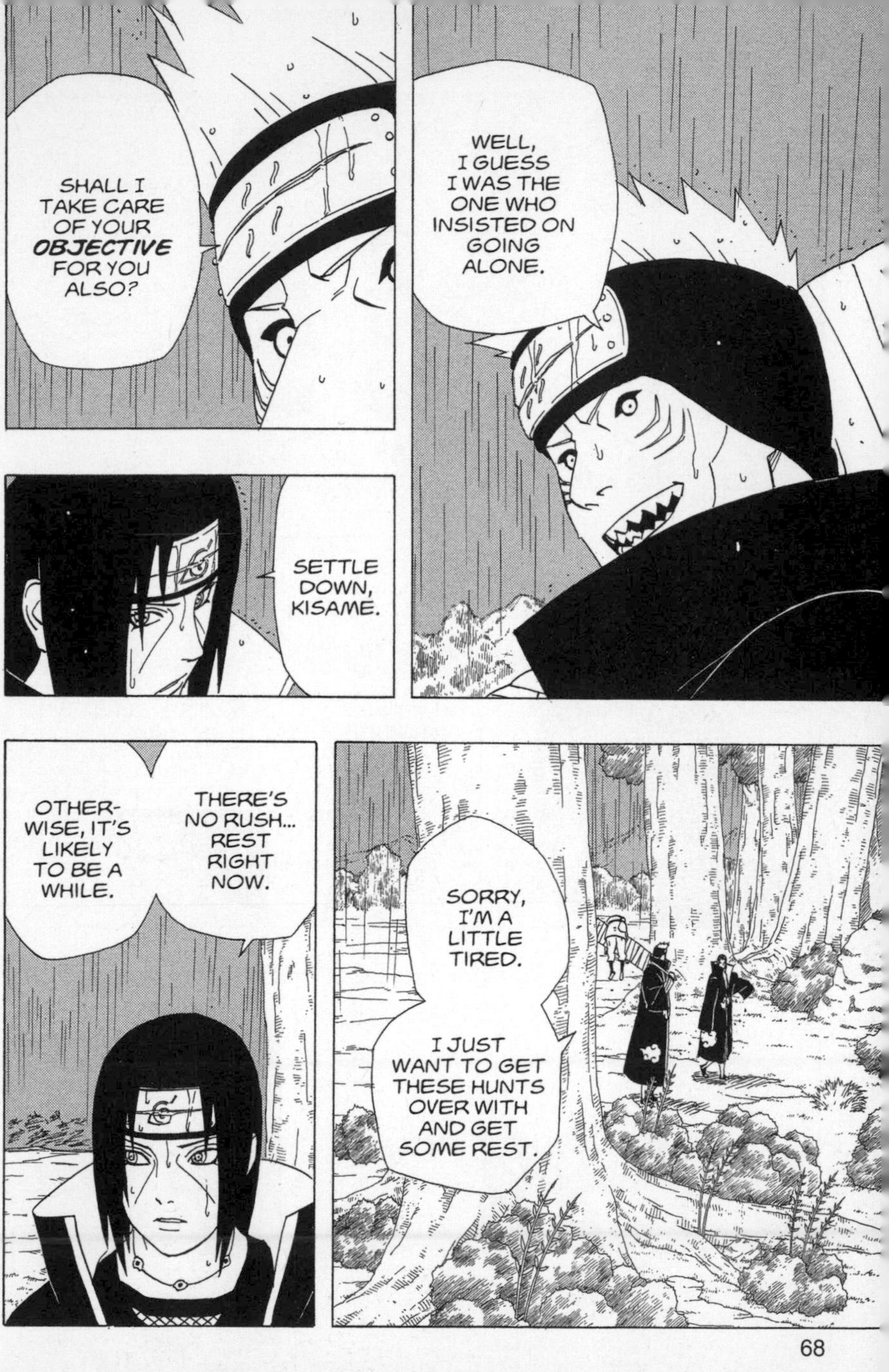
WELL, I GUESS I WAS THE ONE WHO INSISTED ON GOING ALONE.
SHALL I TAKE CARE OF YOUR OBJECTIVE FOR YOU ALSO?
SETTLE DOWN, KISAME.
SORRY, I'M A LITTLE TIRED.
I JUST WANT TO GET THESE HUNTS OVER WITH AND GET SOME REST.
THERE'S NO RUSH... REST RIGHT NOW.
OTHER-WISE, IT'S LIKELY TO BE A WHILE.

READ THIS WAY

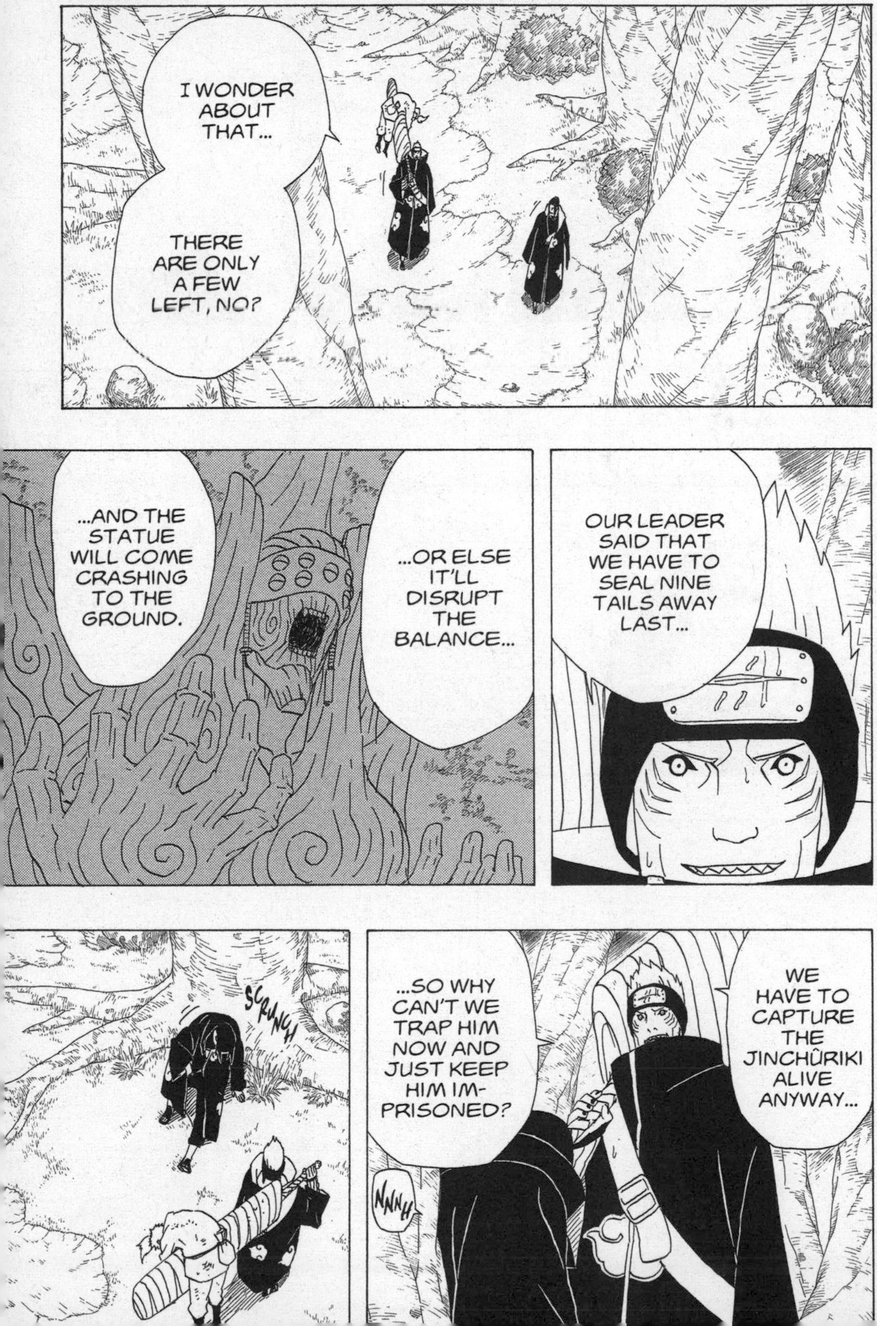
I WONDER ABOUT THAT...
THERE ARE ONLY A FEW LEFT, NO?
OUR LEADER SAID THAT WE HAVE TO SEAL NINE TAILS AWAY LAST...
...OR ELSE IT'LL DISRUPT THE BALANCE...
...AND THE STATUE WILL COME CRASHING TO THE GROUND.
WE HAVE TO CAPTURE THE JINCHÛRIKI ALIVE ANYWAY...
...SO WHY CAN'T WE TRAP HIM NOW AND JUST KEEP HIM IM-PRISONED?
NNNH
SCRUNCH

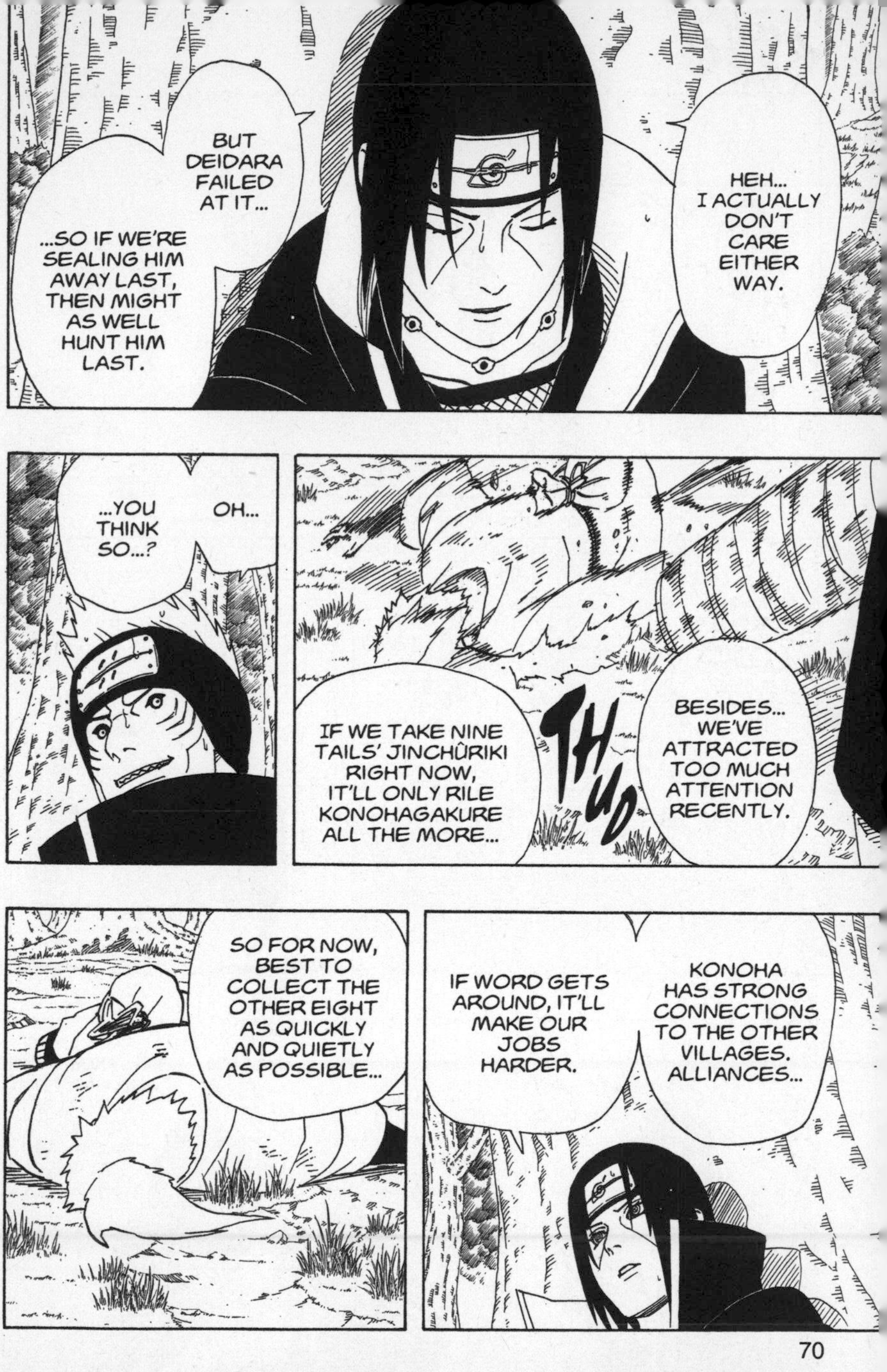
HEH... I ACTUALLY DON'T CARE EITHER WAY.
BUT DEIDARA FAILED AT IT...
...SO IF WE'RE SEALING HIM AWAY LAST, THEN MIGHT AS WELL HUNT HIM LAST.
BESIDES... WE'VE ATTRACTED TOO MUCH ATTENTION RECENTLY.
THUD
IF WE TAKE NINE TAILS' JINCHÛRIKI RIGHT NOW, IT'LL ONLY RILE KONOHAGAKURE ALL THE MORE...
OH...
...YOU THINK SO...?
KONOHA HAS STRONG CONNECTIONS TO THE OTHER VILLAGES. ALLIANCES...
IF WORD GETS AROUND, IT'LL MAKE OUR JOBS HARDER.
SO FOR NOW, BEST TO COLLECT THE OTHER EIGHT AS QUICKLY AND QUIETLY AS POSSIBLE...

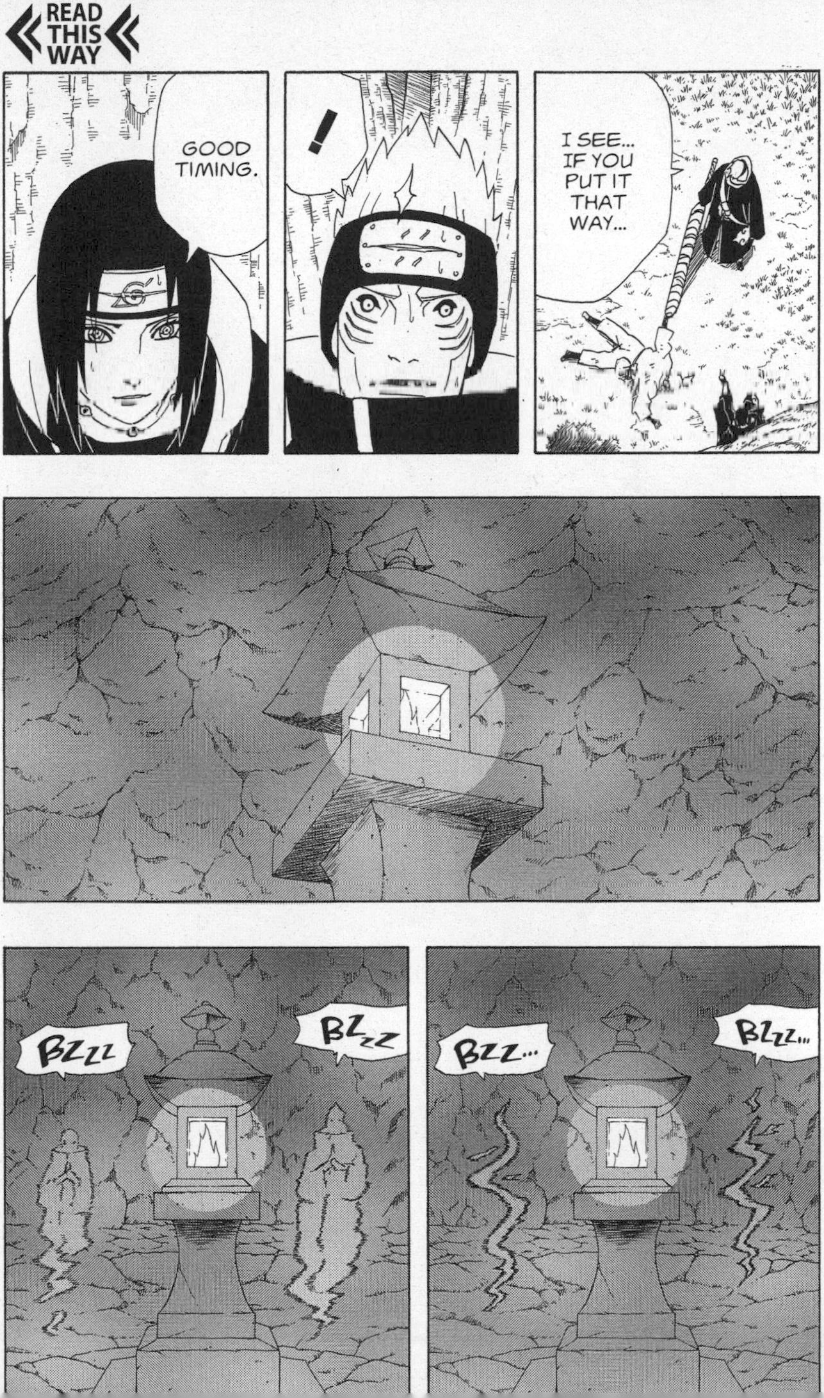
READ THIS WAY
I SEE... IF YOU PUT IT THAT WAY...
!
GOOD TIMING.
BZZZ...
BZZ...
BZZZ
BZZZ

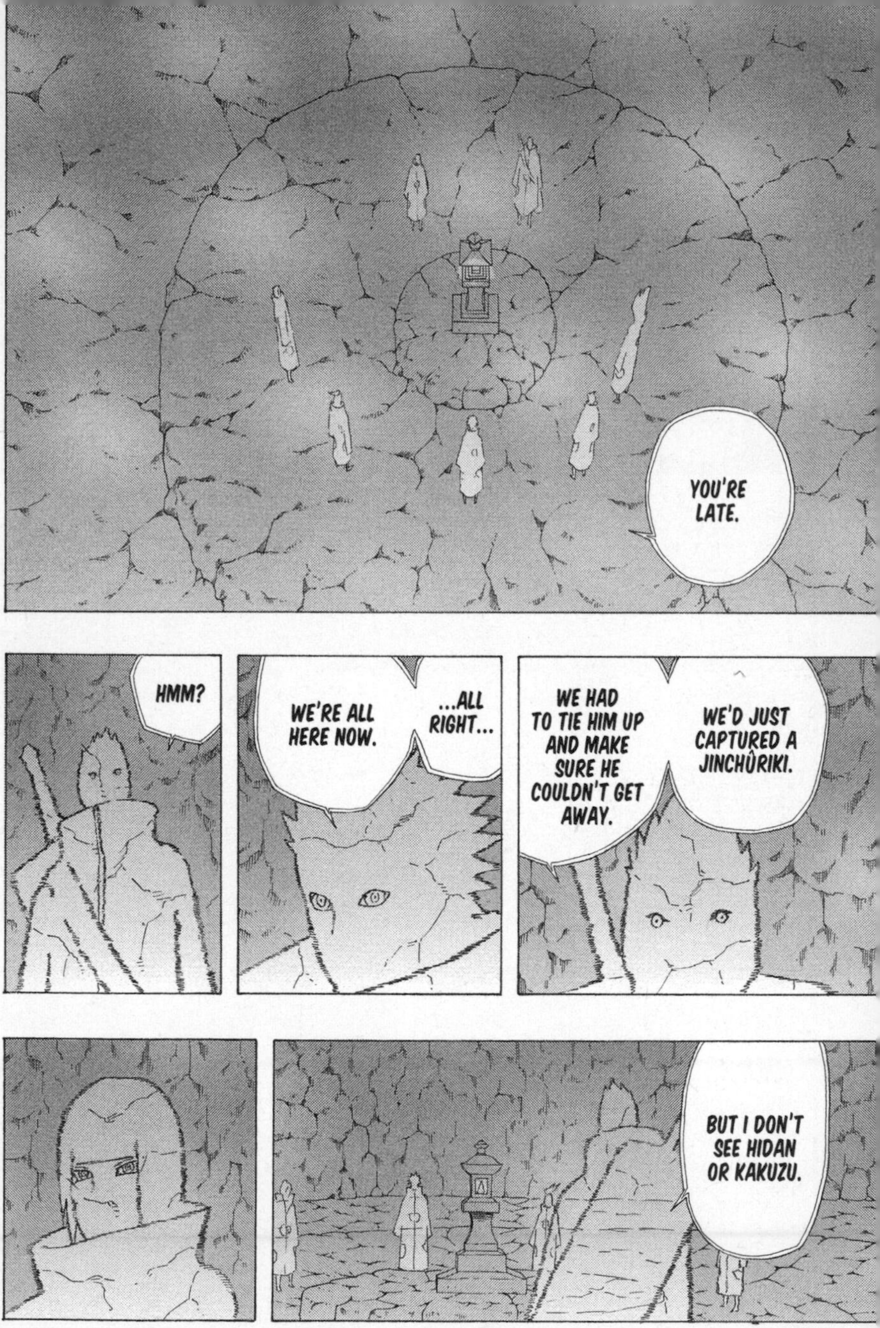
YOU'RE LATE.
WE'D JUST CAPTURED A JINCHÛRIKI.
WE HAD TO TIE HIM UP AND MAKE SURE HE COULDN'T GET AWAY.
...ALL RIGHT...
WE'RE ALL HERE NOW.
HMM?
BUT I DON'T SEE HIDAN OR KAKUZU.

READ THIS WAY

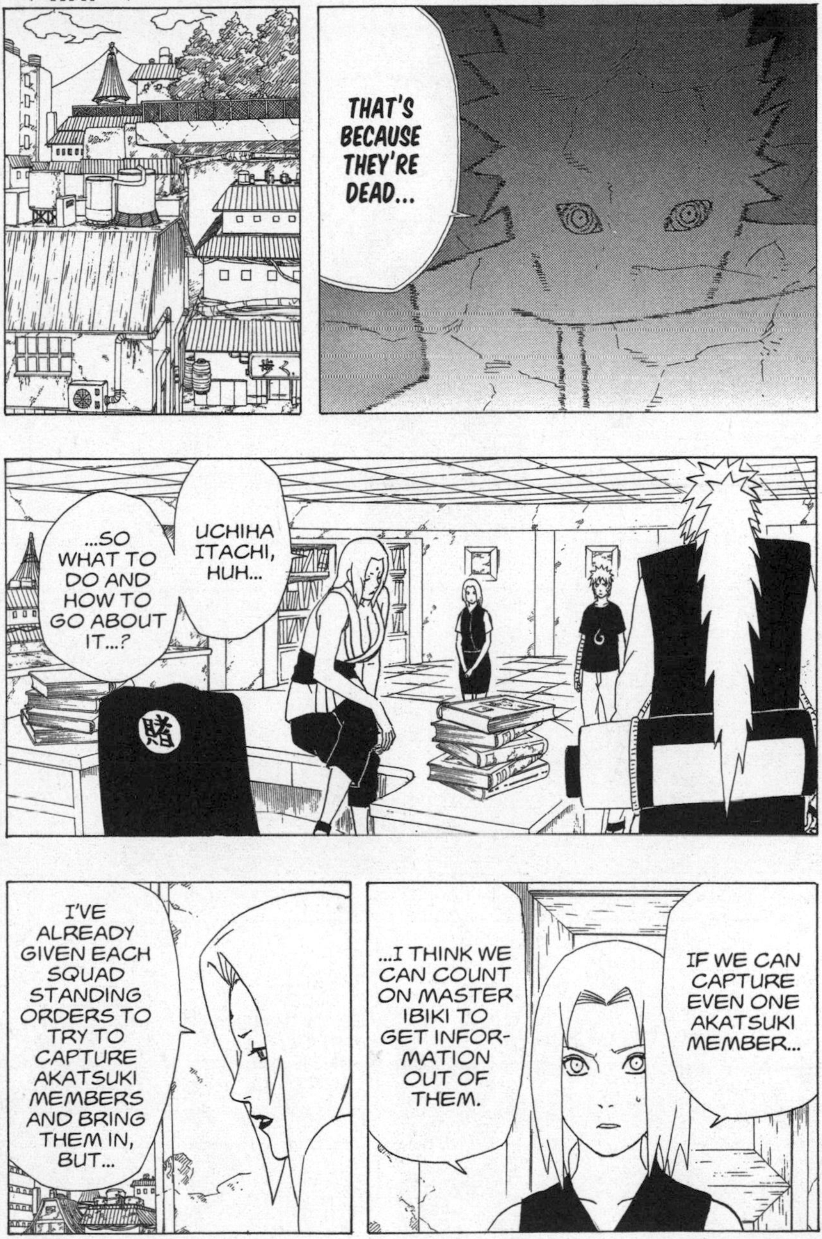
THAT'S BECAUSE THEY'RE DEAD...
UCHIHA ITACHI, HUH...
...SO WHAT TO DO AND HOW TO GO ABOUT IT...?
IF WE CAN CAPTURE EVEN ONE AKATSUKI MEMBER...
...I THINK WE CAN COUNT ON MASTER IBIKI TO GET INFORMATION OUT OF THEM.
I'VE ALREADY GIVEN EACH SQUAD STANDING ORDERS TO TRY TO CAPTURE AKATSUKI MEMBERS AND BRING THEM IN, BUT...

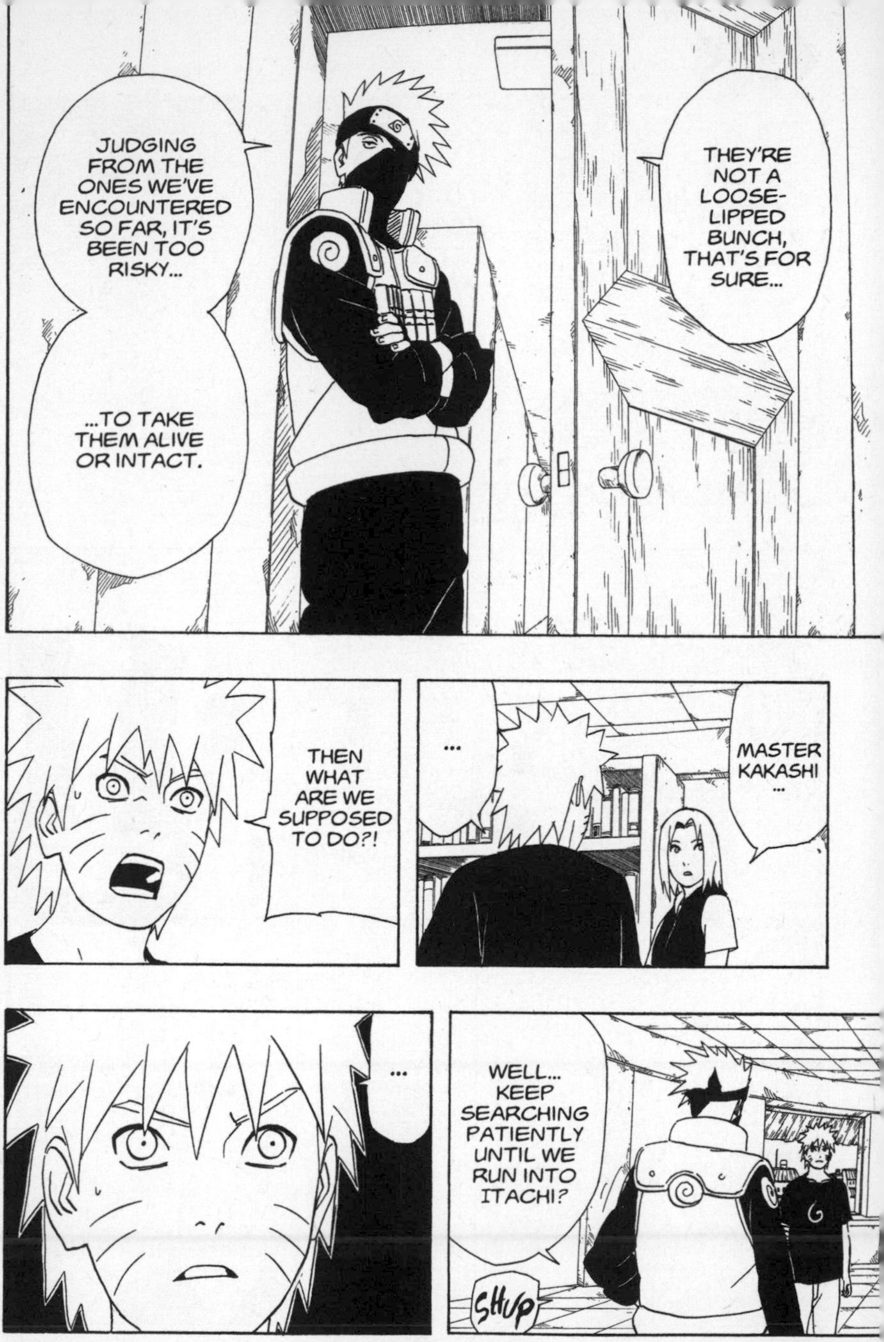
THEY'RE NOT A LOOSE-LIPPED BUNCH, THAT'S FOR SURE...
JUDGING FROM THE ONES WE'VE ENCOUNTERED SO FAR, IT'S BEEN TOO RISKY...
...TO TAKE THEM ALIVE OR INTACT.
MASTER KAKASHI ...
...
THEN WHAT ARE WE SUPPOSED TO DO?!
WELL... KEEP SEARCHING PATIENTLY UNTIL WE RUN INTO ITACHI?
SHUP
...

READ THIS WAY

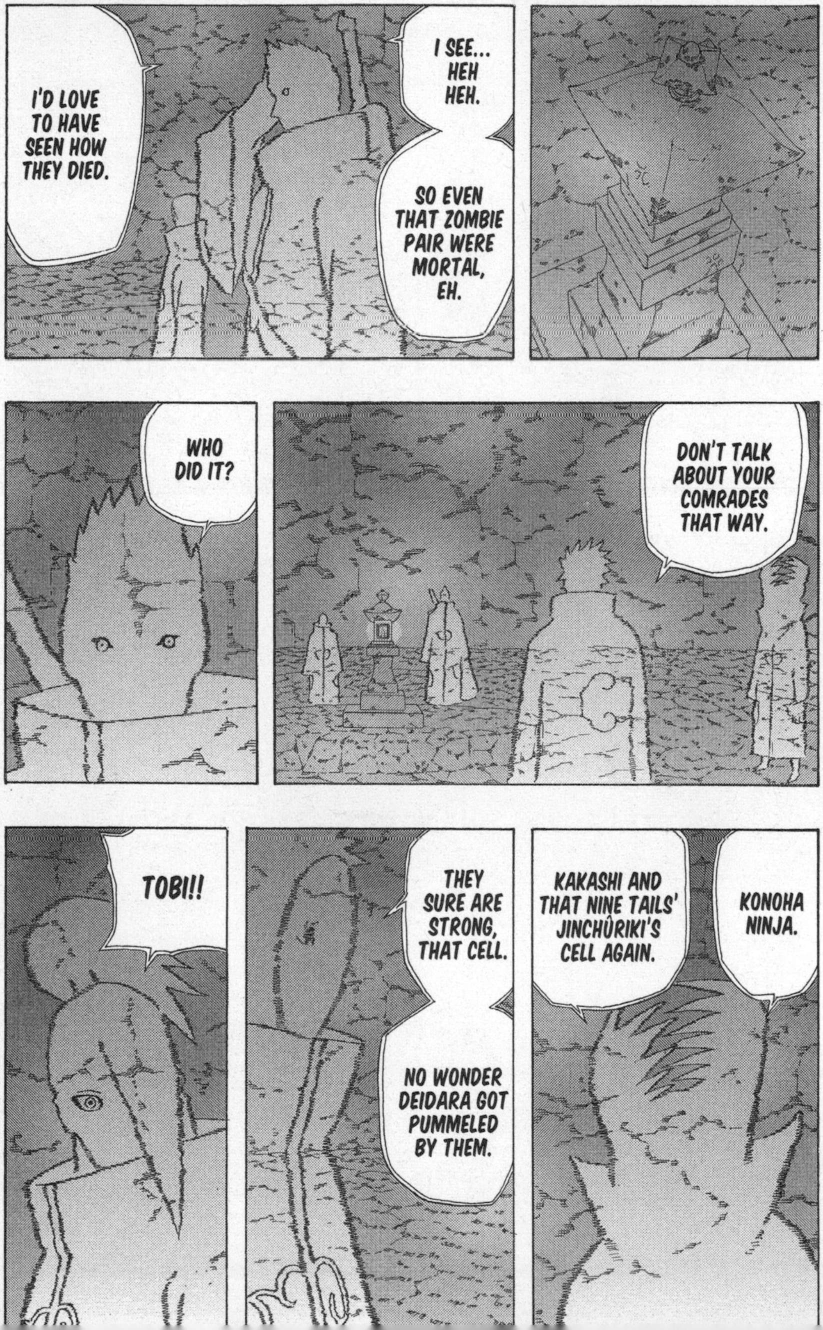

I SEE... HEH HEH.
SO EVEN THAT ZOMBIE PAIR WERE MORTAL, EH.
I'D LOVE TO HAVE SEEN HOW THEY DIED.
DON'T TALK ABOUT YOUR COMRADES THAT WAY.
WHO DID IT?
KONOHA NINJA.
KAKASHI AND THAT NINE TAILS' JINCHÛRIKI'S CELL AGAIN.
THEY SURE ARE STRONG, THAT CELL.
NO WONDER DEIDARA GOT PUMMELED BY THEM.
TOBI!!

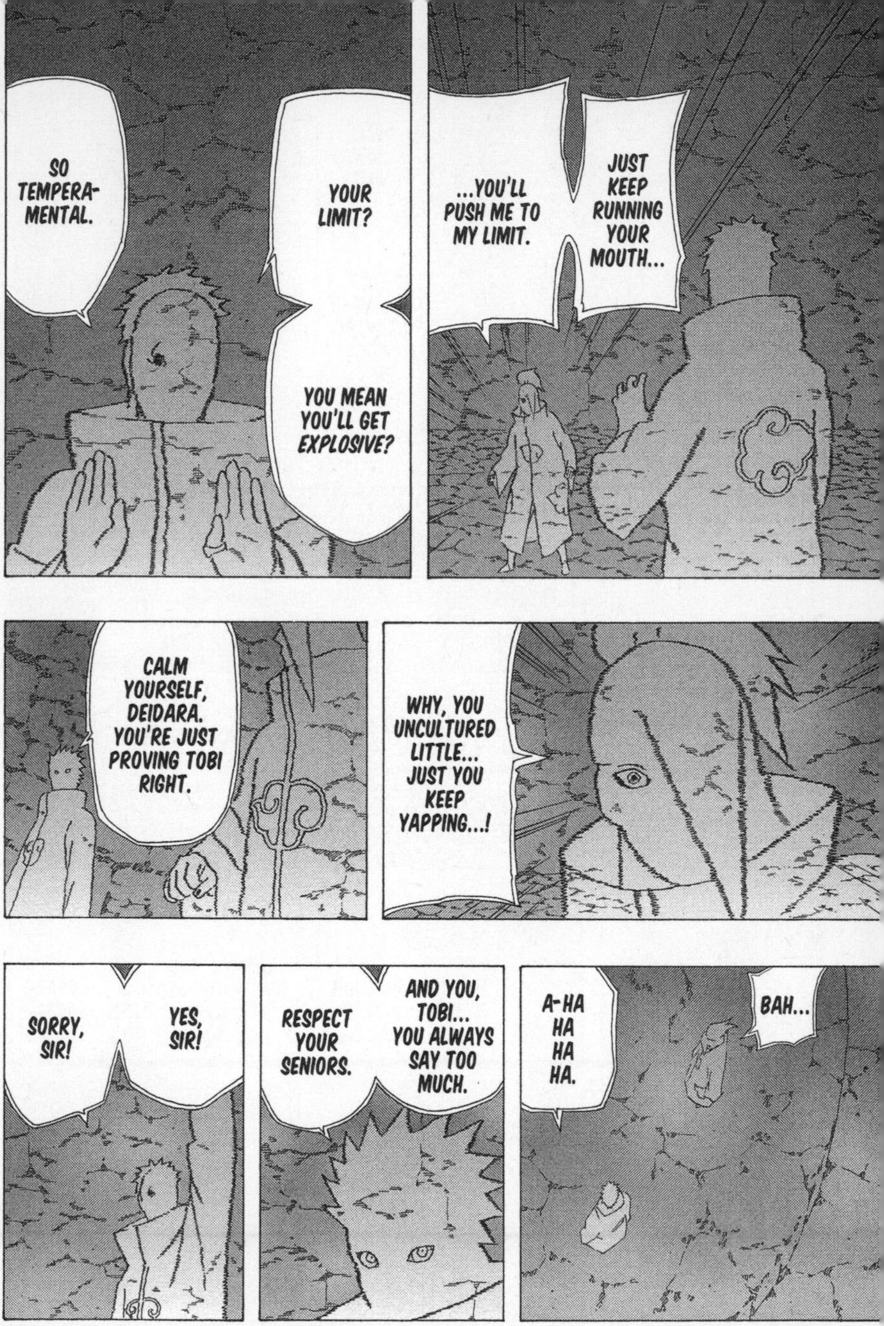
JUST KEEP RUNNING YOUR MOUTH...
...YOU'LL PUSH ME TO MY LIMIT.
YOUR LIMIT?
YOU MEAN YOU'LL GET *EXPLOSIVE?*
SO TEMPERA-MENTAL.
WHY, YOU UNCULTURED LITTLE... JUST YOU KEEP YAPPING...!
CALM YOURSELF, DEIDARA. YOU'RE JUST PROVING TOBI RIGHT.
BAH...
A-HA HA HA HA.
AND YOU, TOBI... YOU ALWAYS SAY TOO MUCH.
RESPECT YOUR SENIORS.
YES, SIR!
SORRY, SIR!

READ THIS WAY

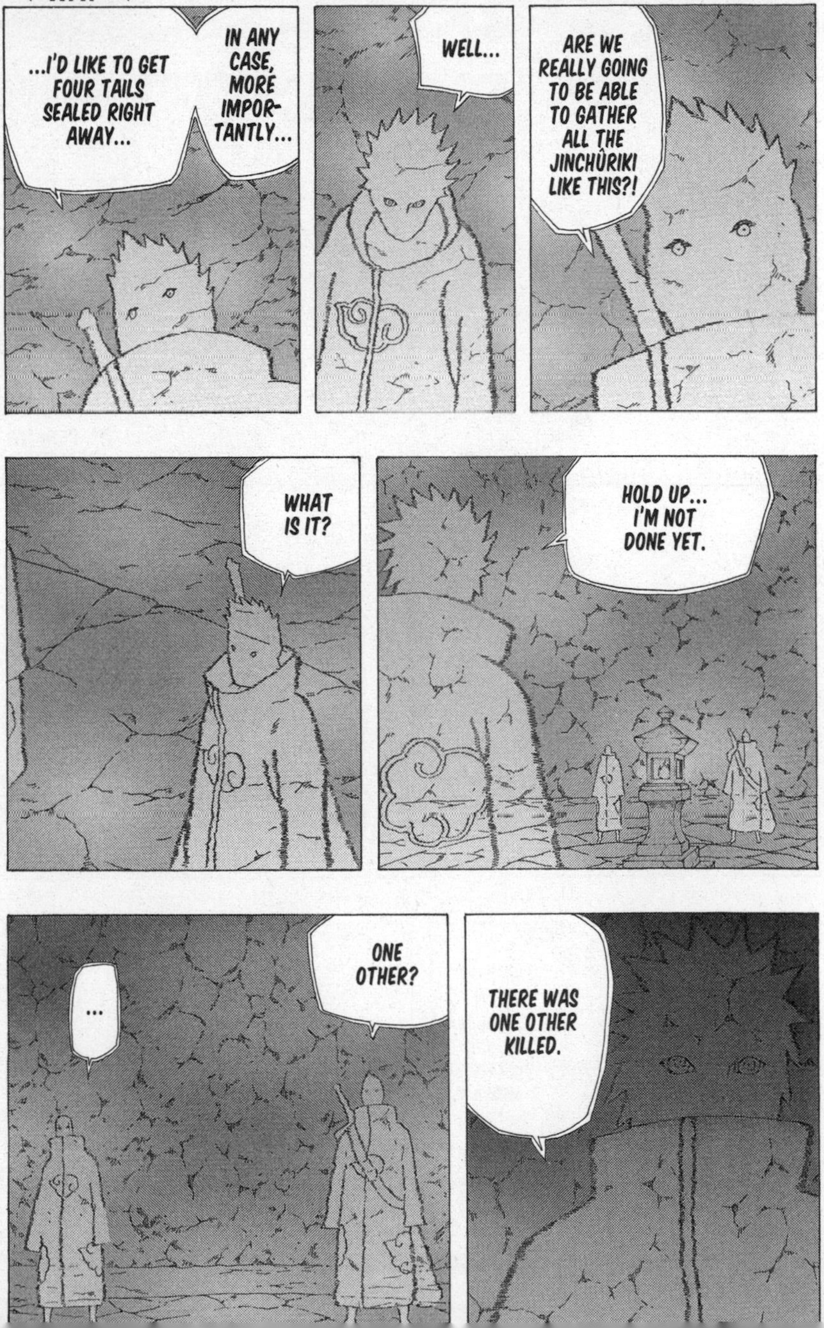
ARE WE REALLY GOING TO BE ABLE TO GATHER ALL THE JINCHÛRIKI LIKE THIS?!
WELL...
IN ANY CASE, MORE IMPORTANTLY...
...I'D LIKE TO GET FOUR TAILS SEALED RIGHT AWAY...
HOLD UP... I'M NOT DONE YET.
WHAT IS IT?
THERE WAS ONE OTHER KILLED.
ONE OTHER?
...

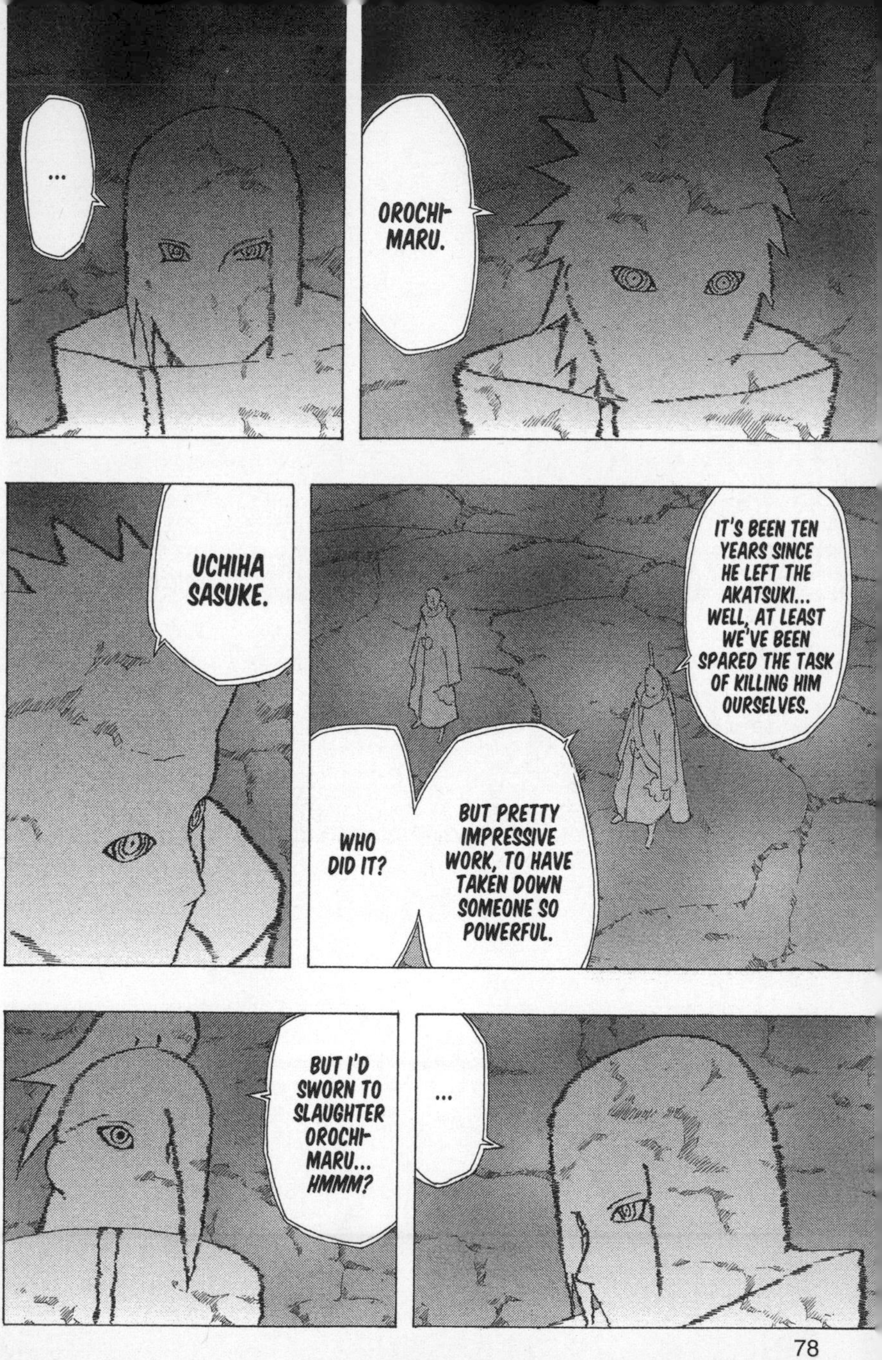
OROCHI-MARU.
...
IT'S BEEN TEN YEARS SINCE HE LEFT THE AKATSUKI... WELL, AT LEAST WE'VE BEEN SPARED THE TASK OF KILLING HIM OURSELVES.
BUT PRETTY IMPRESSIVE WORK, TO HAVE TAKEN DOWN SOMEONE SO POWERFUL.
WHO DID IT?
UCHIHA SASUKE.
...
BUT I'D SWORN TO SLAUGHTER OROCHI-MARU... HMMM?

READ THIS WAY

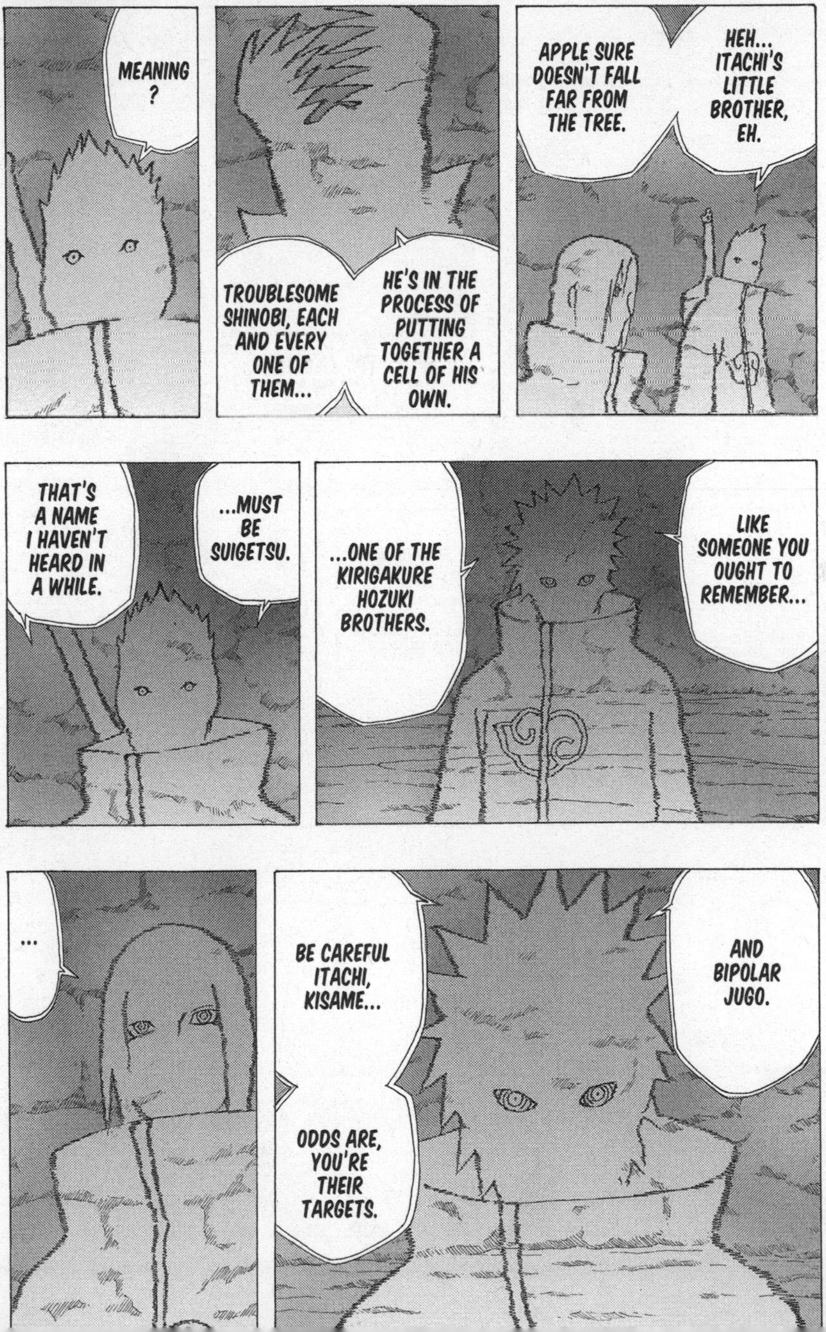
HEH... ITACHI'S LITTLE BROTHER, EH.
APPLE SURE DOESN'T FALL FAR FROM THE TREE.
HE'S IN THE PROCESS OF PUTTING TOGETHER A CELL OF HIS OWN.
TROUBLESOME SHINOBI, EACH AND EVERY ONE OF THEM...
MEANING?
LIKE SOMEONE YOU OUGHT TO REMEMBER...
...ONE OF THE KIRIGAKURE HOZUKI BROTHERS.
...MUST BE SUIGETSU.
THAT'S A NAME I HAVEN'T HEARD IN A WHILE.
AND BIPOLAR JUGO.
BE CAREFUL ITACHI, KISAME...
ODDS ARE, YOU'RE THEIR TARGETS.
...

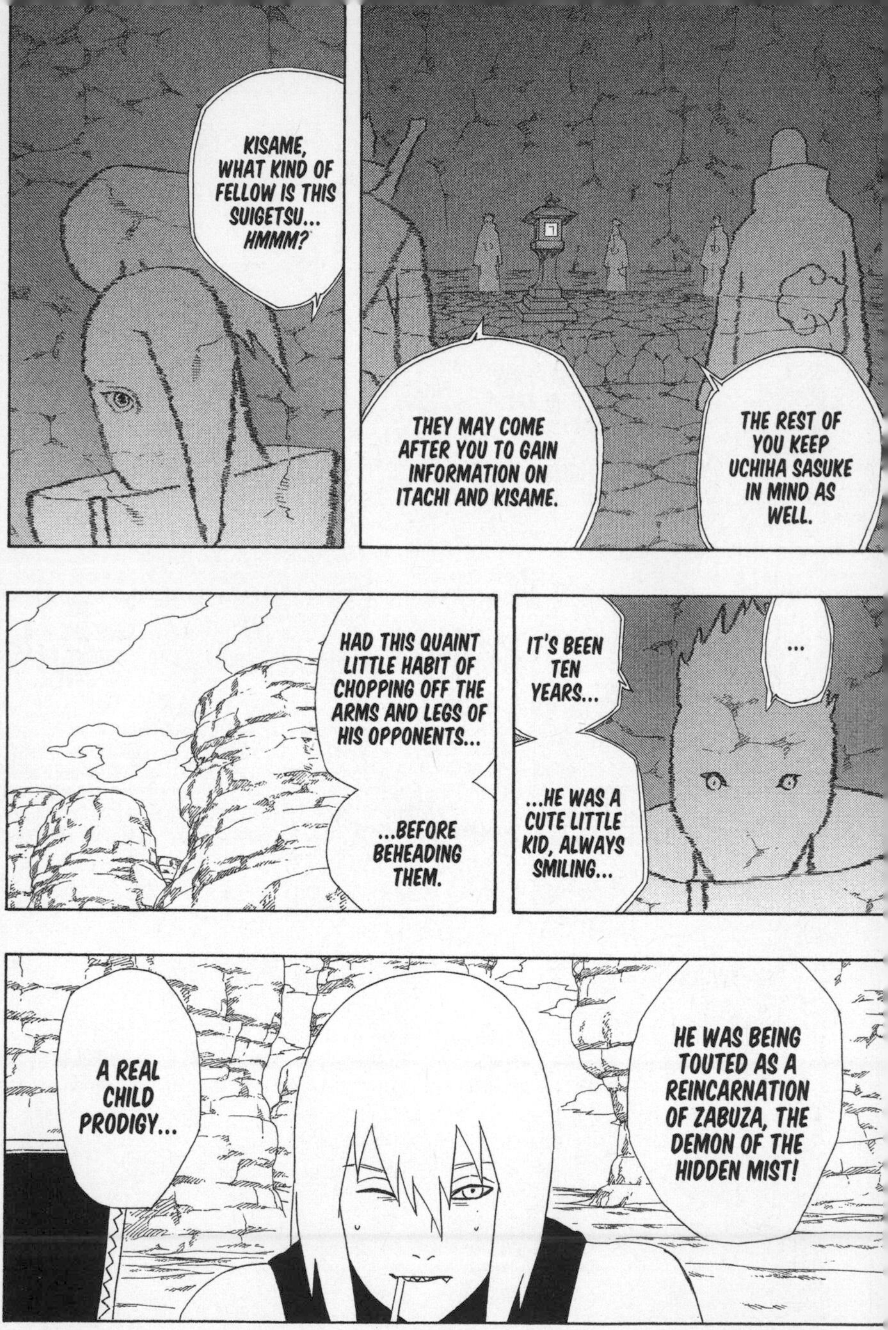
THE REST OF YOU KEEP UCHIHA SASUKE IN MIND AS WELL.
THEY MAY COME AFTER YOU TO GAIN INFORMATION ON ITACHI AND KISAME.
KISAME, WHAT KIND OF FELLOW IS THIS SUIGETSU... HMMM?
...
IT'S BEEN TEN YEARS...
...HE WAS A CUTE LITTLE KID, ALWAYS SMILING...
HAD THIS QUAINT LITTLE HABIT OF CHOPPING OFF THE ARMS AND LEGS OF HIS OPPONENTS...
...BEFORE BEHEADING THEM.
HE WAS BEING TOUTED AS A REINCARNATION OF ZABUZA, THE DEMON OF THE HIDDEN MIST!
A REAL CHILD PRODIGY...

READ THIS WAY

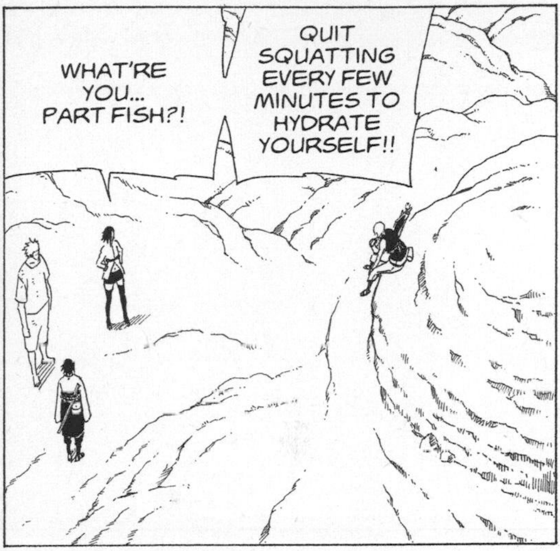
QUIT SQUATTING EVERY FEW MINUTES TO HYDRATE YOURSELF!!
WHAT'RE YOU... PART FISH?!

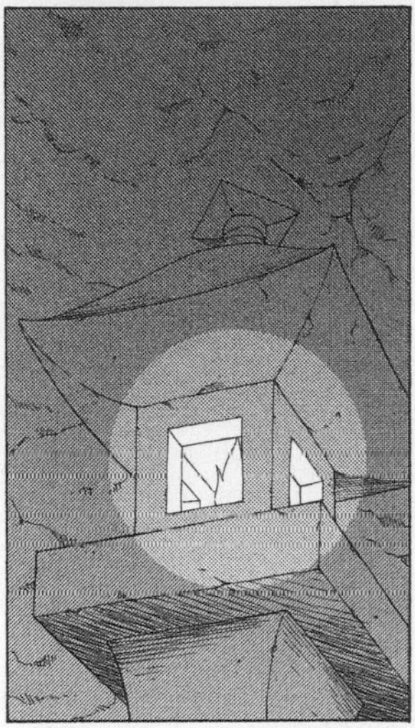

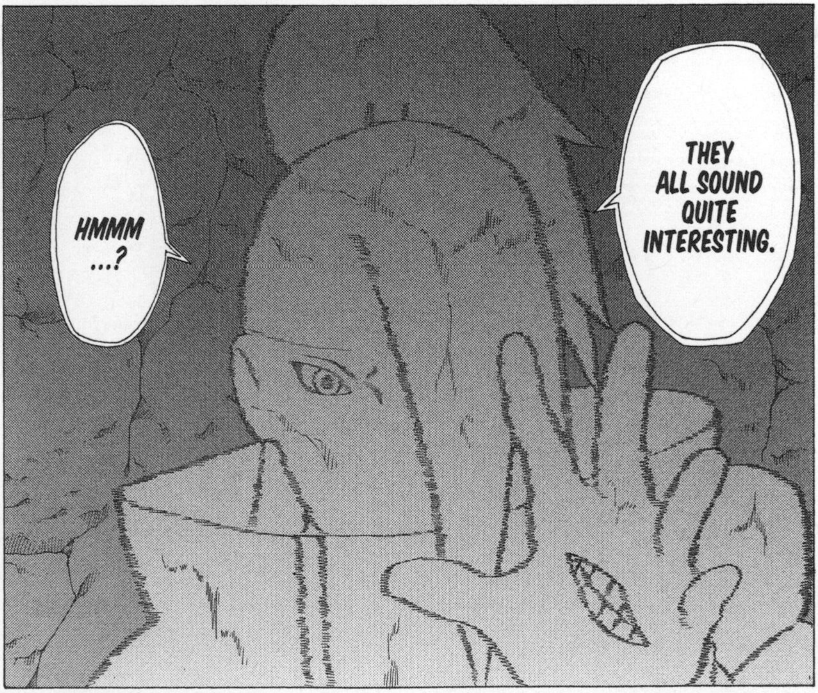
THEY ALL SOUND QUITE INTERESTING.
HMMM ...?

Number 354: On the Move

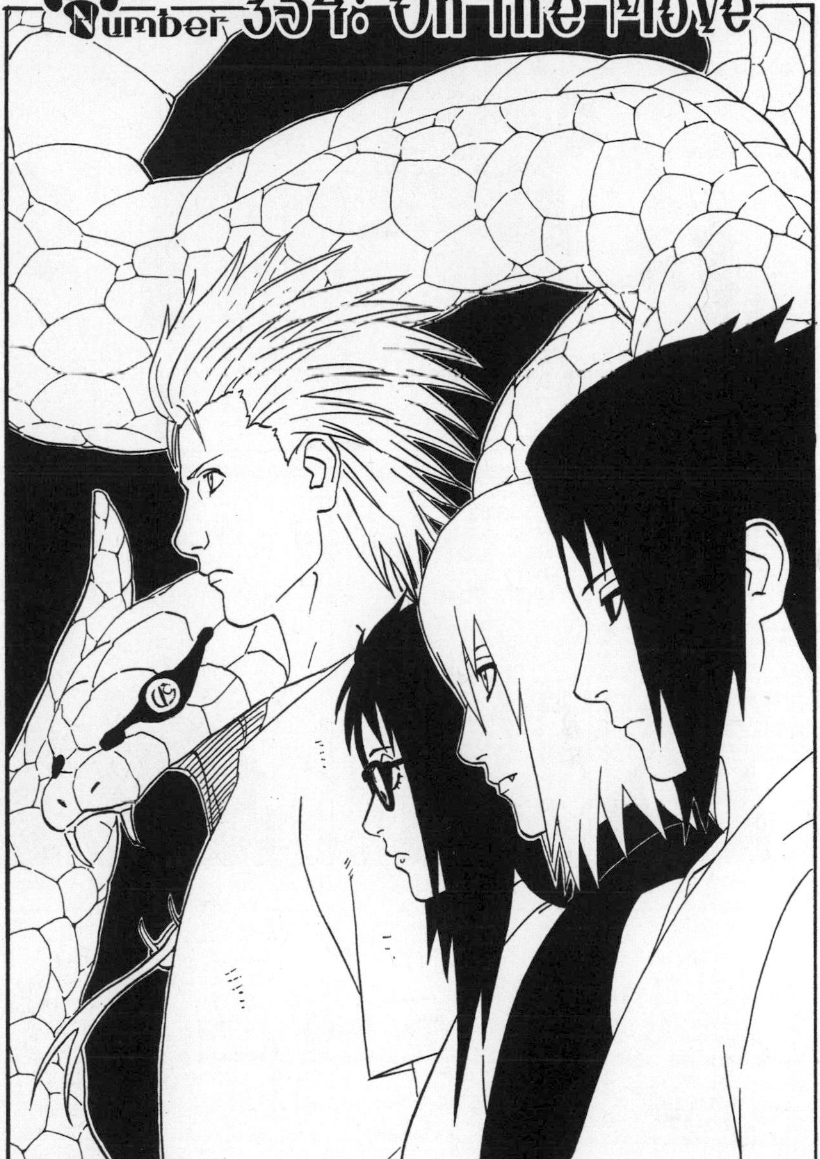

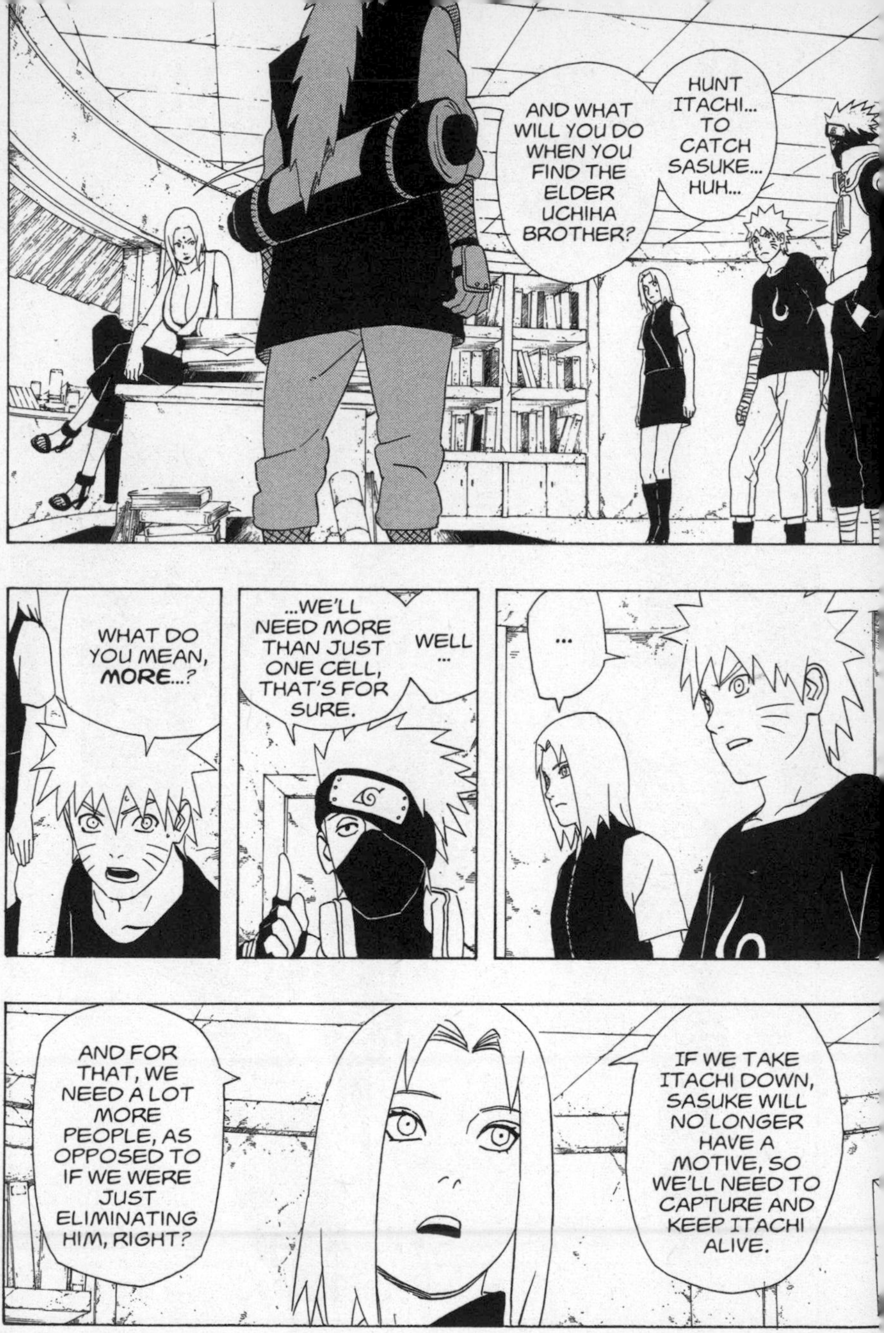
HUNT ITACHI... TO CATCH SASUKE... HUH...
AND WHAT WILL YOU DO WHEN YOU FIND THE ELDER UCHIHA BROTHER?
...
WELL ...
...WE'LL NEED MORE THAN JUST ONE CELL, THAT'S FOR SURE.
WHAT DO YOU MEAN, **MORE**...?
IF WE TAKE ITACHI DOWN, SASUKE WILL NO LONGER HAVE A MOTIVE, SO WE'LL NEED TO CAPTURE AND KEEP ITACHI ALIVE.
AND FOR THAT, WE NEED A LOT MORE PEOPLE, AS OPPOSED TO IF WE WERE JUST ELIMINATING HIM, RIGHT?

READ THIS WAY

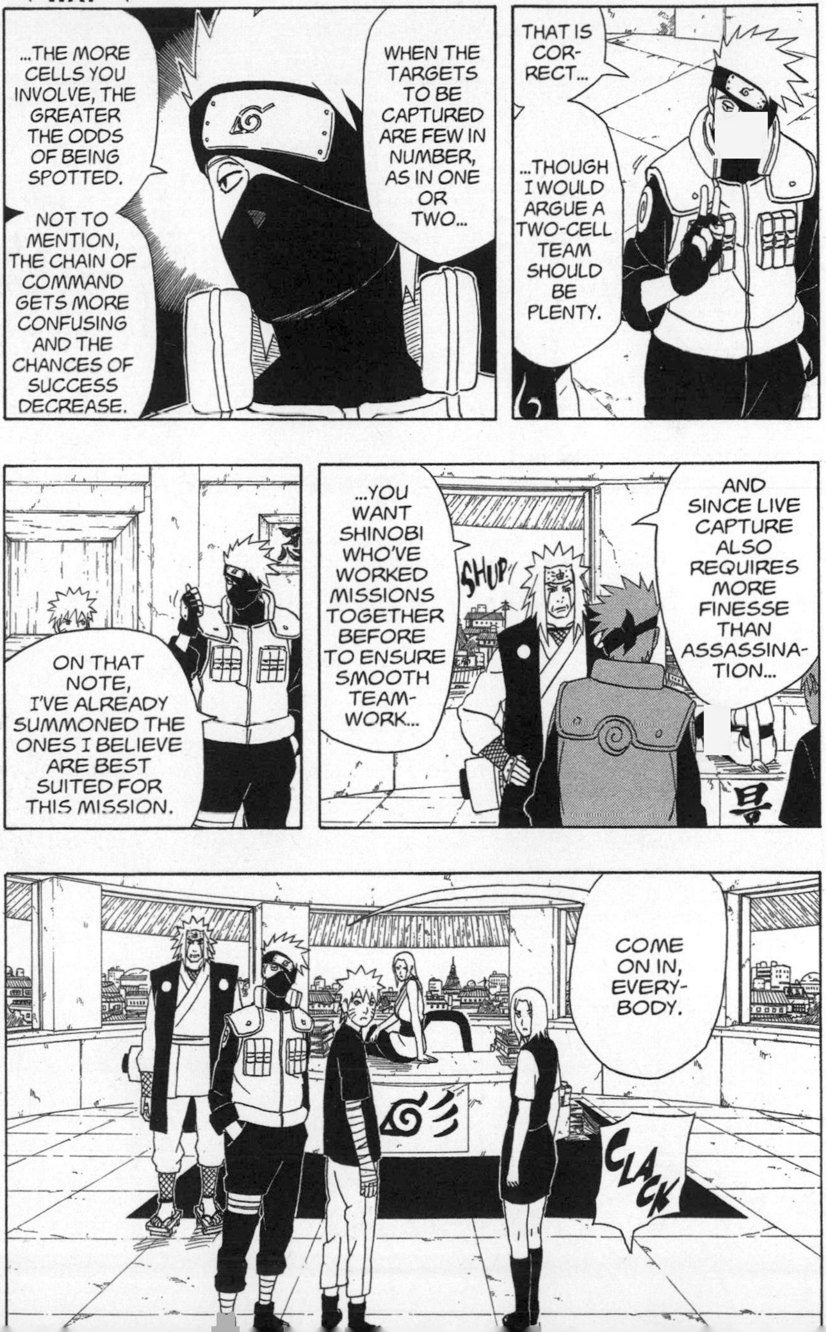
THAT IS COR-RECT...
...THOUGH I WOULD ARGUE A TWO-CELL TEAM SHOULD BE PLENTY.
WHEN THE TARGETS TO BE CAPTURED ARE FEW IN NUMBER, AS IN ONE OR TWO...
...THE MORE CELLS YOU INVOLVE, THE GREATER THE ODDS OF BEING SPOTTED.
NOT TO MENTION, THE CHAIN OF COMMAND GETS MORE CONFUSING AND THE CHANCES OF SUCCESS DECREASE.
AND SINCE LIVE CAPTURE ALSO REQUIRES MORE FINESSE THAN ASSASSINA-TION...
SHUP
...YOU WANT SHINOBI WHO'VE WORKED MISSIONS TOGETHER BEFORE TO ENSURE SMOOTH TEAM-WORK...
ON THAT NOTE, I'VE ALREADY SUMMONED THE ONES I BELIEVE ARE BEST SUITED FOR THIS MISSION.
COME ON IN, EVERY-BODY.
CLACK

(SKY WARD)

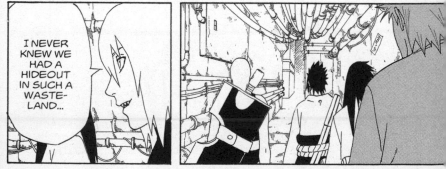

I NEVER KNEW WE HAD A HIDEOUT IN SUCH A WASTELAND...

READ THIS WAY

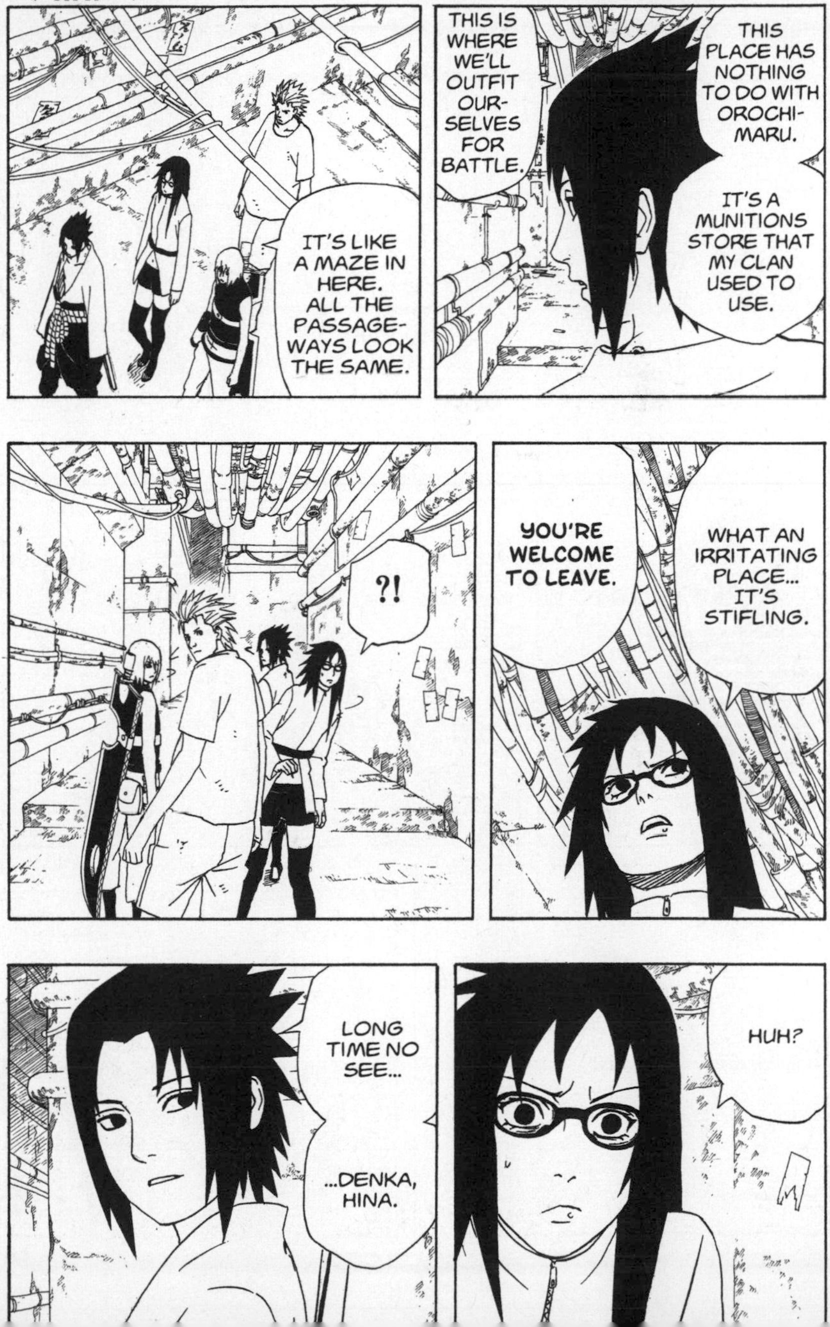
THIS PLACE HAS NOTHING TO DO WITH OROCHIMARU.
IT'S A MUNITIONS STORE THAT MY CLAN USED TO USE.
THIS IS WHERE WE'LL OUTFIT OURSELVES FOR BATTLE.
IT'S LIKE A MAZE IN HERE. ALL THE PASSAGEWAYS LOOK THE SAME.
WHAT AN IRRITATING PLACE... IT'S STIFLING.
YOU'RE WELCOME TO LEAVE.
?!
HUH?
LONG TIME NO SEE...
...DENKA, HINA.

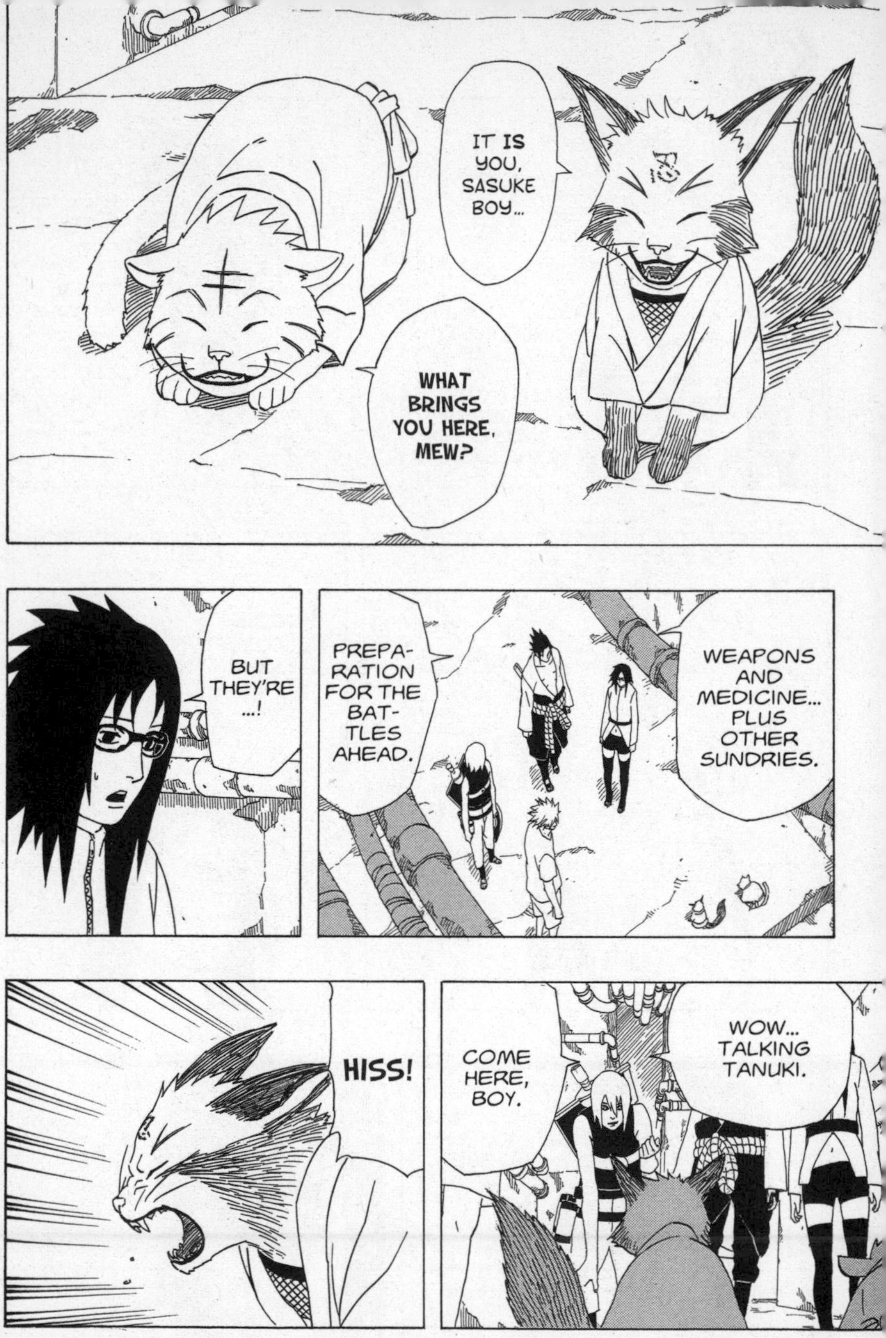
IT IS YOU, SASUKE BOY...
WHAT BRINGS YOU HERE, MEW?
WEAPONS AND MEDICINE... PLUS OTHER SUNDRIES.
PREPARATION FOR THE BATTLES AHEAD.
BUT THEY'RE ...!
WOW... TALKING TANUKI.
COME HERE, BOY.
HISS!

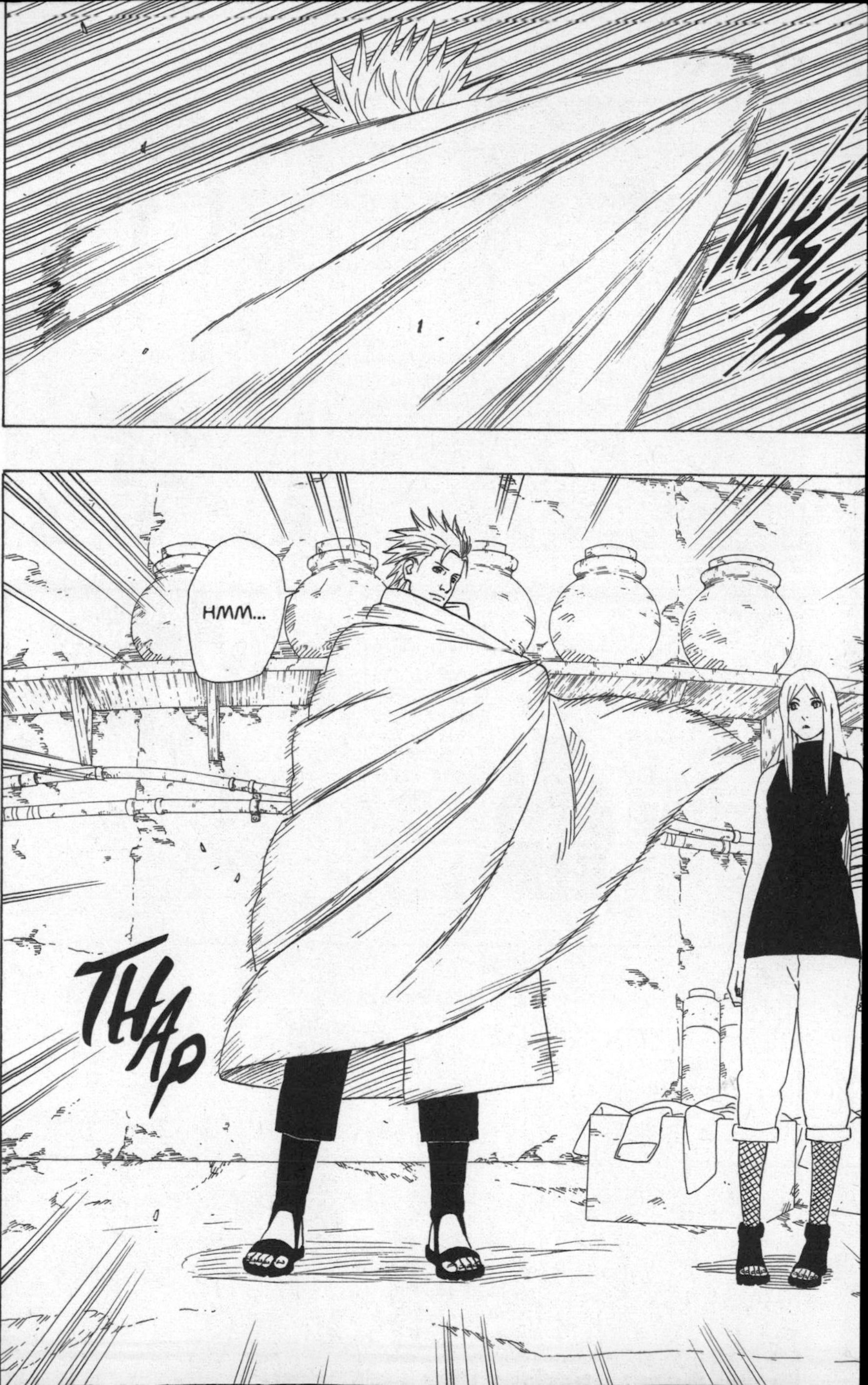
WHSH
HMM...
THAP

READ THIS WAY

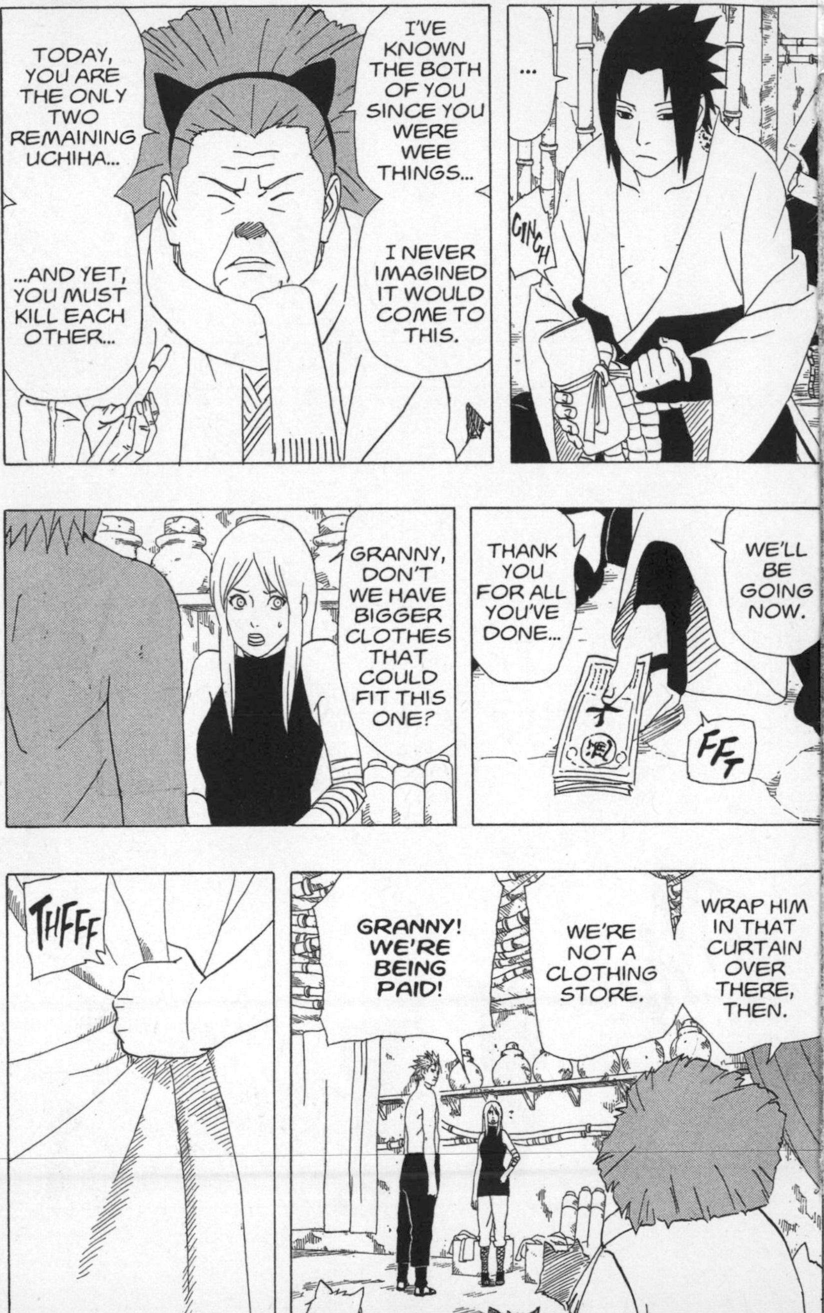

...
CINCH
I'VE KNOWN THE BOTH OF YOU SINCE YOU WERE WEE THINGS...
I NEVER IMAGINED IT WOULD COME TO THIS.
TODAY, YOU ARE THE ONLY TWO REMAINING UCHIHA...
...AND YET, YOU MUST KILL EACH OTHER...
WE'LL BE GOING NOW.
THANK YOU FOR ALL YOU'VE DONE...
FFT
GRANNY, DON'T WE HAVE BIGGER CLOTHES THAT COULD FIT THIS ONE?
WRAP HIM IN THAT CURTAIN OVER THERE, THEN.
WE'RE NOT A CLOTHING STORE.
GRANNY! WE'RE BEING PAID!
THFFF

HISS

I AM TRULY GRATEFUL, GRANNY CAT.

SO, YOU'RE STILL GOING AFTER ITACHI?

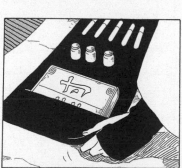

READ THIS WAY

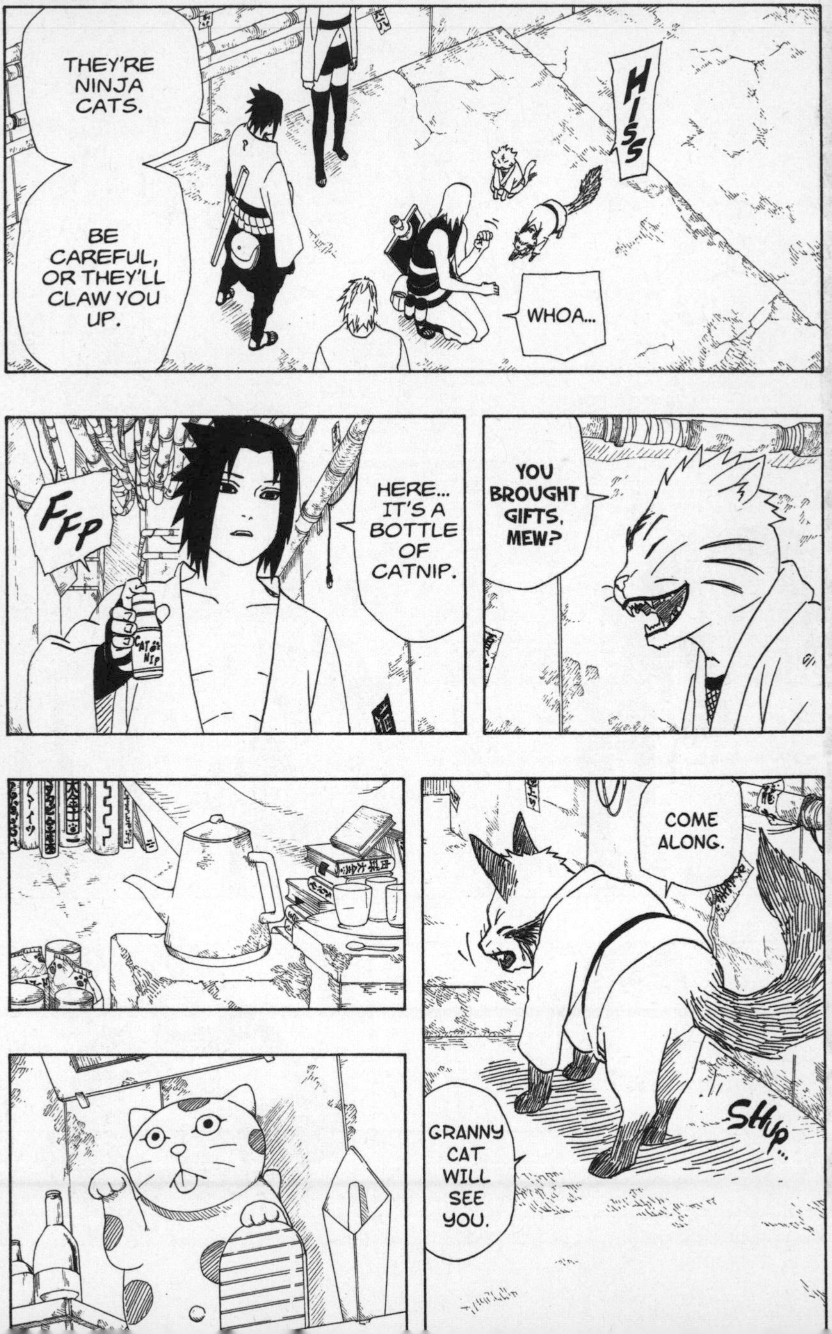
HISS
WHOA...
THEY'RE NINJA CATS.
BE CAREFUL, OR THEY'LL CLAW YOU UP.
YOU BROUGHT GIFTS, MEW?
HERE... IT'S A BOTTLE OF CATNIP.
FFP
CAT NIP
COME ALONG.
SHUP...
GRANNY CAT WILL SEE YOU.

READ THIS WAY

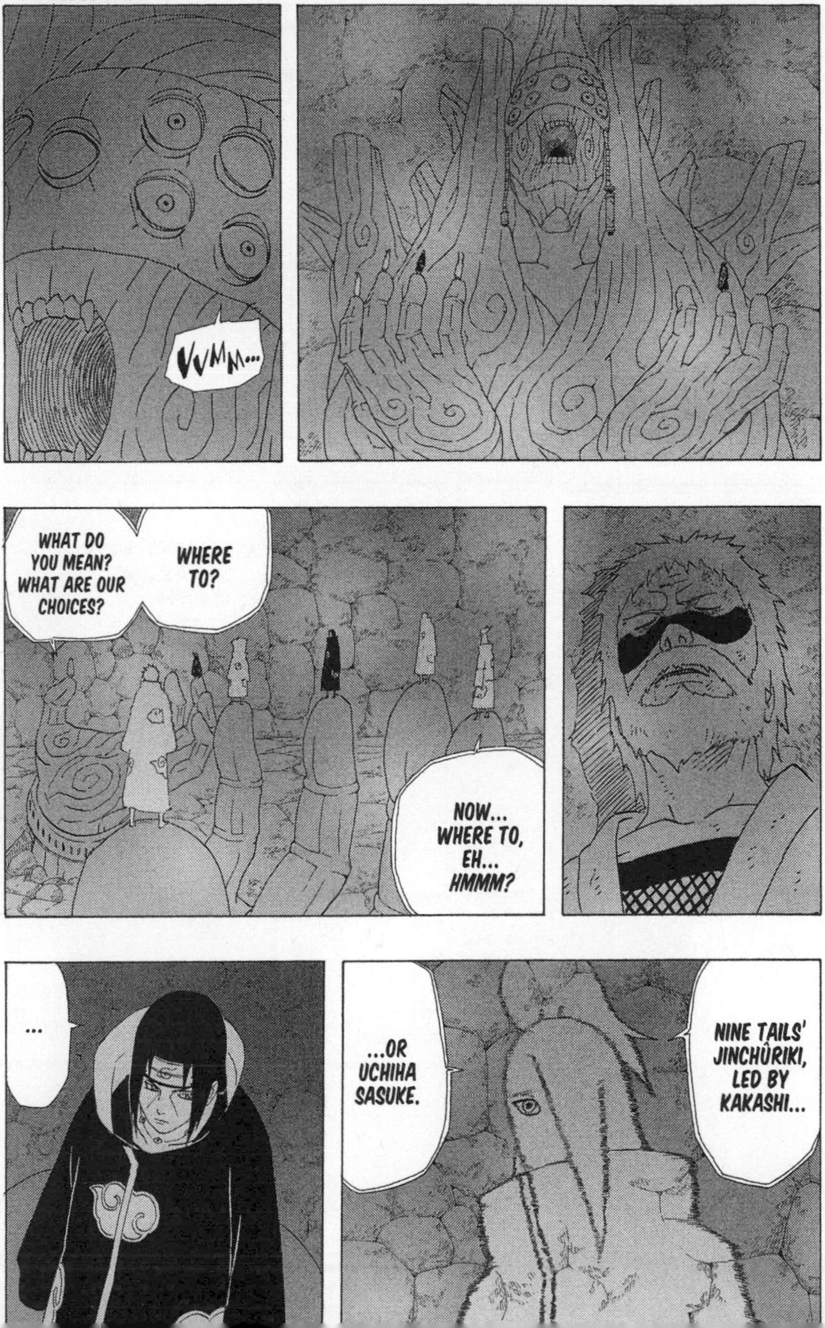
VVMM...
WHERE TO?
WHAT DO YOU MEAN? WHAT ARE OUR CHOICES?
NOW... WHERE TO, EH... HMMM?
NINE TAILS' JINCHÛRIKI, LED BY KAKASHI...
...OR UCHIHA SASUKE.
...

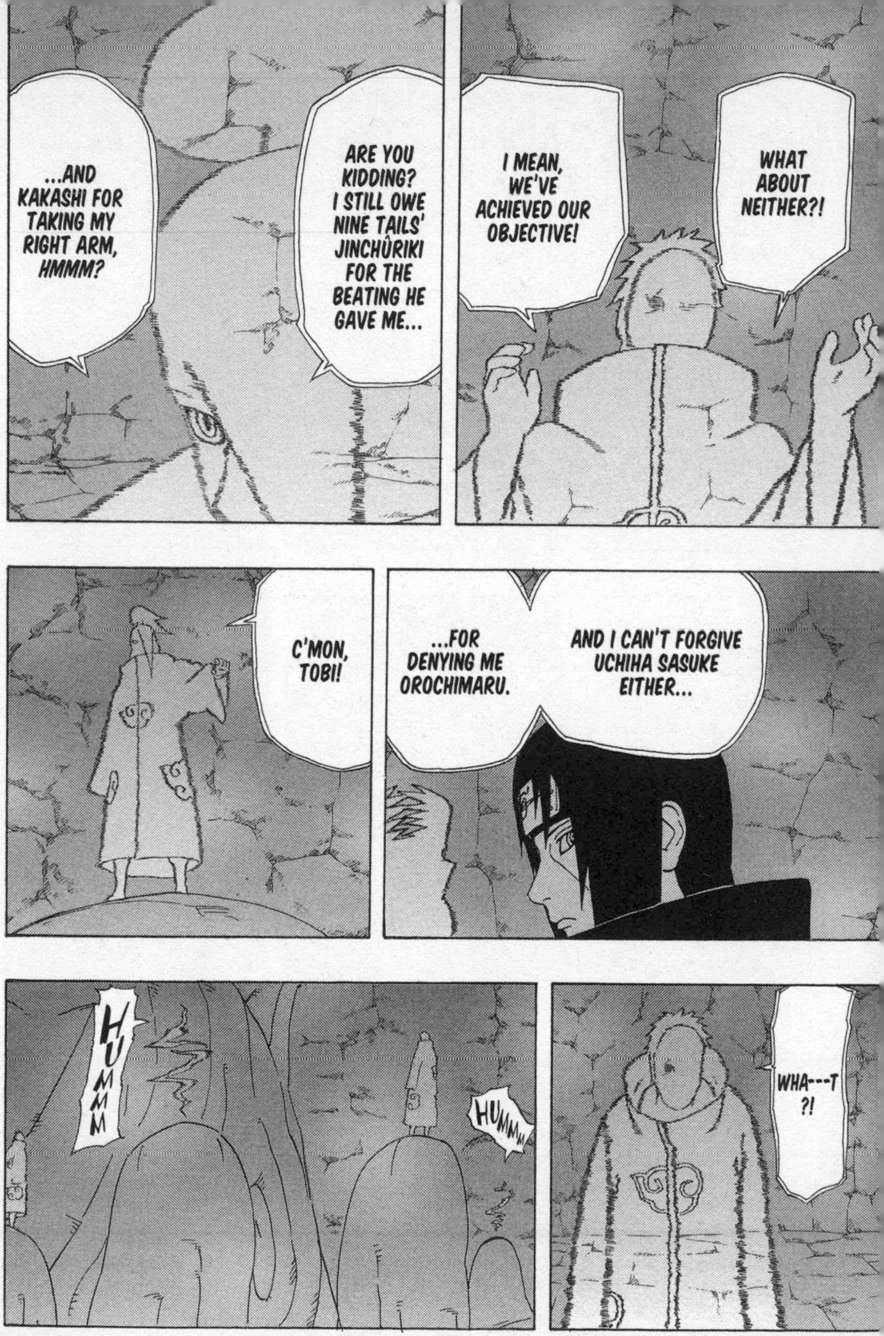
WHAT ABOUT NEITHER?!
I MEAN, WE'VE ACHIEVED OUR OBJECTIVE!
ARE YOU KIDDING? I STILL OWE NINE TAILS' JINCHÛRIKI FOR THE BEATING HE GAVE ME...
...AND KAKASHI FOR TAKING MY RIGHT ARM, HMMM?
AND I CAN'T FORGIVE UCHIHA SASUKE EITHER...
...FOR DENYING ME OROCHIMARU.
C'MON, TOBI!
WHA---T ?!
HUMMM
HUMMM

READ THIS WAY

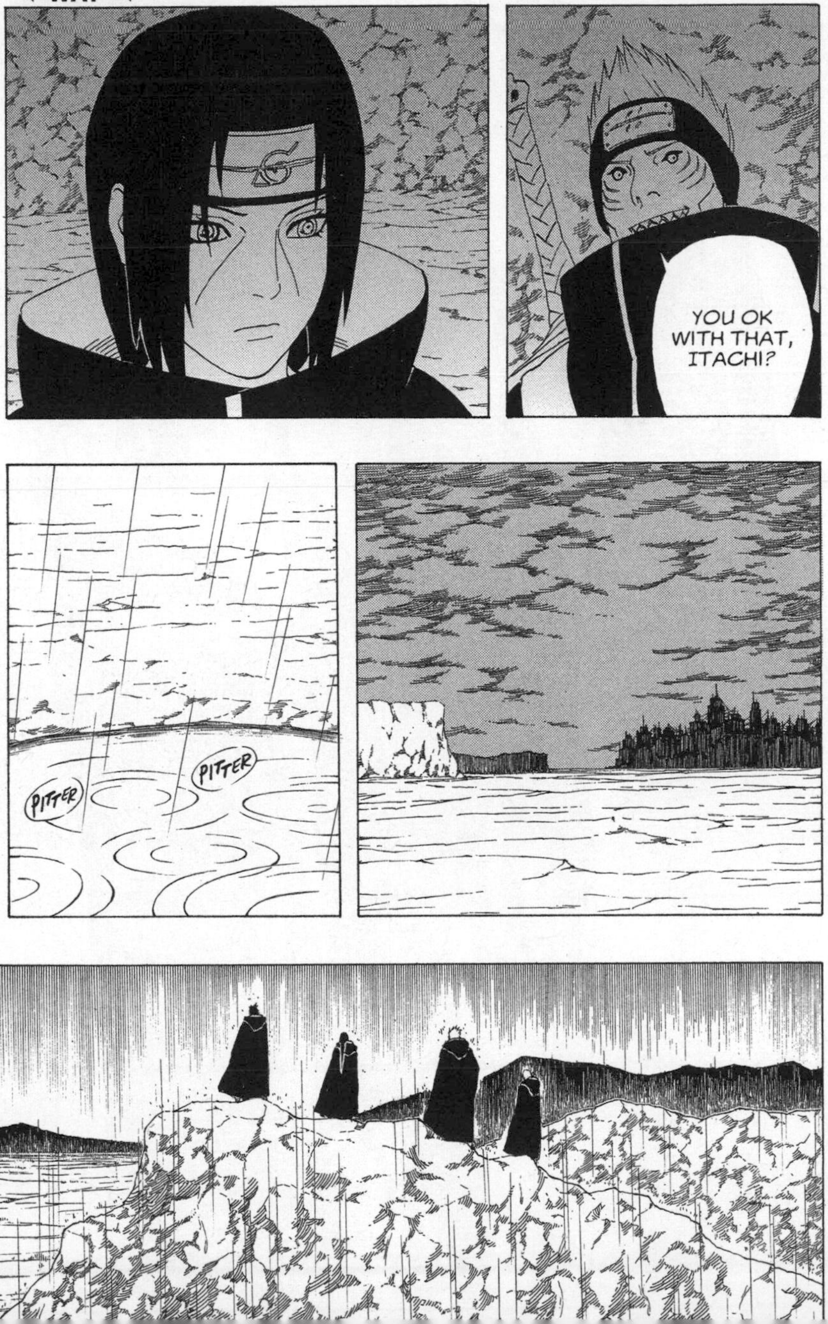
YOU OK WITH THAT, ITACHI?
PITTER
PITTER

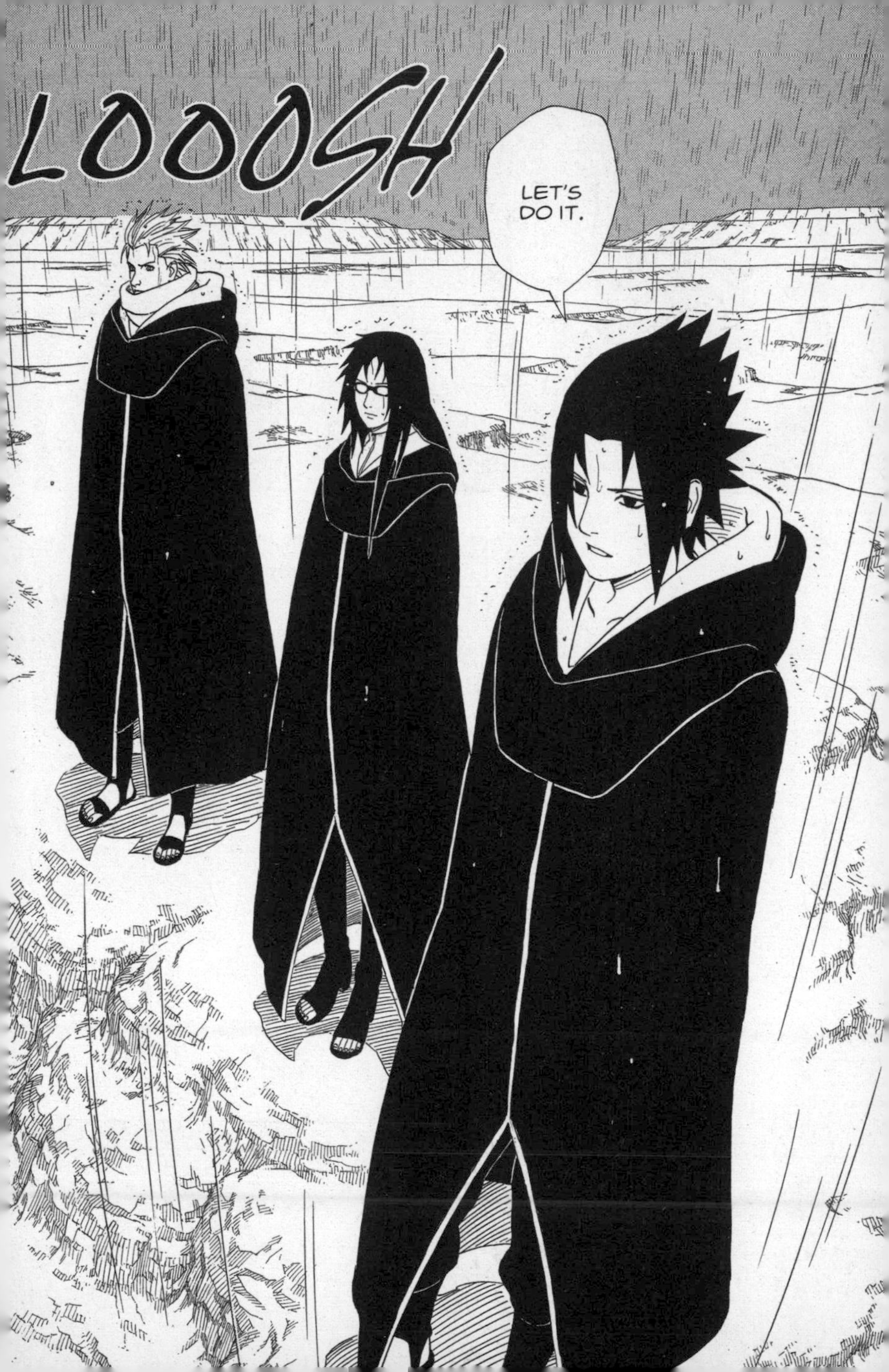
LOOOSH
LET'S DO IT.

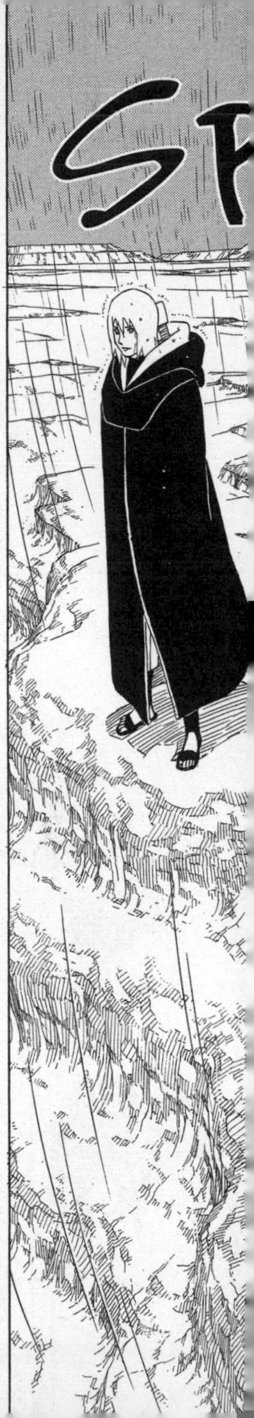

READ THIS WAY

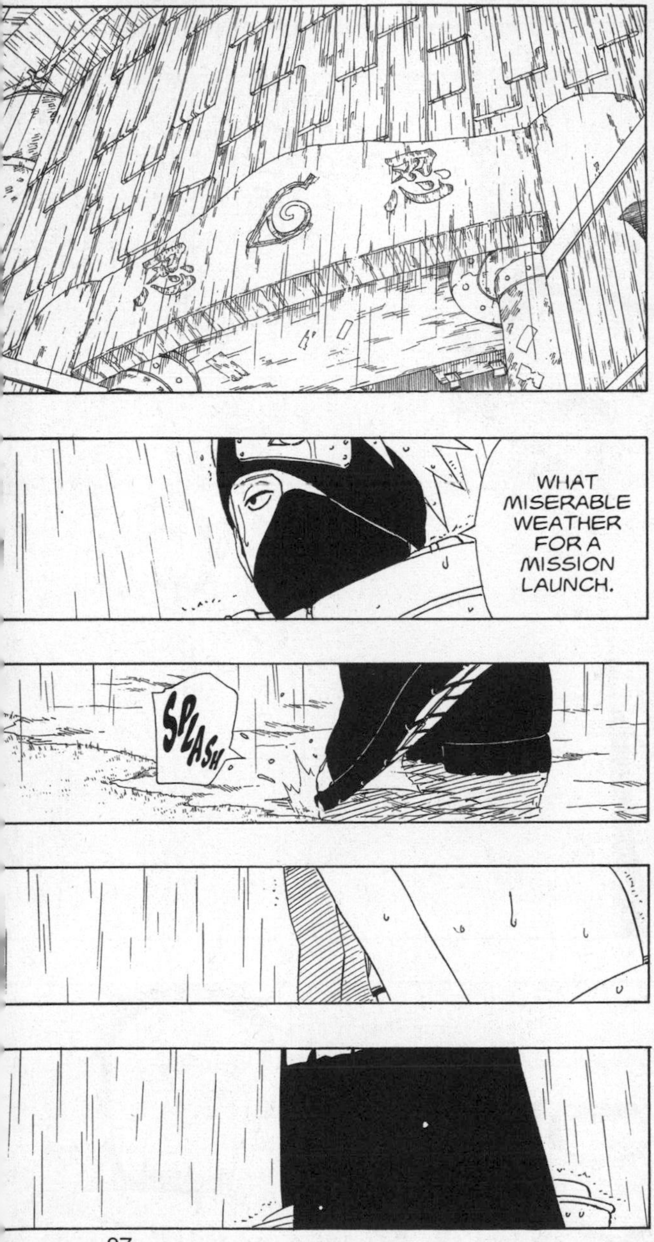
WHAT MISERABLE WEATHER FOR A MISSION LAUNCH.
SPLASH

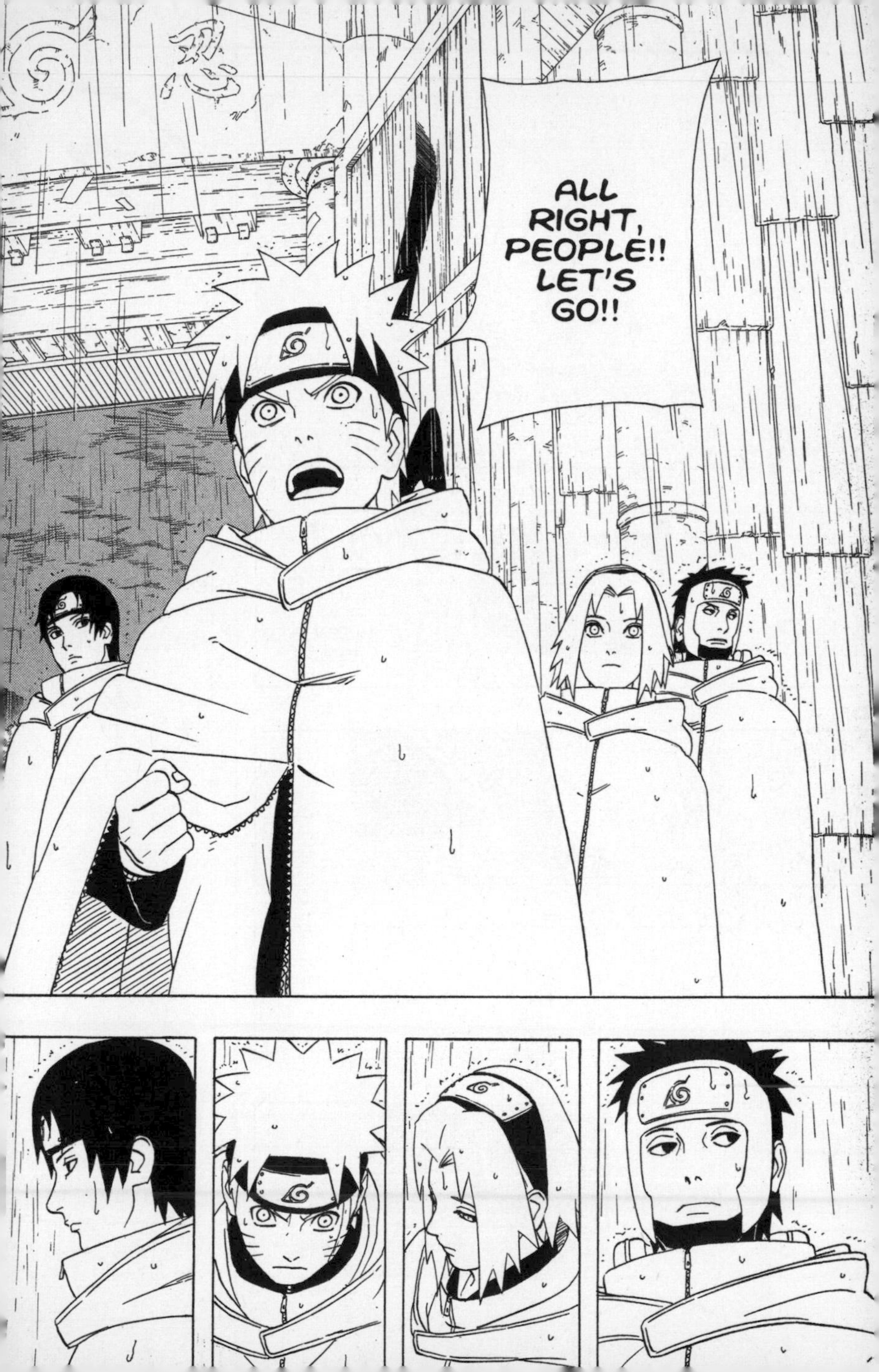
ALL RIGHT, PEOPLE!! LET'S GO!!

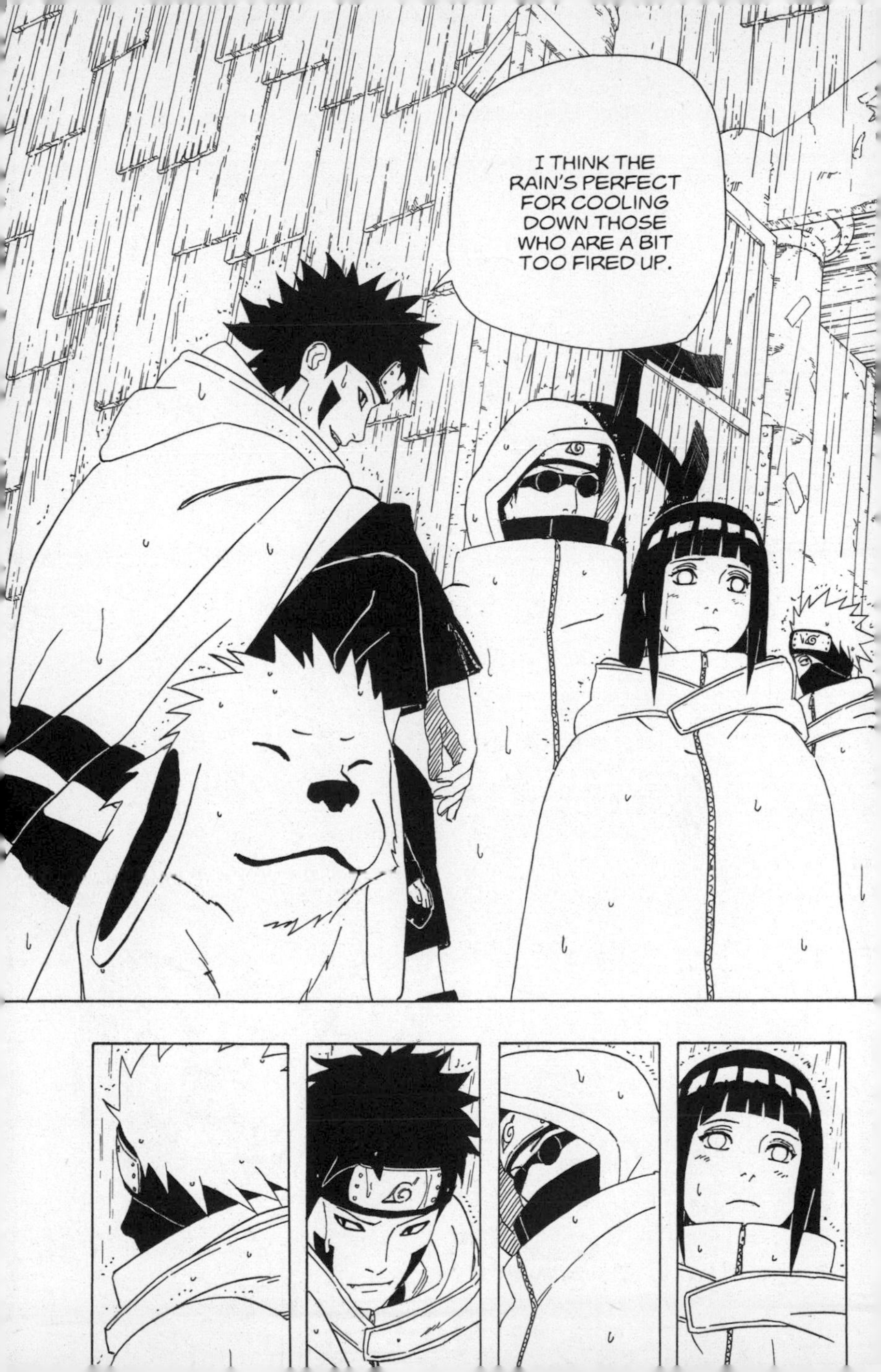
I THINK THE RAIN'S PERFECT FOR COOLING DOWN THOSE WHO ARE A BIT TOO FIRED UP.

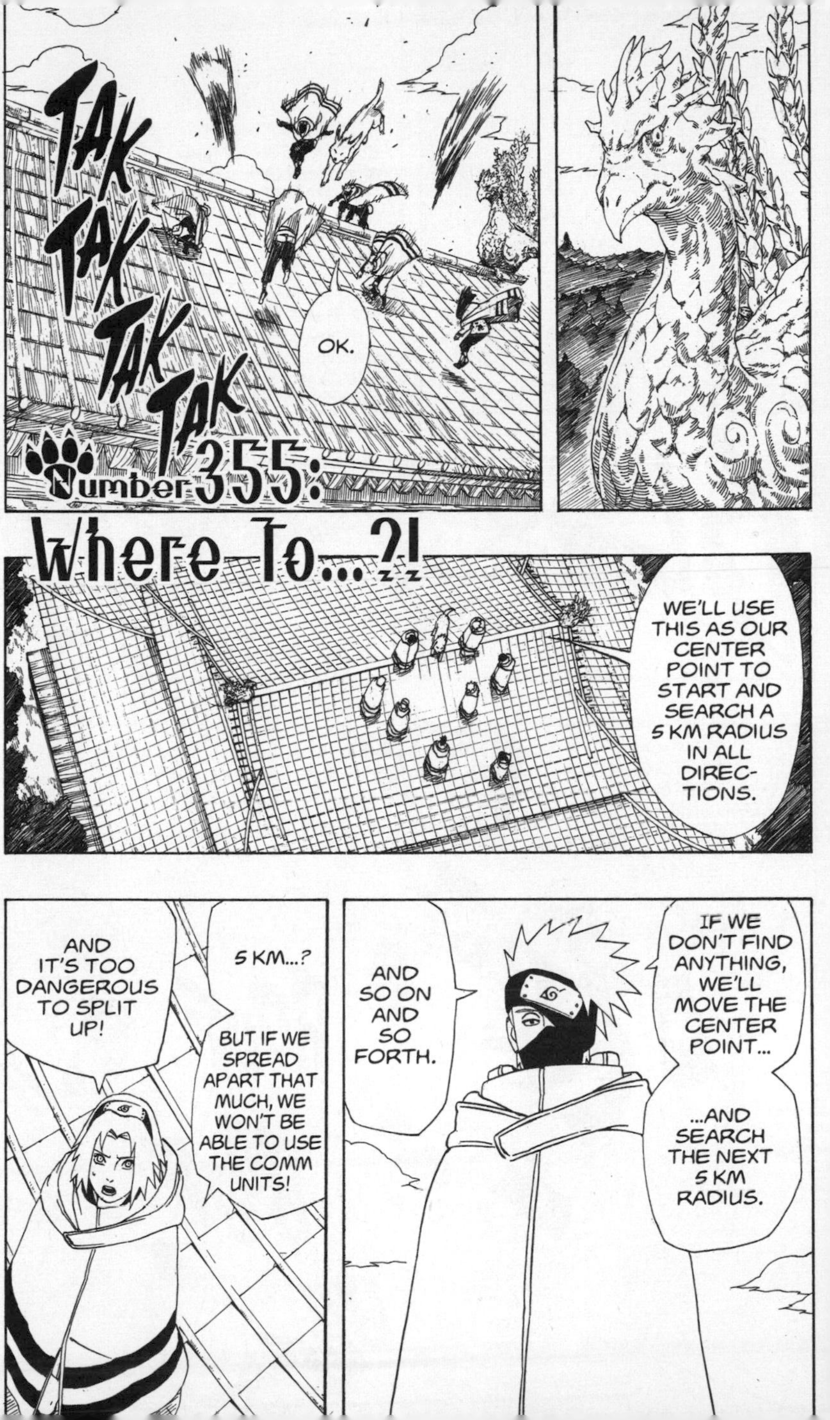
TAK TAK TAK TAK
OK.
Number 355: Where To...?!
WE'LL USE THIS AS OUR CENTER POINT TO START AND SEARCH A 5 KM RADIUS IN ALL DIREC-TIONS.
IF WE DON'T FIND ANYTHING, WE'LL MOVE THE CENTER POINT...
...AND SEARCH THE NEXT 5 KM RADIUS.
AND SO ON AND SO FORTH.
5 KM...?
BUT IF WE SPREAD APART THAT MUCH, WE WON'T BE ABLE TO USE THE COMM UNITS!
AND IT'S TOO DANGEROUS TO SPLIT UP!

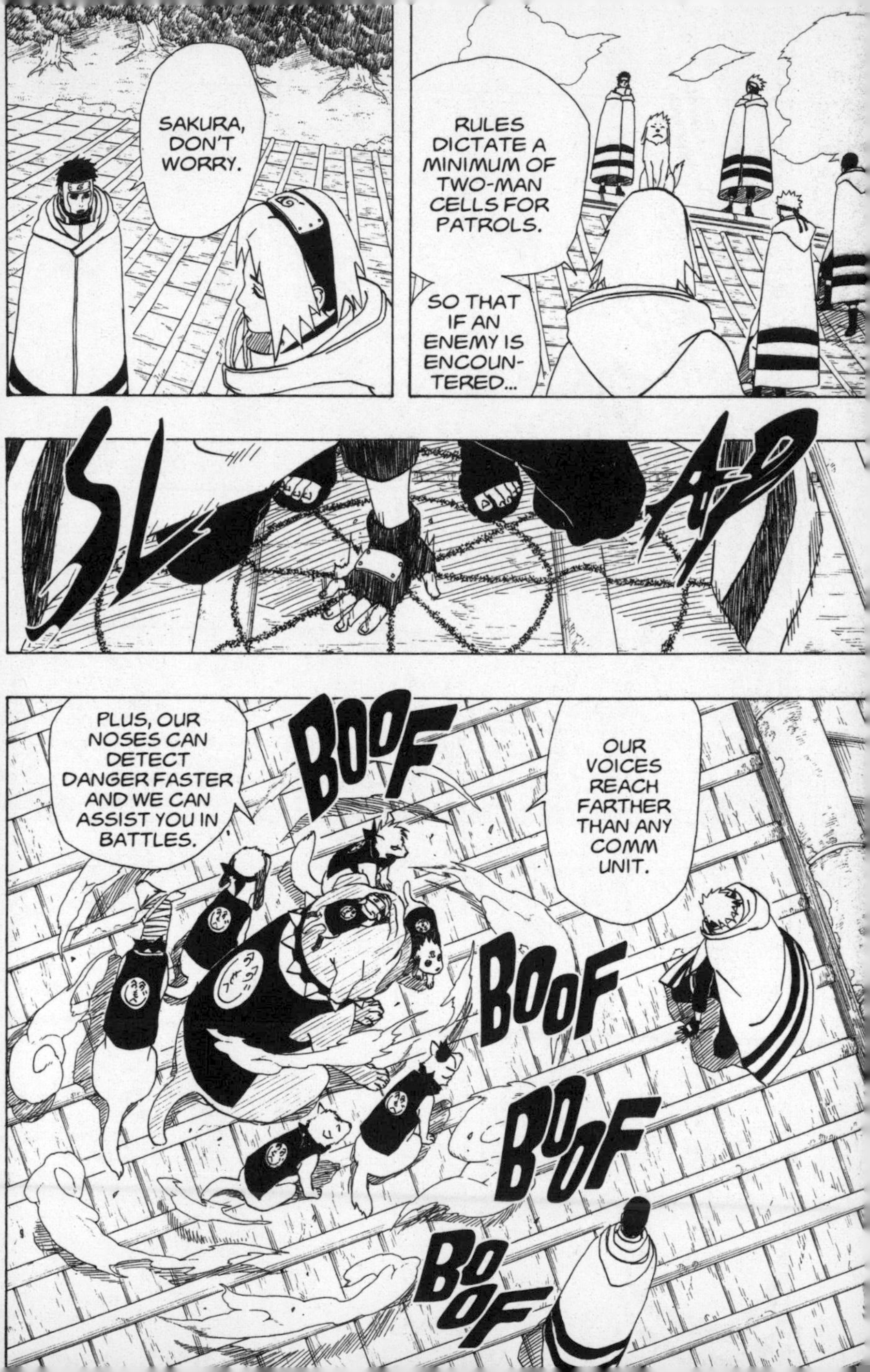
RULES DICTATE A MINIMUM OF TWO-MAN CELLS FOR PATROLS.
SO THAT IF AN ENEMY IS ENCOUN-TERED...
SAKURA, DON'T WORRY.
SLAP
OUR VOICES REACH FARTHER THAN ANY COMM UNIT.
PLUS, OUR NOSES CAN DETECT DANGER FASTER AND WE CAN ASSIST YOU IN BATTLES.
BOOF
BOOF
BOOF
BOOF

READ THIS WAY

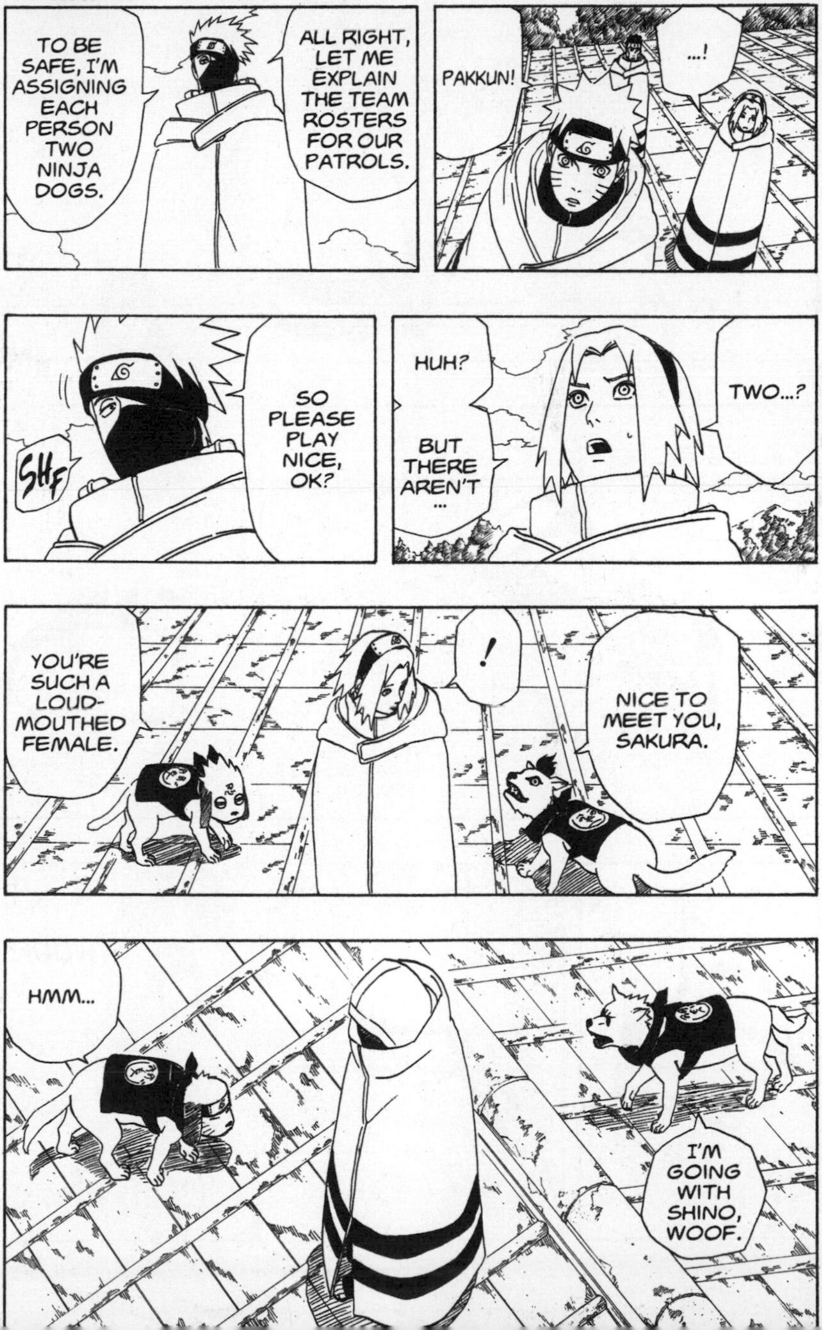
PAKKUN!
...!
ALL RIGHT, LET ME EXPLAIN THE TEAM ROSTERS FOR OUR PATROLS.
TO BE SAFE, I'M ASSIGNING EACH PERSON TWO NINJA DOGS.
TWO...?
HUH?
BUT THERE AREN'T ...
SO PLEASE PLAY NICE, OK?
SHF
NICE TO MEET YOU, SAKURA.
!
YOU'RE SUCH A LOUD-MOUTHED FEMALE.
HMM...
I'M GOING WITH SHINO, WOOF.

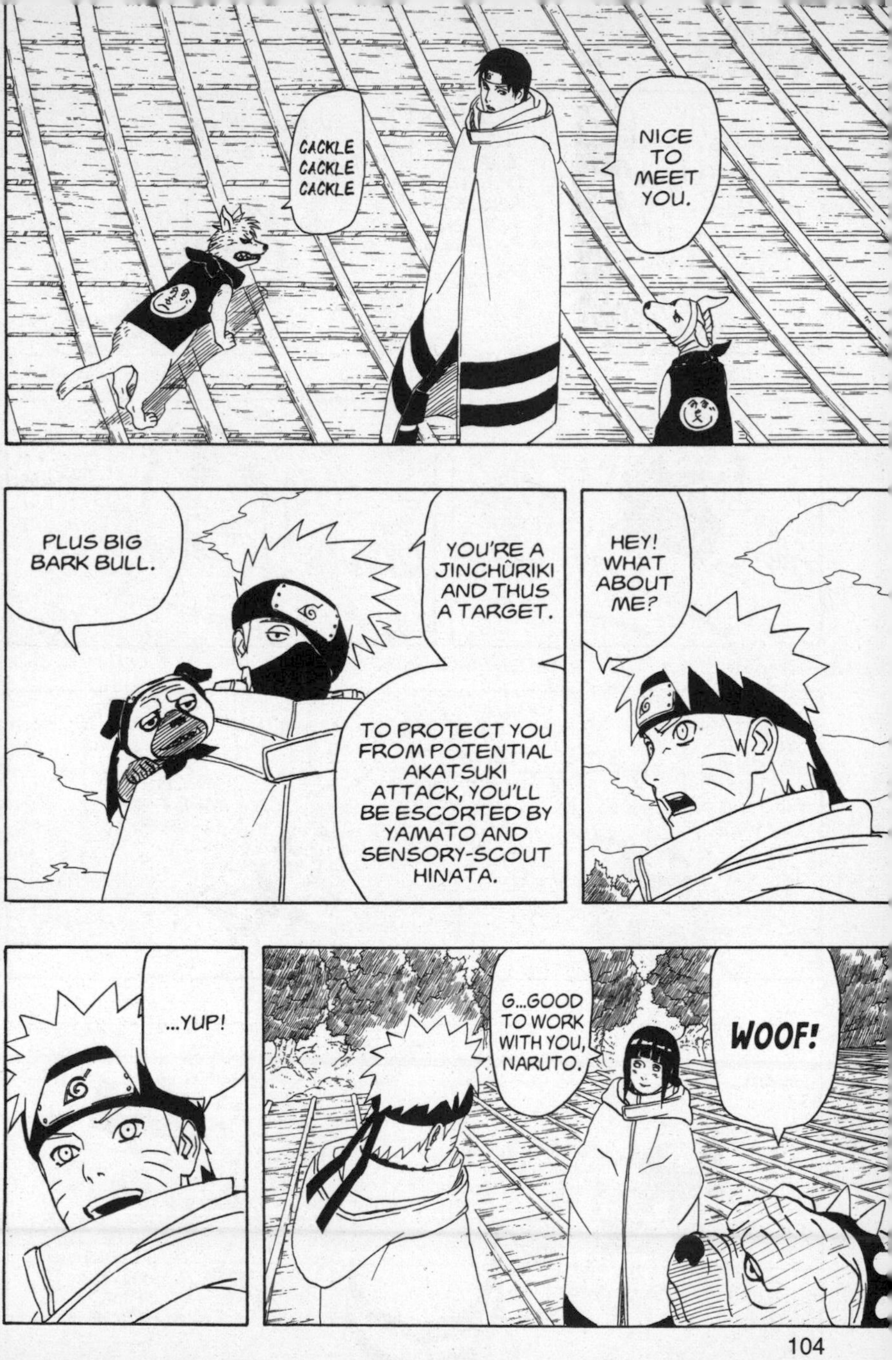
NICE TO MEET YOU.
CACKLE CACKLE CACKLE
HEY! WHAT ABOUT ME?
YOU'RE A JINCHŪRIKI AND THUS A TARGET.
TO PROTECT YOU FROM POTENTIAL AKATSUKI ATTACK, YOU'LL BE ESCORTED BY YAMATO AND SENSORY-SCOUT HINATA.
PLUS BIG BARK BULL.
WOOF!
G...GOOD TO WORK WITH YOU, NARUTO.
...YUP!

READ THIS WAY

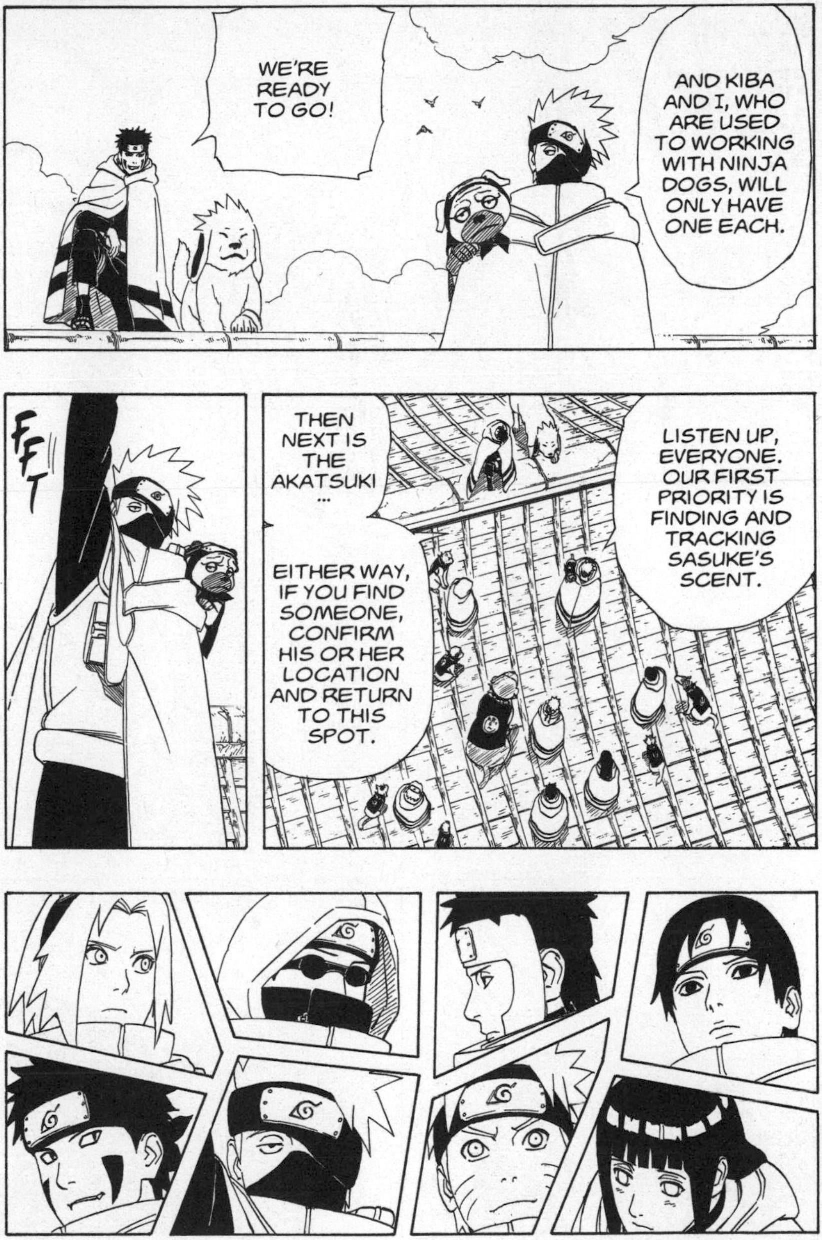
AND KIBA AND I, WHO ARE USED TO WORKING WITH NINJA DOGS, WILL ONLY HAVE ONE EACH.
WE'RE READY TO GO!
LISTEN UP, EVERYONE. OUR FIRST PRIORITY IS FINDING AND TRACKING SASUKE'S SCENT.
THEN NEXT IS THE AKATSUKI ...
EITHER WAY, IF YOU FIND SOMEONE, CONFIRM HIS OR HER LOCATION AND RETURN TO THIS SPOT.
FFT

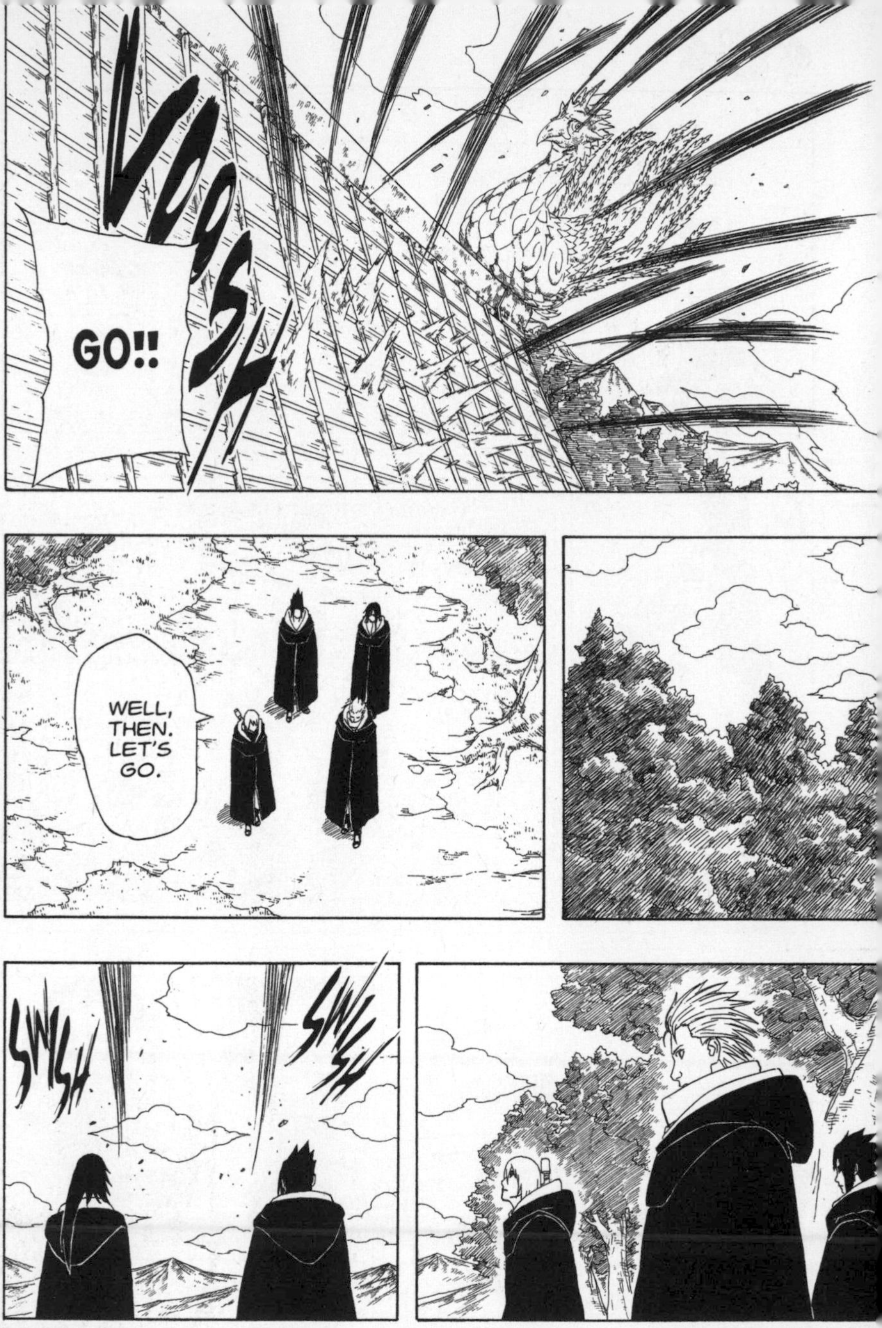
VOOSH
GO!!
WELL, THEN. LET'S GO.
SWISH
SWISH

READ THIS WAY

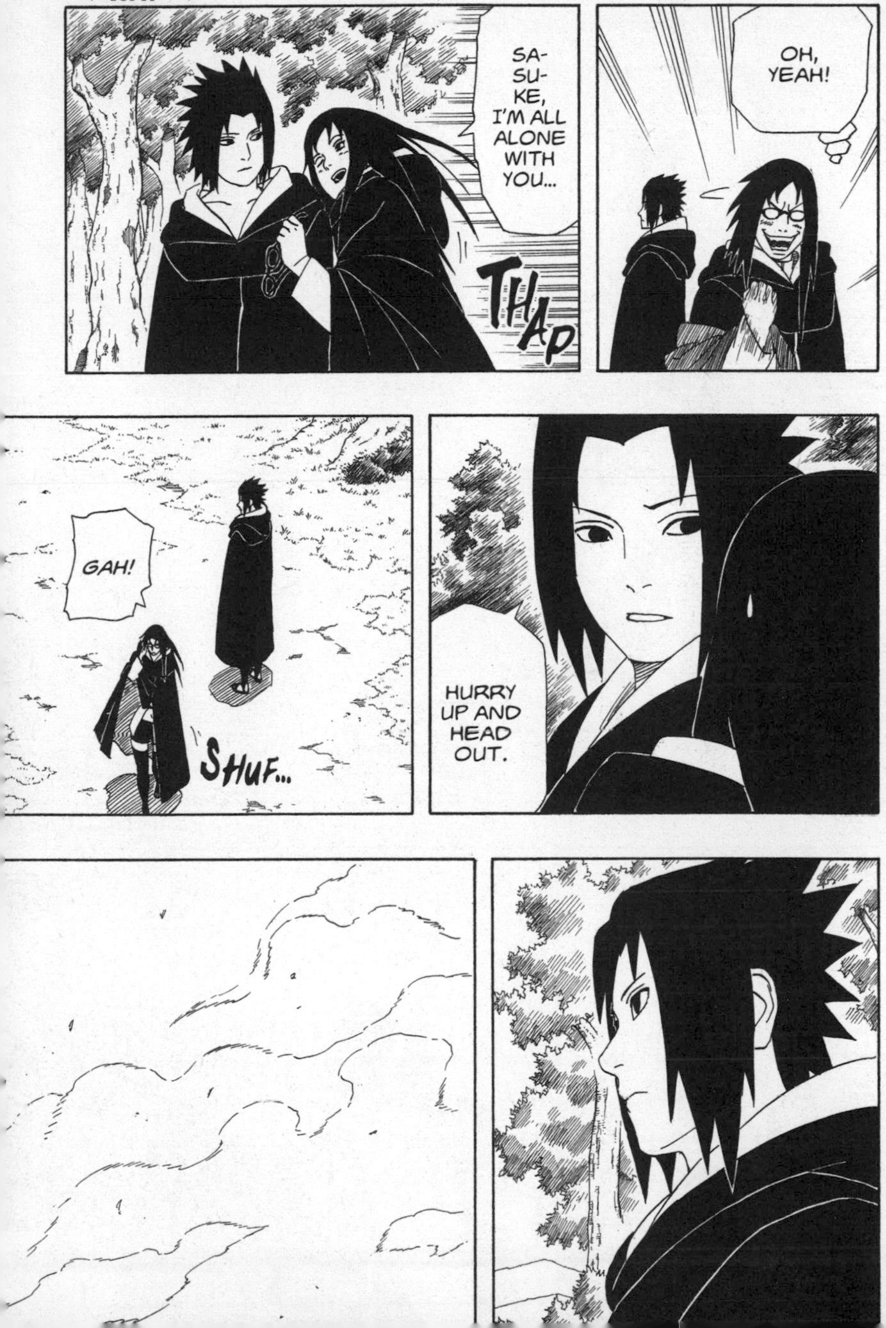
OH, YEAH!
SA-SU-KE, I'M ALL ALONE WITH YOU...
THAP
HURRY UP AND HEAD OUT.
GAH!
SHUF...

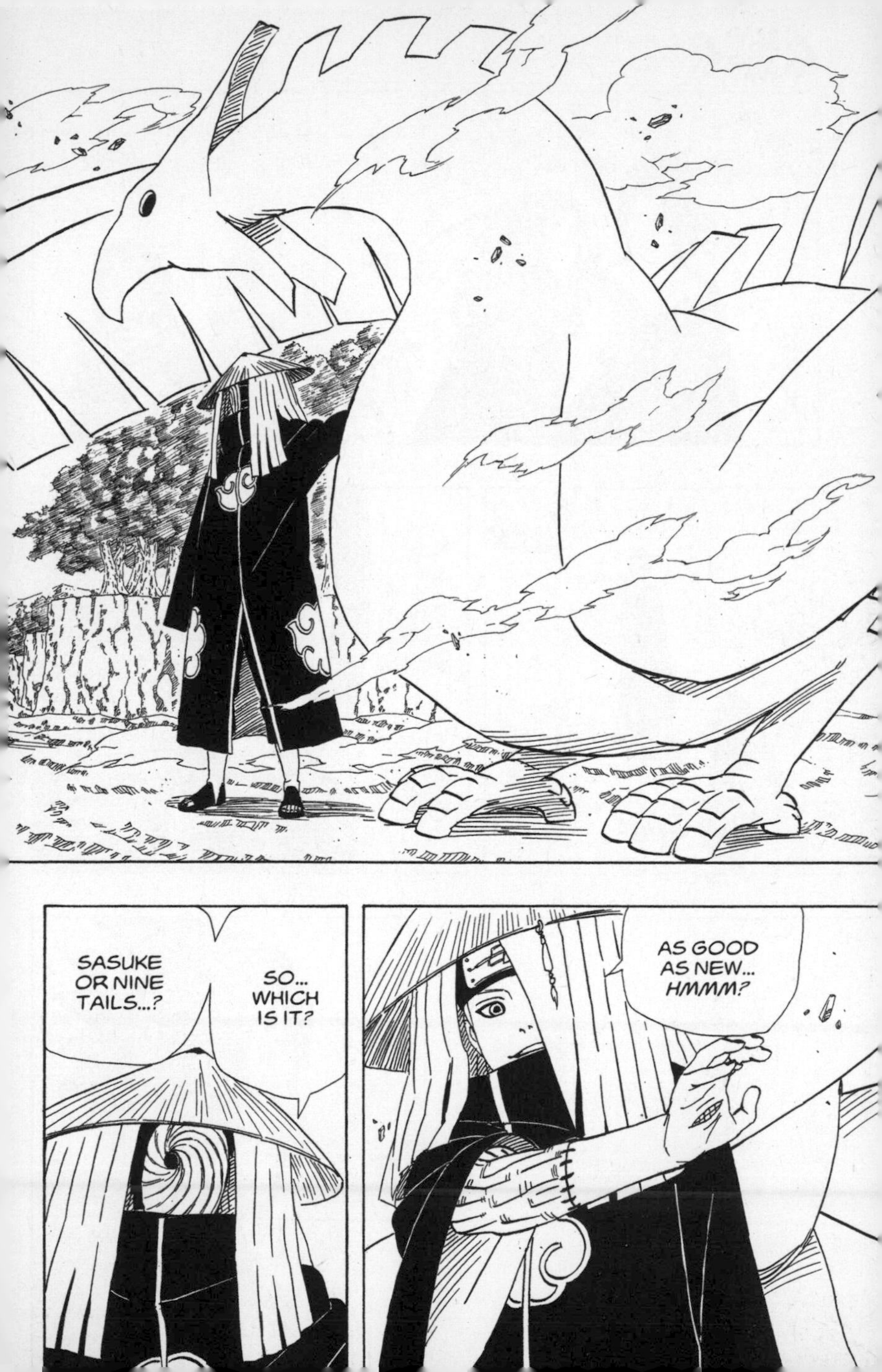
AS GOOD AS NEW... HMMM?
SO... WHICH IS IT?
SASUKE OR NINE TAILS...?

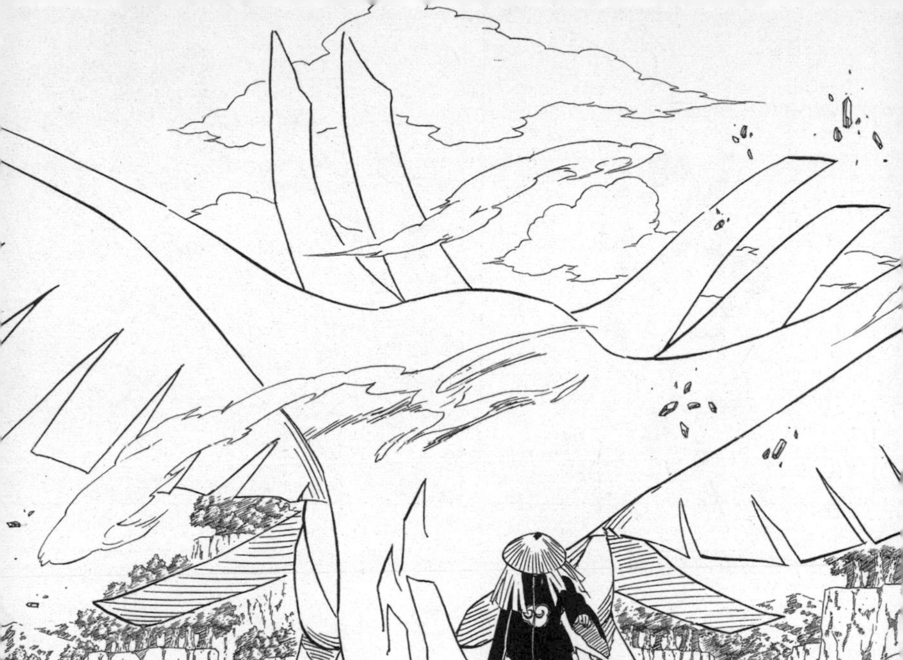

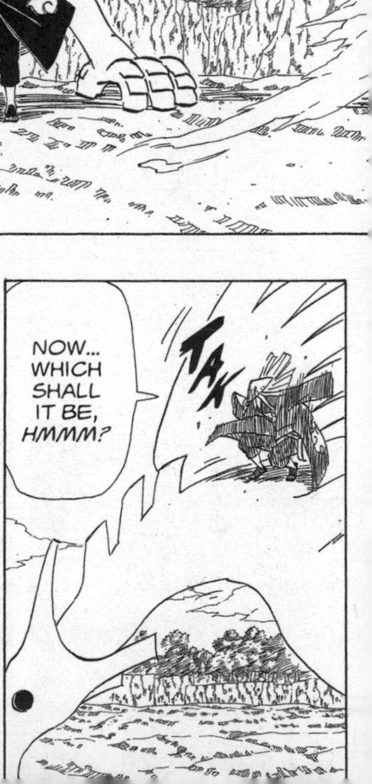
NOW... WHICH SHALL IT BE, HMMM?
TAK

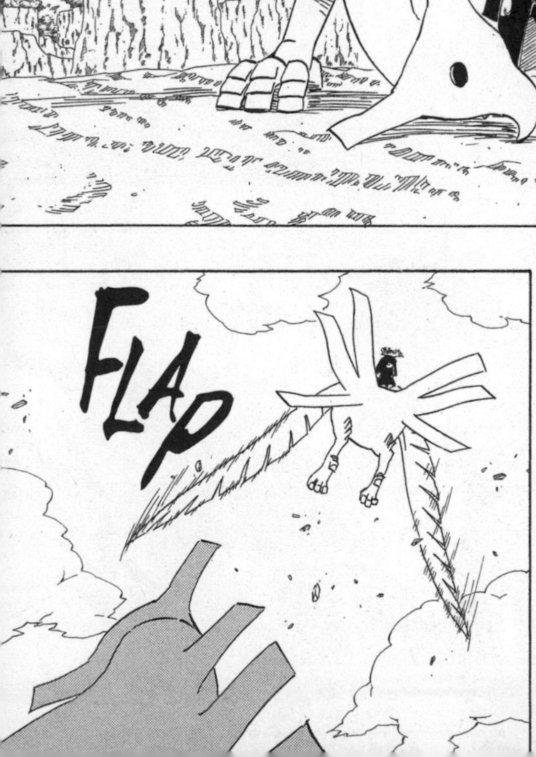
FLAP

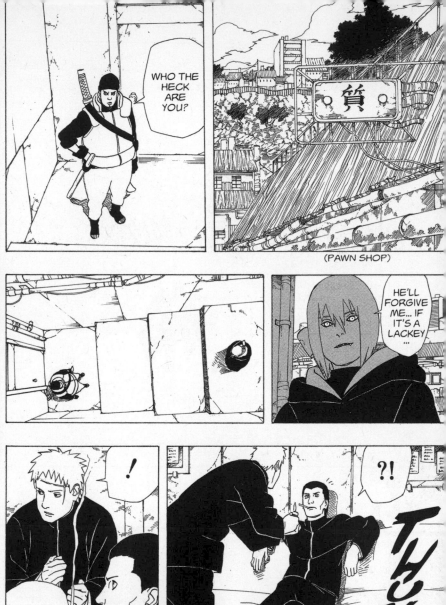

WHO THE HECK ARE YOU?

(PAWN SHOP)

HE'LL FORGIVE ME... IF IT'S A LACKEY...

!

GO TAKE A LOOK.

?!

THUNK

110

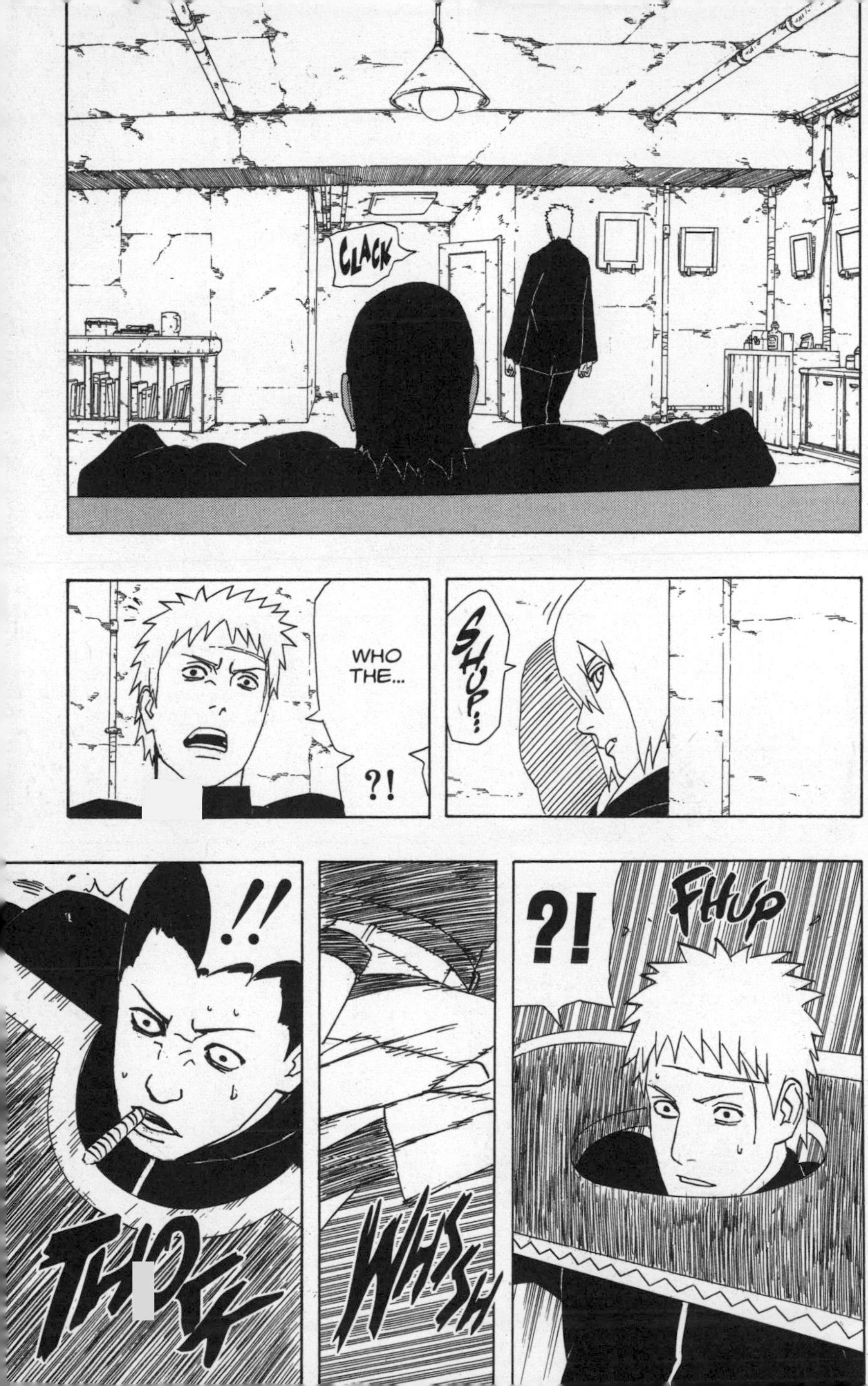
CLACK
SHUP...
WHO THE...
?!
FHUP
?!
WHSH
!!
THOCK

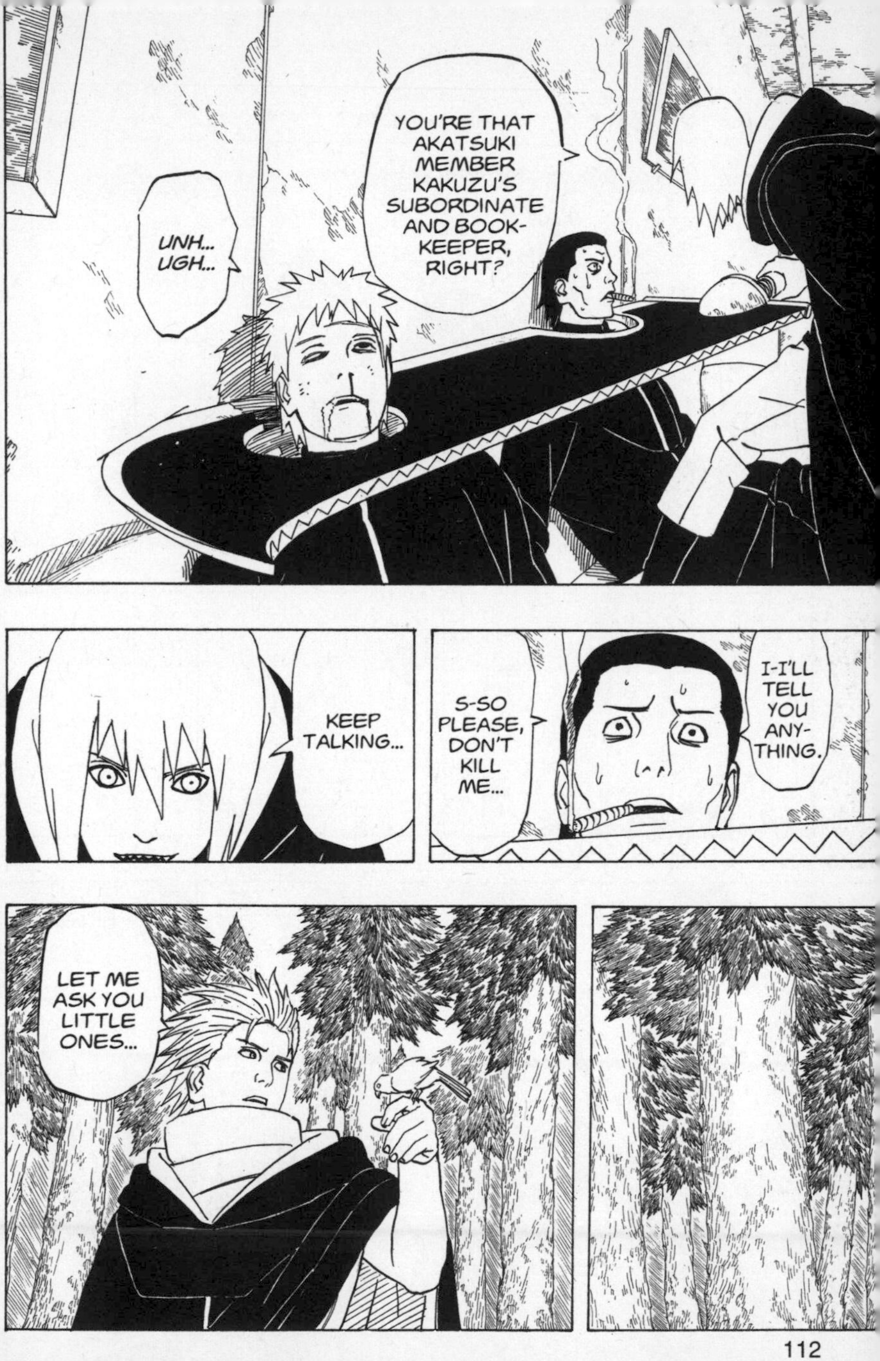
YOU'RE THAT AKATSUKI MEMBER KAKUZU'S SUBORDINATE AND BOOK-KEEPER, RIGHT?
UNH... UGH...
I-I'LL TELL YOU ANY-THING.
S-SO PLEASE, DON'T KILL ME...
KEEP TALKING...
LET ME ASK YOU LITTLE ONES...

READ THIS WAY

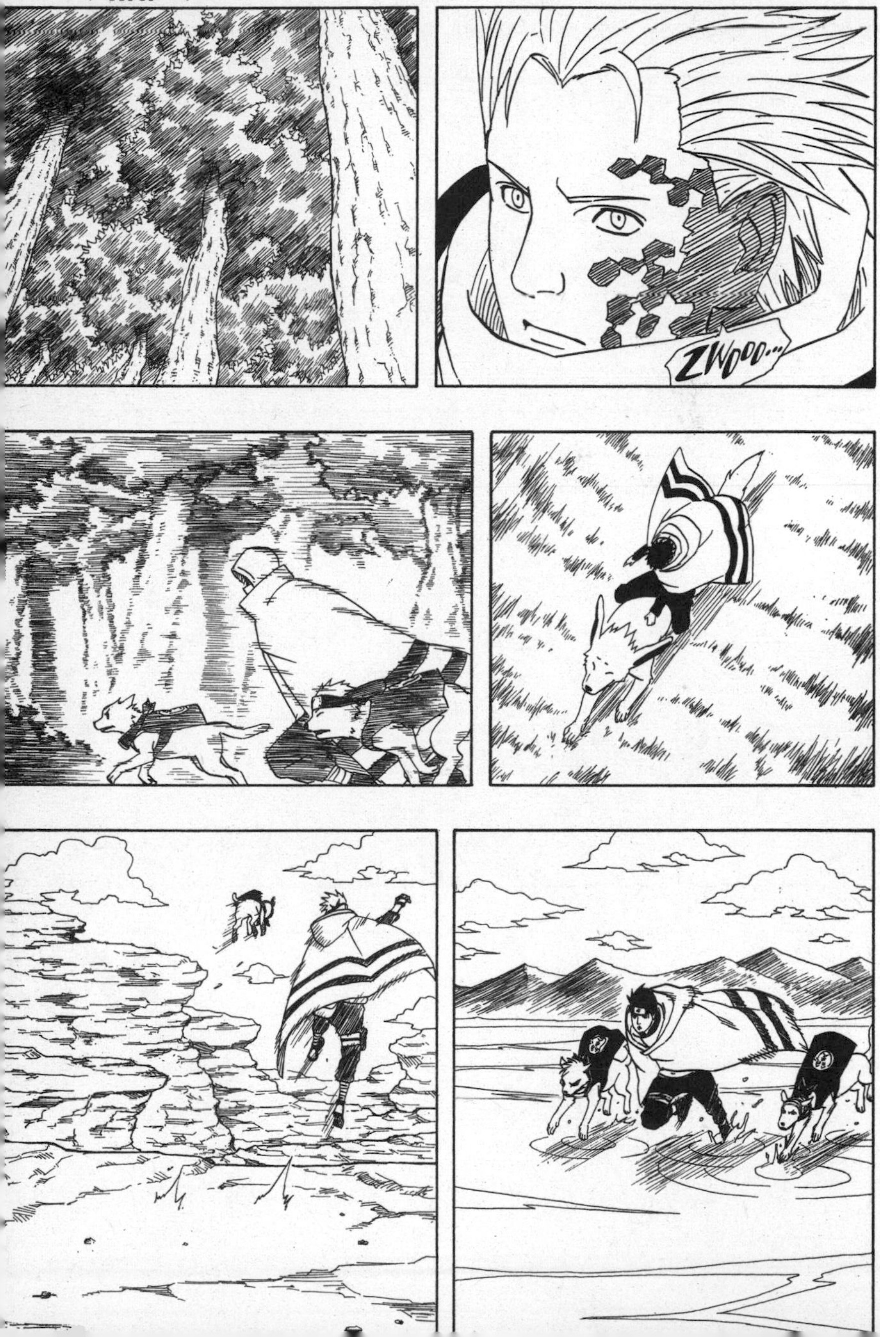
ZWOOO...

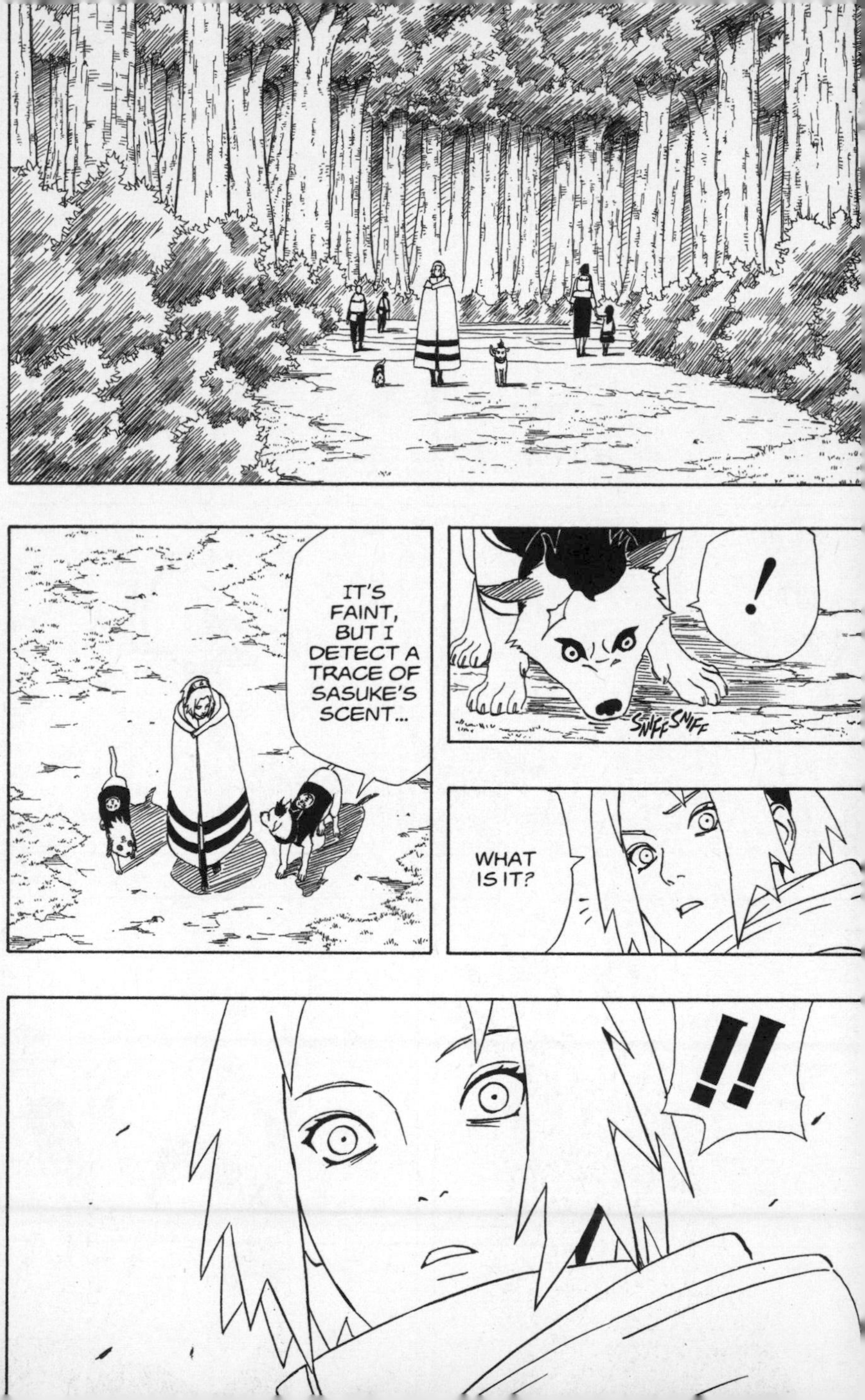
!
SNIFF SNIFF
WHAT IS IT?
IT'S FAINT, BUT I DETECT A TRACE OF SASUKE'S SCENT...
!!

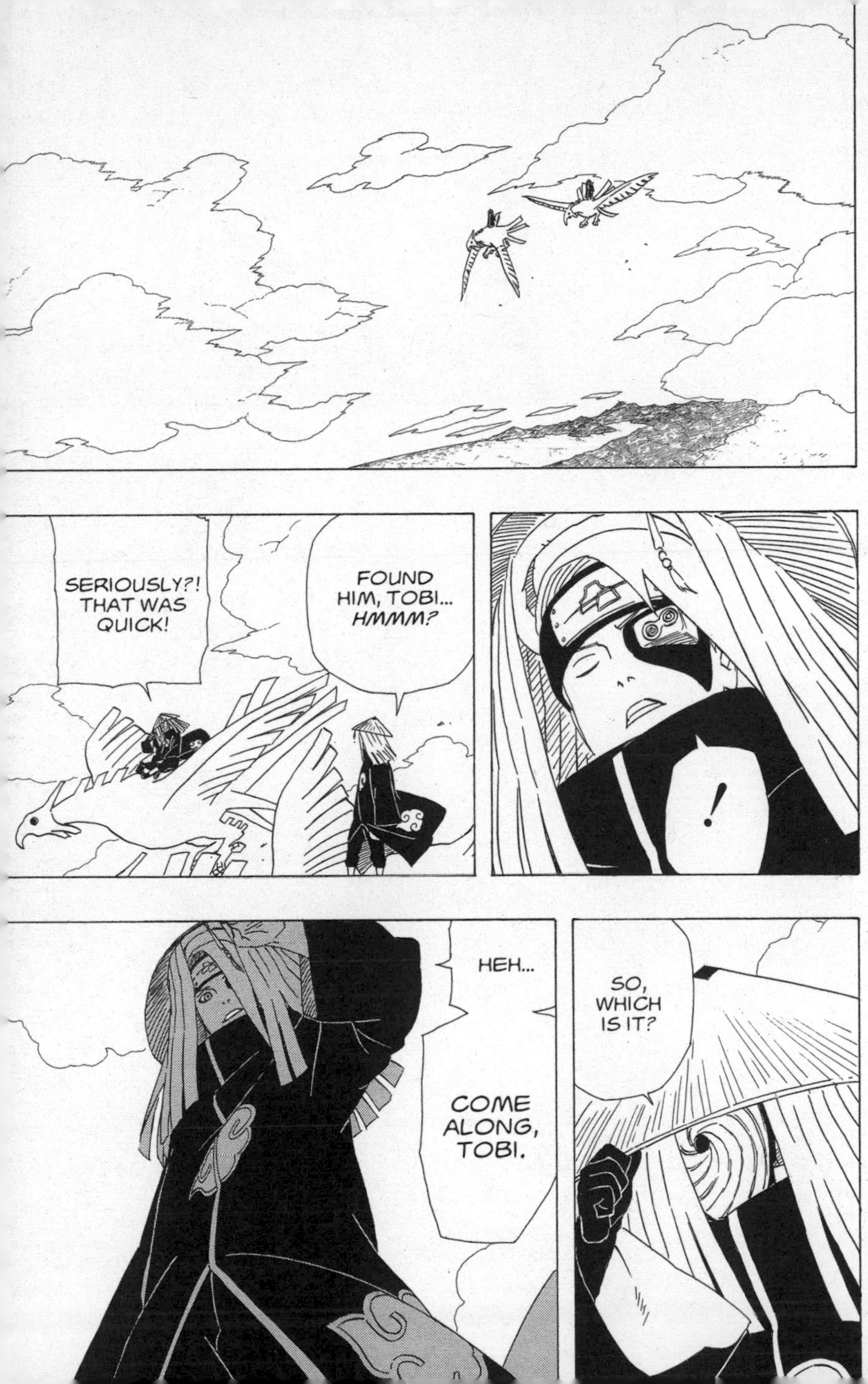
!
FOUND HIM, TOBI... *HMMM?*
SERIOUSLY?! THAT WAS QUICK!
SO, WHICH IS IT?
HEH...
COME ALONG, TOBI.

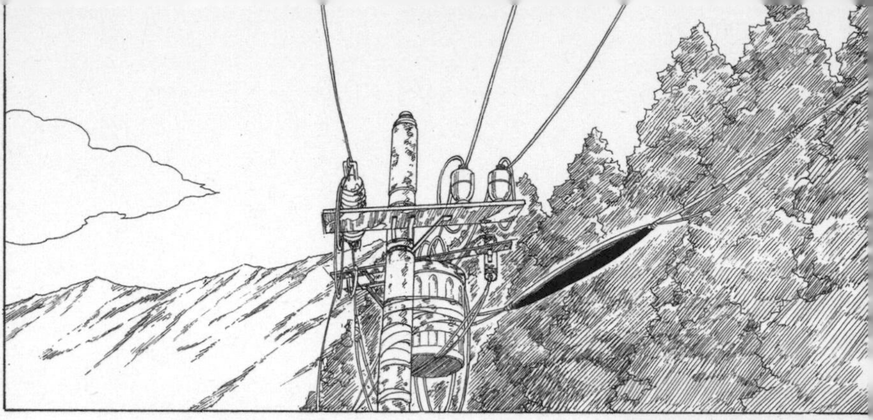

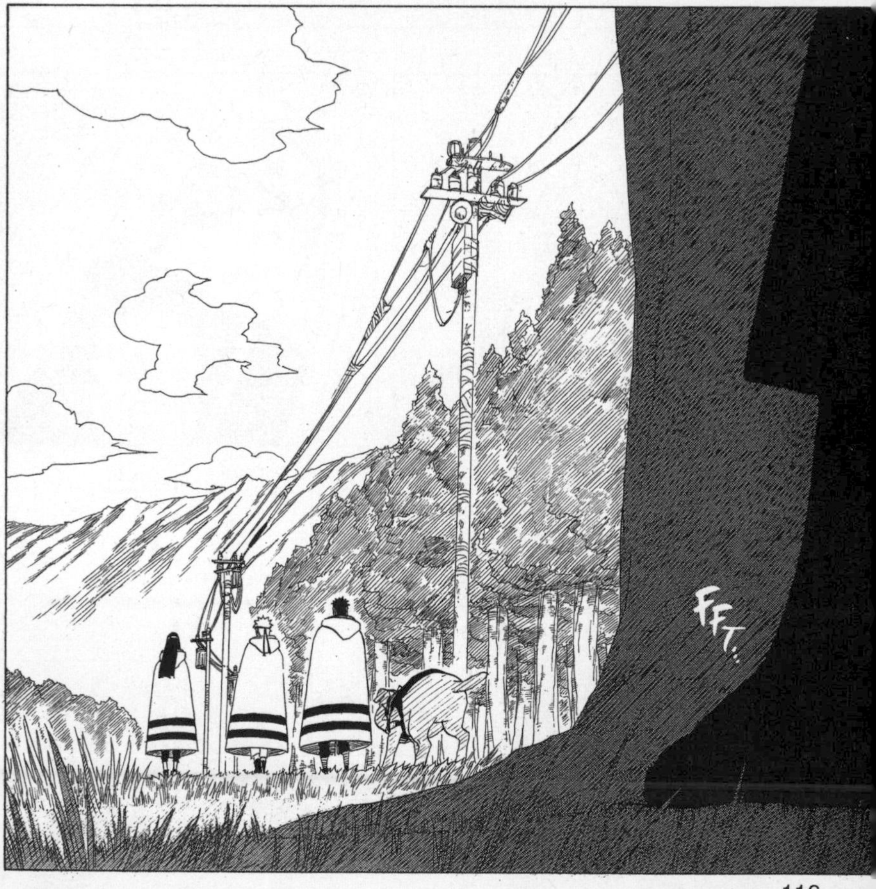
FFT..

READ THIS WAY

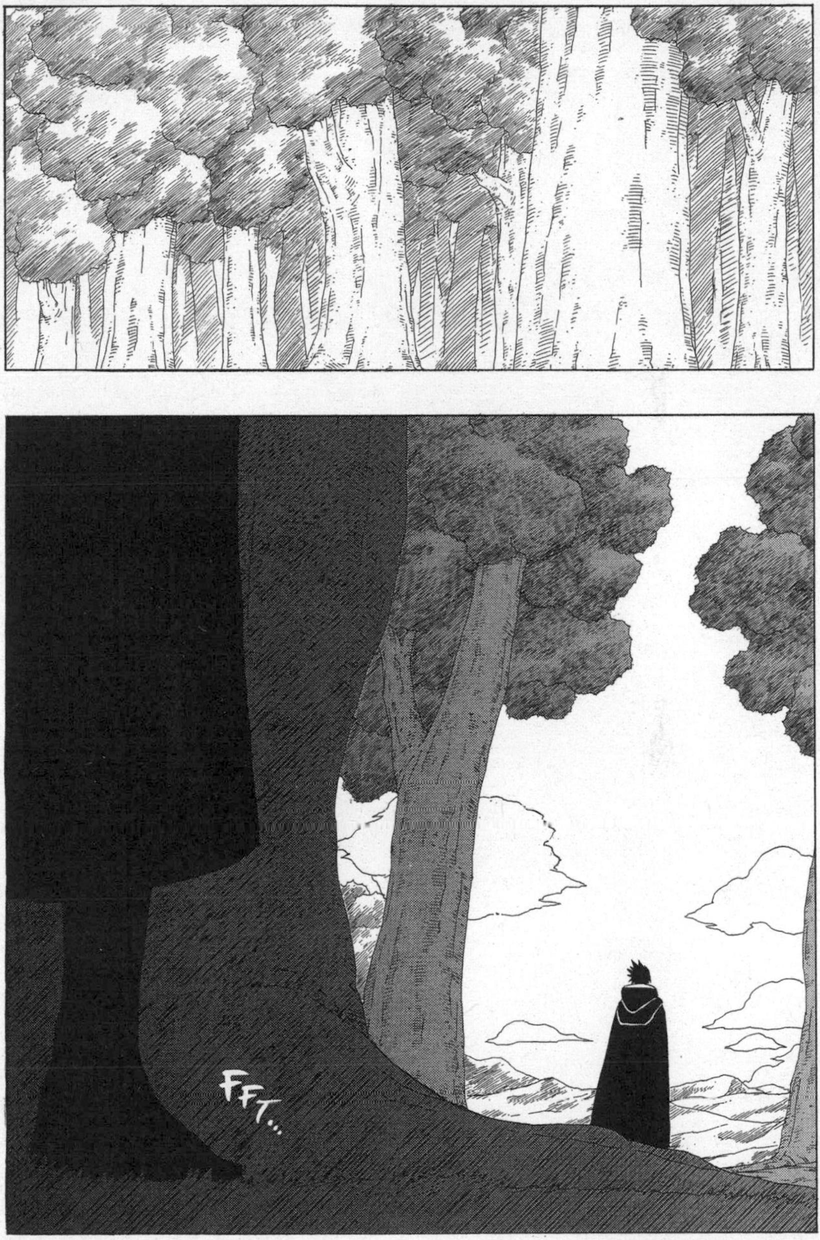
FFT...

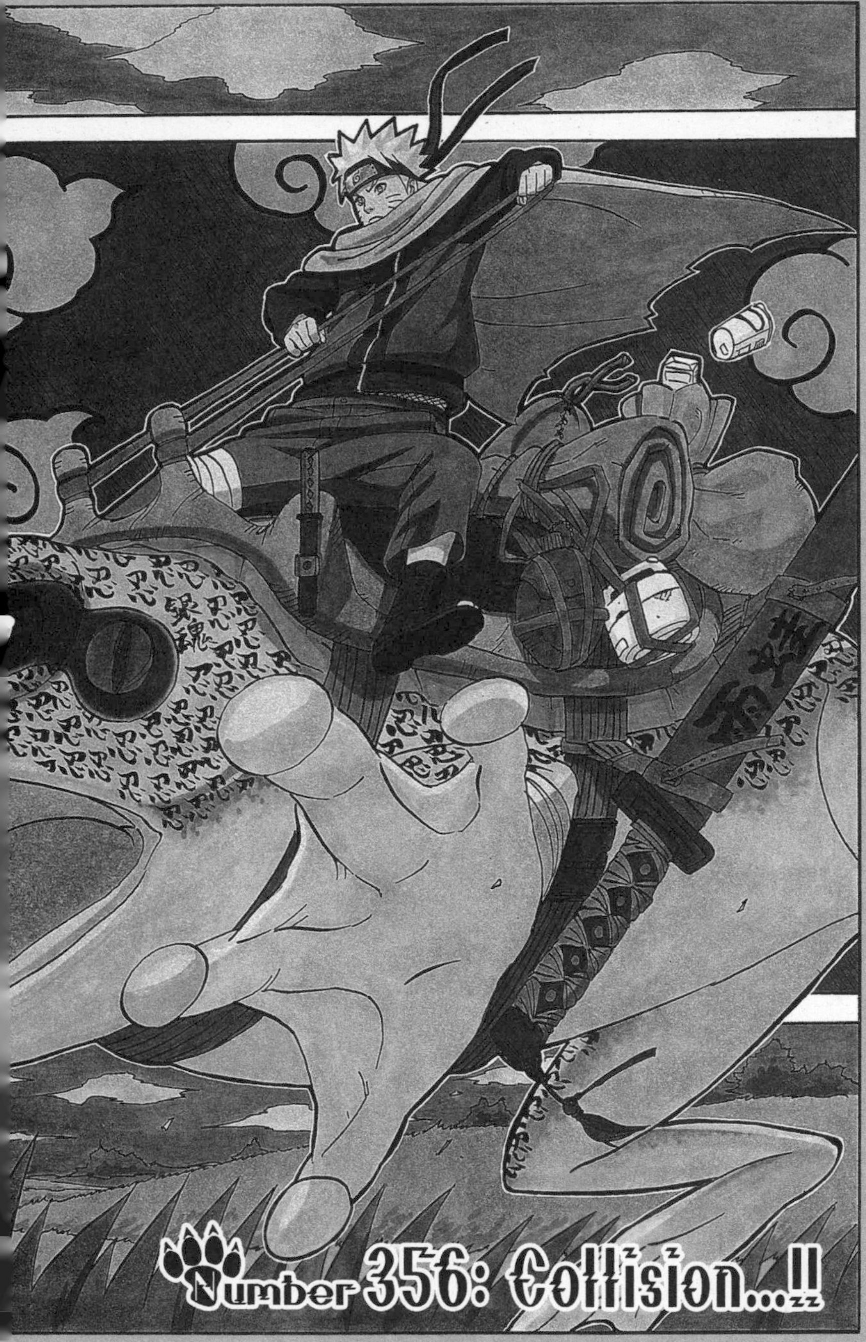
Number 356: Collision...!!

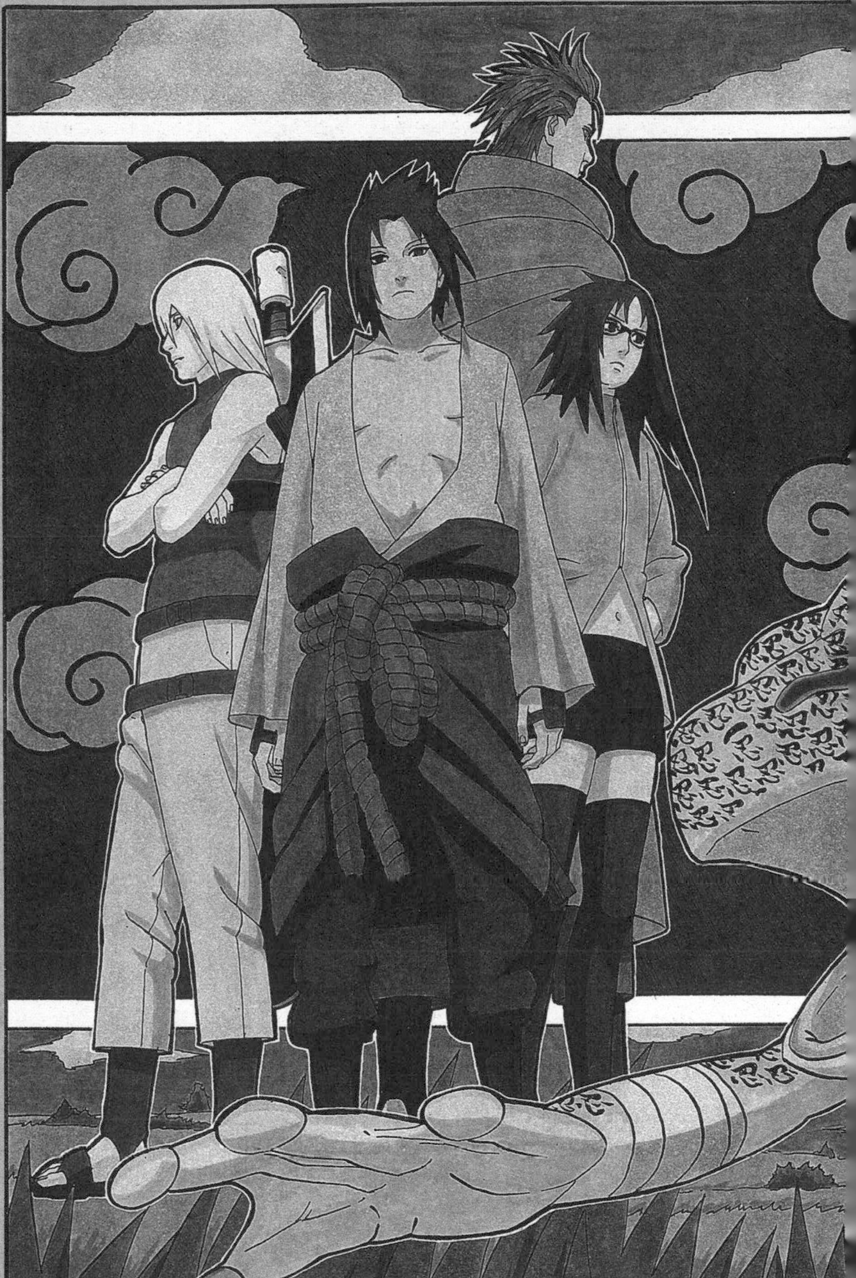

NARUTO

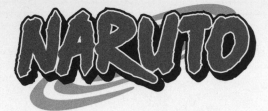

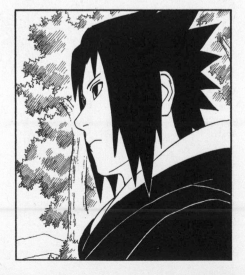

Number 356: Collision...!!

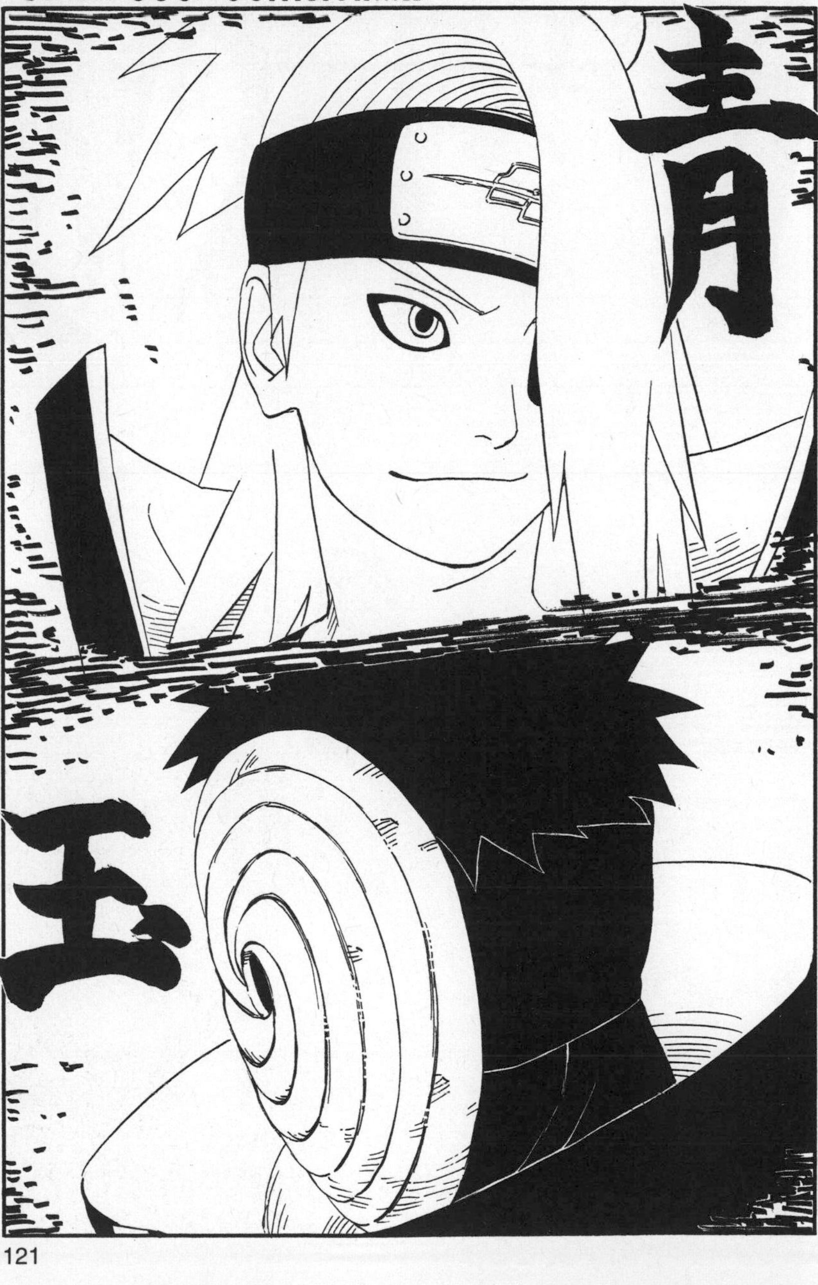
青
玉

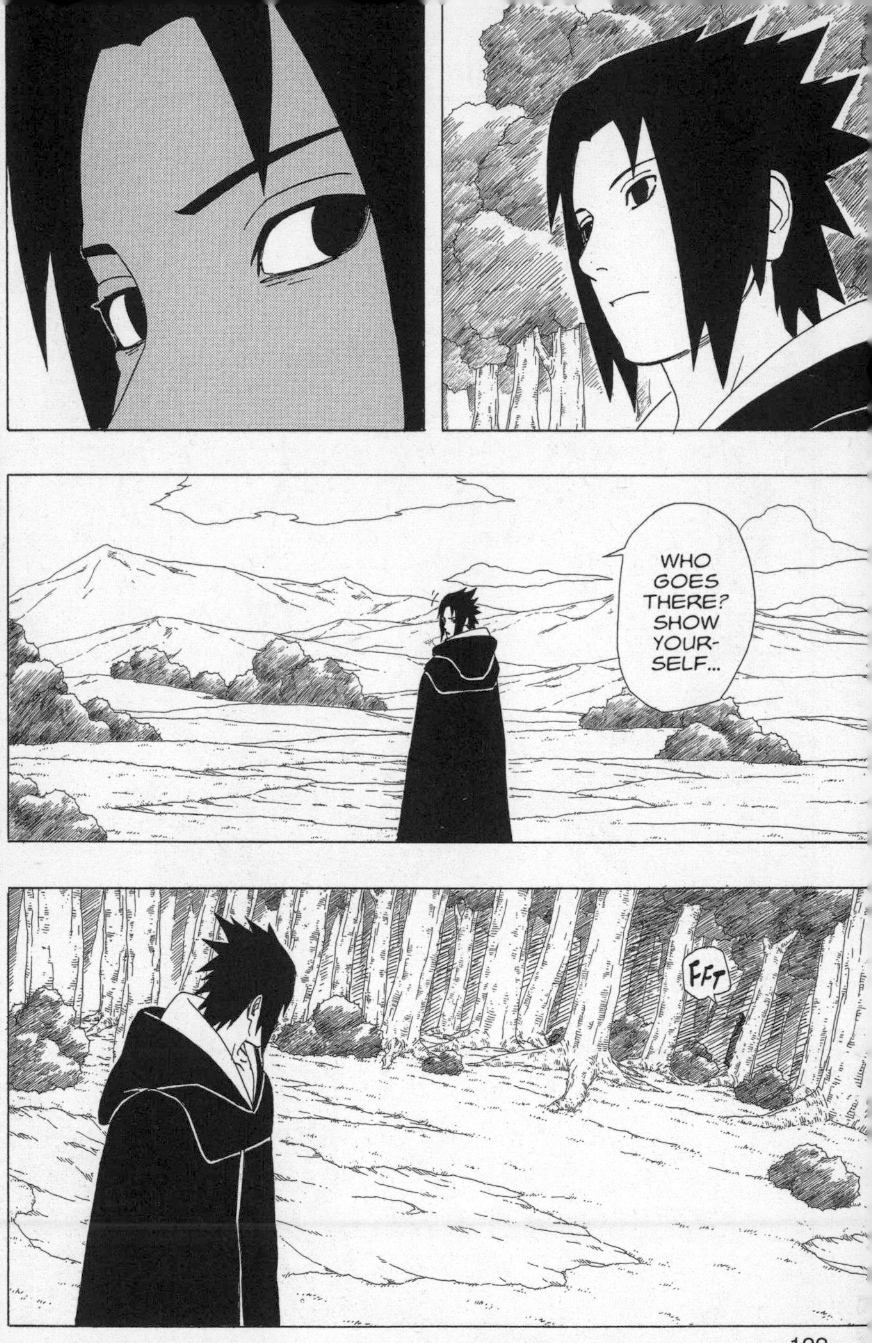
WHO GOES THERE? SHOW YOUR-SELF...
FFT

READ THIS WAY

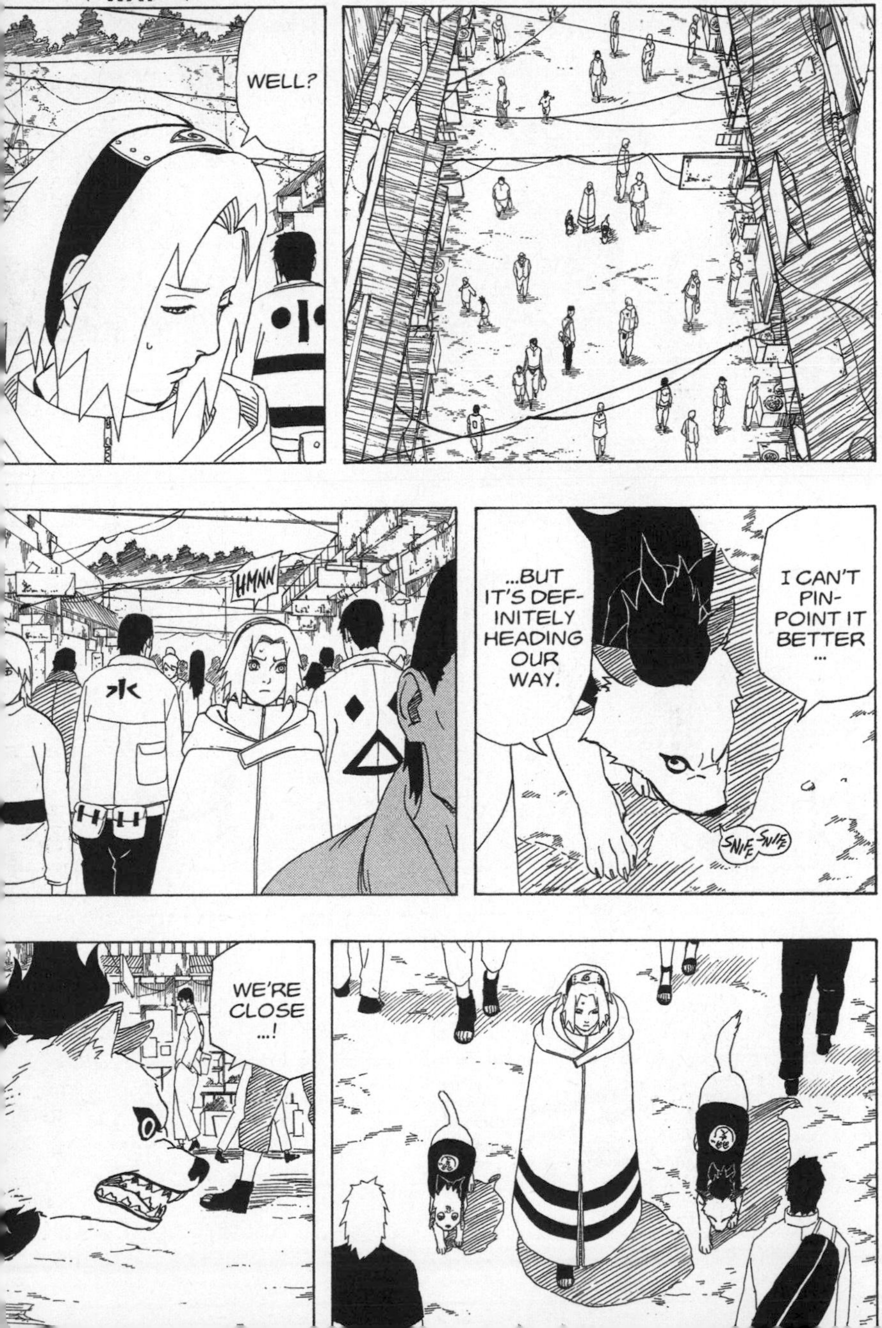
WELL?
I CAN'T PIN-POINT IT BETTER ...
...BUT IT'S DEF-INITELY HEADING OUR WAY.
SNIFF SNIFF
HMNN
WE'RE CLOSE ...!

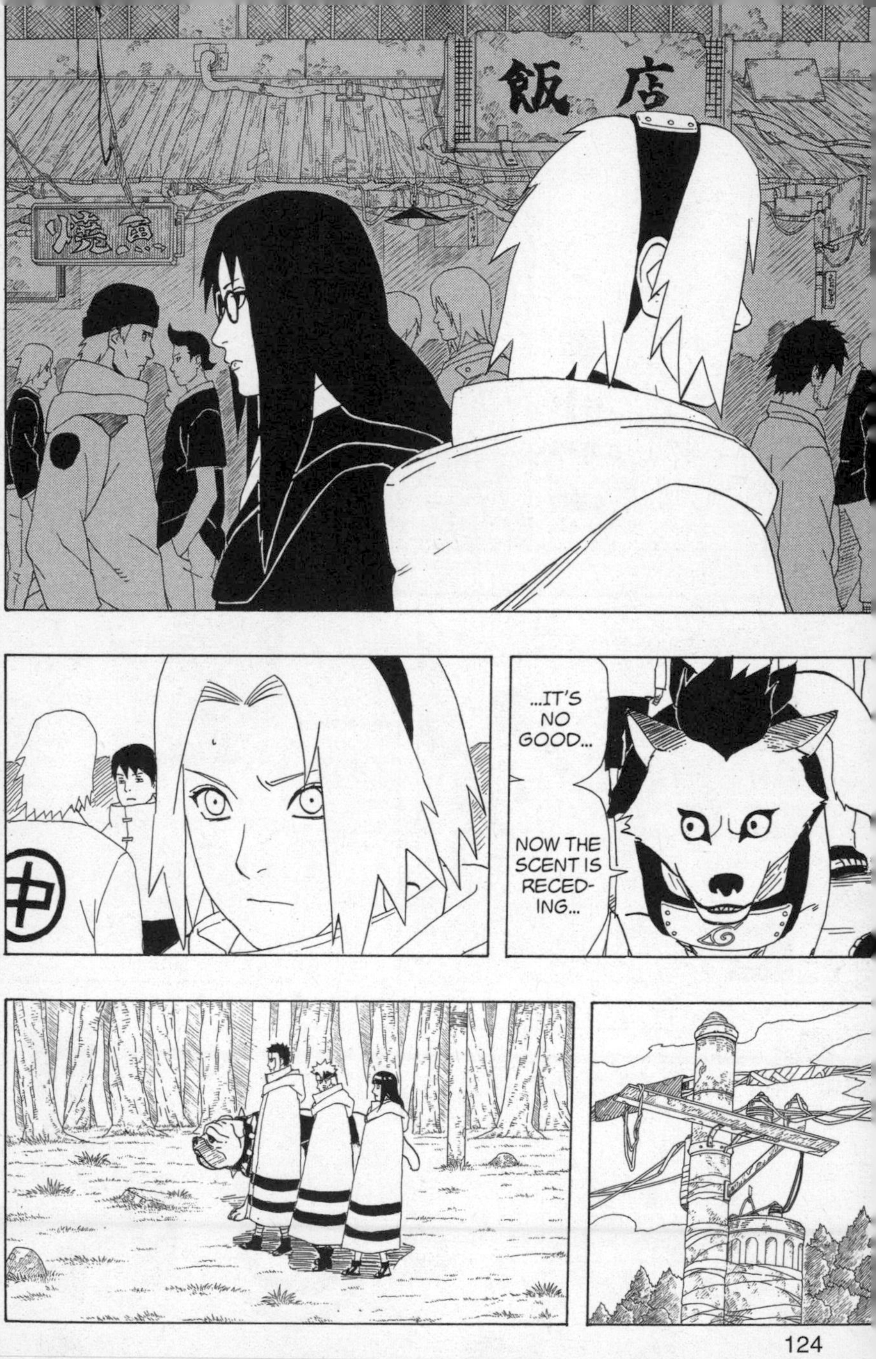
飯店
...IT'S NO GOOD...
NOW THE SCENT IS RECEDING...

READ THIS WAY

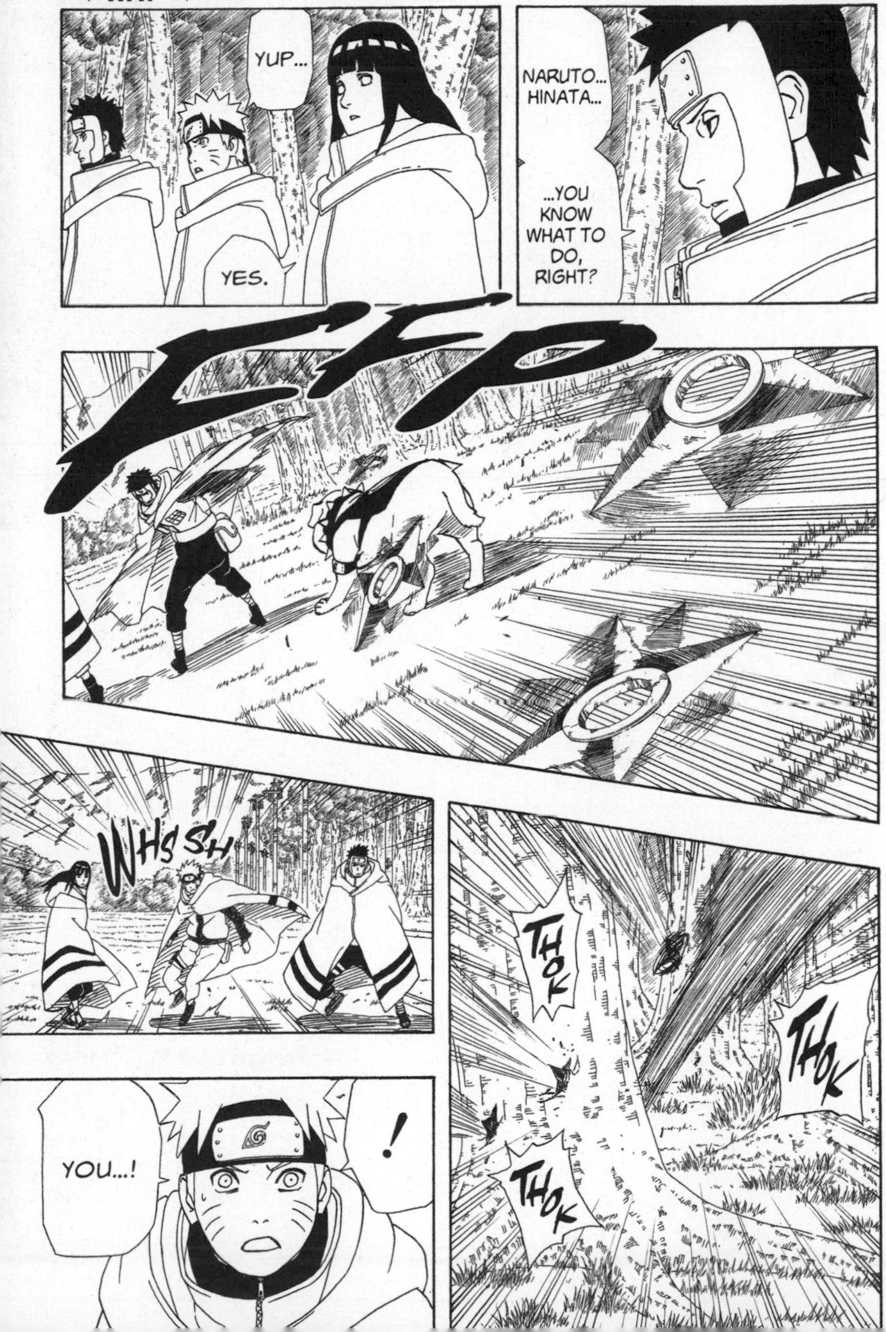
NARUTO... HINATA...
...YOU KNOW WHAT TO DO, RIGHT?
YUP...
YES.
FFP
THOK
THOK
THOK
WHSSH
!
YOU...!

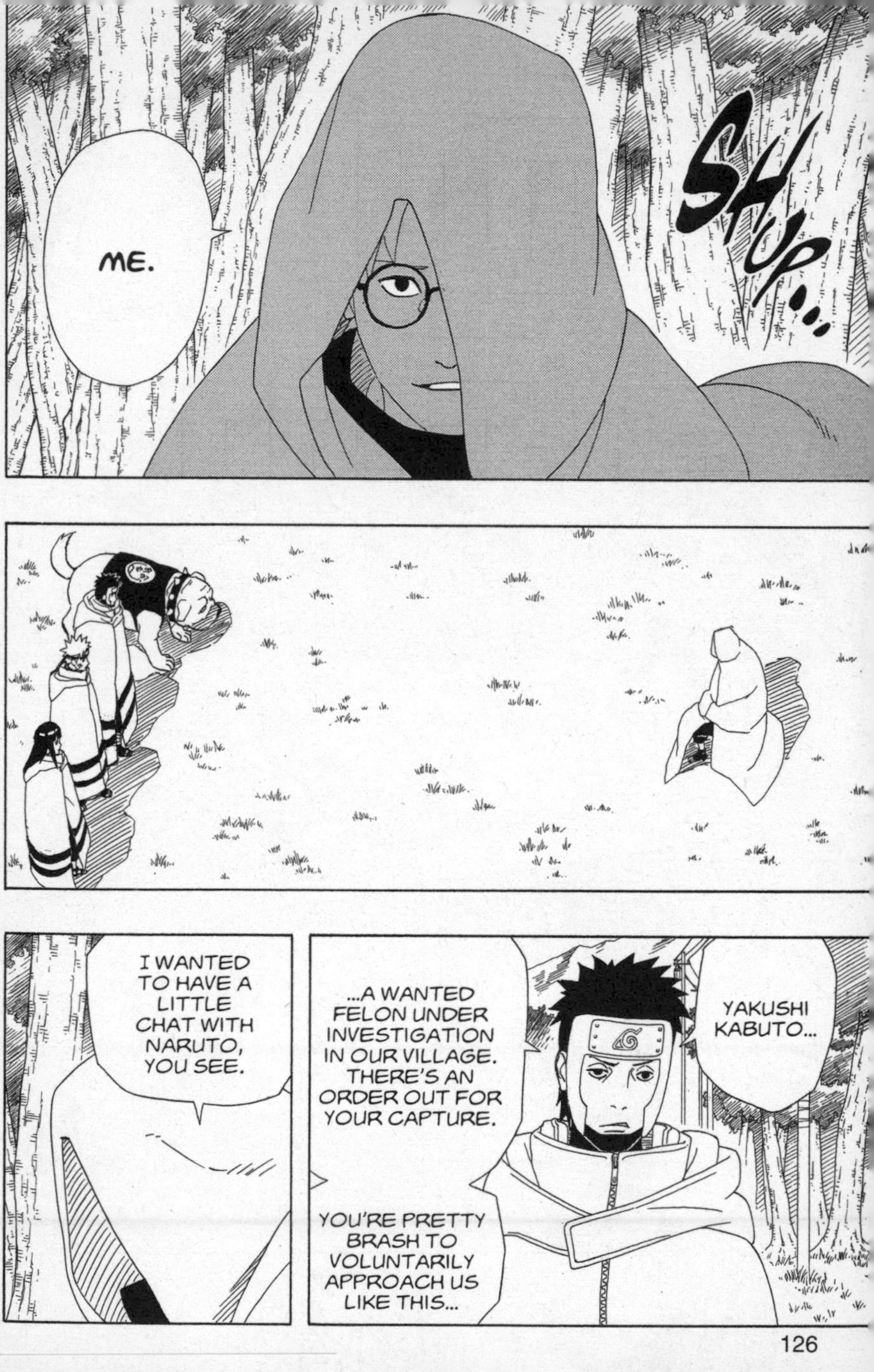
SHUP...
ME.
YAKUSHI KABUTO...
...A WANTED FELON UNDER INVESTIGATION IN OUR VILLAGE. THERE'S AN ORDER OUT FOR YOUR CAPTURE.
YOU'RE PRETTY BRASH TO VOLUNTARILY APPROACH US LIKE THIS...
I WANTED TO HAVE A LITTLE CHAT WITH NARUTO, YOU SEE.

READ THIS WAY

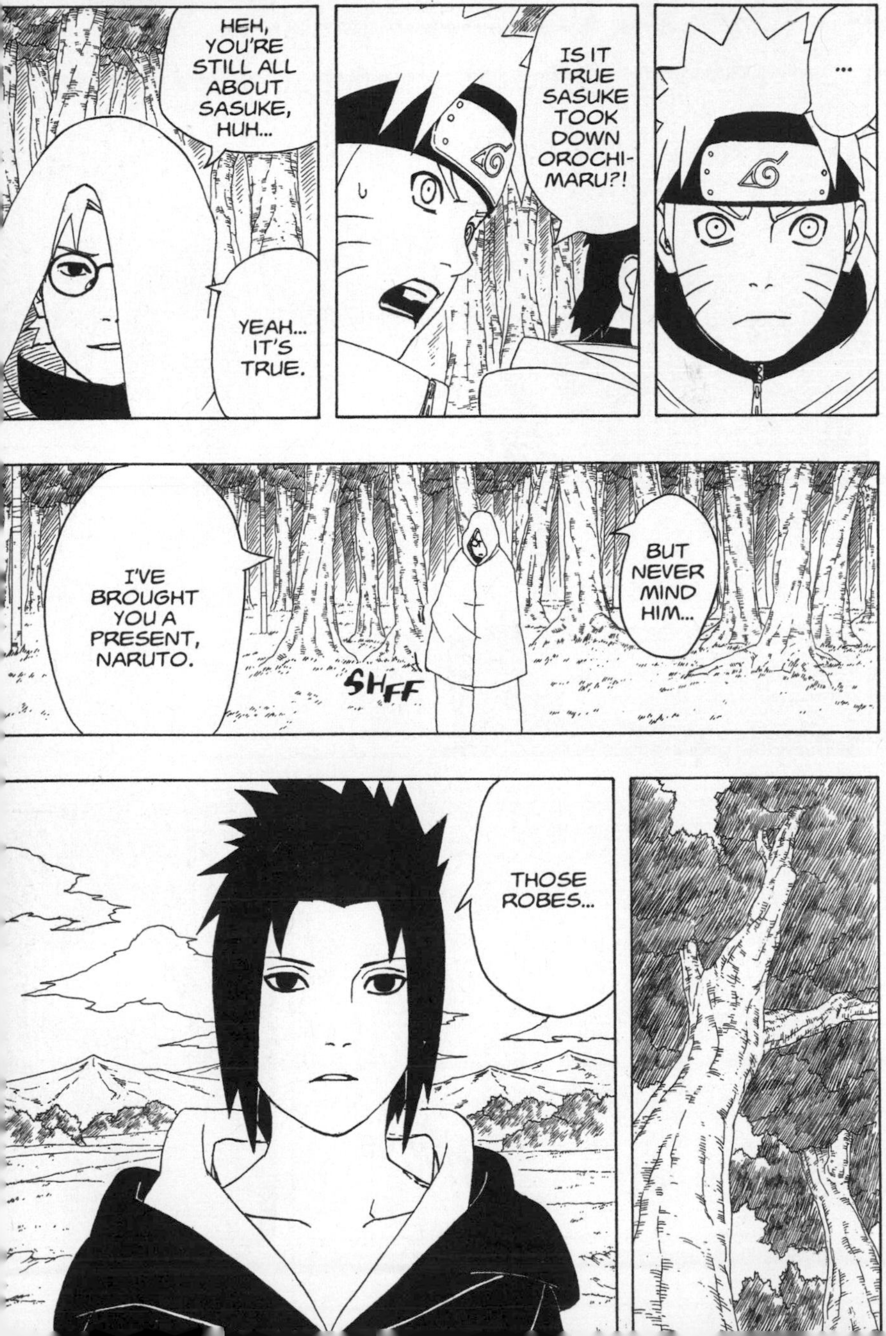
...
IS IT TRUE SASUKE TOOK DOWN OROCHIMARU?!
HEH, YOU'RE STILL ALL ABOUT SASUKE, HUH...
YEAH... IT'S TRUE.
BUT NEVER MIND HIM...
I'VE BROUGHT YOU A PRESENT, NARUTO.
SHFF
THOSE ROBES...

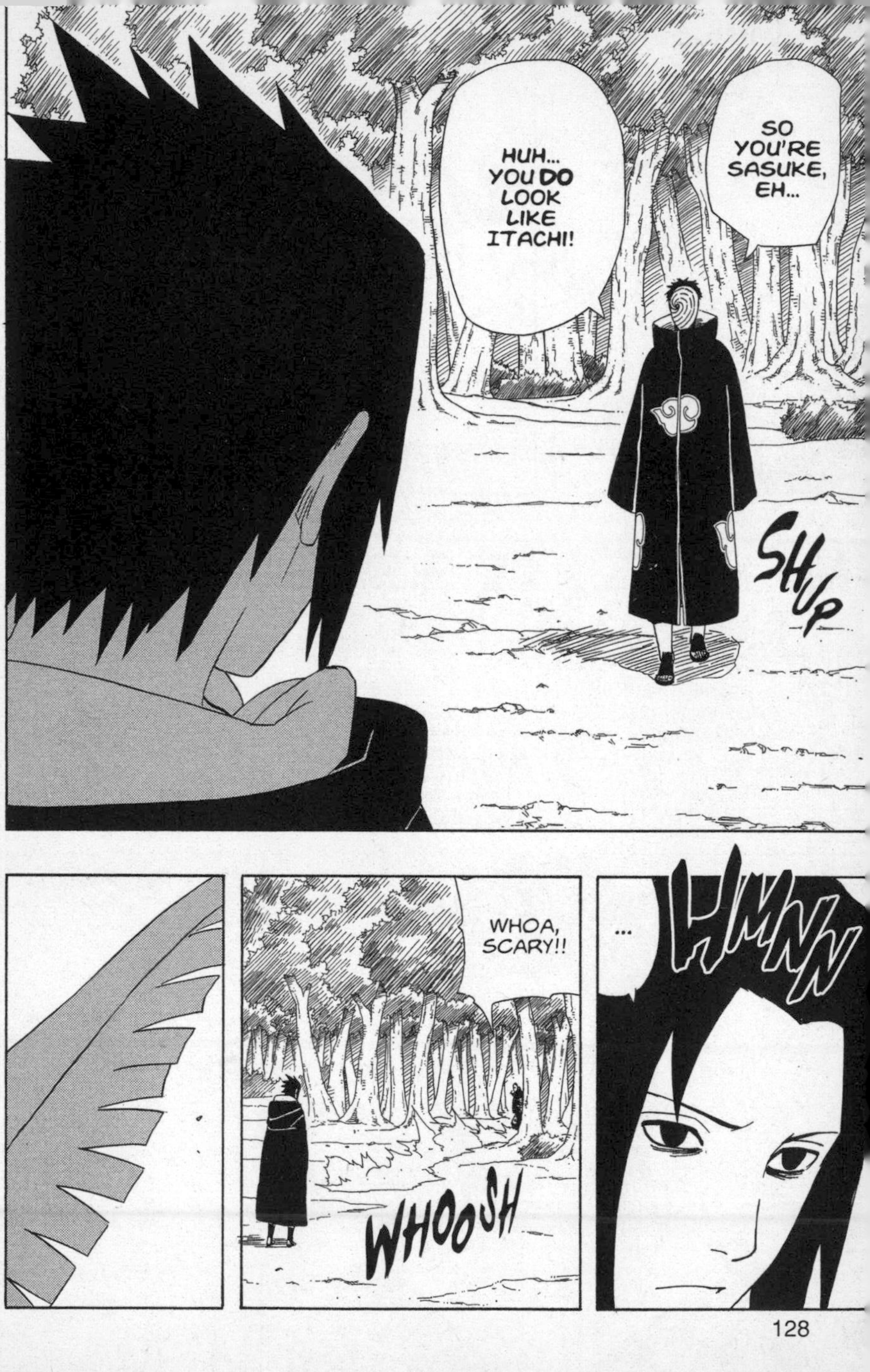
SO YOU'RE SASUKE, EH...
HUH... YOU DO LOOK LIKE ITACHI!
SHUP
...
HMMN
WHOA, SCARY!!
WHOOSH

READ THIS WAY

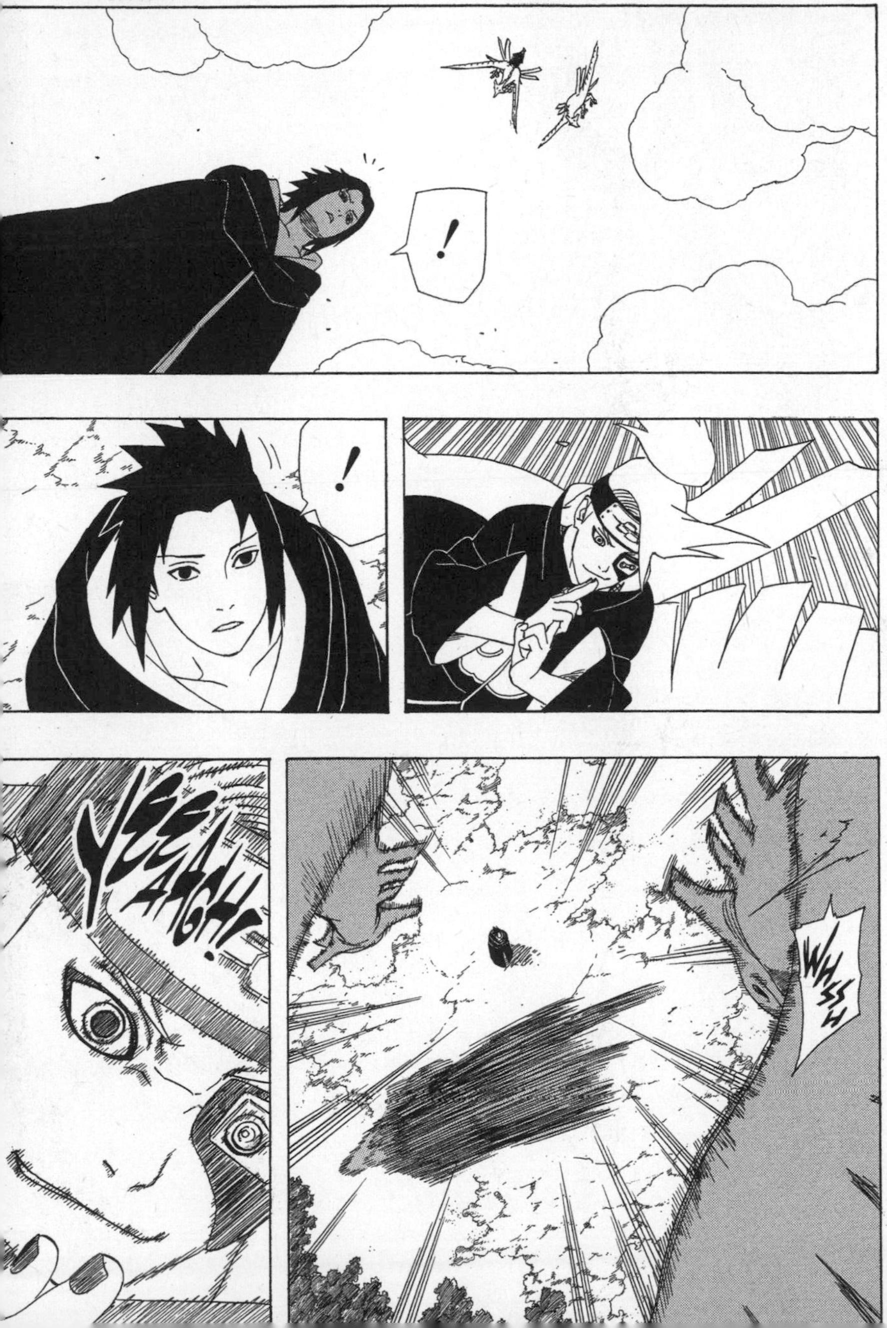
!
!
WHSSH
YEEAAAGH!!

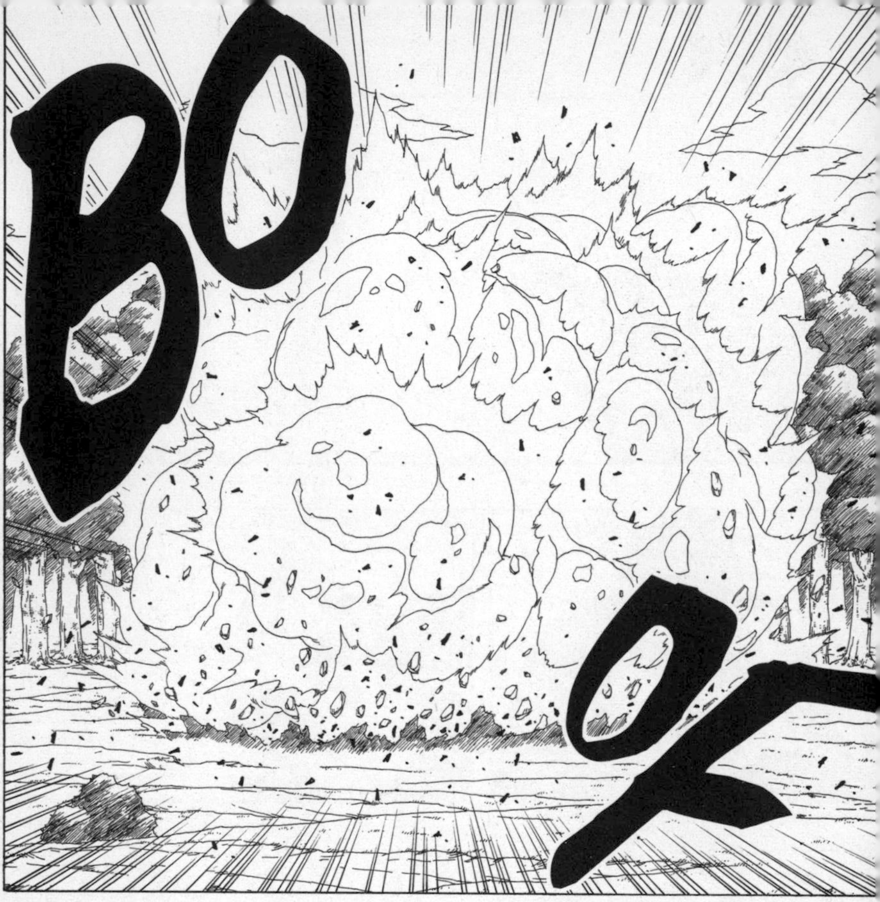
BOOM
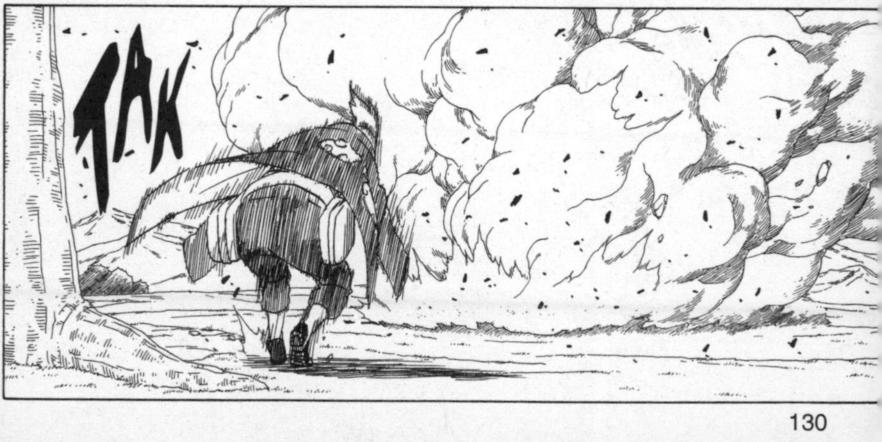
TAK

READ THIS WAY

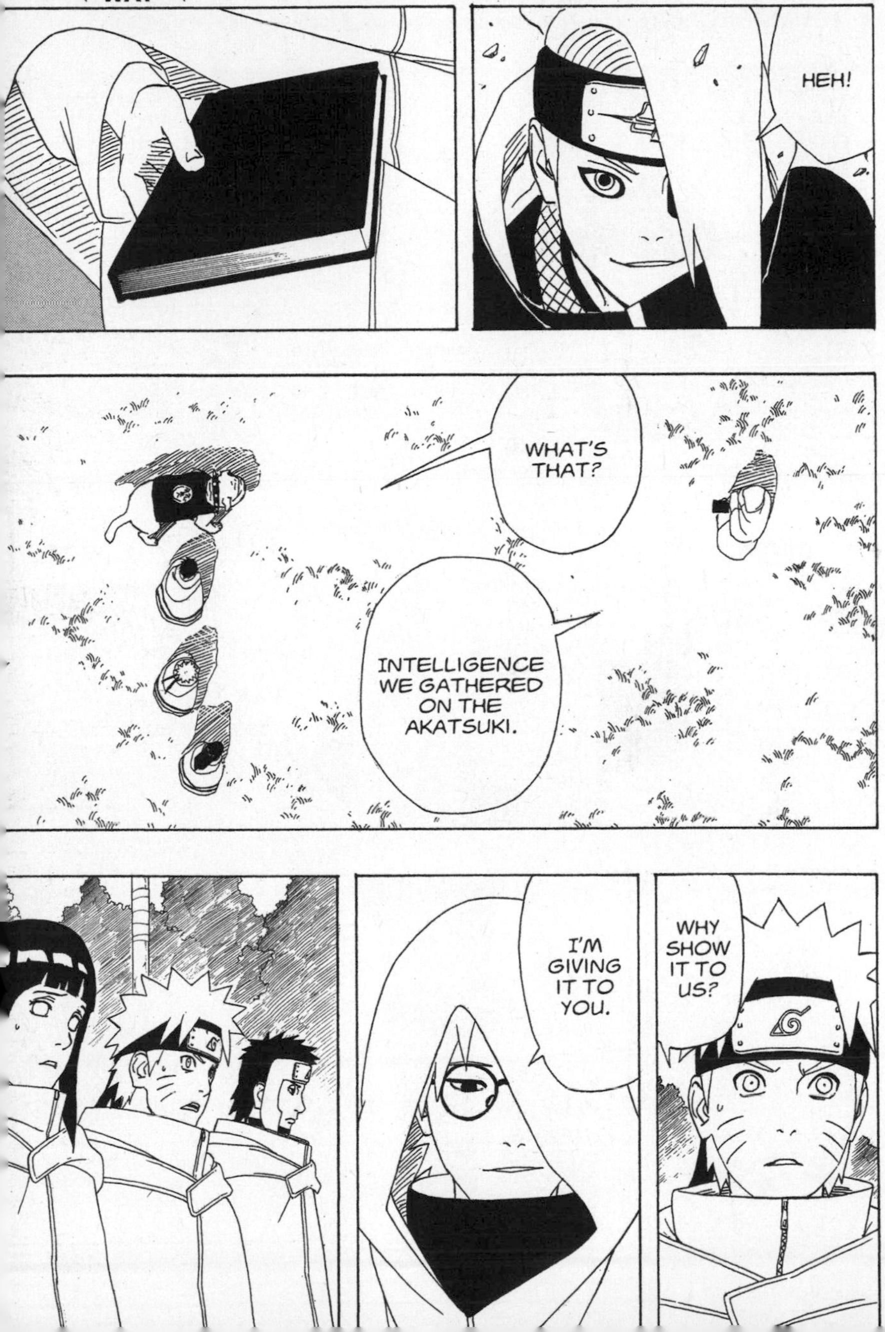
HEH!
WHAT'S THAT?
INTELLIGENCE WE GATHERED ON THE AKATSUKI.
WHY SHOW IT TO US?
I'M GIVING IT TO YOU.

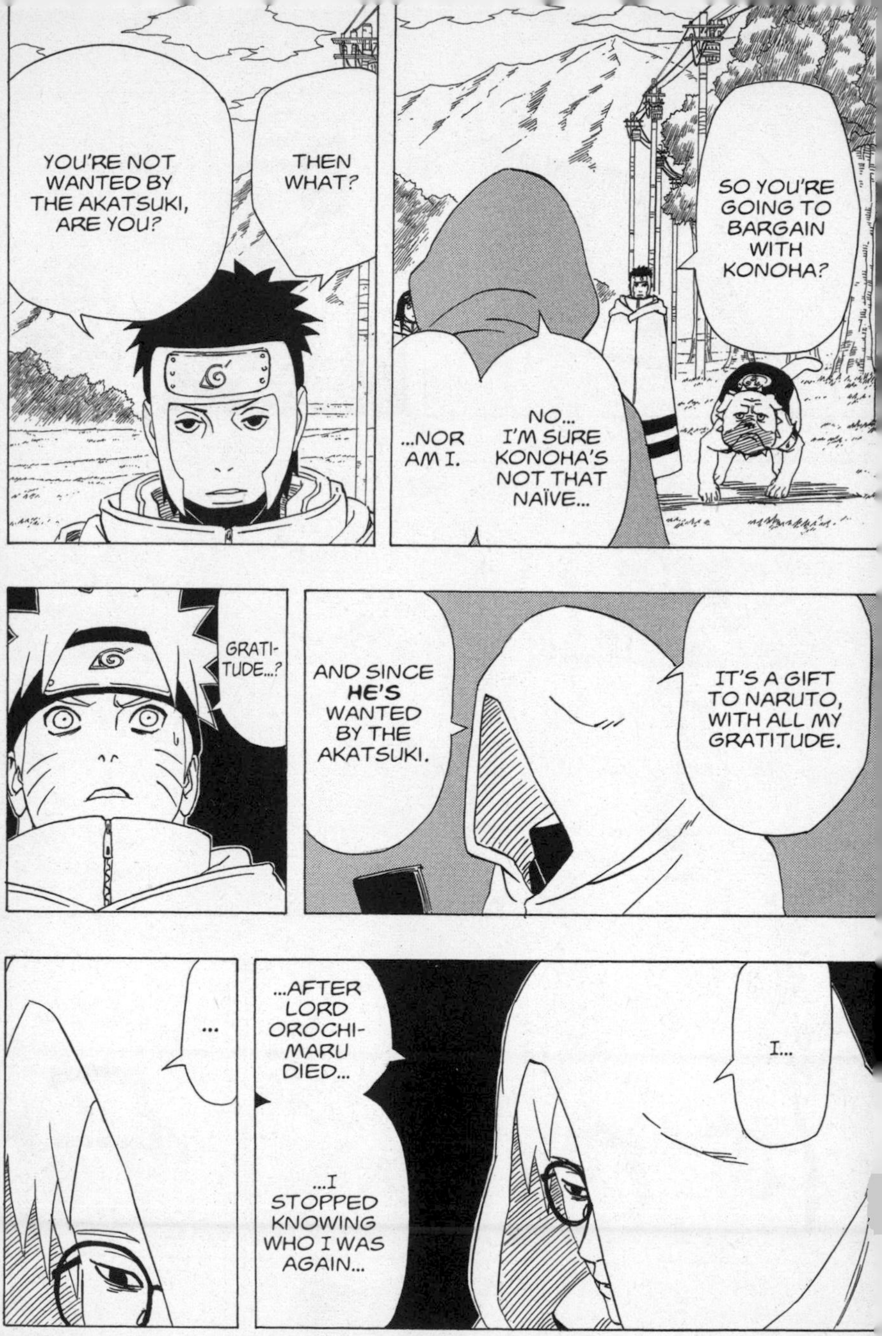
SO YOU'RE GOING TO BARGAIN WITH KONOHA?
NO... I'M SURE KONOHA'S NOT THAT NAÏVE...
...NOR AM I.
THEN WHAT?
YOU'RE NOT WANTED BY THE AKATSUKI, ARE YOU?
IT'S A GIFT TO NARUTO, WITH ALL MY GRATITUDE.
AND SINCE **HE'S** WANTED BY THE AKATSUKI.
GRATI-TUDE...?
I...
...AFTER LORD OROCHI-MARU DIED...
...I STOPPED KNOWING WHO I WAS AGAIN...
...

READ THIS WAY

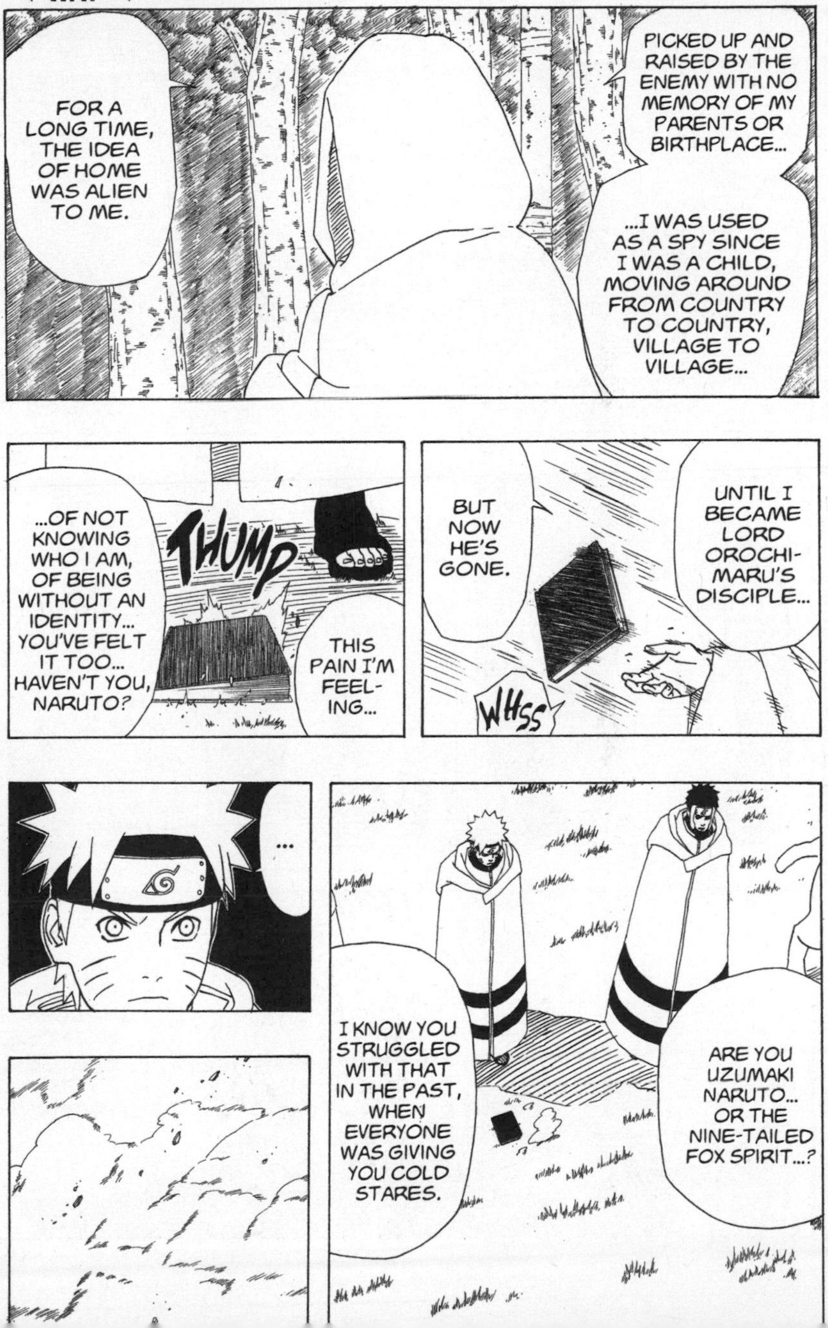
PICKED UP AND RAISED BY THE ENEMY WITH NO MEMORY OF MY PARENTS OR BIRTHPLACE...
...I WAS USED AS A SPY SINCE I WAS A CHILD, MOVING AROUND FROM COUNTRY TO COUNTRY, VILLAGE TO VILLAGE...
FOR A LONG TIME, THE IDEA OF HOME WAS ALIEN TO ME.
UNTIL I BECAME LORD OROCHIMARU'S DISCIPLE...
BUT NOW HE'S GONE.
WHSS
THUMP
THIS PAIN I'M FEELING...
...OF NOT KNOWING WHO I AM, OF BEING WITHOUT AN IDENTITY... YOU'VE FELT IT TOO... HAVEN'T YOU, NARUTO?
ARE YOU UZUMAKI NARUTO... OR THE NINE-TAILED FOX SPIRIT...?
I KNOW YOU STRUGGLED WITH THAT IN THE PAST, WHEN EVERYONE WAS GIVING YOU COLD STARES.
...

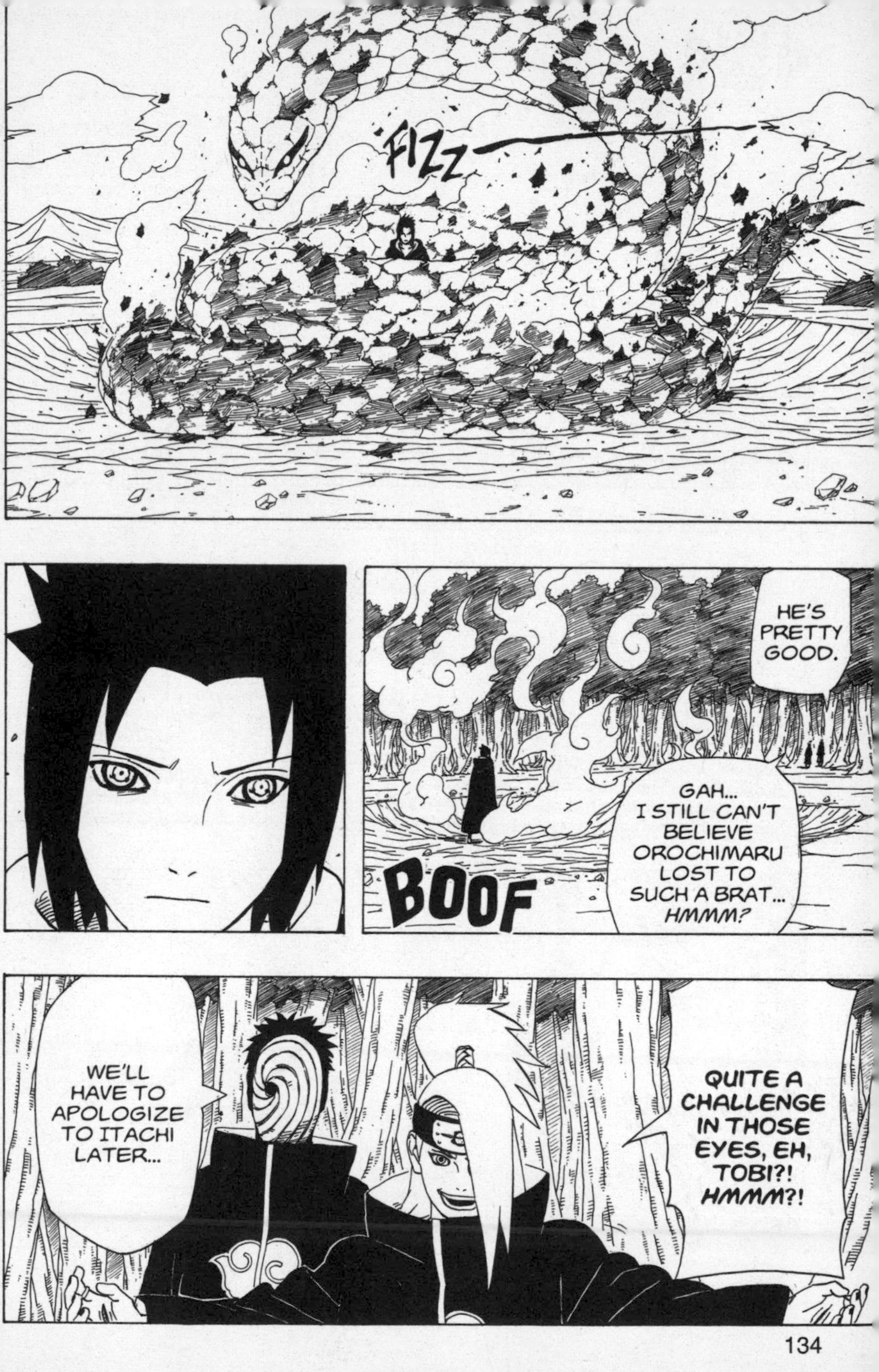
FIZZ
HE'S PRETTY GOOD.
GAH... I STILL CAN'T BELIEVE OROCHIMARU LOST TO SUCH A BRAT... HMMM?
BOOF
QUITE A CHALLENGE IN THOSE EYES, EH, TOBI?! HMMM?!
WE'LL HAVE TO APOLOGIZE TO ITACHI LATER...

READ THIS WAY

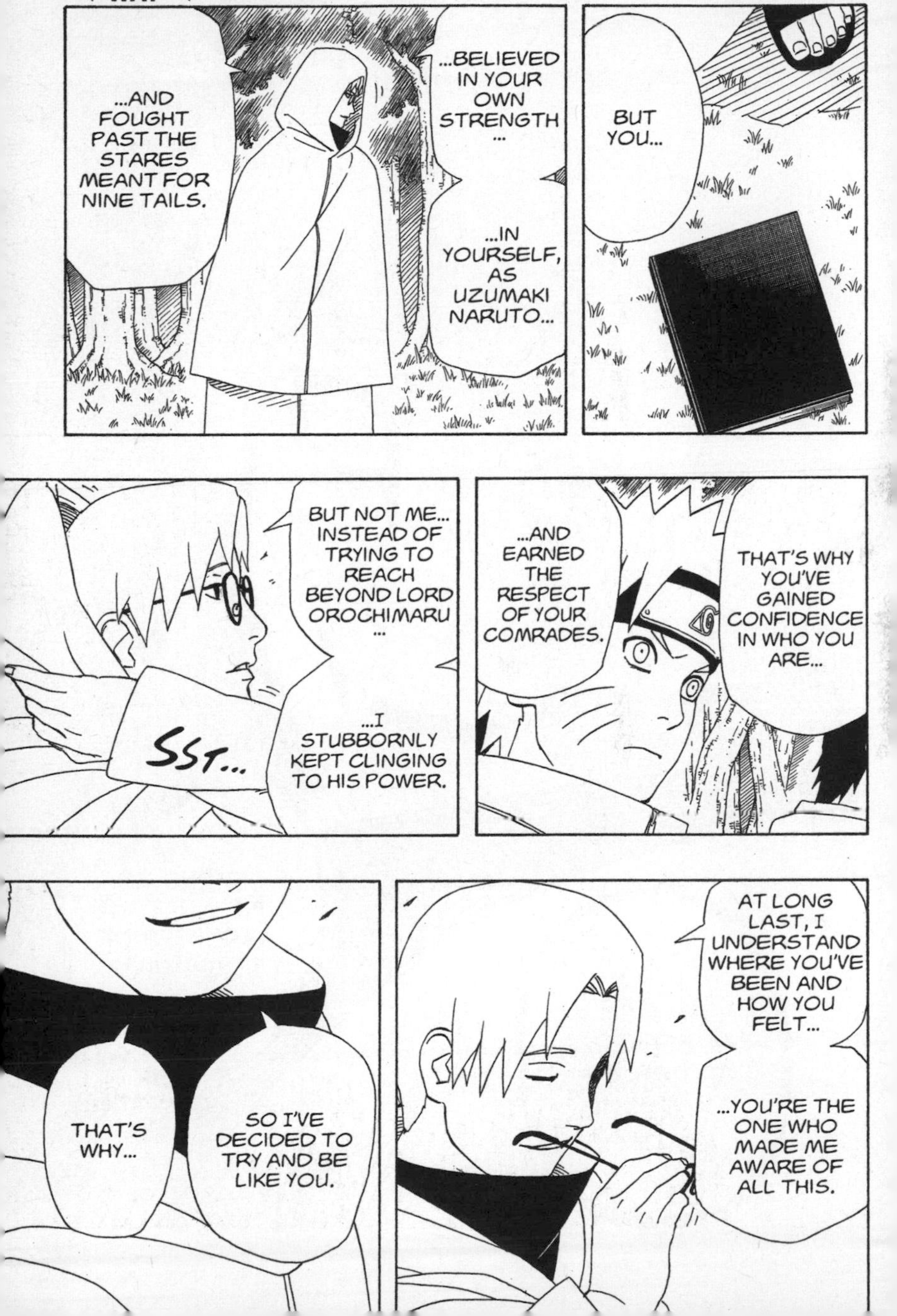
BUT YOU...
...BELIEVED IN YOUR OWN STRENGTH...
...IN YOURSELF, AS UZUMAKI NARUTO...
...AND FOUGHT PAST THE STARES MEANT FOR NINE TAILS.
...AND EARNED THE RESPECT OF YOUR COMRADES.
THAT'S WHY YOU'VE GAINED CONFIDENCE IN WHO YOU ARE...
BUT NOT ME... INSTEAD OF TRYING TO REACH BEYOND LORD OROCHIMARU...
...I STUBBORNLY KEPT CLINGING TO HIS POWER.
SST...
AT LONG LAST, I UNDERSTAND WHERE YOU'VE BEEN AND HOW YOU FELT...
...YOU'RE THE ONE WHO MADE ME AWARE OF ALL THIS.
THAT'S WHY...
SO I'VE DECIDED TO TRY AND BE LIKE YOU.

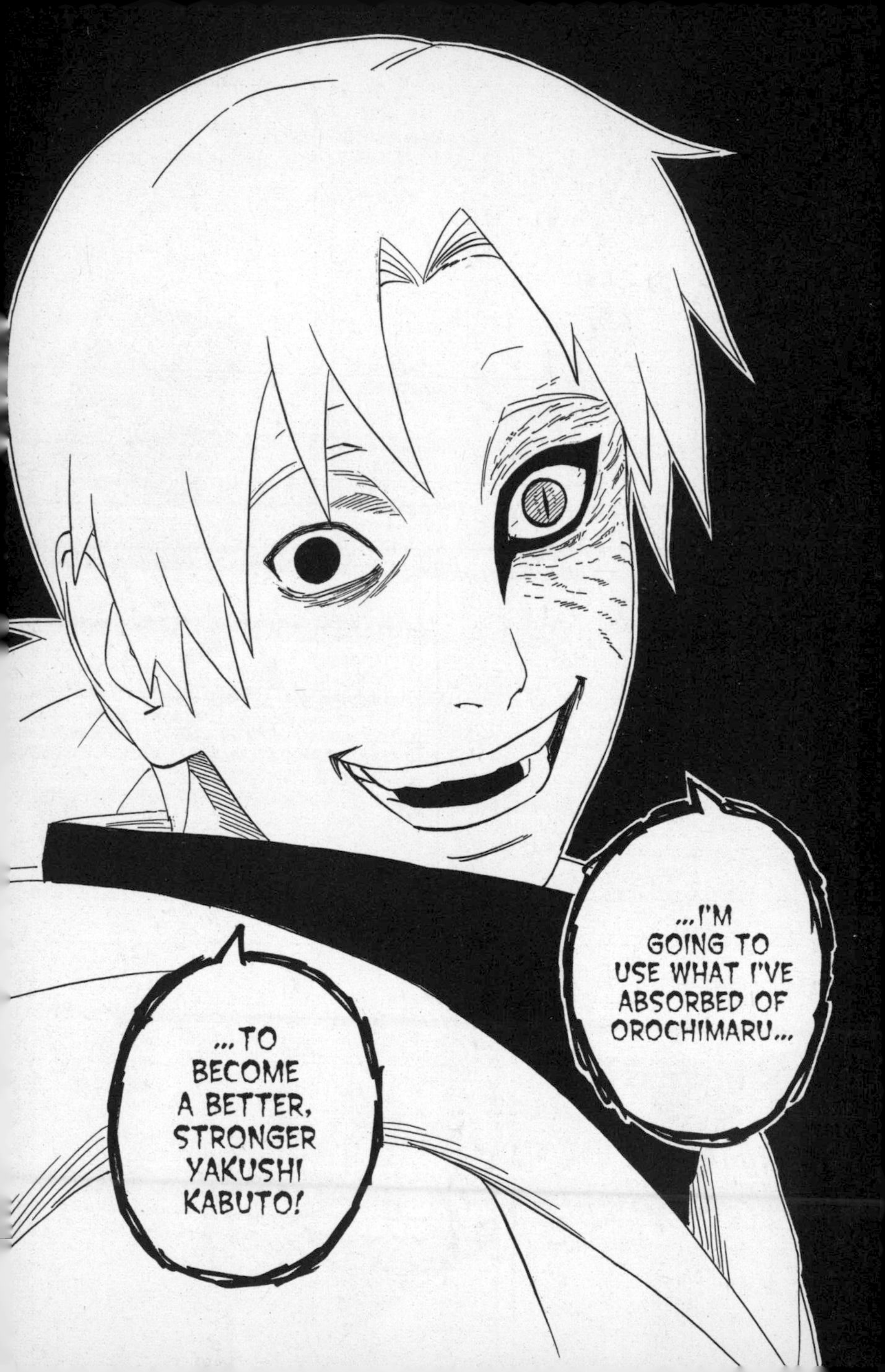
...I'M GOING TO USE WHAT I'VE ABSORBED OF OROCHIMARU...
...TO BECOME A BETTER, STRONGER YAKUSHI KABUTO!

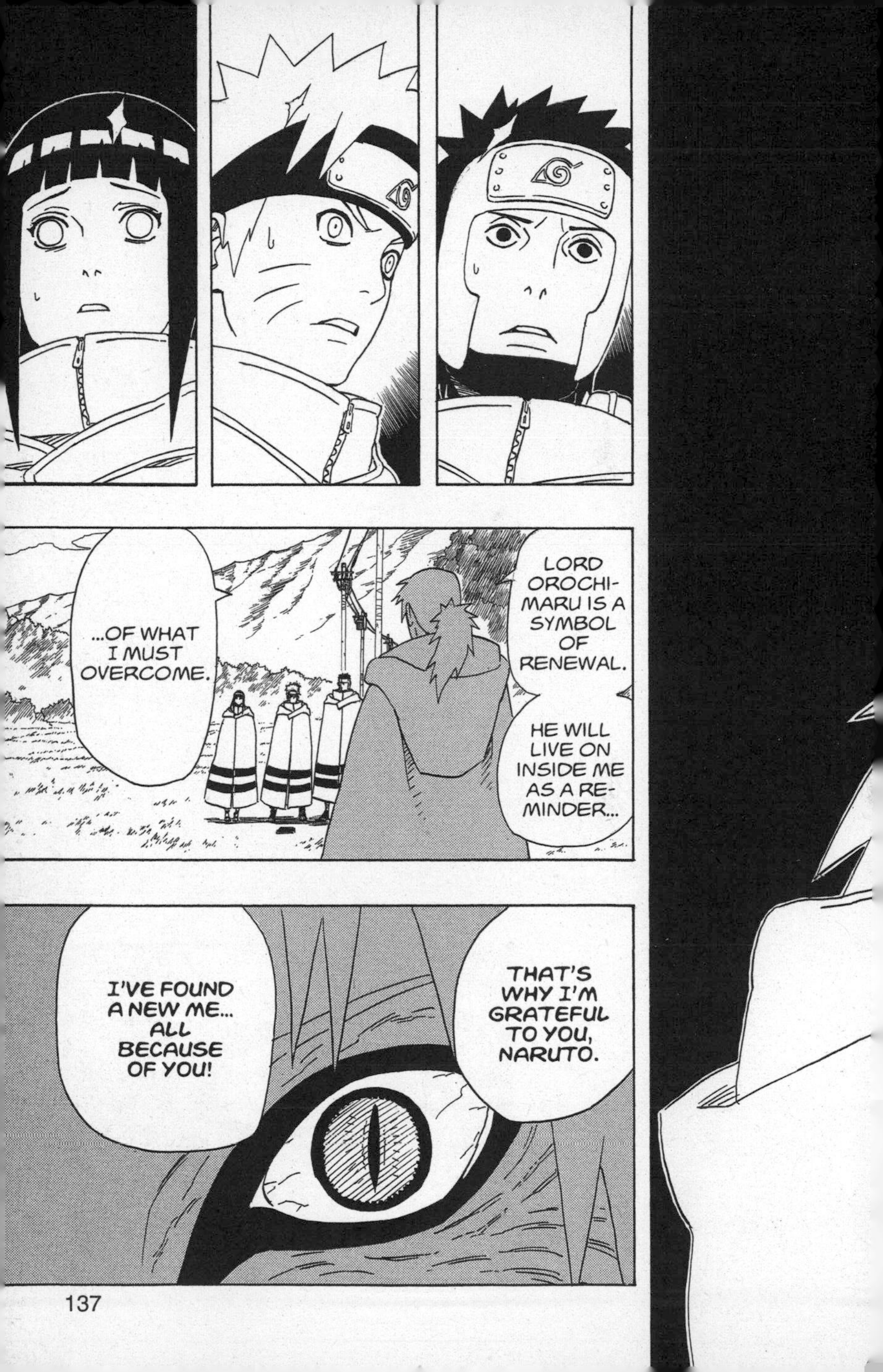
LORD OROCHIMARU IS A SYMBOL OF RENEWAL.
HE WILL LIVE ON INSIDE ME AS A REMINDER...
...OF WHAT I MUST OVERCOME.
THAT'S WHY I'M GRATEFUL TO YOU, NARUTO.
I'VE FOUND A NEW ME... ALL BECAUSE OF YOU!

Number 357: Deidara VS. Sasuke!!

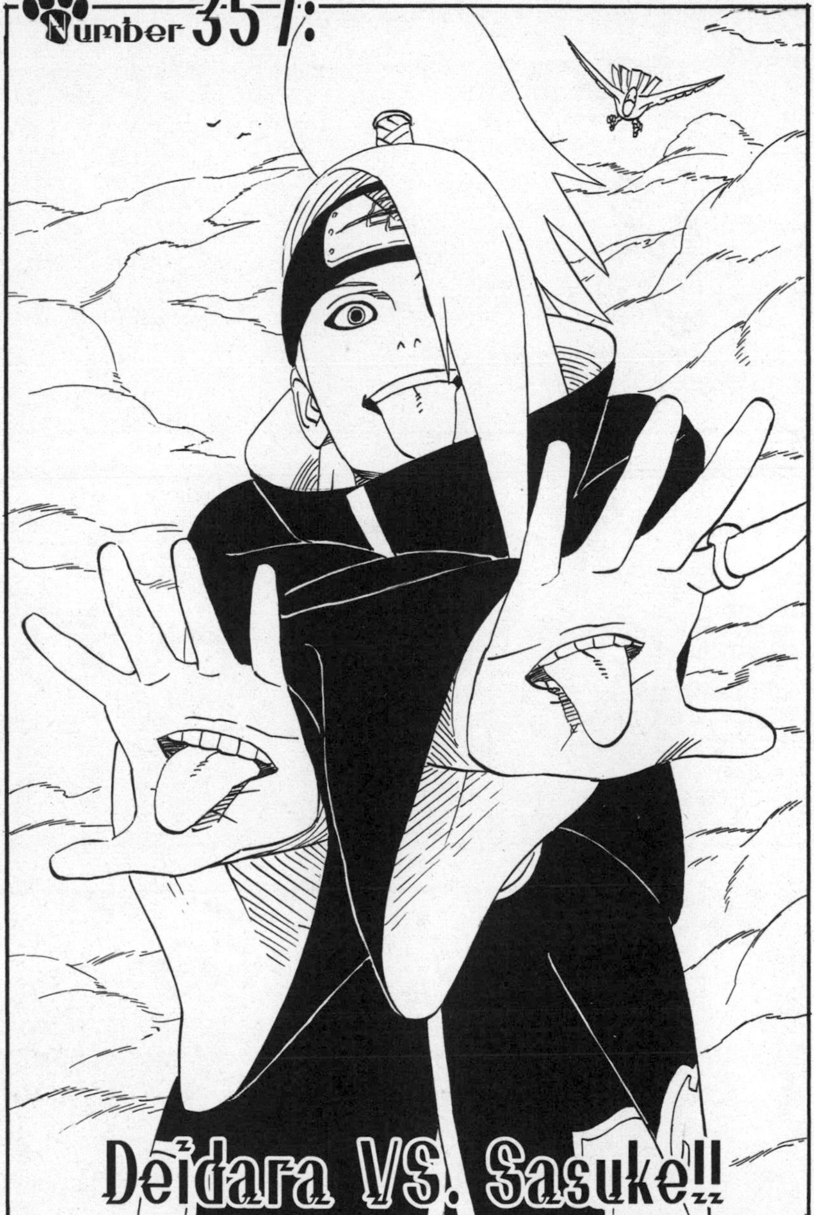

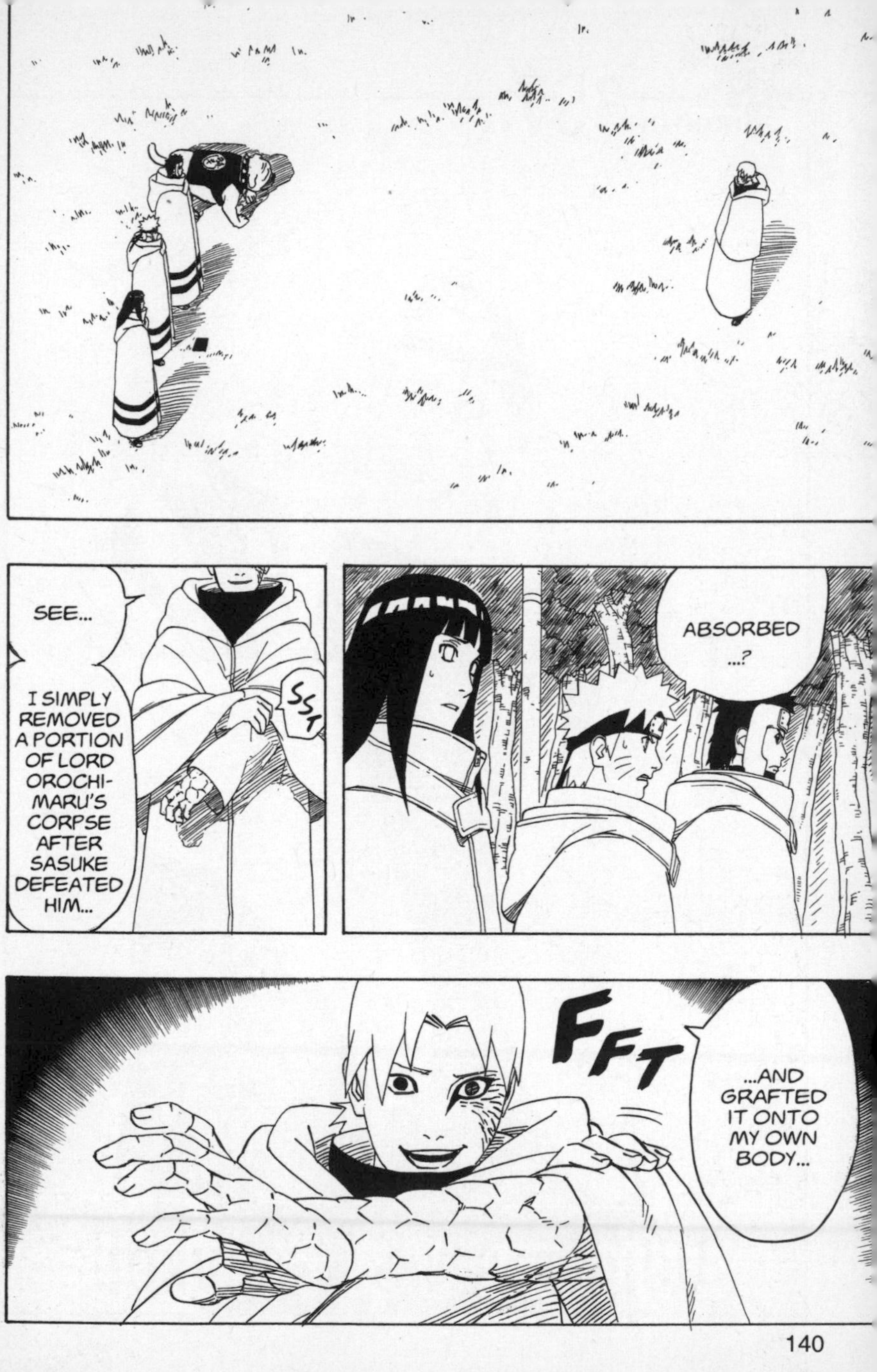
ABSORBED ...?
SEE...
SST
I SIMPLY REMOVED A PORTION OF LORD OROCHI-MARU'S CORPSE AFTER SASUKE DEFEATED HIM...
FFT
...AND GRAFTED IT ONTO MY OWN BODY...

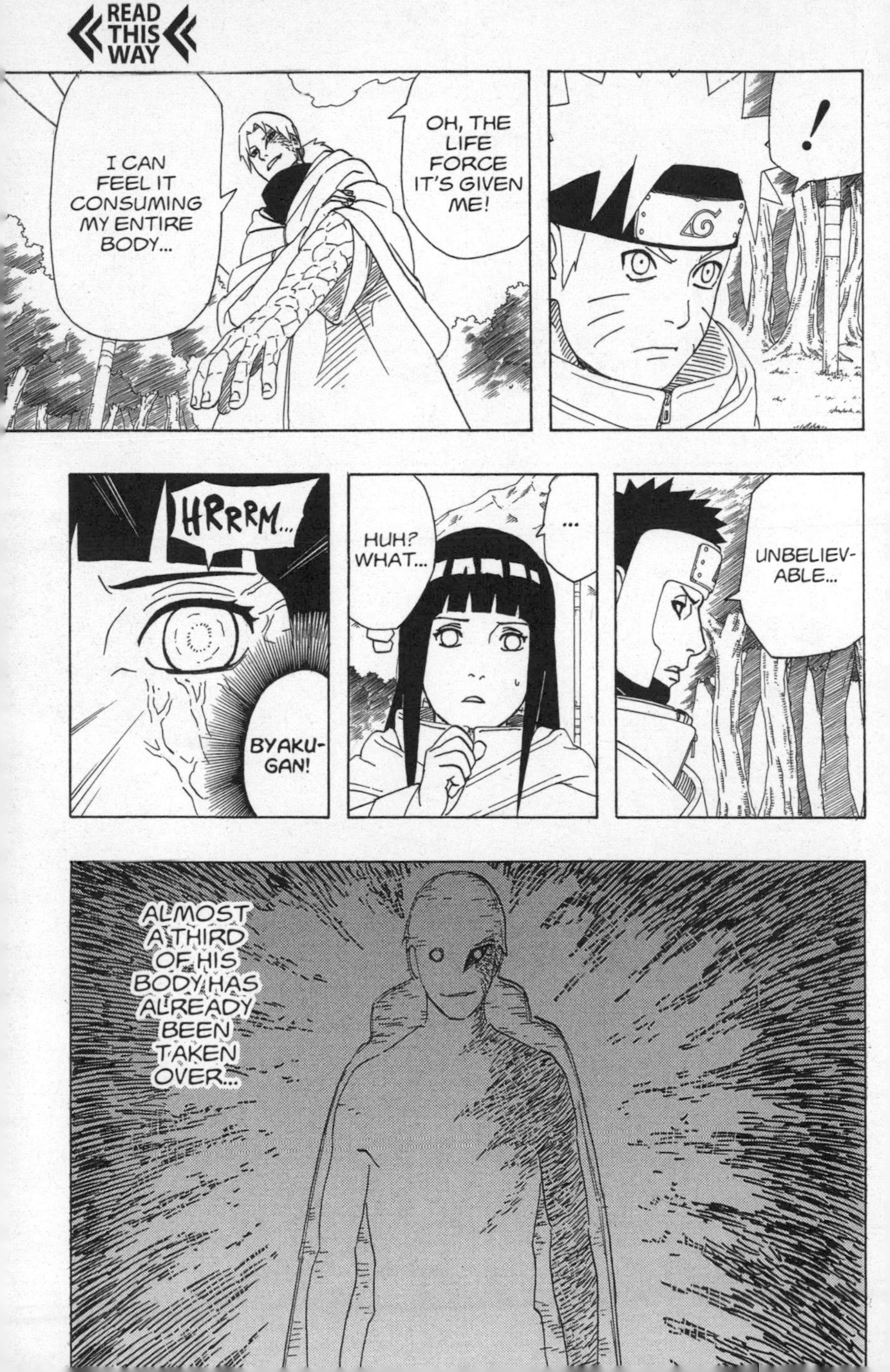
READ THIS WAY
!
OH, THE LIFE FORCE IT'S GIVEN ME!
I CAN FEEL IT CONSUMING MY ENTIRE BODY...
UNBELIEV-ABLE...
...
HUH? WHAT...
HRRRM...
BYAKU-GAN!
ALMOST A THIRD OF HIS BODY HAS ALREADY BEEN TAKEN OVER...

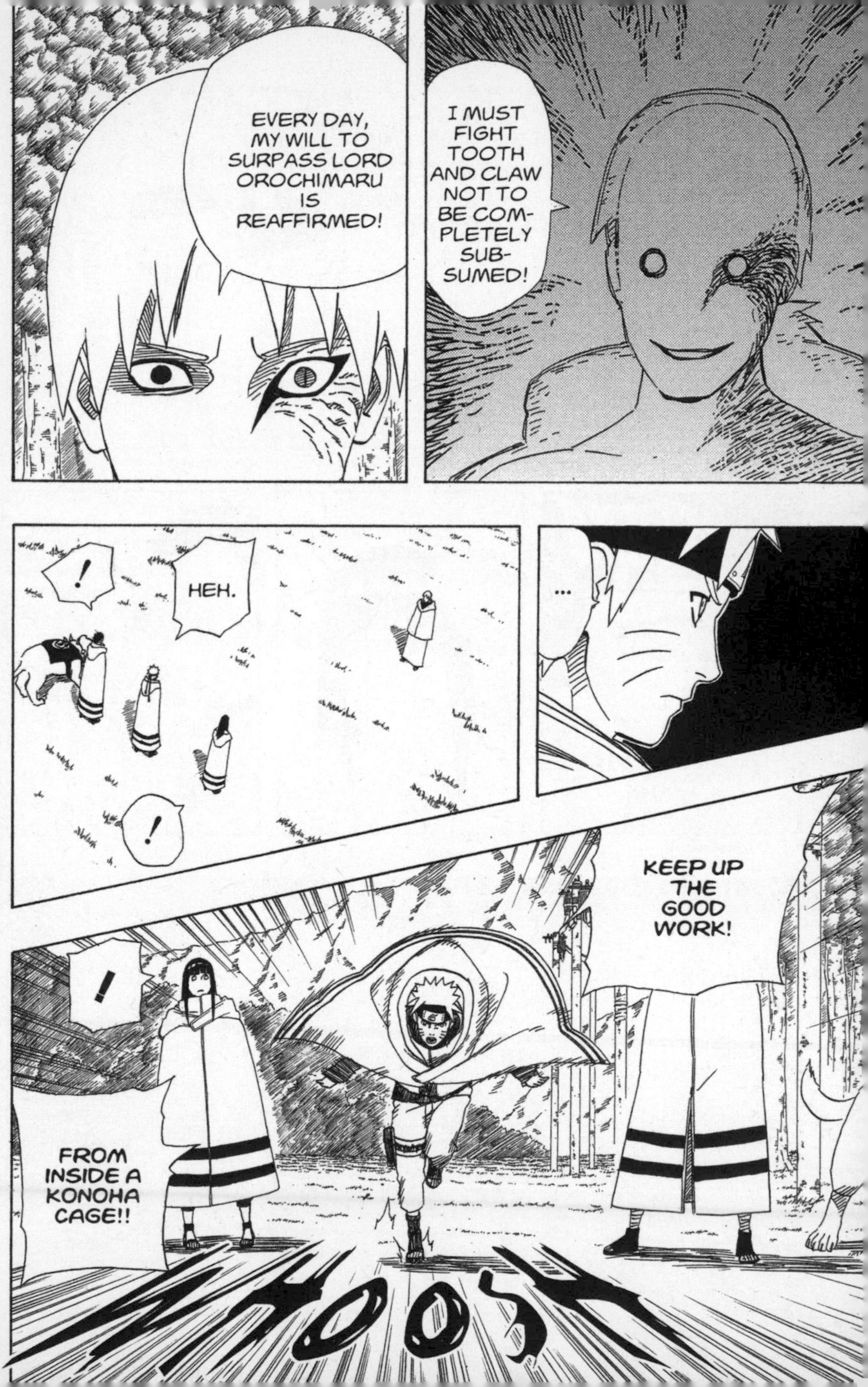
I MUST FIGHT TOOTH AND CLAW NOT TO BE COMPLETELY SUBSUMED!
EVERY DAY, MY WILL TO SURPASS LORD OROCHIMARU IS REAFFIRMED!
...
HEH.
!
!
KEEP UP THE GOOD WORK!
!
FROM INSIDE A KONOHA CAGE!!
WHOOSH

READ THIS WAY

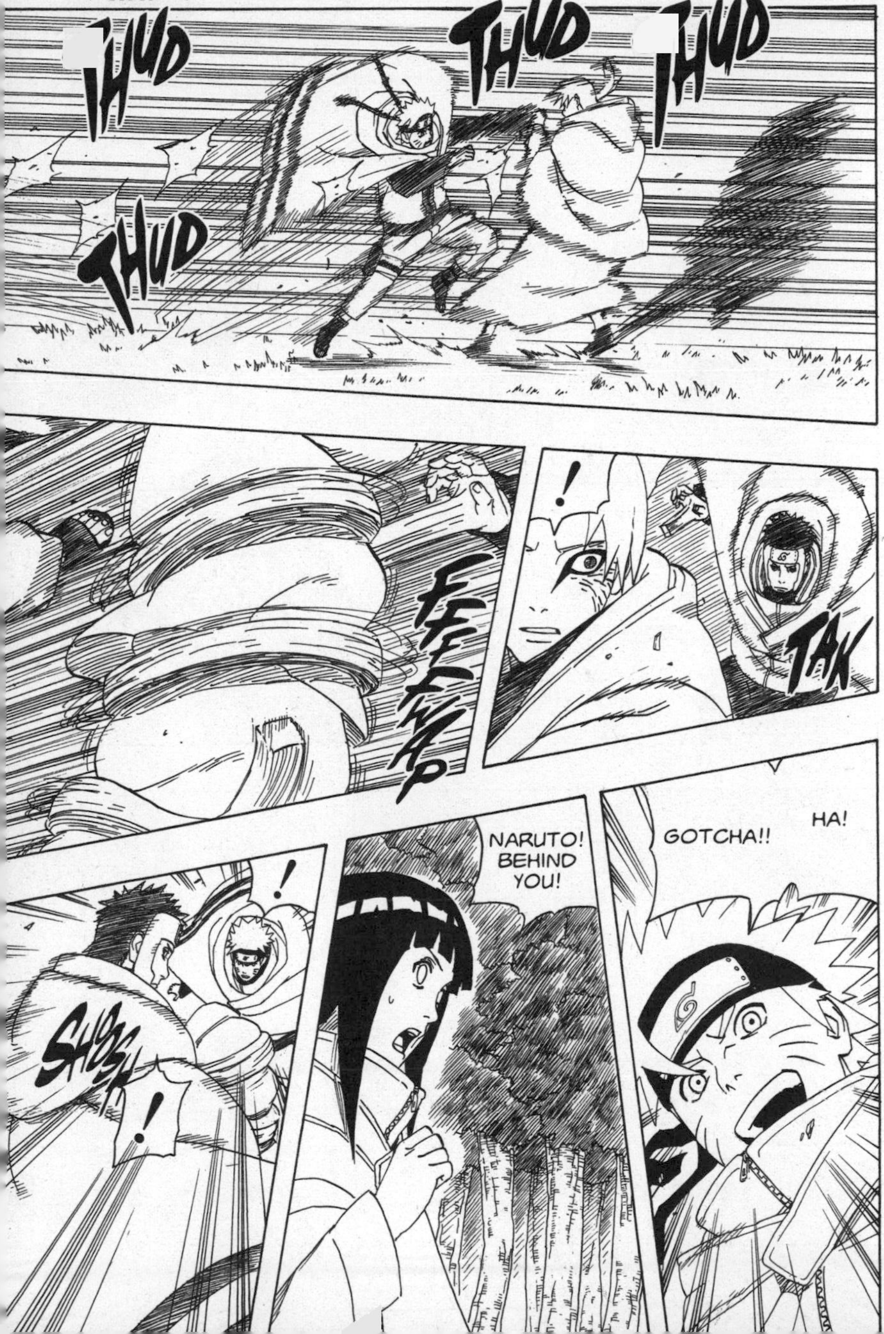
THUD
THUD
THUD
THUD
!
TAK
FFFWAP
HA!
GOTCHA!!
NARUTO! BEHIND YOU!
!
SHOOSH
!

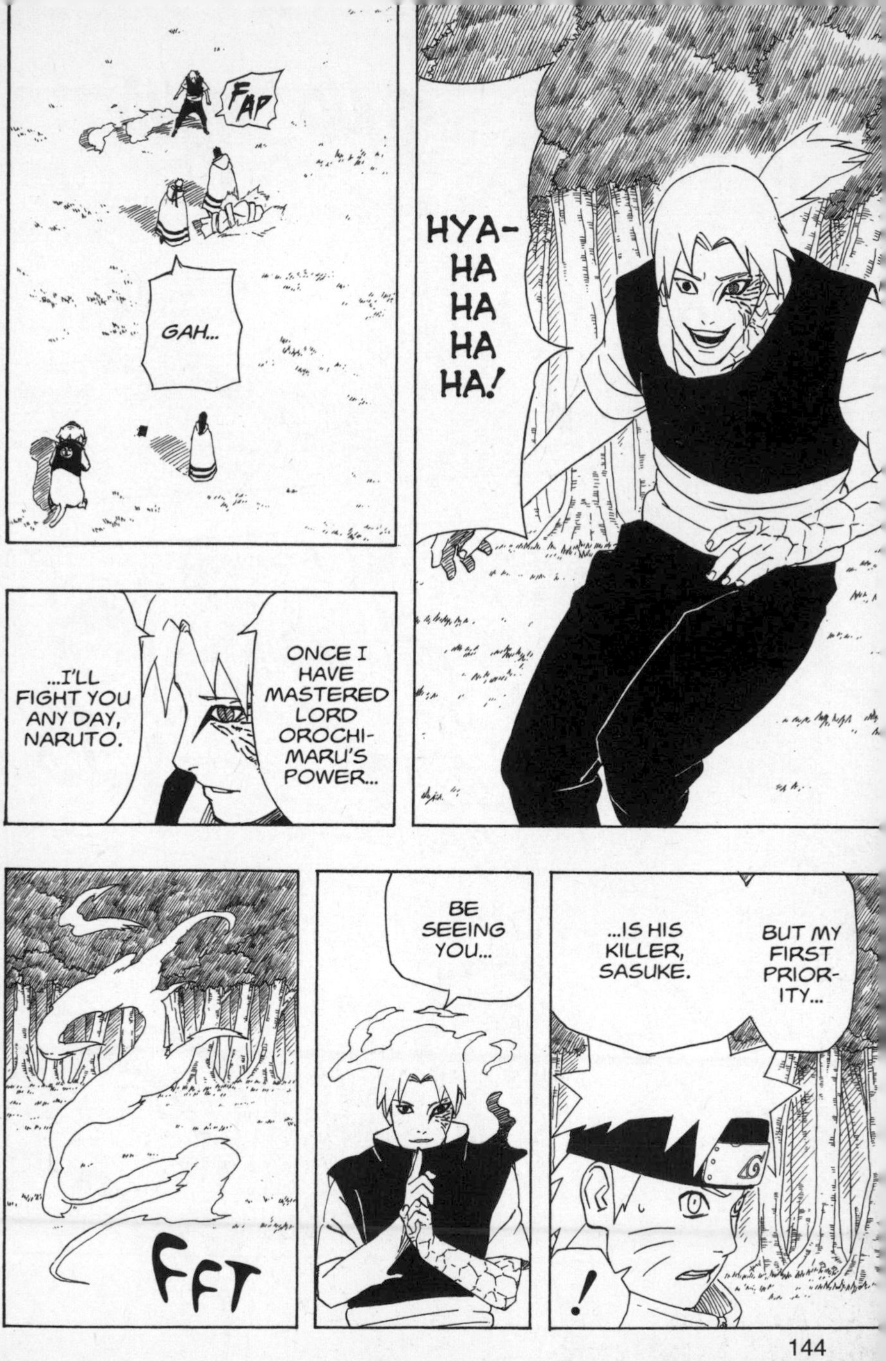
HYA-
HA
HA
HA
HA!
FAP
GAH...
ONCE I HAVE MASTERED LORD OROCHIMARU'S POWER...
...I'LL FIGHT YOU ANY DAY, NARUTO.
BUT MY FIRST PRIORITY...
...IS HIS KILLER, SASUKE.
!
BE SEEING YOU...
FFT

READ THIS WAY

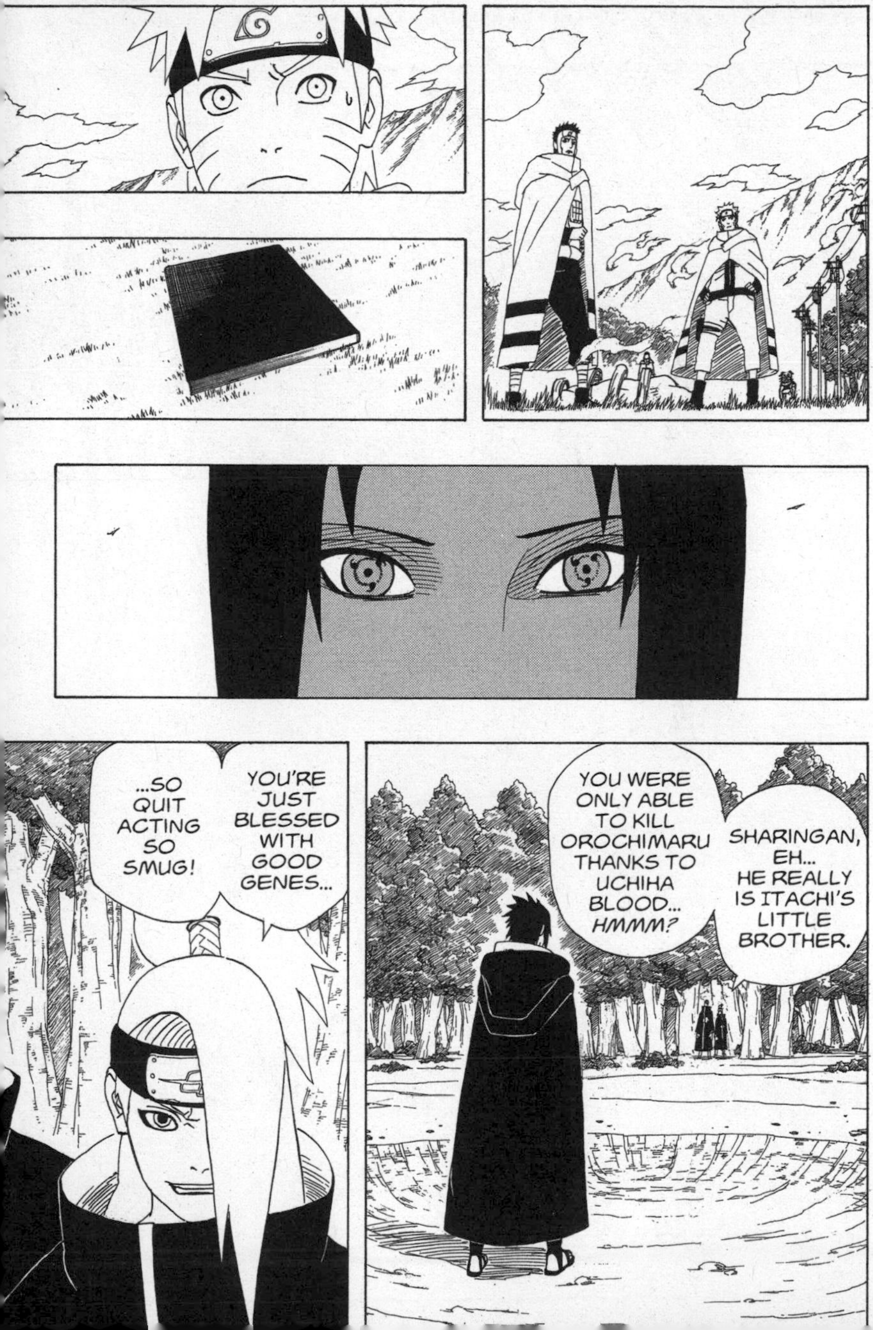
SHARINGAN, EH... HE REALLY IS ITACHI'S LITTLE BROTHER.
YOU WERE ONLY ABLE TO KILL OROCHIMARU THANKS TO UCHIHA BLOOD... HMMM?
YOU'RE JUST BLESSED WITH GOOD GENES...
...SO QUIT ACTING SO SMUG!

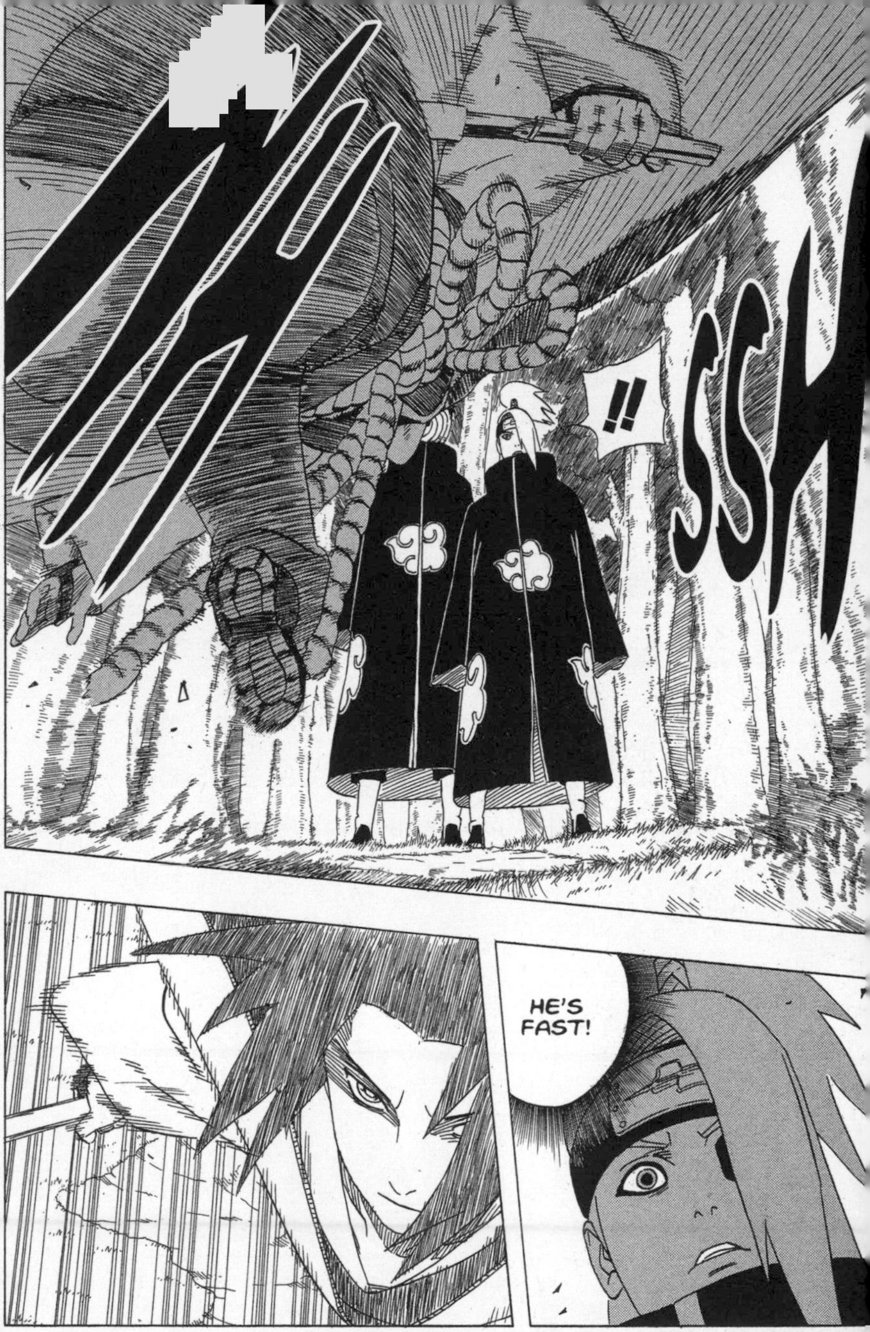
SSH
!!
HE'S FAST!

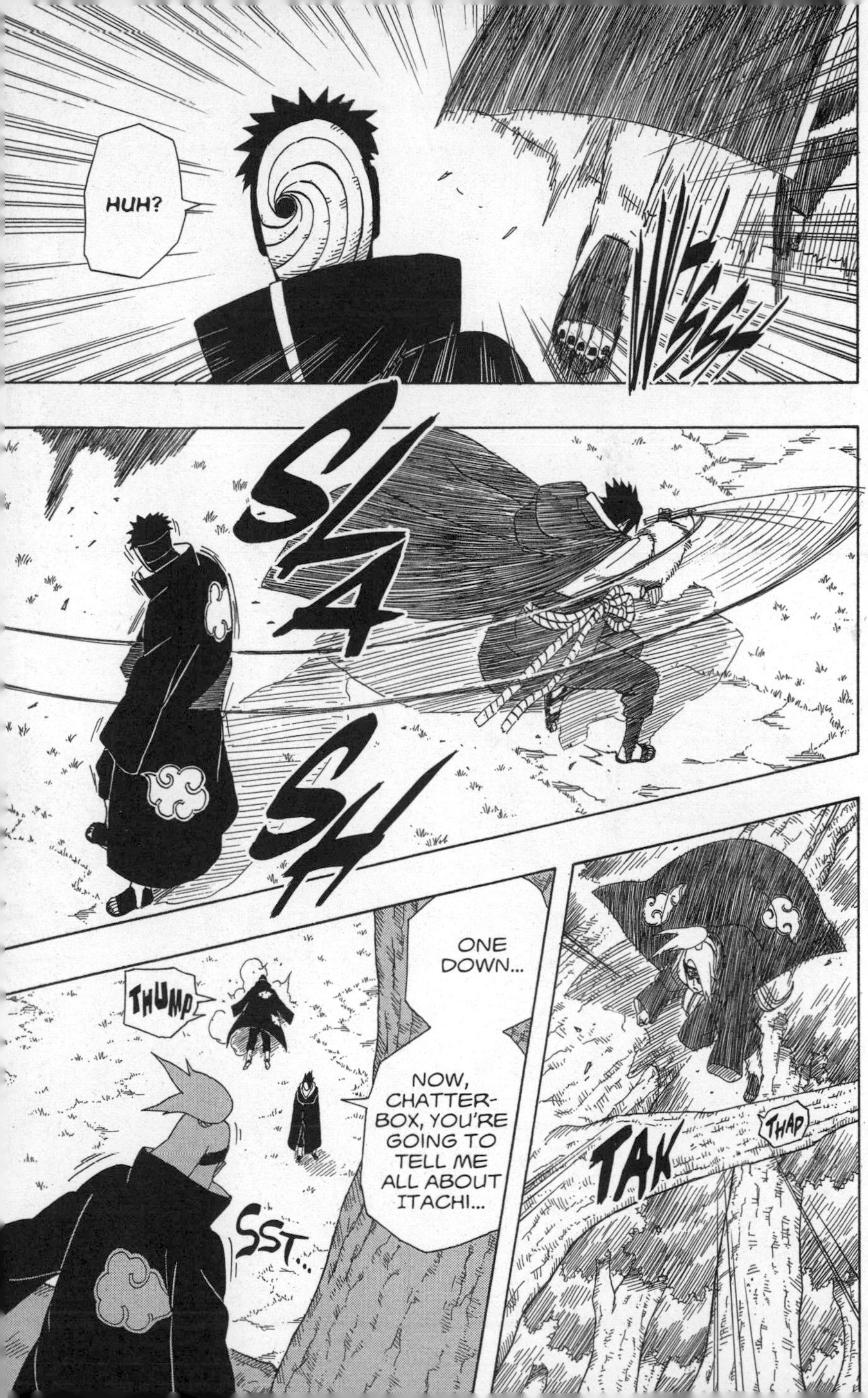
WSSH
HUH?
SLASH
TAK
THAP
ONE DOWN...
NOW, CHATTER-BOX, YOU'RE GOING TO TELL ME ALL ABOUT ITACHI...
THUMP
SST...

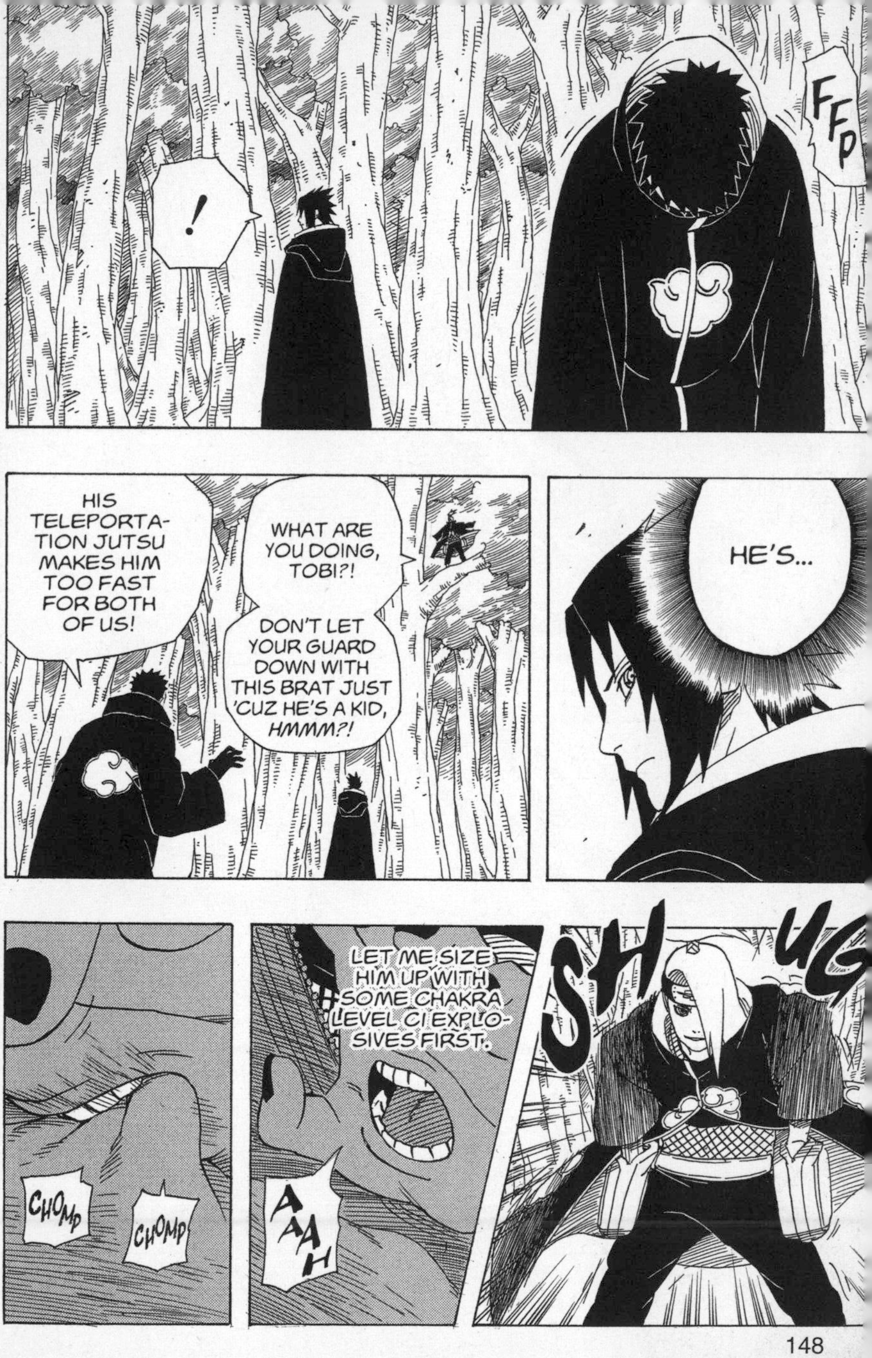
FFP
!
HE'S...
WHAT ARE YOU DOING, TOBI?!
DON'T LET YOUR GUARD DOWN WITH THIS BRAT JUST 'CUZ HE'S A KID, *HMMM?!*
HIS TELEPORTATION JUTSU MAKES HIM TOO FAST FOR BOTH OF US!
SHUG
LET ME SIZE HIM UP WITH SOME CHAKRA LEVEL C1 EXPLOSIVES FIRST.
AAAH
CHOMP
CHOMP

READ THIS WAY

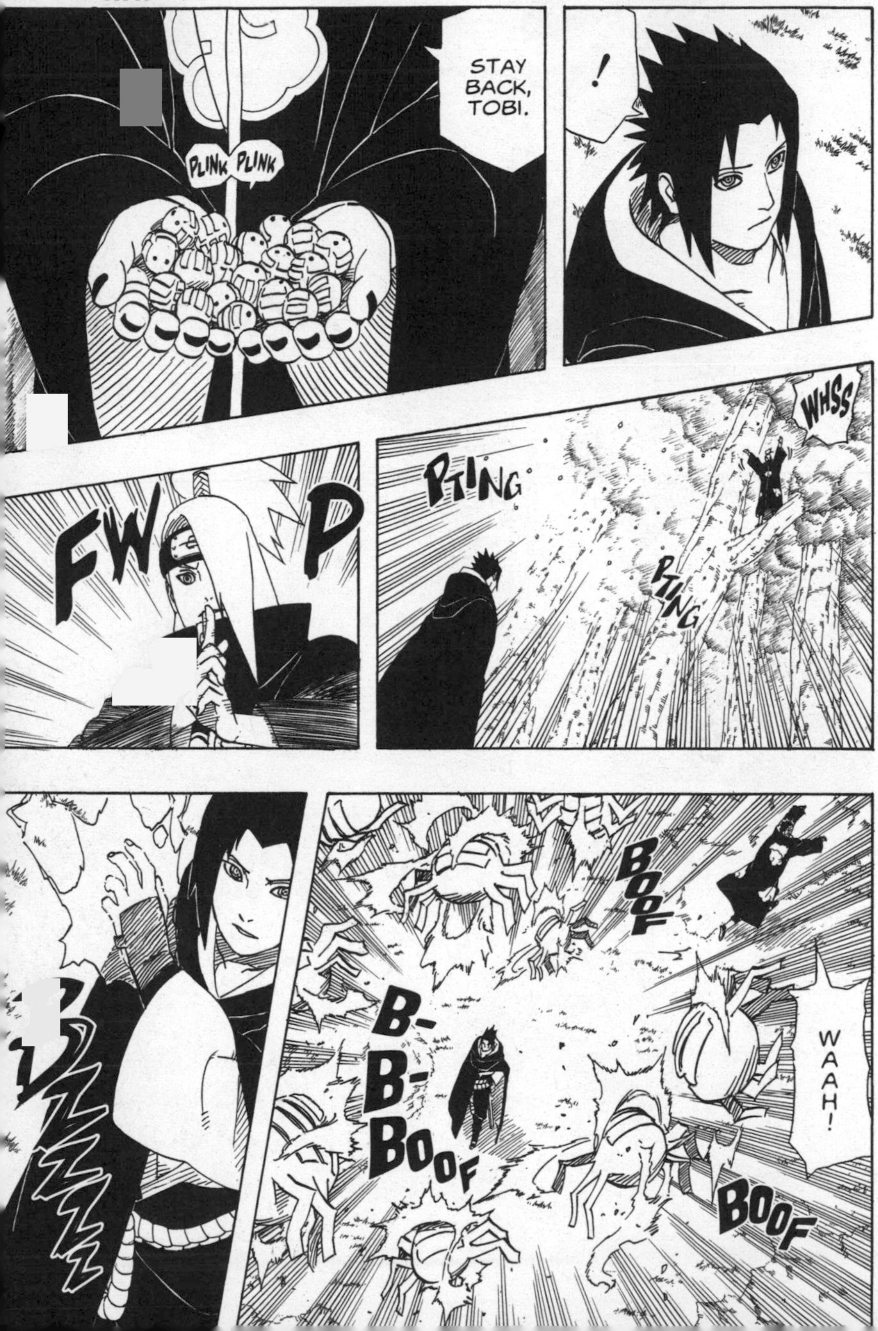
!
STAY BACK, TOBI.
PLINK PLINK
WHSS
PTING
PTING
FWP
BOOF
WAAH!
B-B-BOOOF
BOOF

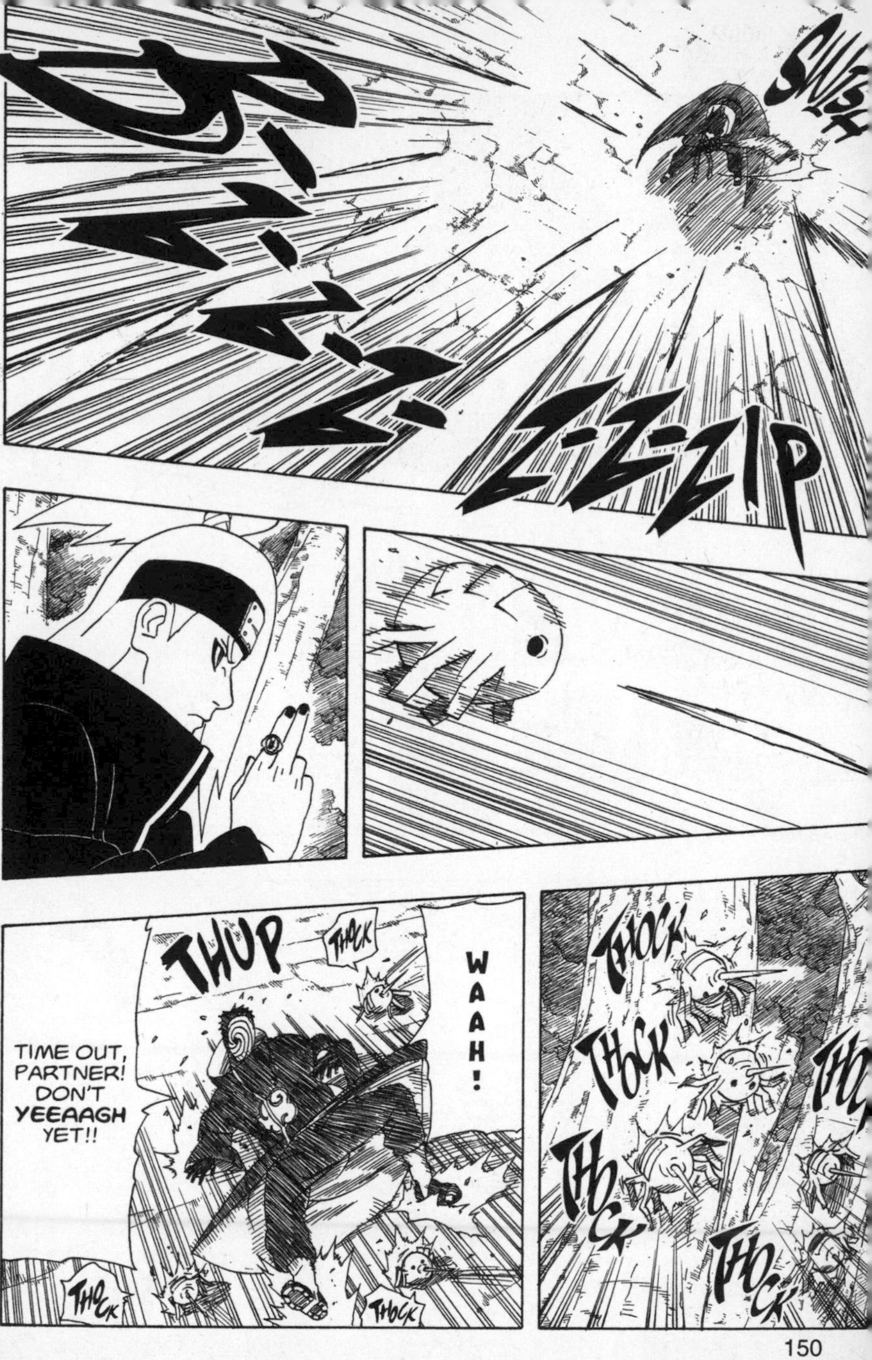
SWISH
ZI-ZI-ZIP
THOCK
THOCK
THOCK
THOCK
THUP
THOCK
WAAAH!
TIME OUT, PARTNER! DON'T YEEAAGH YET!!
THOCK
THOCK

READ THIS WAY

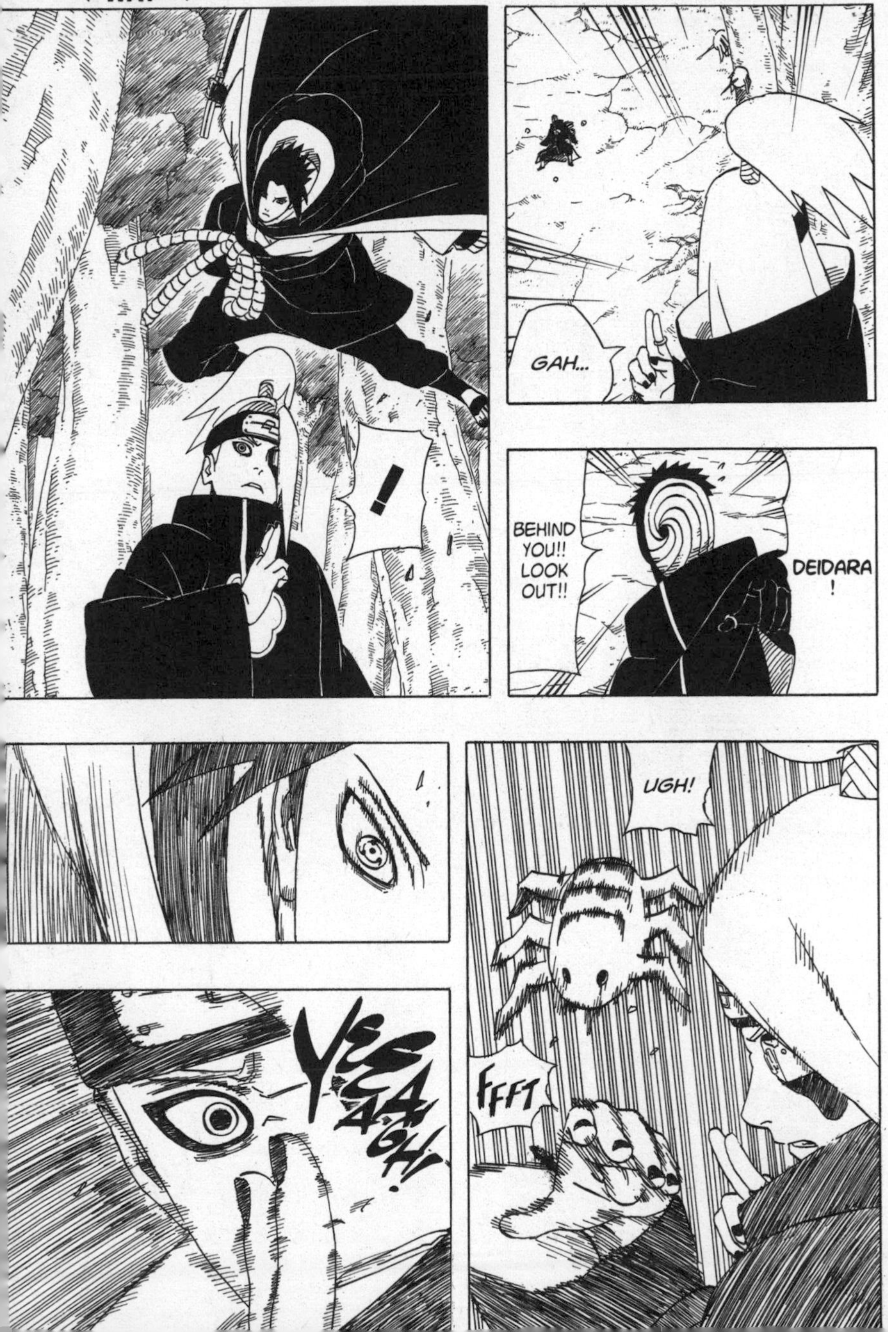
GAH...
DEIDARA!
BEHIND YOU!! LOOK OUT!!
!
UGH!
FFFT
YEEAAGH!

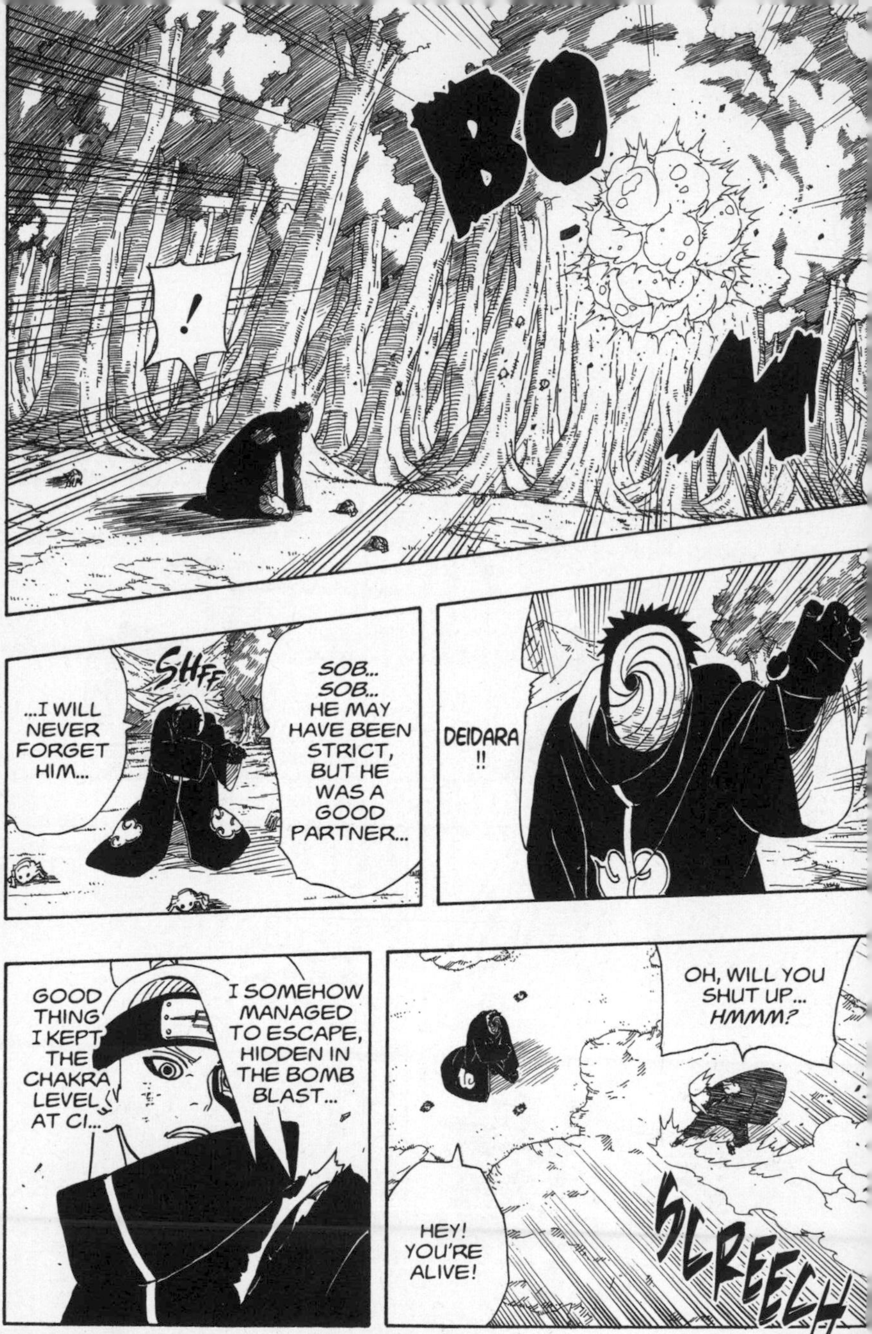
BOOM
!
DEIDARA !!
SOB... SOB... HE MAY HAVE BEEN STRICT, BUT HE WAS A GOOD PARTNER...
SHFF
...I WILL NEVER FORGET HIM...
OH, WILL YOU SHUT UP... *HMMM?*
HEY! YOU'RE ALIVE!
SCREECH
I SOMEHOW MANAGED TO ESCAPE, HIDDEN IN THE BOMB BLAST...
GOOD THING I KEPT THE CHAKRA LEVEL AT C1...

READ THIS WAY

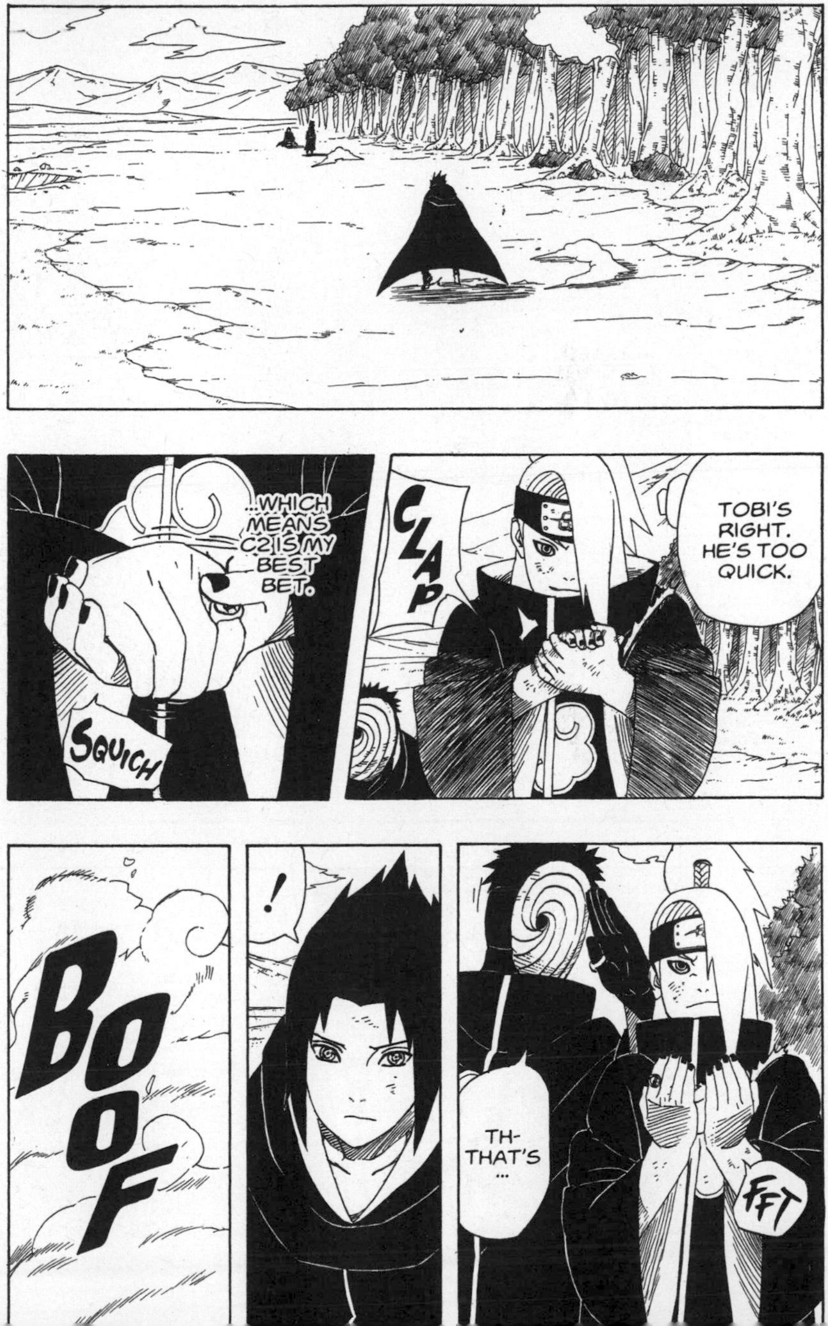
TOBI'S RIGHT. HE'S TOO QUICK.
CLAP
...WHICH MEANS C2 IS MY BEST BET.
SQUICH
TH- THAT'S ...
FFT
!
BOOF

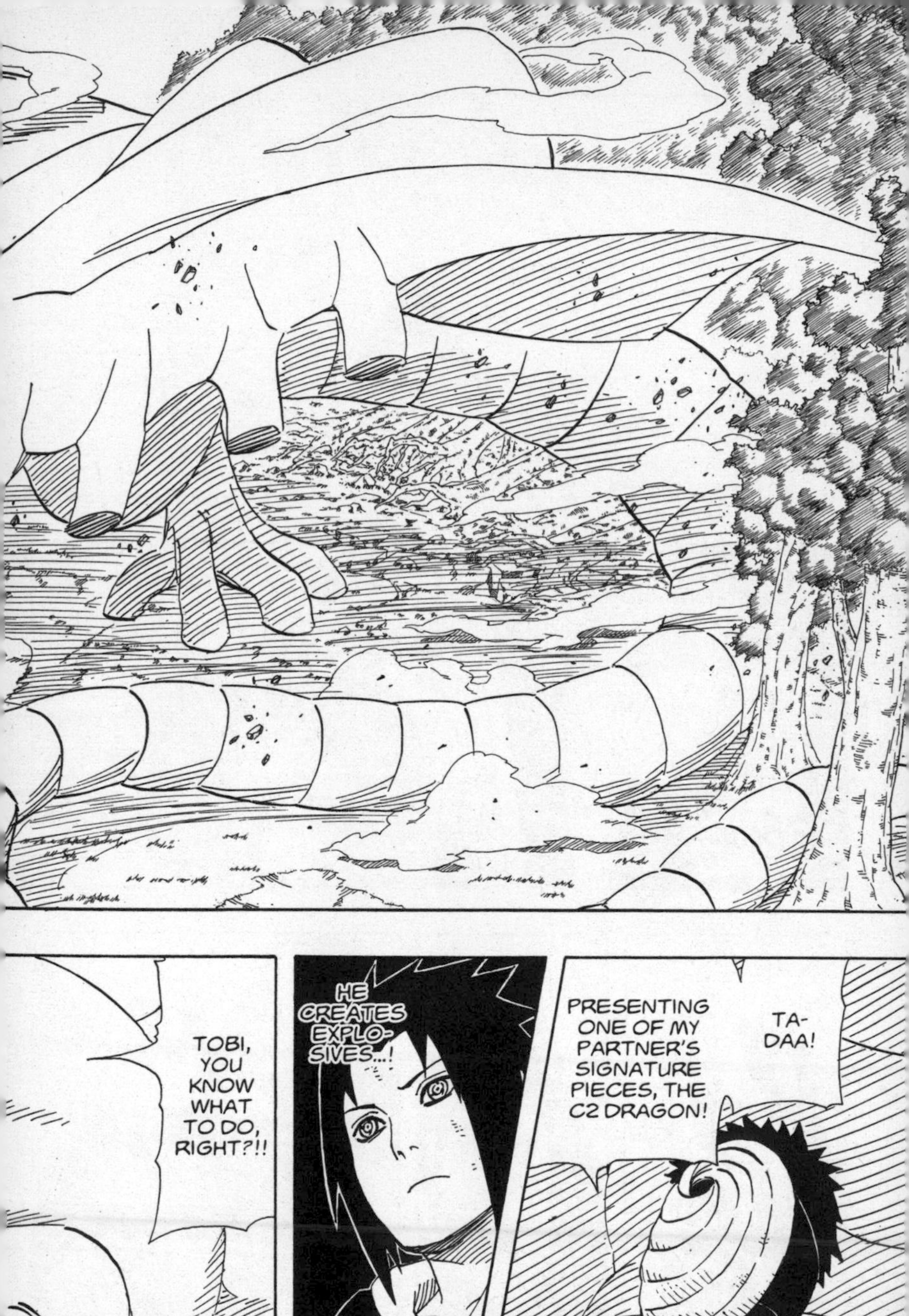
TA-DAA!
PRESENTING ONE OF MY PARTNER'S SIGNATURE PIECES, THE C2 DRAGON!
HE CREATES EXPLOSIVES...!
TOBI, YOU KNOW WHAT TO DO, RIGHT?!!

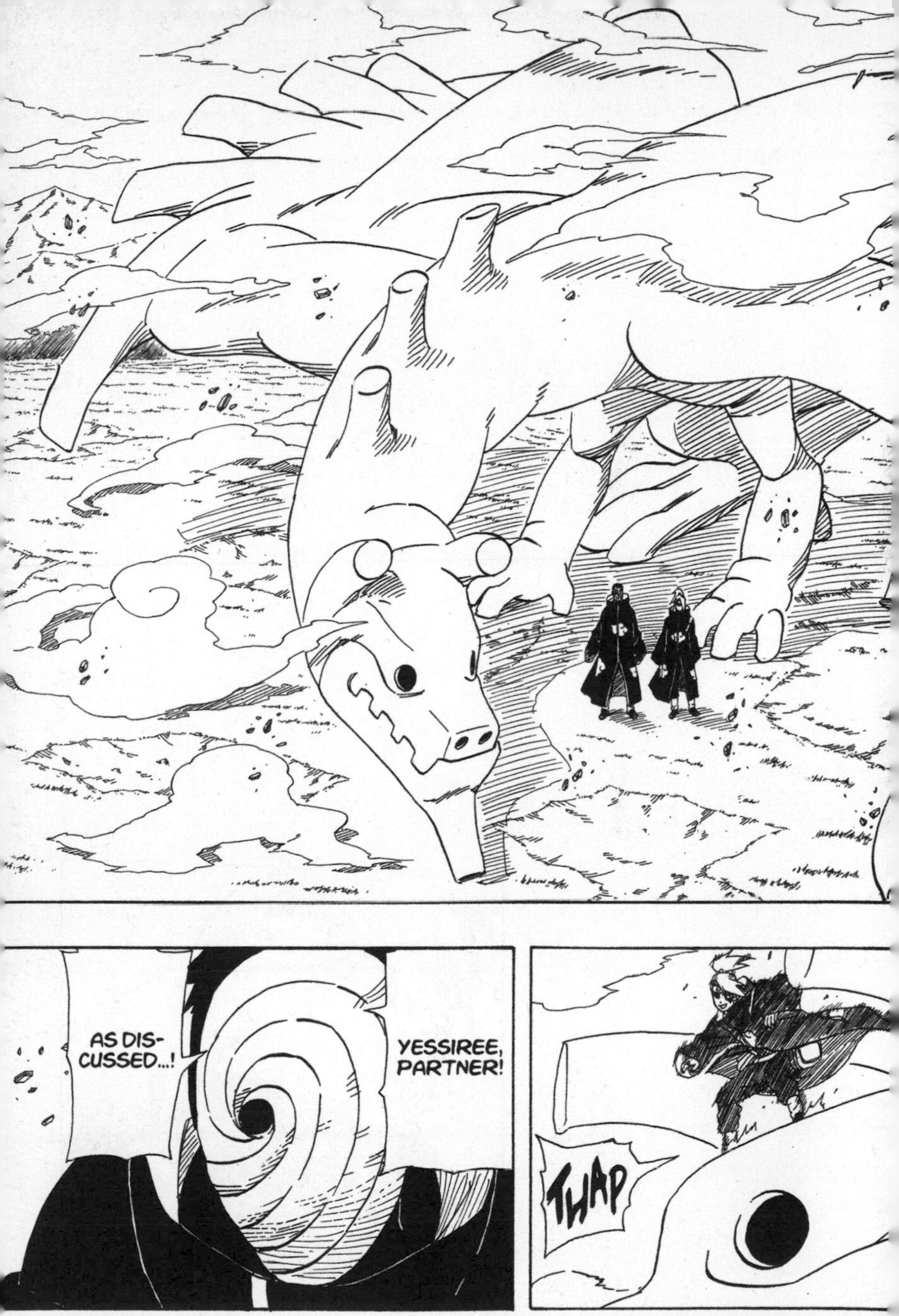
THAP
AS DIS-CUSSED...!
YESSIREE, PARTNER!

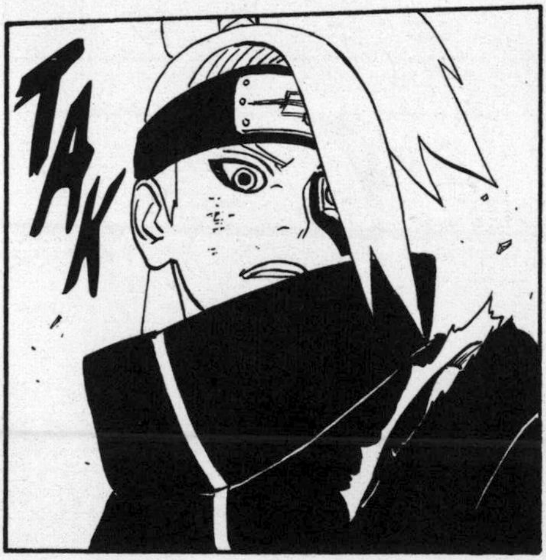
TAK

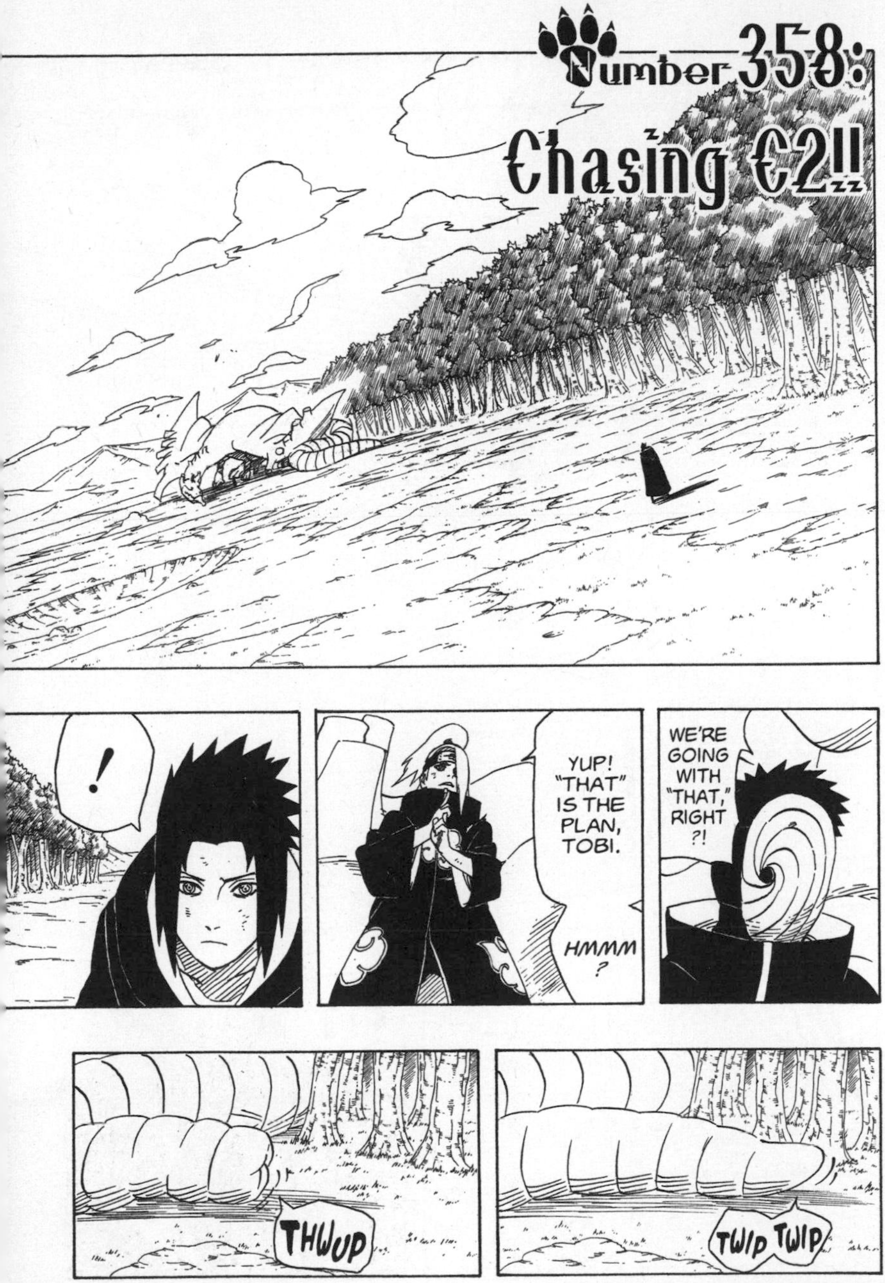
Number 358: Chasing C2!!
WE'RE GOING WITH "THAT," RIGHT ?!
YUP! "THAT" IS THE PLAN, TOBI.
HMMM ?
!
TWIP TWIP
THWUP

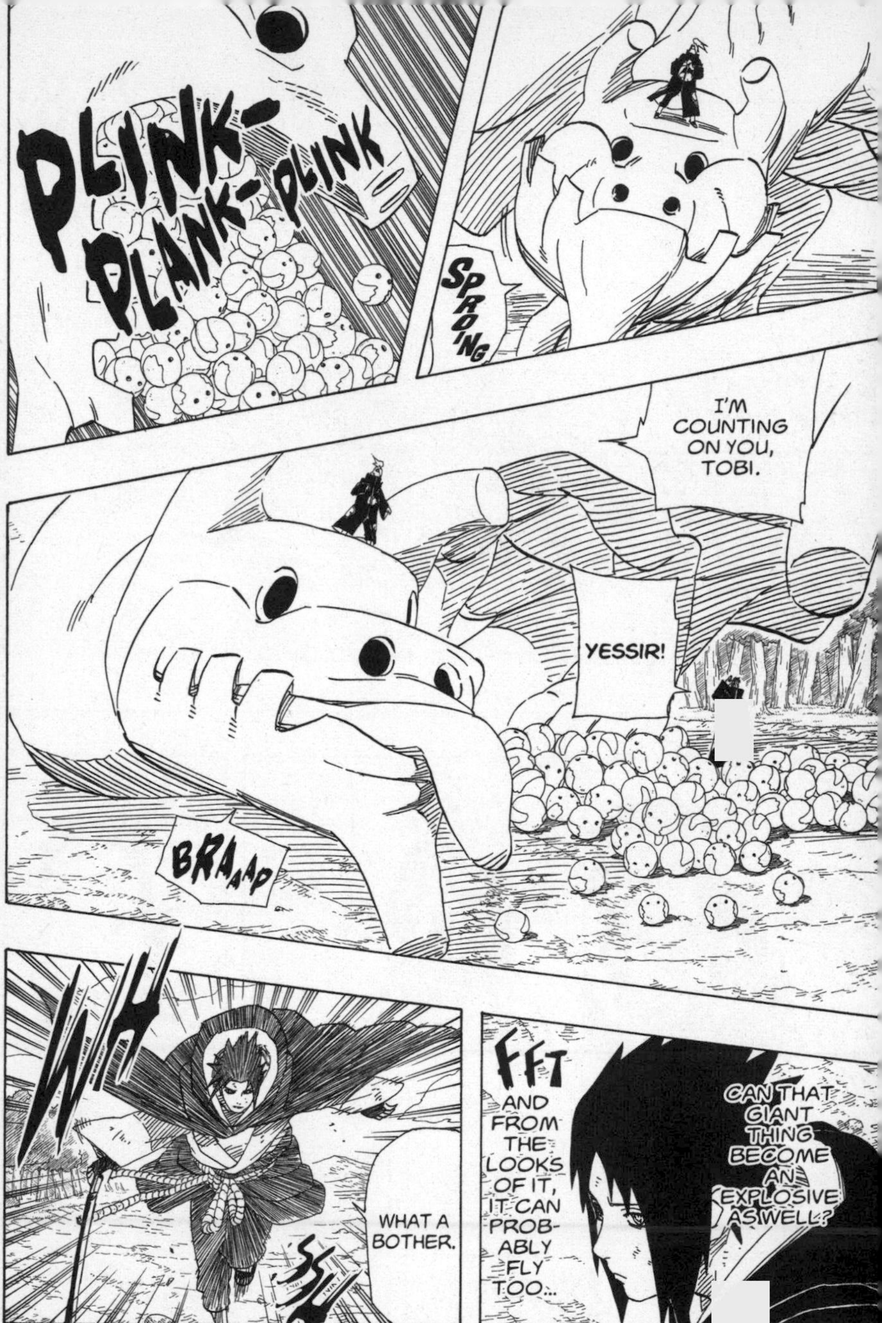

SPROING
PLINK-PLANK-PLINK
I'M COUNTING ON YOU, TOBI.
YESSIR!
BRAAAP
FFT
CAN THAT GIANT THING BECOME AN EXPLOSIVE AS WELL?
AND FROM THE LOOKS OF IT, IT CAN PROBABLY FLY TOO...
WH
WHAT A BOTHER.
SSH

READ THIS WAY

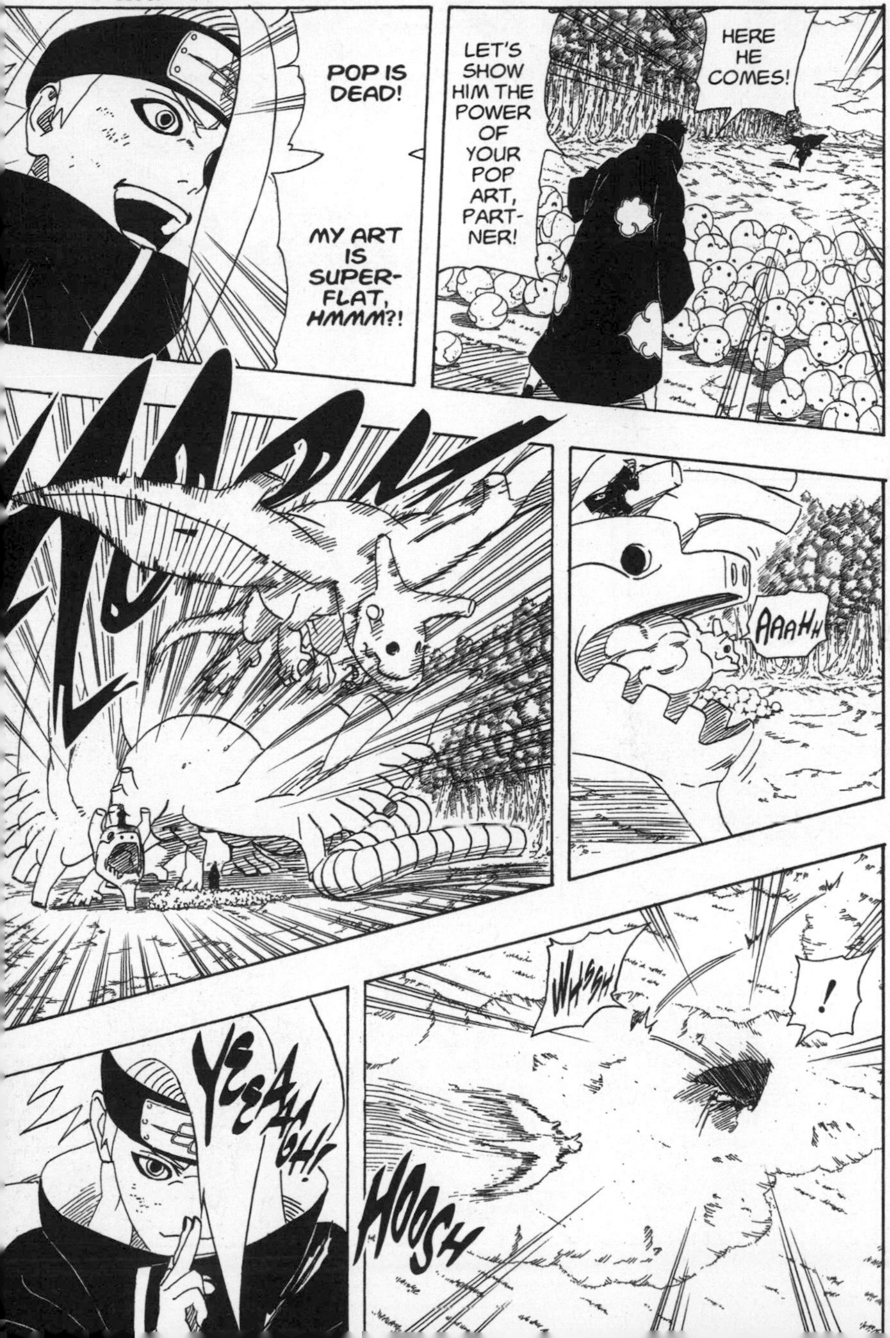
HERE HE COMES!
LET'S SHOW HIM THE POWER OF YOUR POP ART, PARTNER!
POP IS DEAD!
MY ART IS SUPER-FLAT, HMMM?!
AAAHH
WHSSH
!
HOOSH
YEEAAAGH!

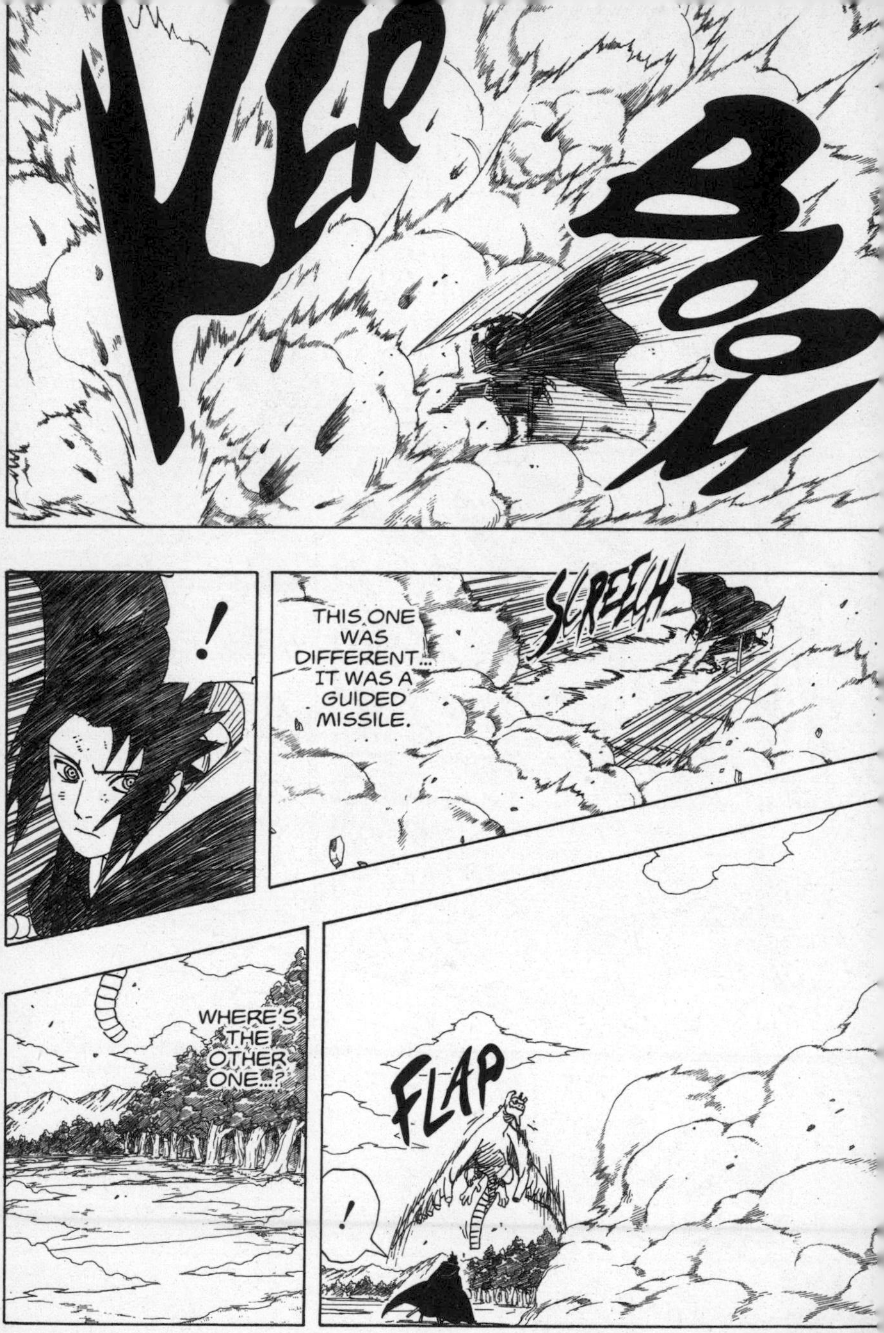
VKER
BOOM
SCREECH
THIS ONE WAS DIFFERENT... IT WAS A GUIDED MISSILE.
!
FLAP
!
WHERE'S THE OTHER ONE...?

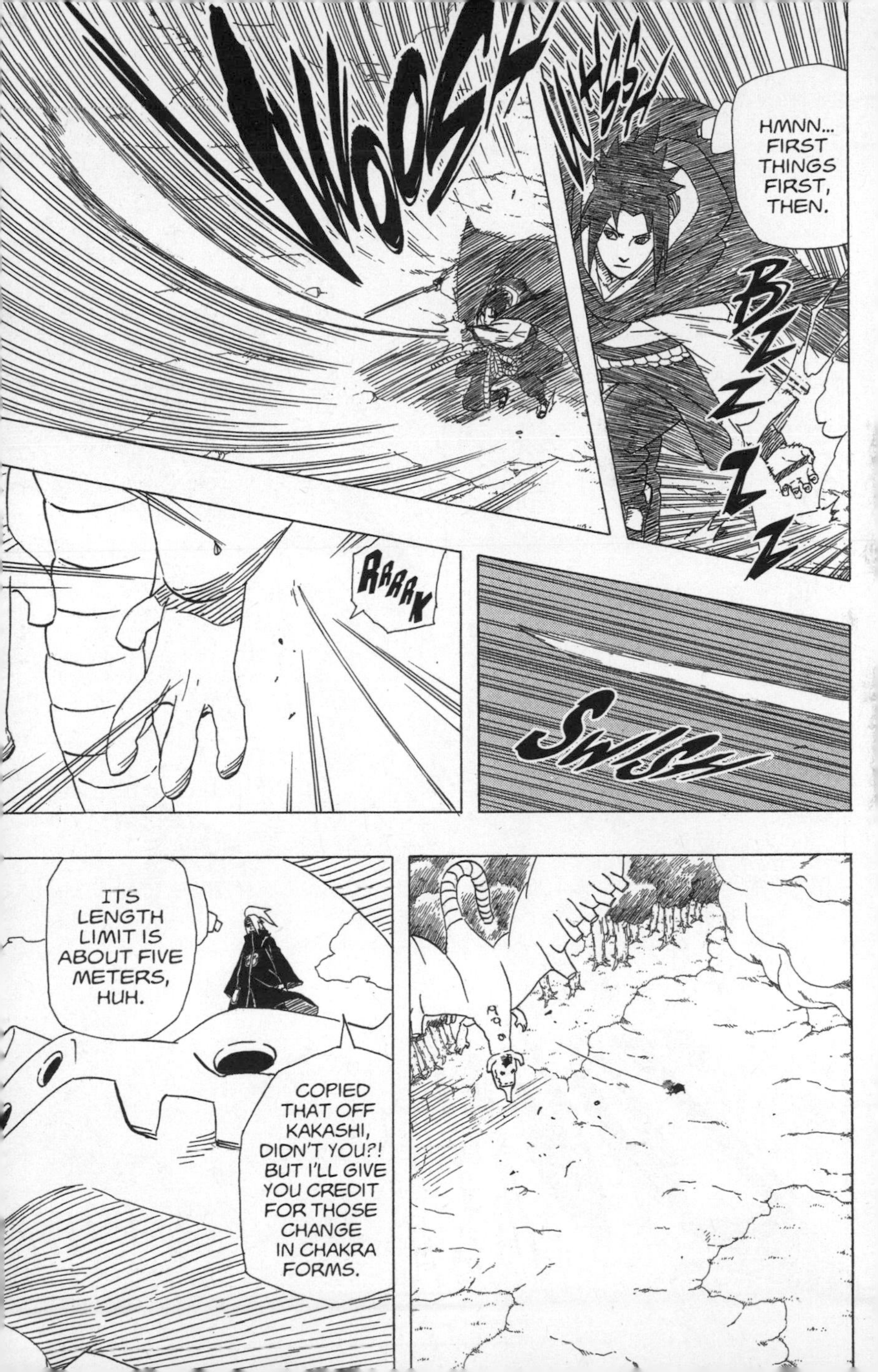
HMNN... FIRST THINGS FIRST, THEN.
BZZZZ
WHSSH
WOOSH
SWISH
RRRRK
ITS LENGTH LIMIT IS ABOUT FIVE METERS, HUH.
COPIED THAT OFF KAKASHI, DIDN'T YOU?! BUT I'LL GIVE YOU CREDIT FOR THOSE CHANGE IN CHAKRA FORMS.

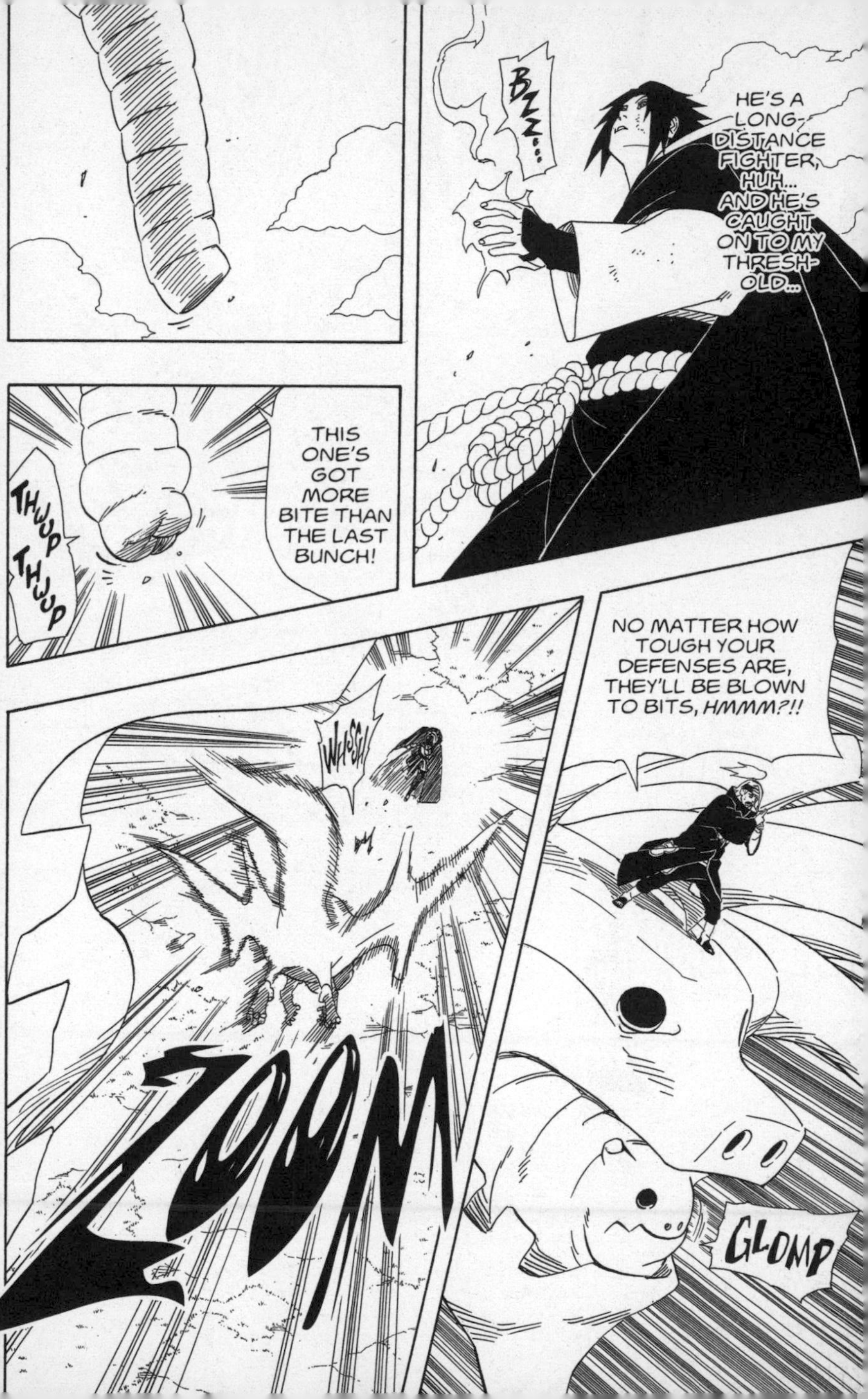
BZZZ...
HE'S A LONG-DISTANCE FIGHTER, HUH... AND HE'S CAUGHT ON TO MY THRESH-OLD...
THWUP THWUP
THIS ONE'S GOT MORE BITE THAN THE LAST BUNCH!
NO MATTER HOW TOUGH YOUR DEFENSES ARE, THEY'LL BE BLOWN TO BITS, *HMMM?!!*
GLOMP
WHOOSH
ZOOM

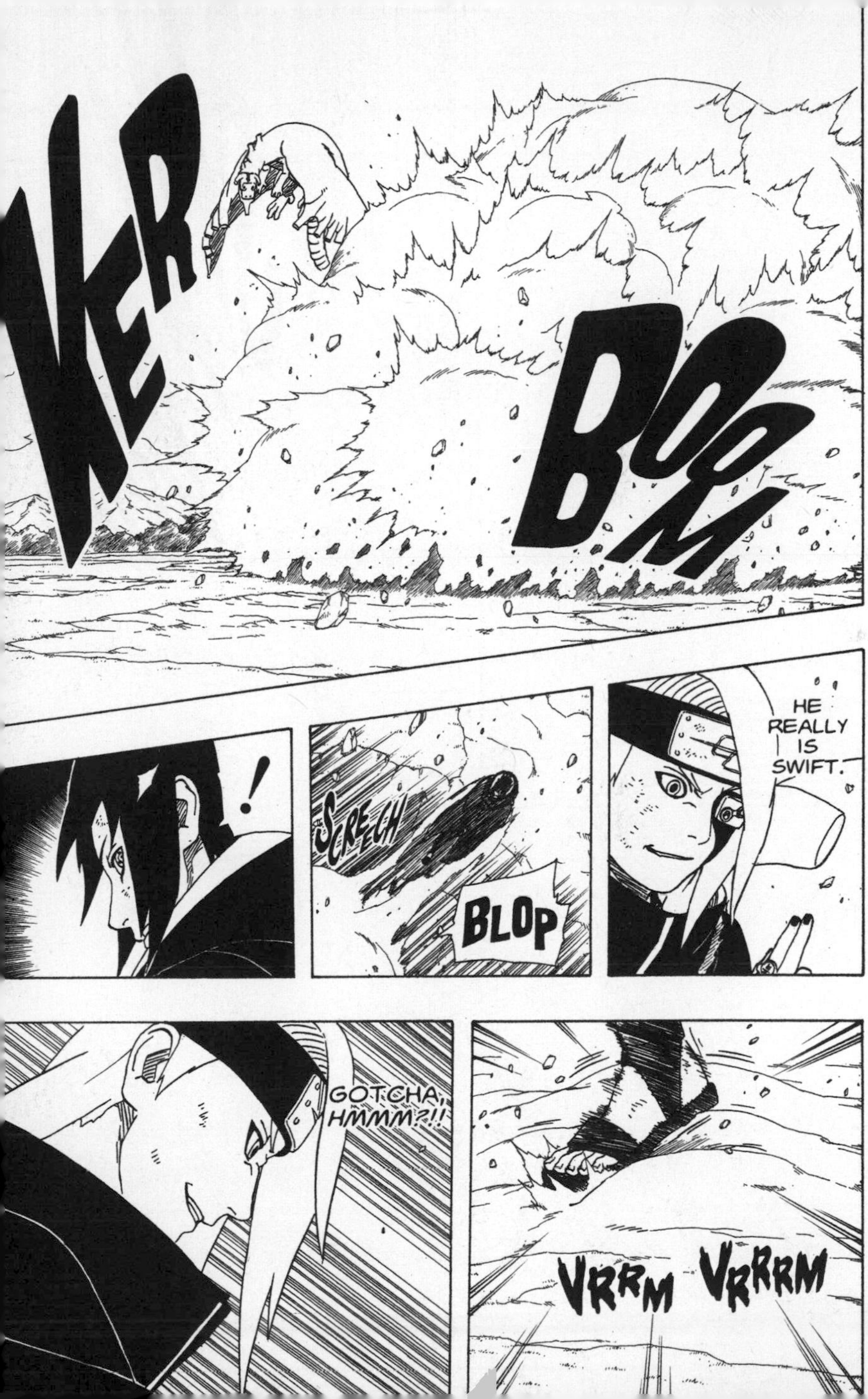
KER
BOOM
HE REALLY IS SWIFT.
SCREECH
BLOP
!
VRRM VRRRM
GOTCHA, HMMM?!!

IS IT
DONE...?!

SHA-
BOW

READ THIS WAY

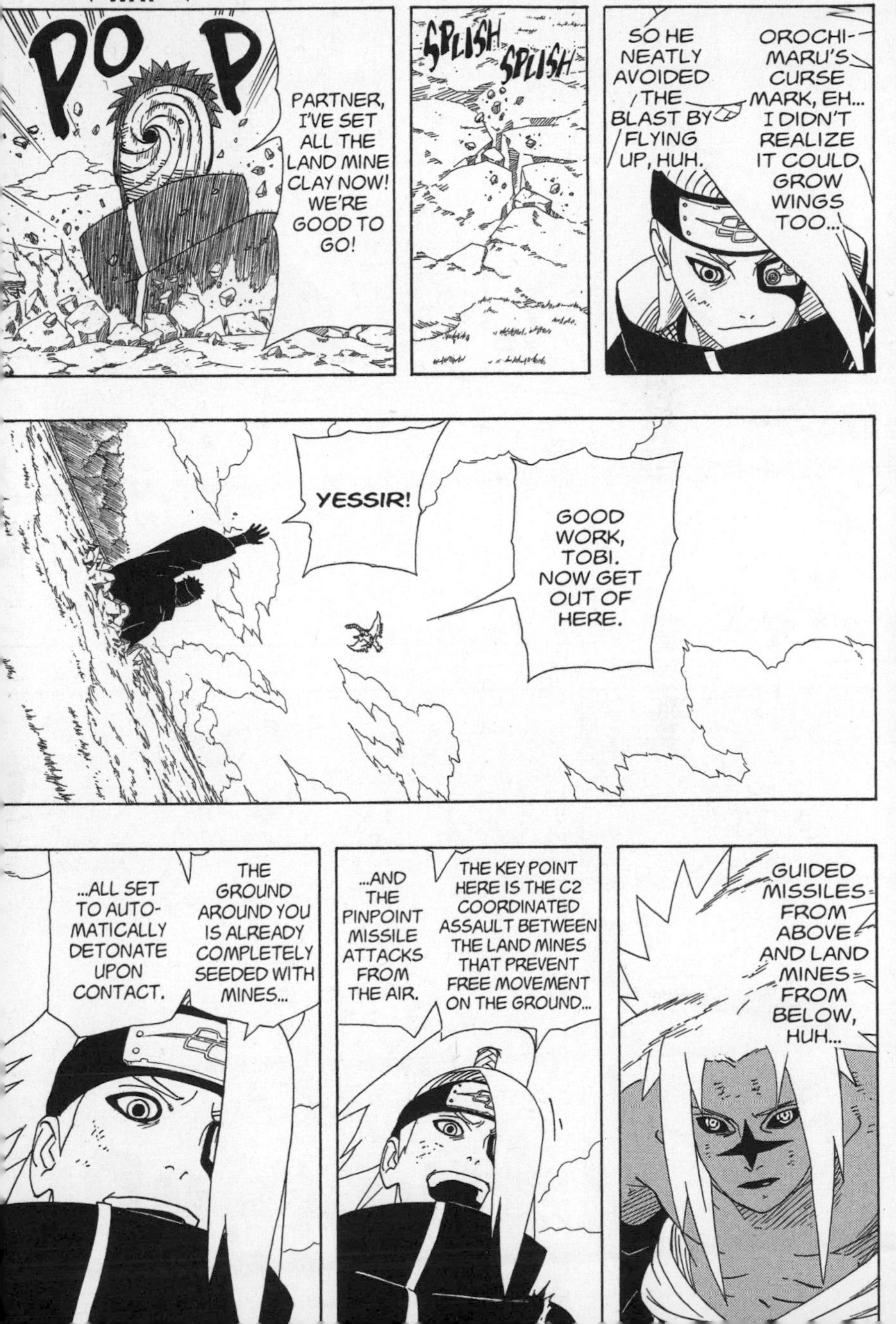
OROCHIMARU'S CURSE MARK, EH... I DIDN'T REALIZE IT COULD GROW WINGS TOO...
SO HE NEATLY AVOIDED THE BLAST BY FLYING UP, HUH.
SPLISH
SPLISH
POP
PARTNER, I'VE SET ALL THE LAND MINE CLAY NOW! WE'RE GOOD TO GO!
GOOD WORK, TOBI. NOW GET OUT OF HERE.
YESSIR!
GUIDED MISSILES FROM ABOVE AND LAND MINES FROM BELOW, HUH...
THE KEY POINT HERE IS THE C2 COORDINATED ASSAULT BETWEEN THE LAND MINES THAT PREVENT FREE MOVEMENT ON THE GROUND...
...AND THE PINPOINT MISSILE ATTACKS FROM THE AIR.
THE GROUND AROUND YOU IS ALREADY COMPLETELY SEEDED WITH MINES...
...ALL SET TO AUTOMATICALLY DETONATE UPON CONTACT.

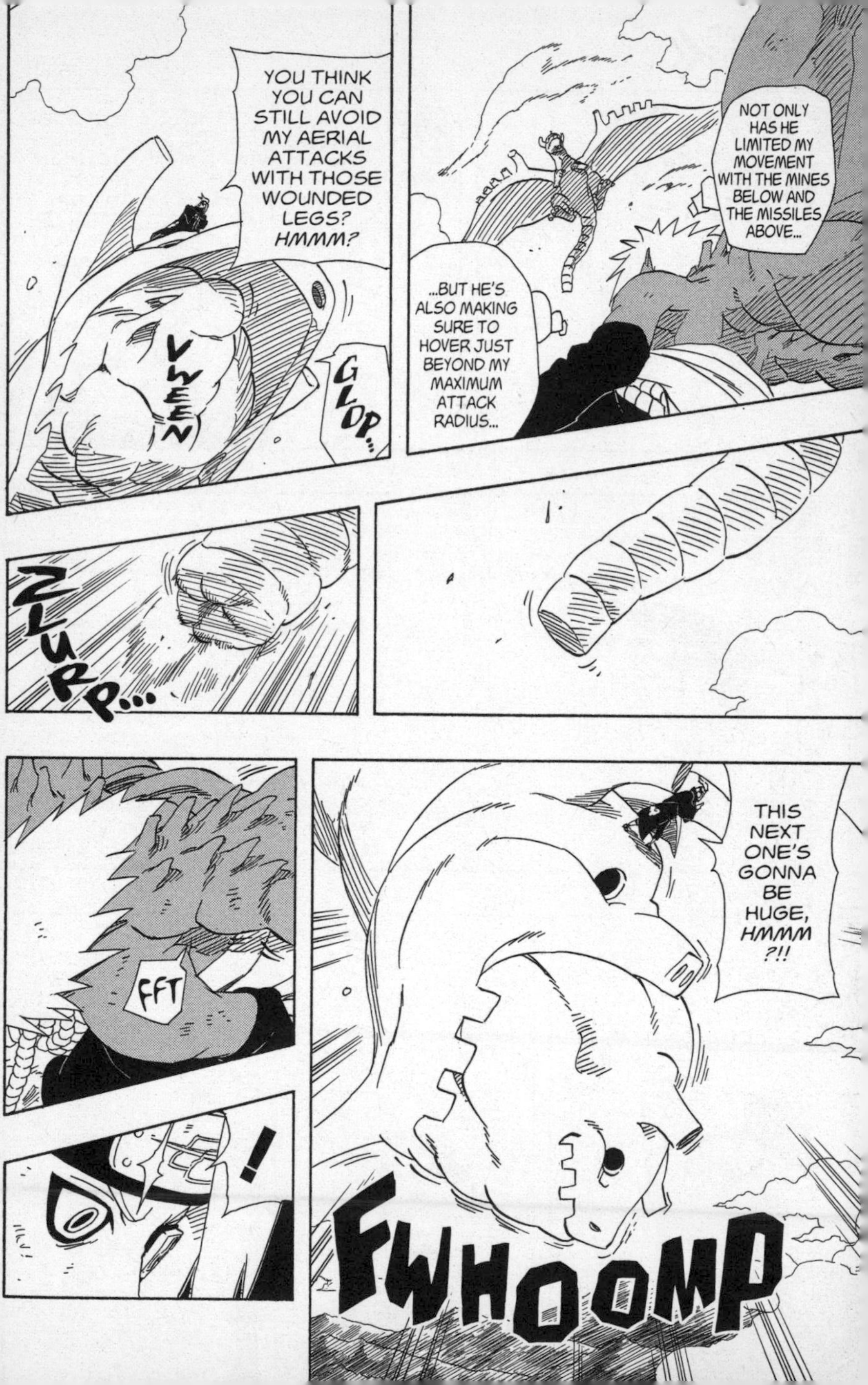
NOT ONLY HAS HE LIMITED MY MOVEMENT WITH THE MINES BELOW AND THE MISSILES ABOVE...
...BUT HE'S ALSO MAKING SURE TO HOVER JUST BEYOND MY MAXIMUM ATTACK RADIUS...
YOU THINK YOU CAN STILL AVOID MY AERIAL ATTACKS WITH THOSE WOUNDED LEGS? HMMM?
VWEEN
GLOP...
ZLURP...
THIS NEXT ONE'S GONNA BE HUGE, HMMM?!!
FWHOOMP
FFT
!

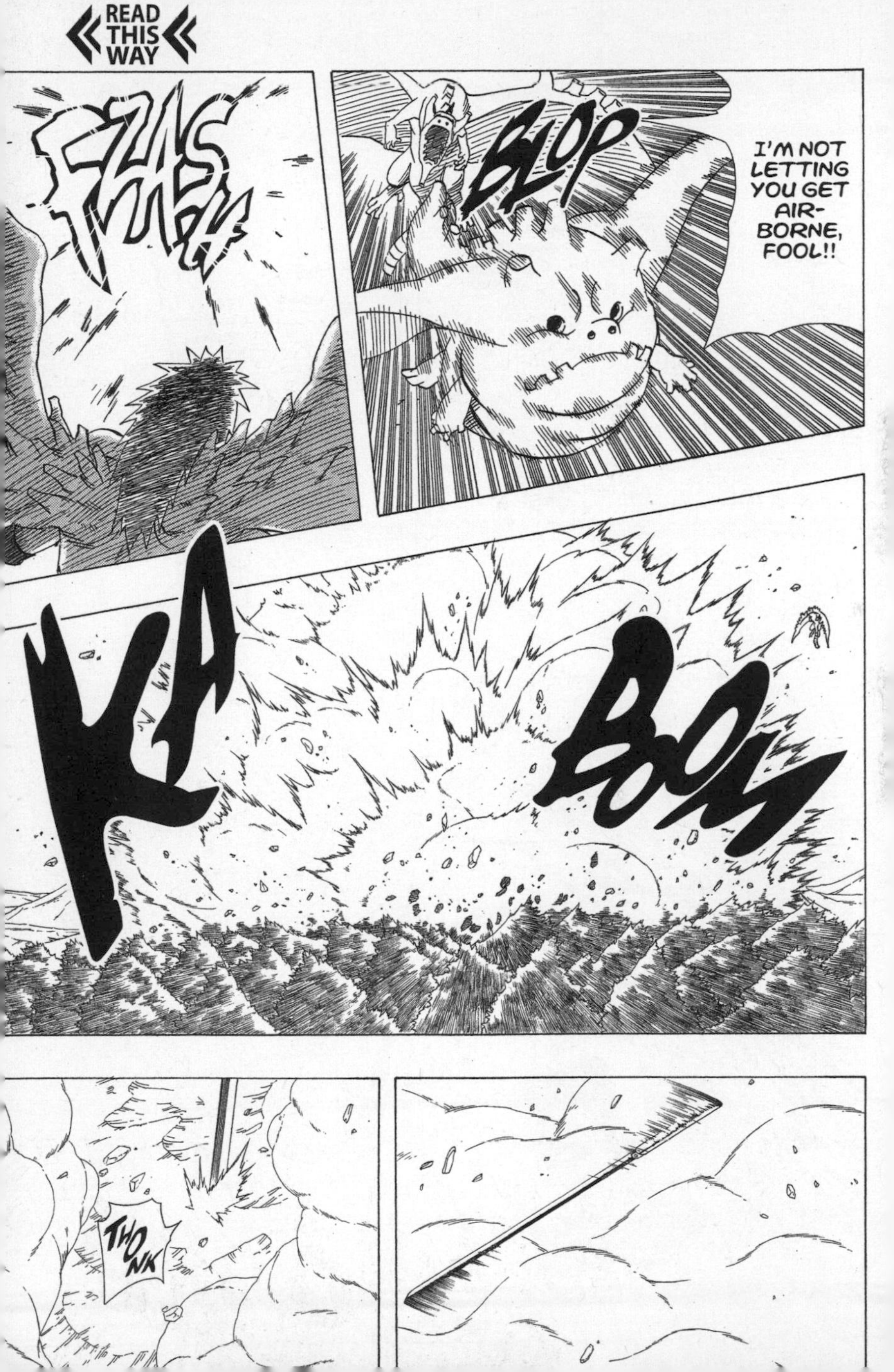
READ THIS WAY
BLOP
I'M NOT LETTING YOU GET AIR-BORNE, FOOL!!
KA BOOM
THONK

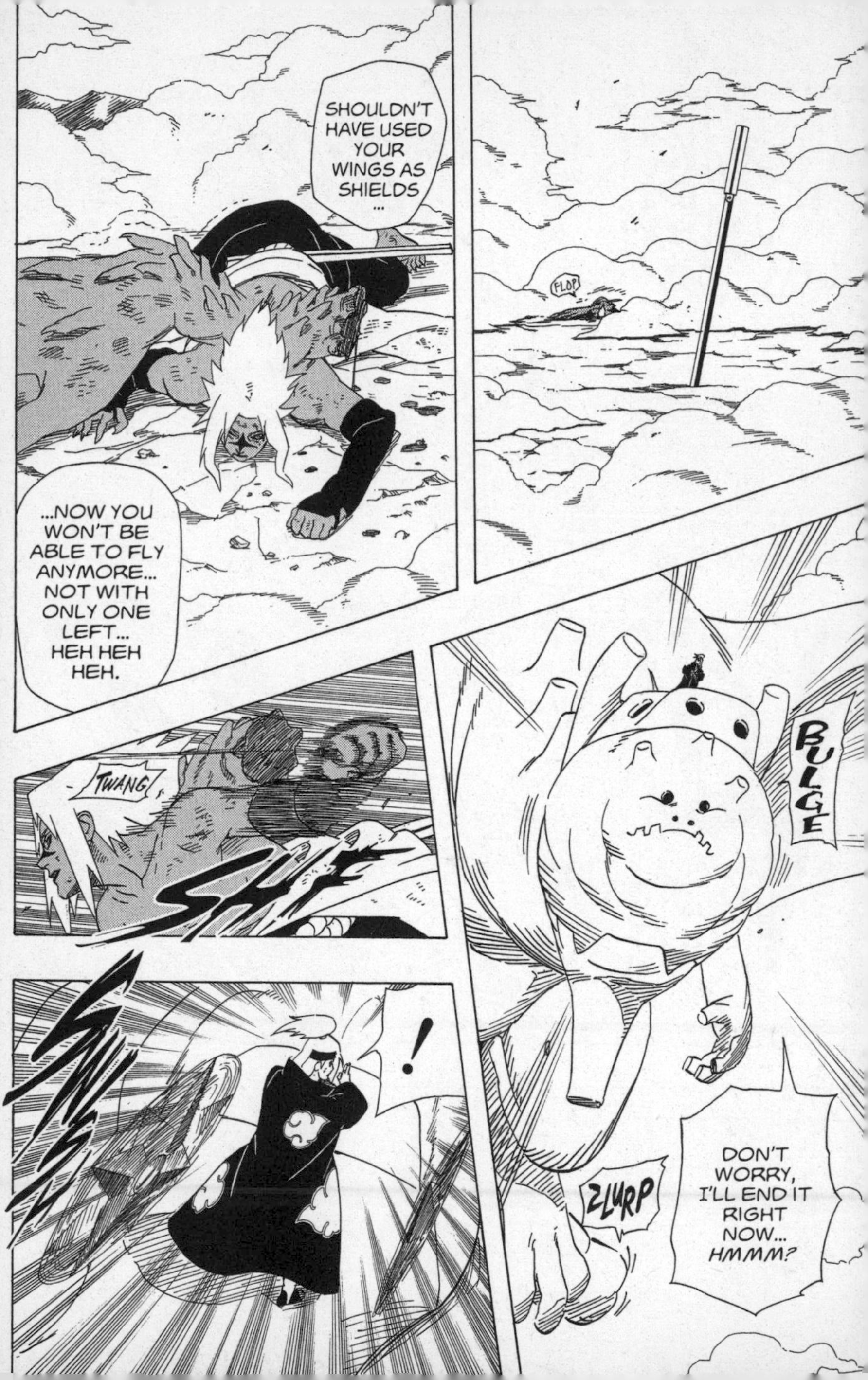
FLOP
SHOULDN'T HAVE USED YOUR WINGS AS SHIELDS...
...NOW YOU WON'T BE ABLE TO FLY ANYMORE... NOT WITH ONLY ONE LEFT... HEH HEH HEH.
BULGE
ZLURP
DON'T WORRY, I'LL END IT RIGHT NOW... *HMMM?*
TWANG
!

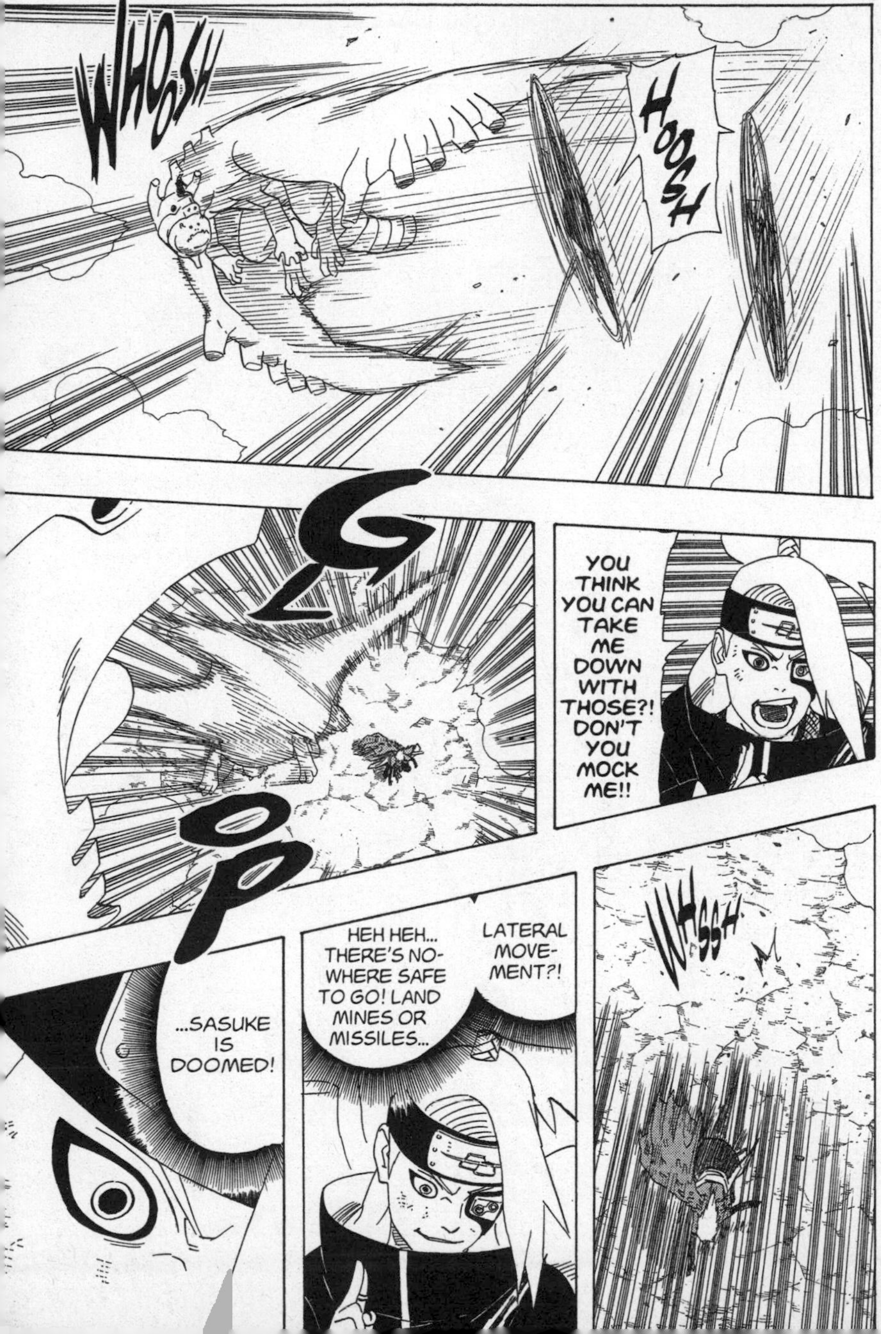
HOOSH
WHOOSH
YOU THINK YOU CAN TAKE ME DOWN WITH THOSE?! DON'T YOU MOCK ME!!
GLOP
WHSSH
LATERAL MOVE-MENT?!
HEH HEH... THERE'S NO-WHERE SAFE TO GO! LAND MINES OR MISSILES...
...SASUKE IS DOOMED!

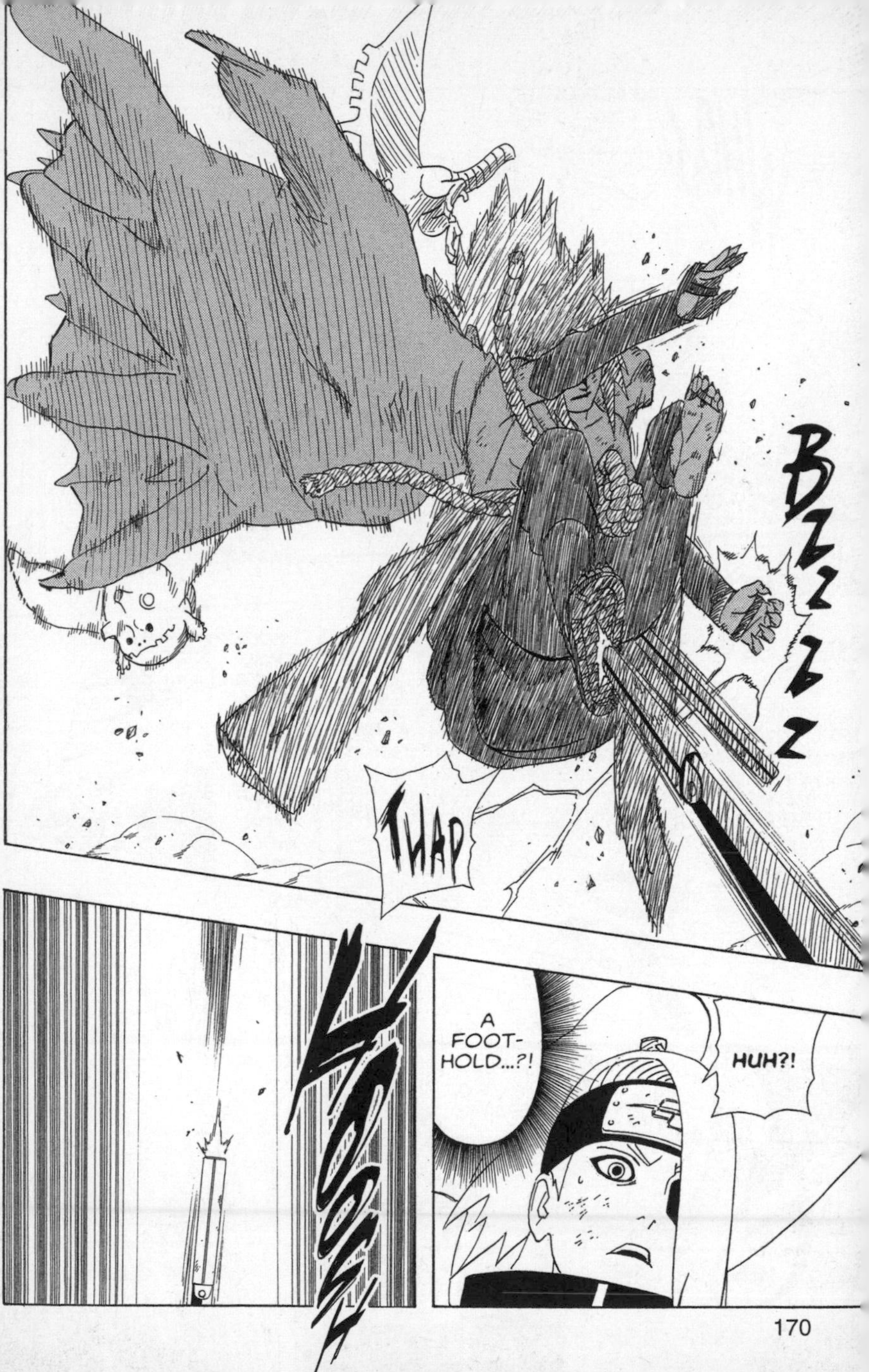
BZZZZ
THAP
HUH?!
A FOOT-HOLD...?!

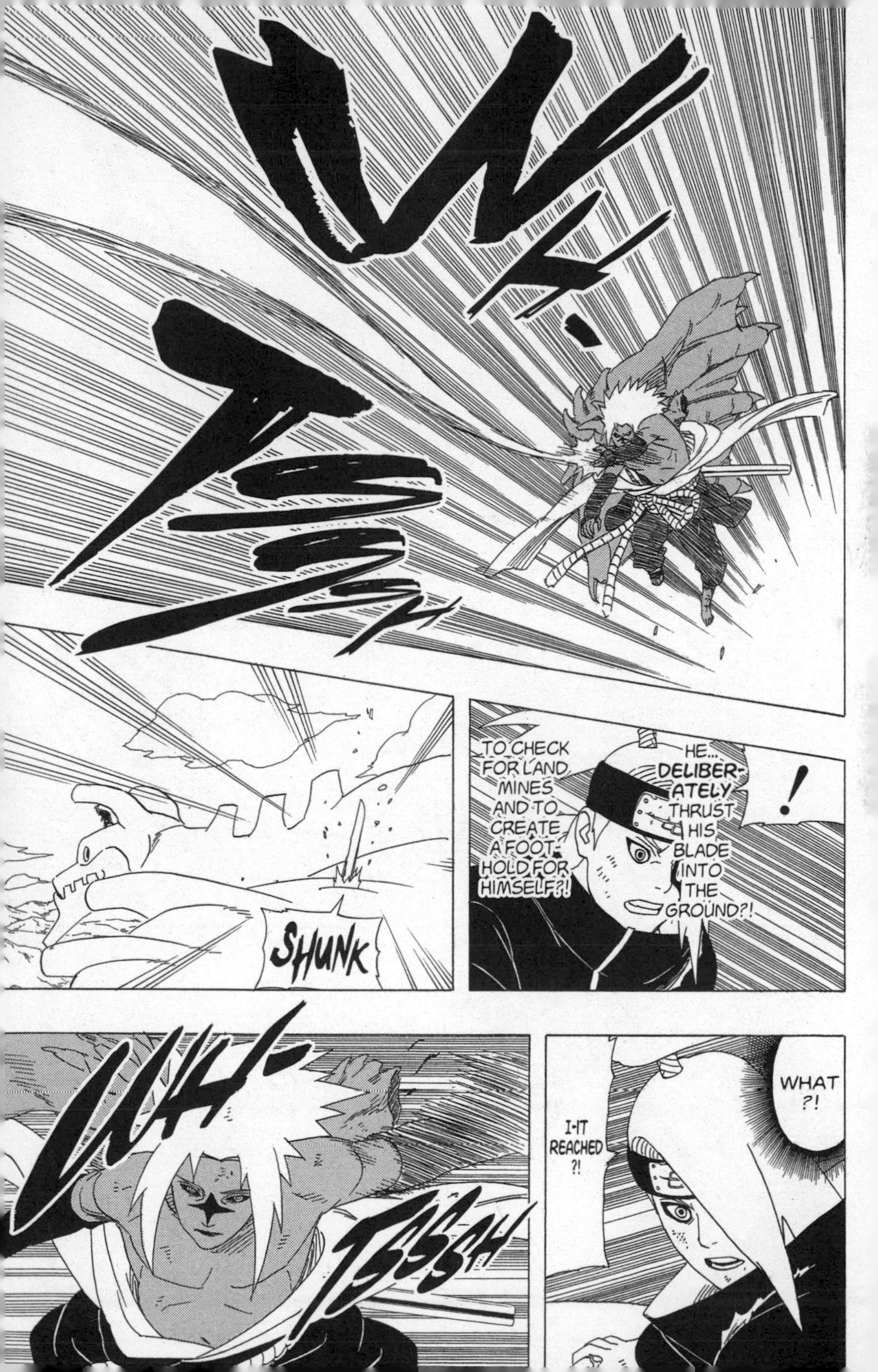

HE... DELIBERATELY THRUST HIS BLADE INTO THE GROUND?!
!
TO CHECK FOR LAND MINES AND TO CREATE A FOOTHOLD FOR HIMSELF?!
SHUNK
WHAT?!
I-IT REACHED?!

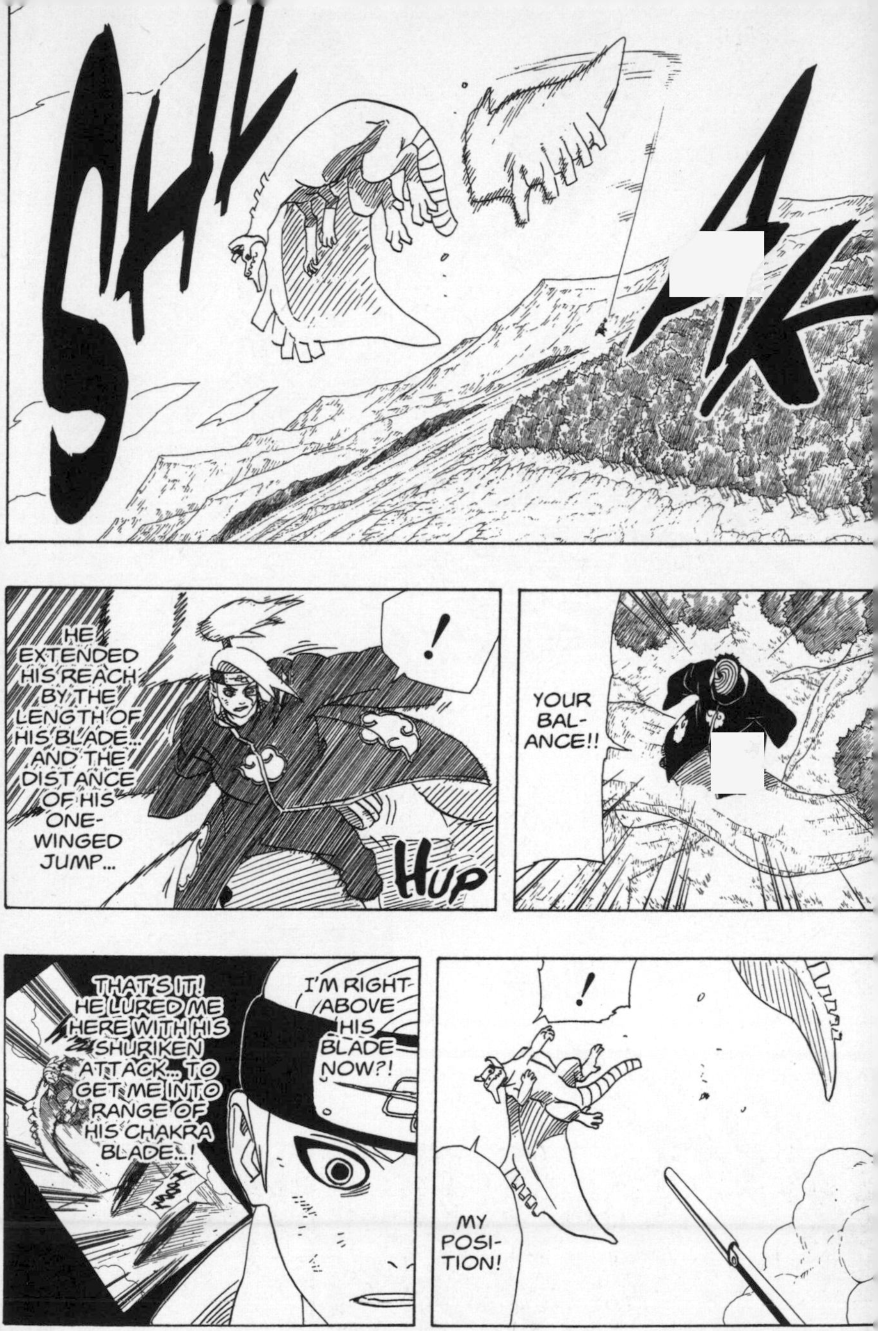
SHAK
YOUR BAL-ANCE!!
!
HE EXTENDED HIS REACH BY THE LENGTH OF HIS BLADE... AND THE DISTANCE OF HIS ONE-WINGED JUMP...
HUP
!
MY POSI-TION!
I'M RIGHT ABOVE HIS BLADE NOW?!
THAT'S IT! HE LURED ME HERE WITH HIS SHURIKEN ATTACK... TO GET ME INTO RANGE OF HIS CHAKRA BLADE...!

READ THIS WAY

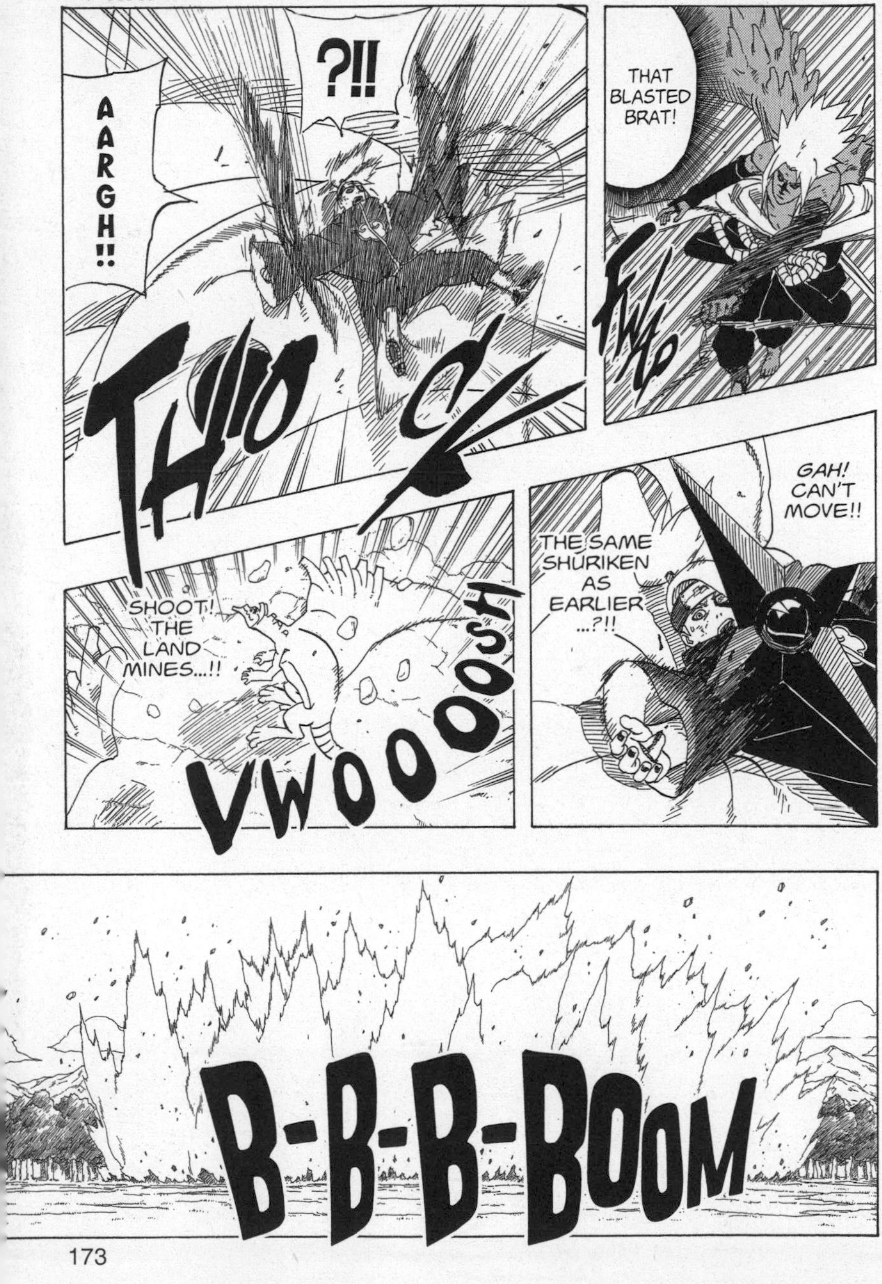
THAT BLASTED BRAT!
FWAP
?!!
AARGH!!
THWOCK
GAH! CAN'T MOVE!!
THE SAME SHURIKEN AS EARLIER ...?!!
SHOOT! THE LAND MINES...!!
VWOOOOSH
B-B-B-BOOM

NARUTO

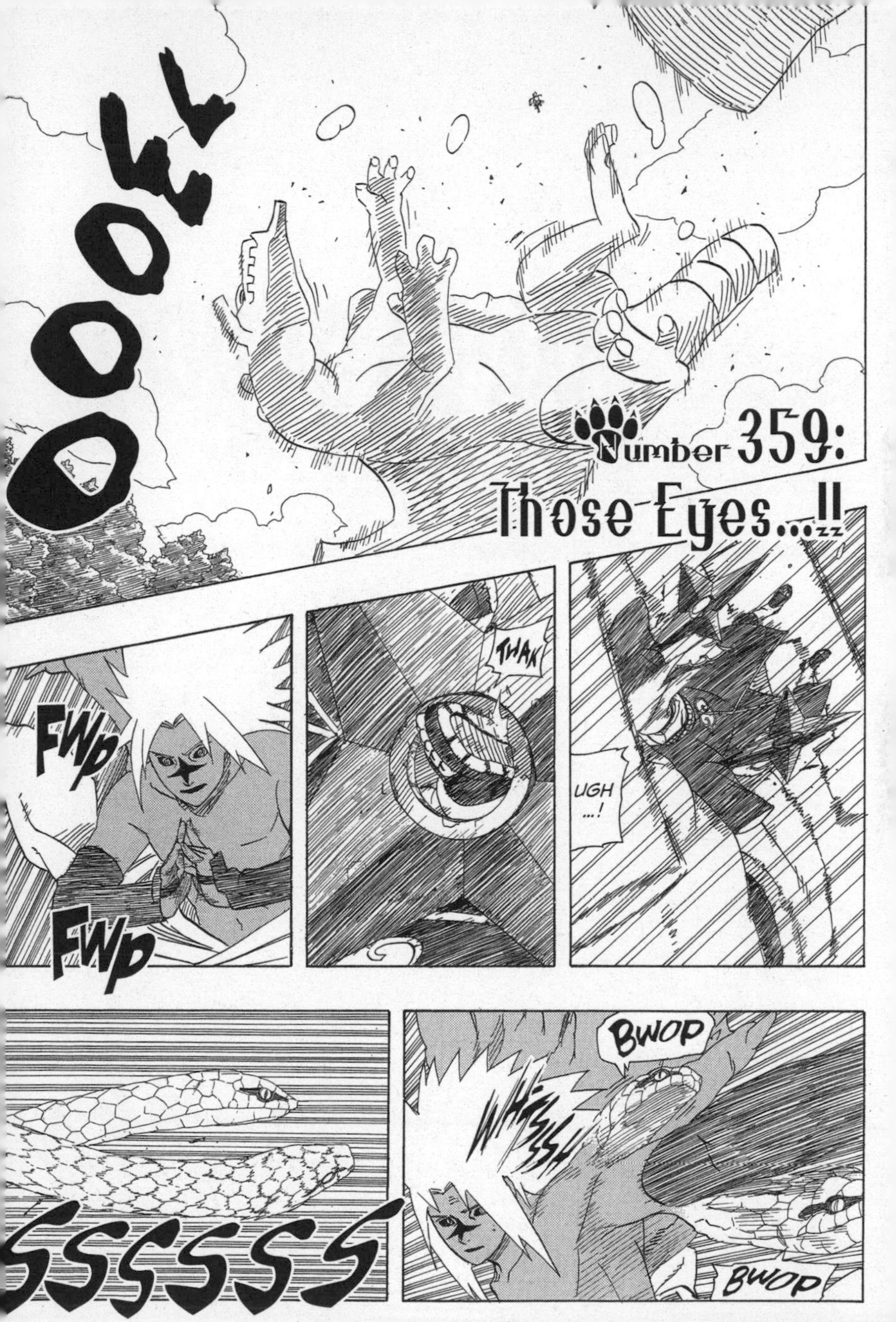
Number 359:
Those Eyes...!!
OOOF
UGH
...!
THAK
FWP
FWP
BWOP
WHASSH
BWOP
SSSSSS

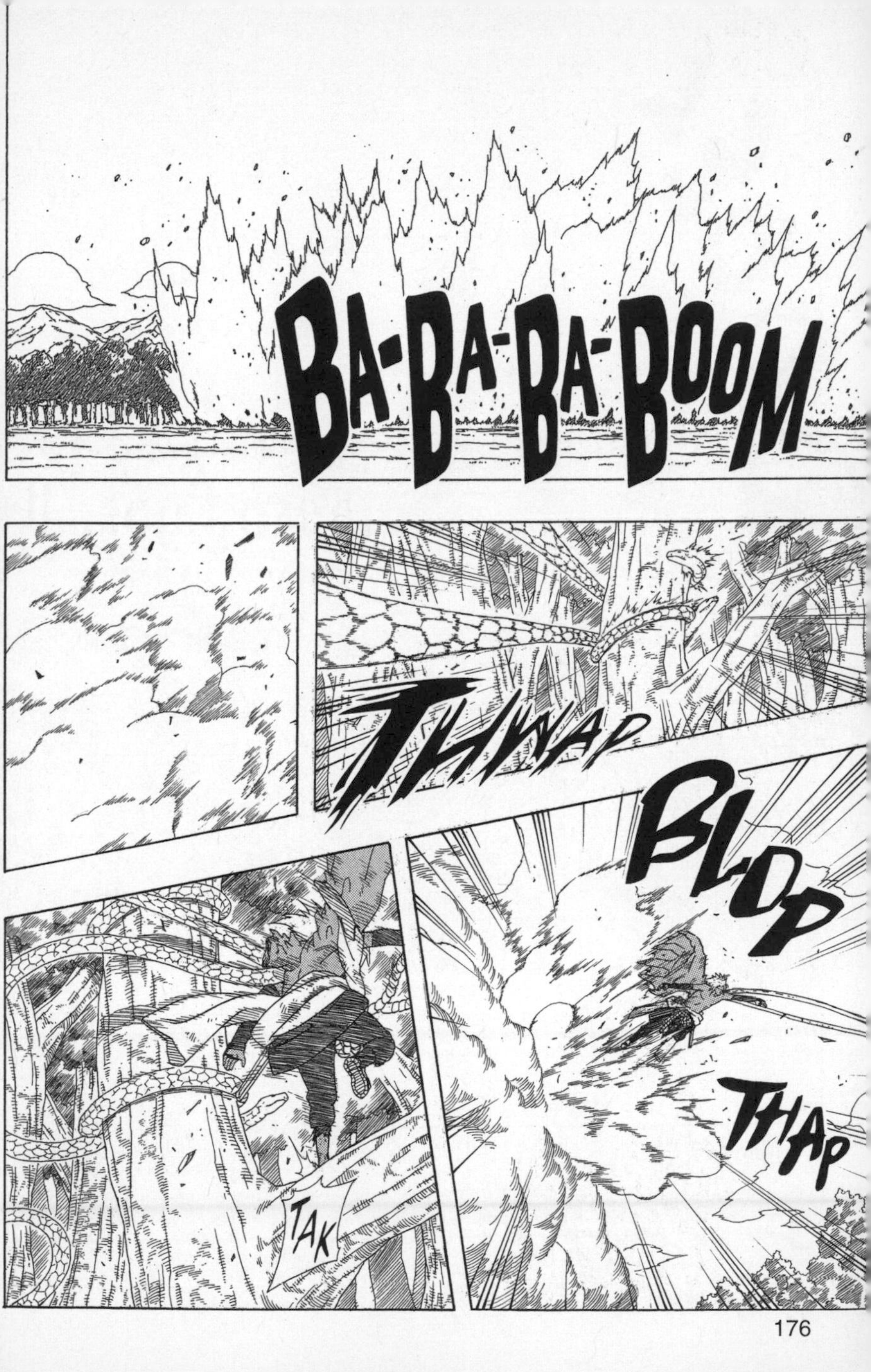
BA-BA-BA-BOOM
THWAP
BLOP
THAP
TAK

READ THIS WAY

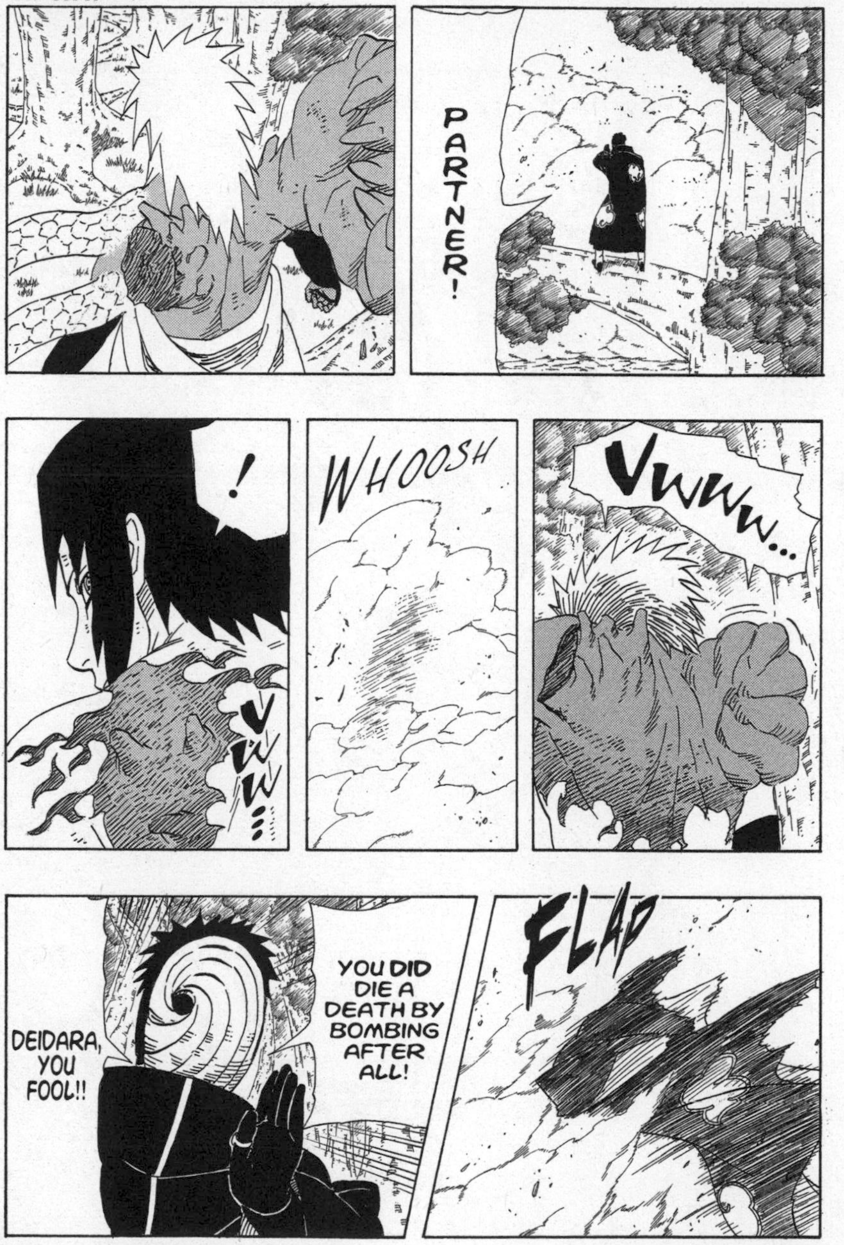
PARTNER!
VWWW...
WHOOSH
!
VWW...
FLAP
YOU DID DIE A DEATH BY BOMBING AFTER ALL!
DEIDARA, YOU FOOL!!

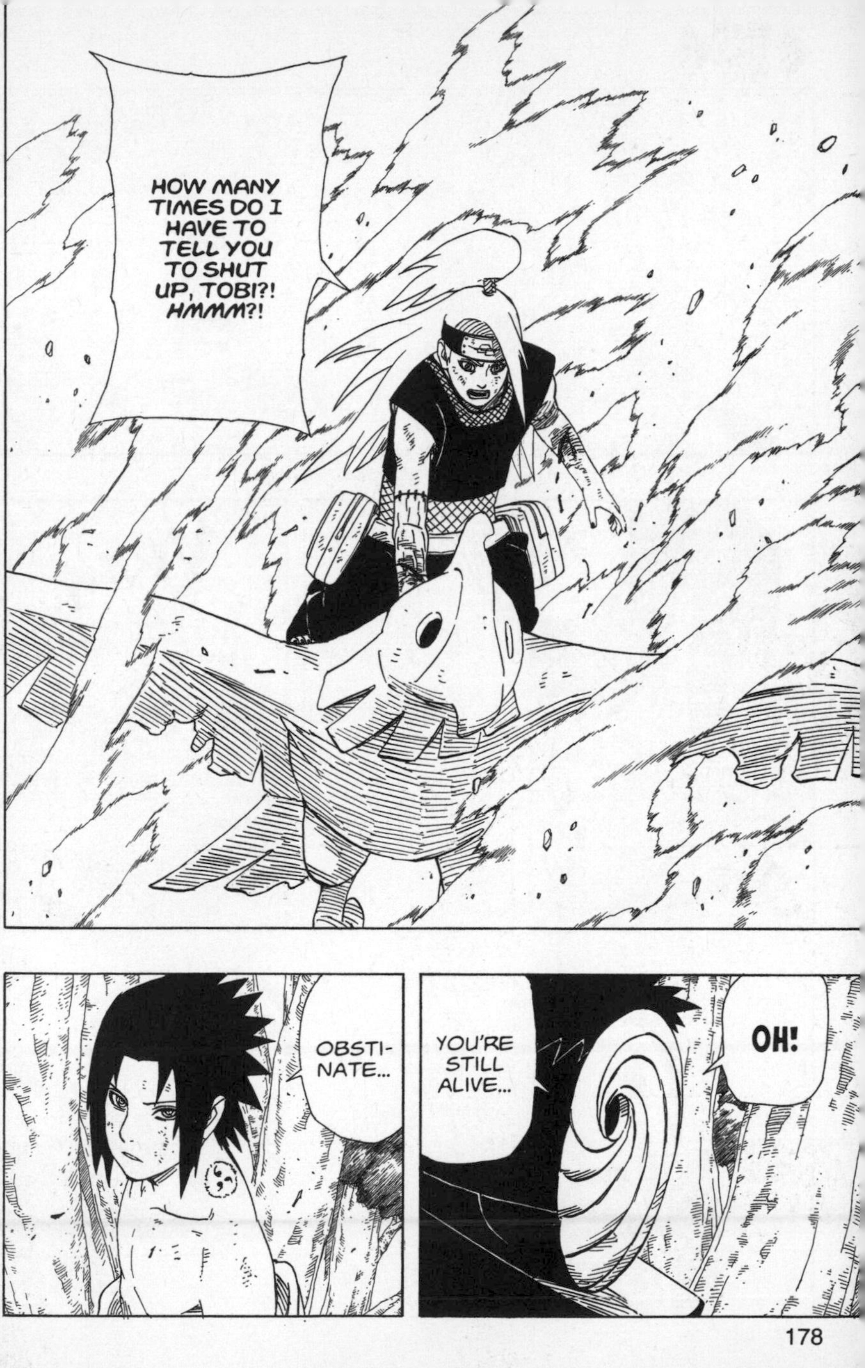
HOW MANY TIMES DO I HAVE TO TELL YOU TO SHUT UP, TOBI?! HMMM?!
OH!
YOU'RE STILL ALIVE...
OBSTI-NATE...

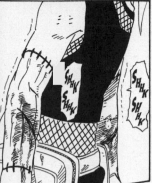

SHHK
SHHK

SHHK
SHHK

THOSE
EYES...

IT'S
THOSE
SAME
EYES...

AARGH...!

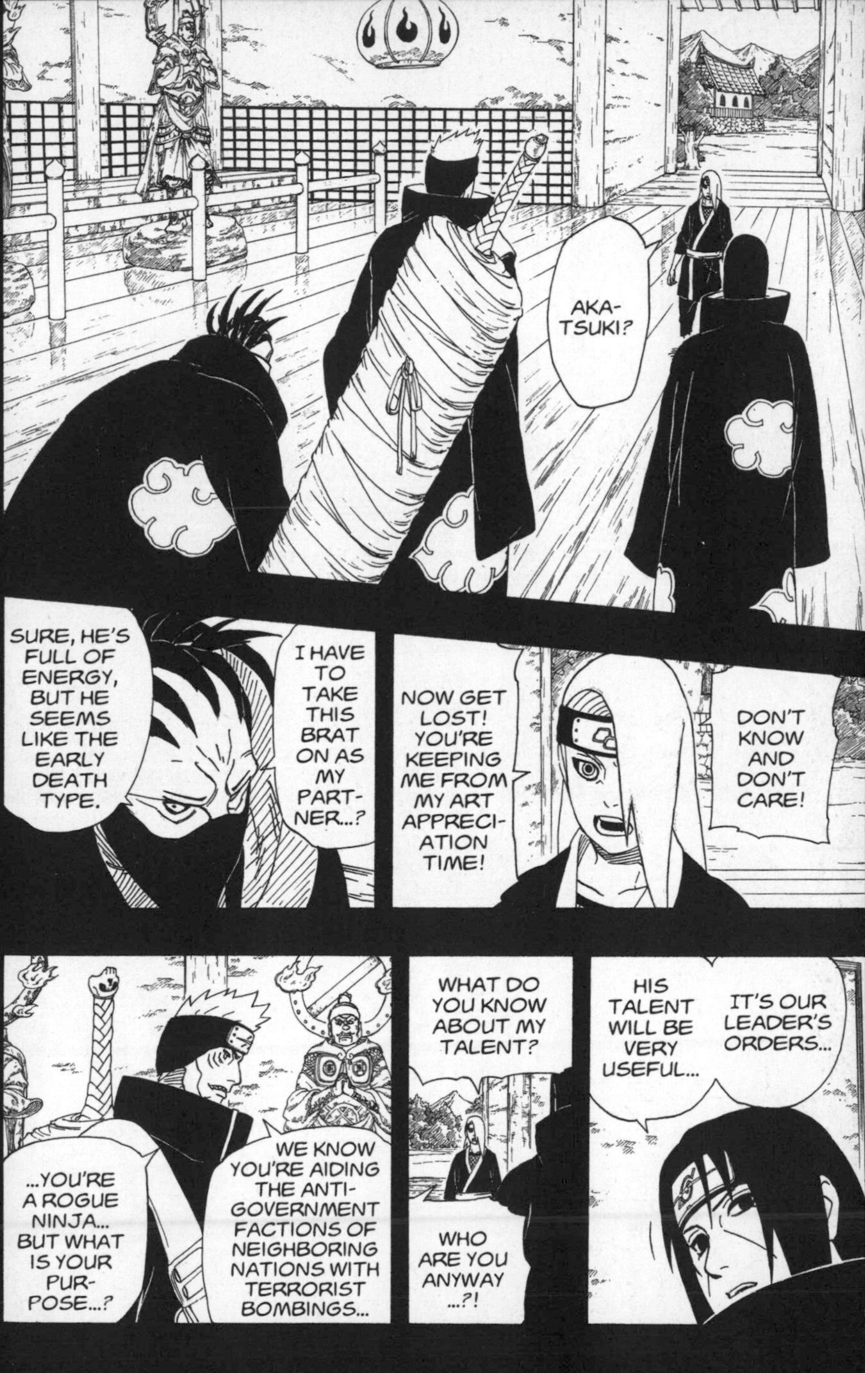
AKA-TSUKI?
DON'T KNOW AND DON'T CARE!
NOW GET LOST! YOU'RE KEEPING ME FROM MY ART APPRECIATION TIME!
I HAVE TO TAKE THIS BRAT ON AS MY PARTNER...?
SURE, HE'S FULL OF ENERGY, BUT HE SEEMS LIKE THE EARLY DEATH TYPE.
IT'S OUR LEADER'S ORDERS...
HIS TALENT WILL BE VERY USEFUL...
WHAT DO YOU KNOW ABOUT MY TALENT?
WHO ARE YOU ANYWAY...?!
WE KNOW YOU'RE AIDING THE ANTI-GOVERNMENT FACTIONS OF NEIGHBORING NATIONS WITH TERRORIST BOMBINGS...
...YOU'RE A ROGUE NINJA... BUT WHAT IS YOUR PURPOSE...?

READ THIS WAY

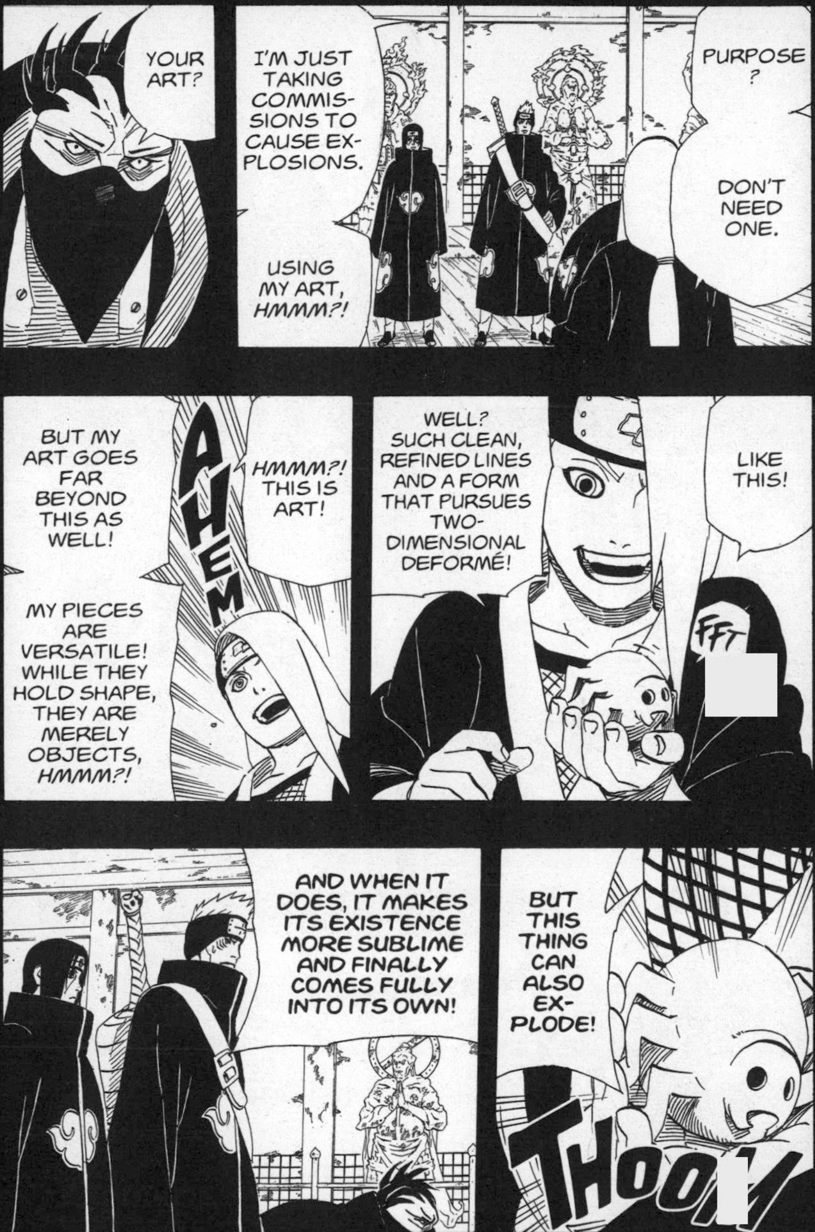
PURPOSE ?
DON'T NEED ONE.
I'M JUST TAKING COMMISSIONS TO CAUSE EXPLOSIONS.
USING MY ART, HMMM?!
YOUR ART?
LIKE THIS!
WELL? SUCH CLEAN, REFINED LINES AND A FORM THAT PURSUES TWO-DIMENSIONAL DEFORMÉ!
FFT
HMMM?! THIS IS ART!
AHEM
BUT MY ART GOES FAR BEYOND THIS AS WELL!
MY PIECES ARE VERSATILE! WHILE THEY HOLD SHAPE, THEY ARE MERELY OBJECTS, HMMM?!
BUT THIS THING CAN ALSO EXPLODE!
THOOM
AND WHEN IT DOES, IT MAKES ITS EXISTENCE MORE SUBLIME AND FINALLY COMES FULLY INTO ITS OWN!

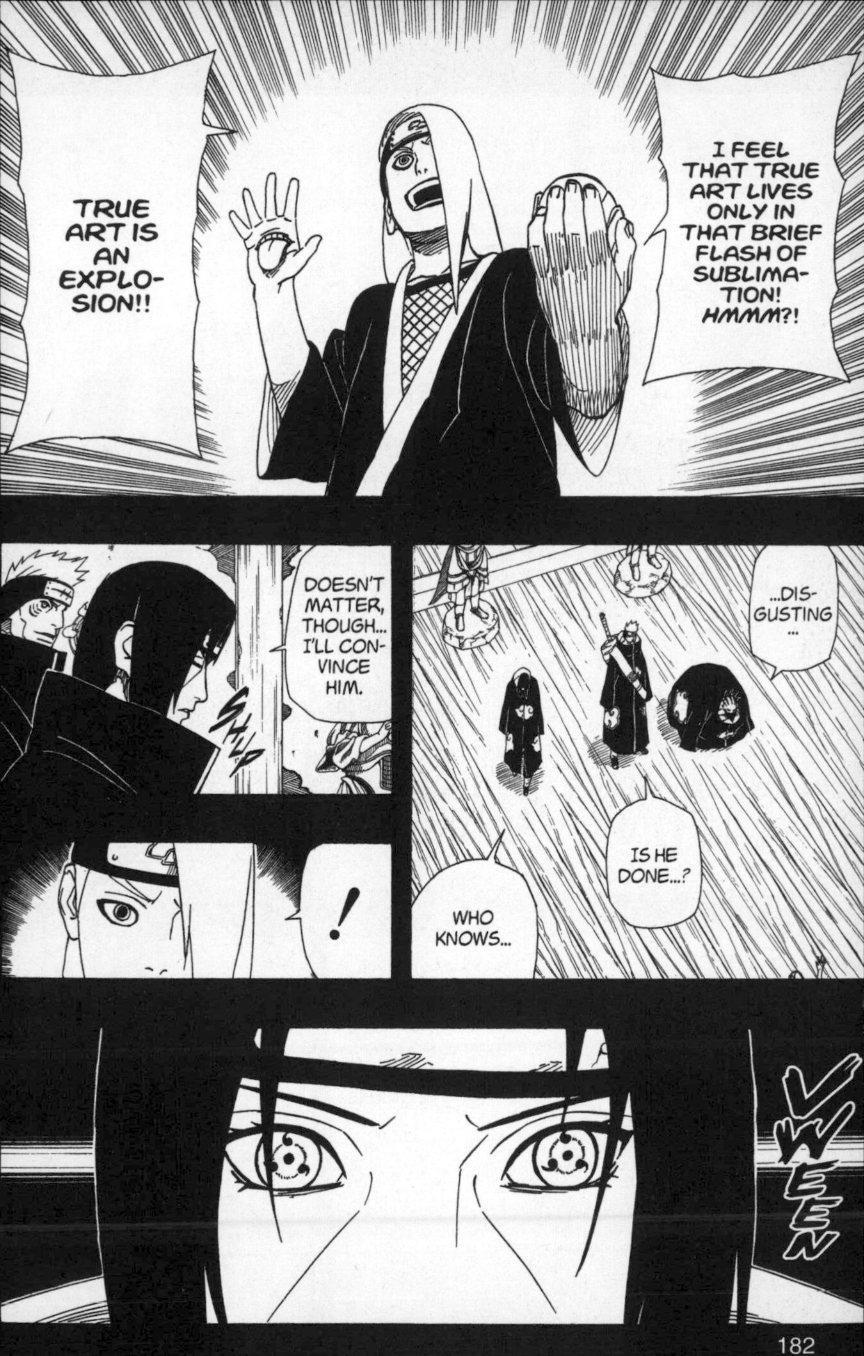
I FEEL THAT TRUE ART LIVES ONLY IN THAT BRIEF FLASH OF SUBLIMATION! HMMM?!
TRUE ART IS AN EXPLOSION!!
...DISGUSTING...
IS HE DONE...?
WHO KNOWS...
DOESN'T MATTER, THOUGH... I'LL CONVINCE HIM.
SHP
!
VWEEN

READ THIS WAY

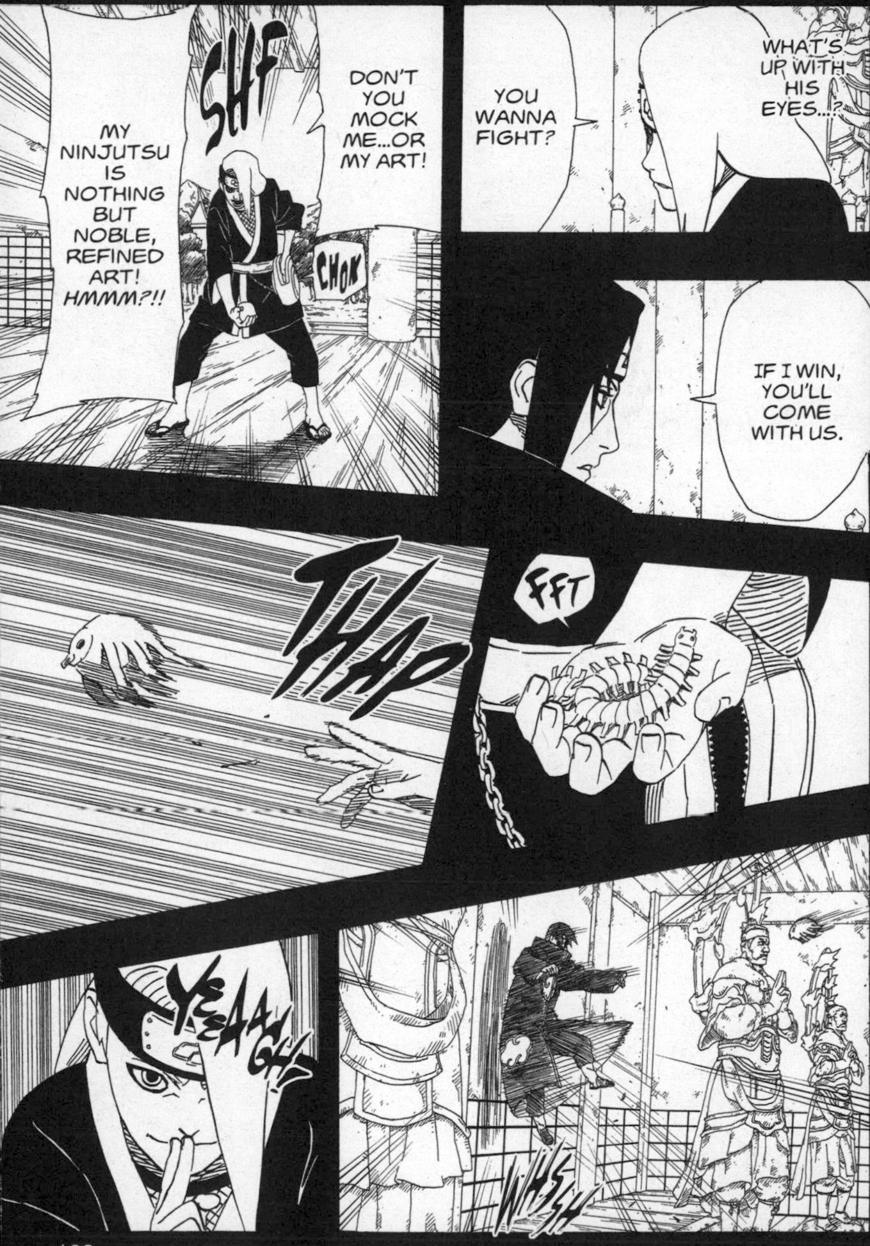

WHAT'S UP WITH HIS EYES...?
YOU WANNA FIGHT?
IF I WIN, YOU'LL COME WITH US.
DON'T YOU MOCK ME...OR MY ART!
SHF
CHOK
MY NINJUTSU IS NOTHING BUT NOBLE, REFINED ART! HMMM?!!
FFT
THAP
WHSH
YEAAAGH!

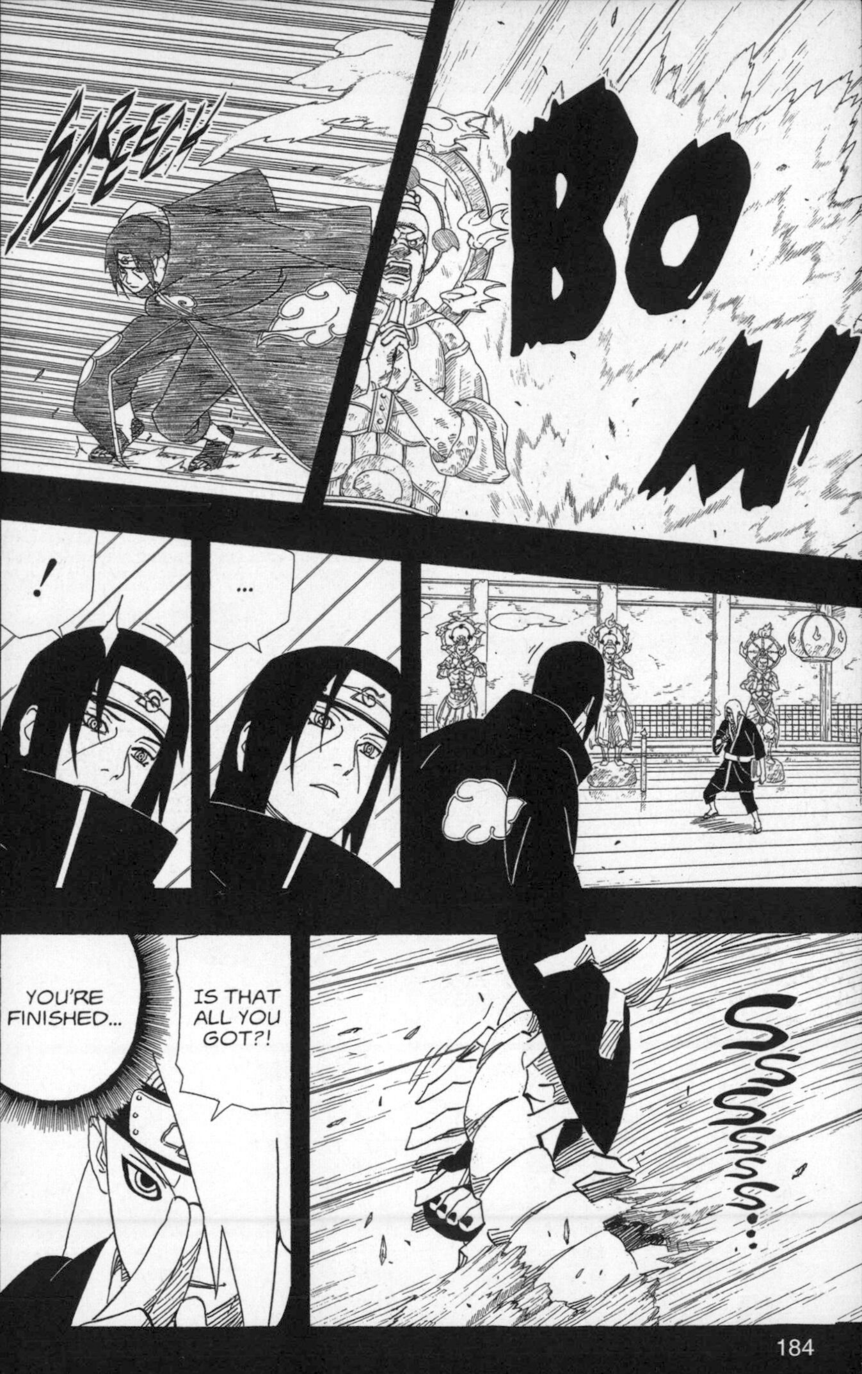
BOOM
SKREECH
...
!
SSSSSS...
IS THAT ALL YOU GOT?!
YOU'RE FINISHED...

READ THIS WAY

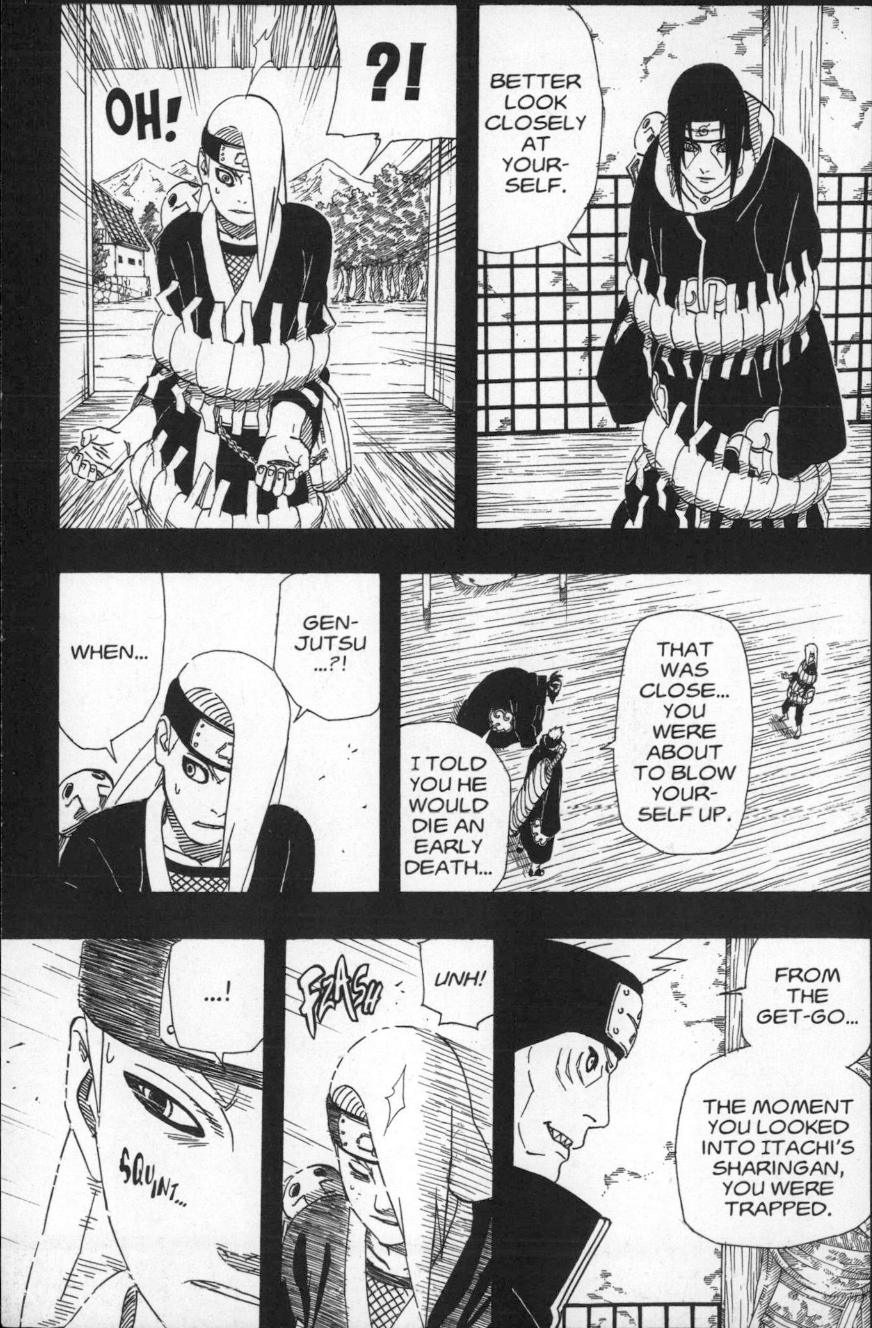

BETTER LOOK CLOSELY AT YOUR-SELF.
?!
OH!
THAT WAS CLOSE... YOU WERE ABOUT TO BLOW YOUR-SELF UP.
I TOLD YOU HE WOULD DIE AN EARLY DEATH...
GEN-JUTSU ...?!
WHEN...
FROM THE GET-GO...
THE MOMENT YOU LOOKED INTO ITACHI'S SHARINGAN, YOU WERE TRAPPED.
UNH!
FZASH
...!
SQUINT...

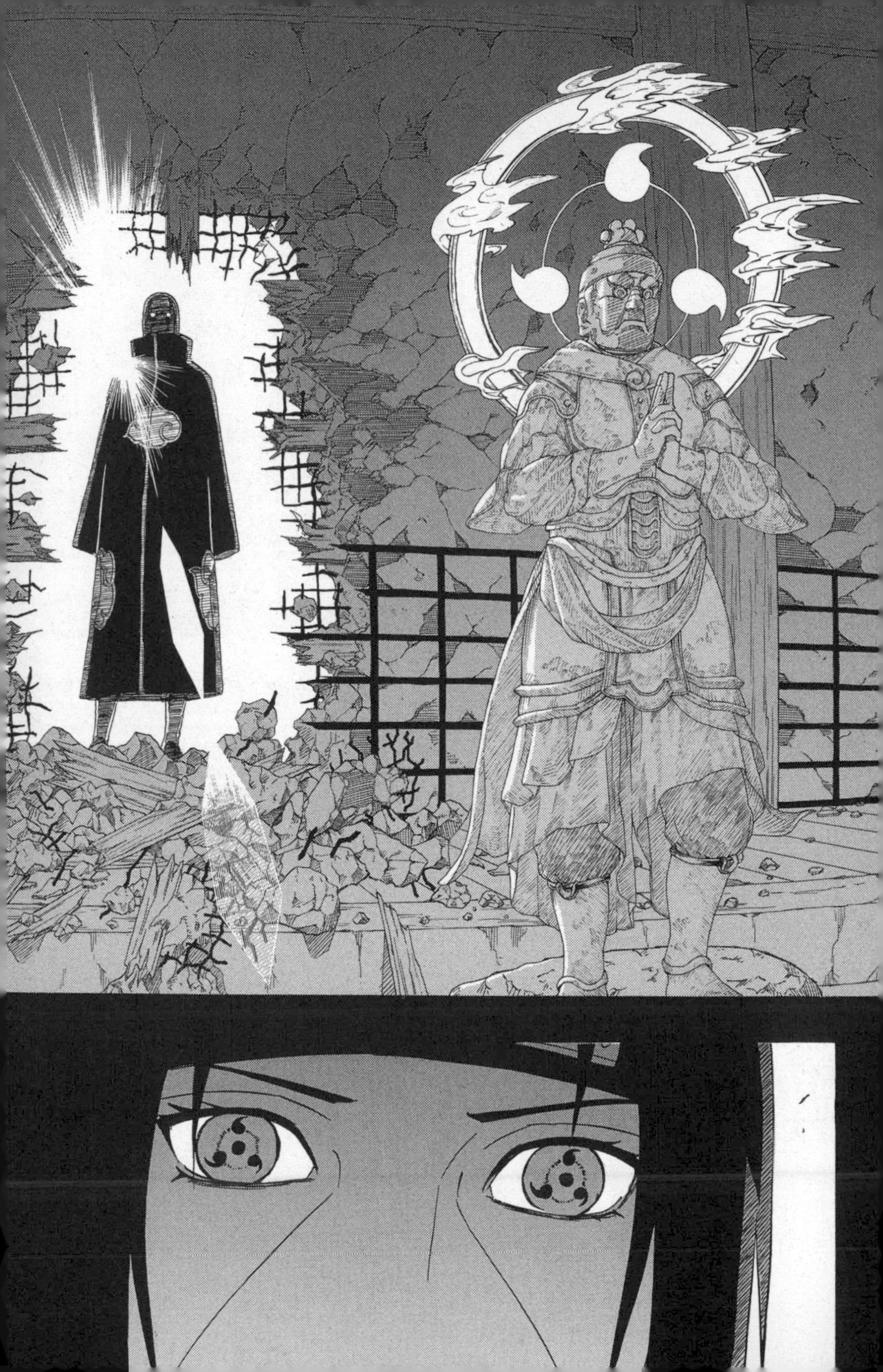

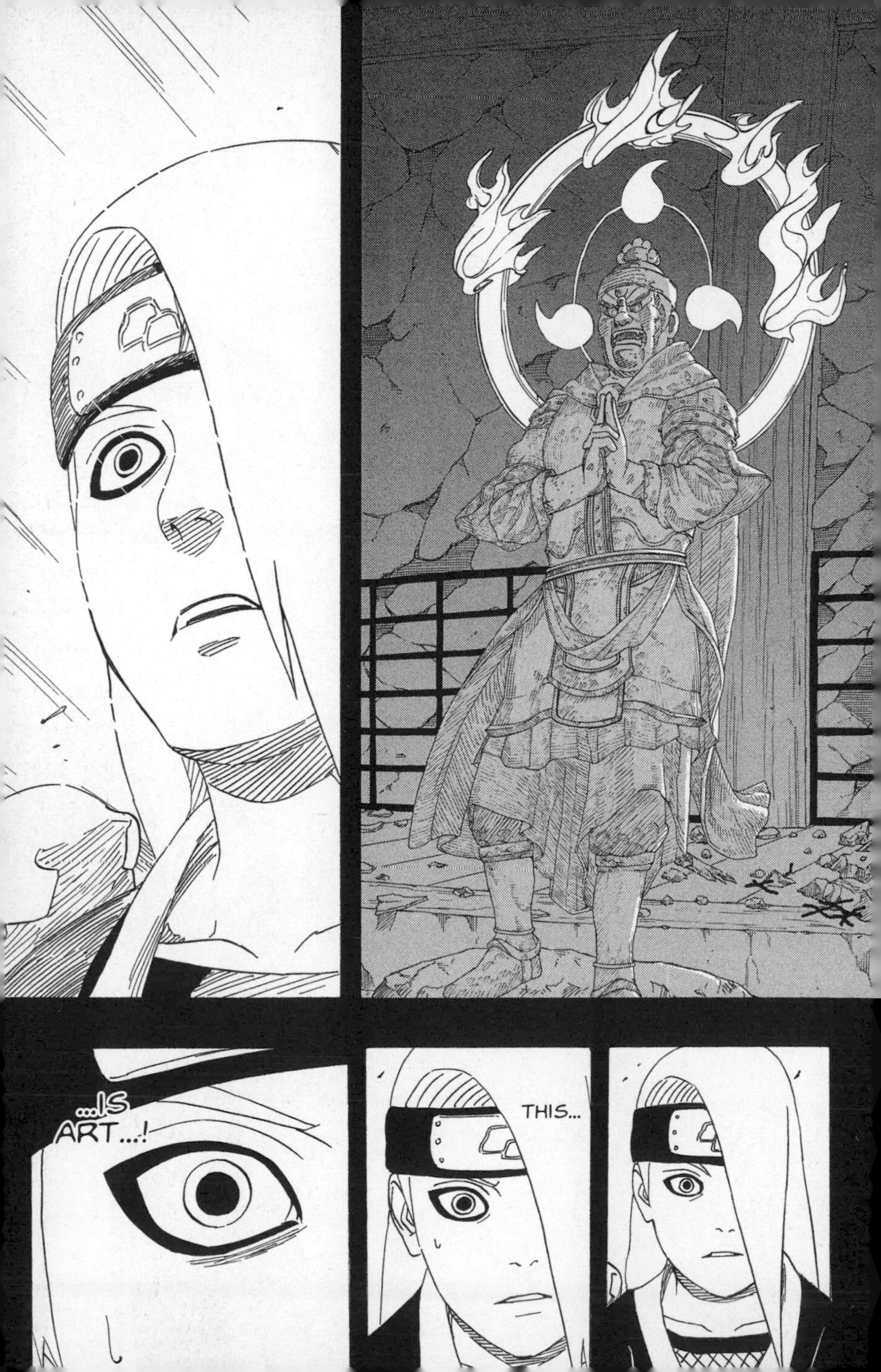
THIS...
...IS ART...!

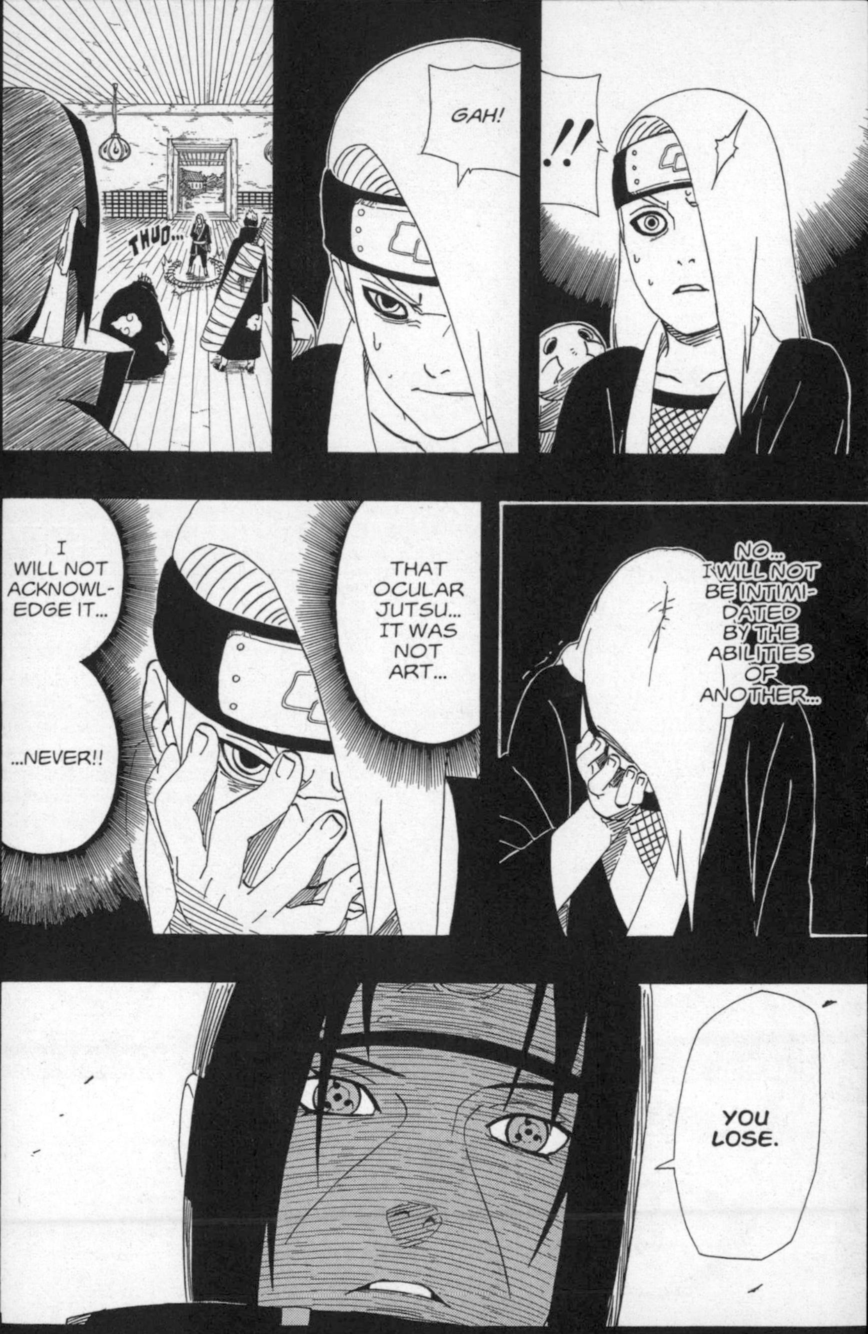
!!
GAH!
THUD...
NO... I WILL NOT BE INTIMIDATED BY THE ABILITIES OF ANOTHER...
THAT OCULAR JUTSU... IT WAS NOT ART...
I WILL NOT ACKNOWLEDGE IT...
...NEVER!!
YOU LOSE.

READ THIS WAY

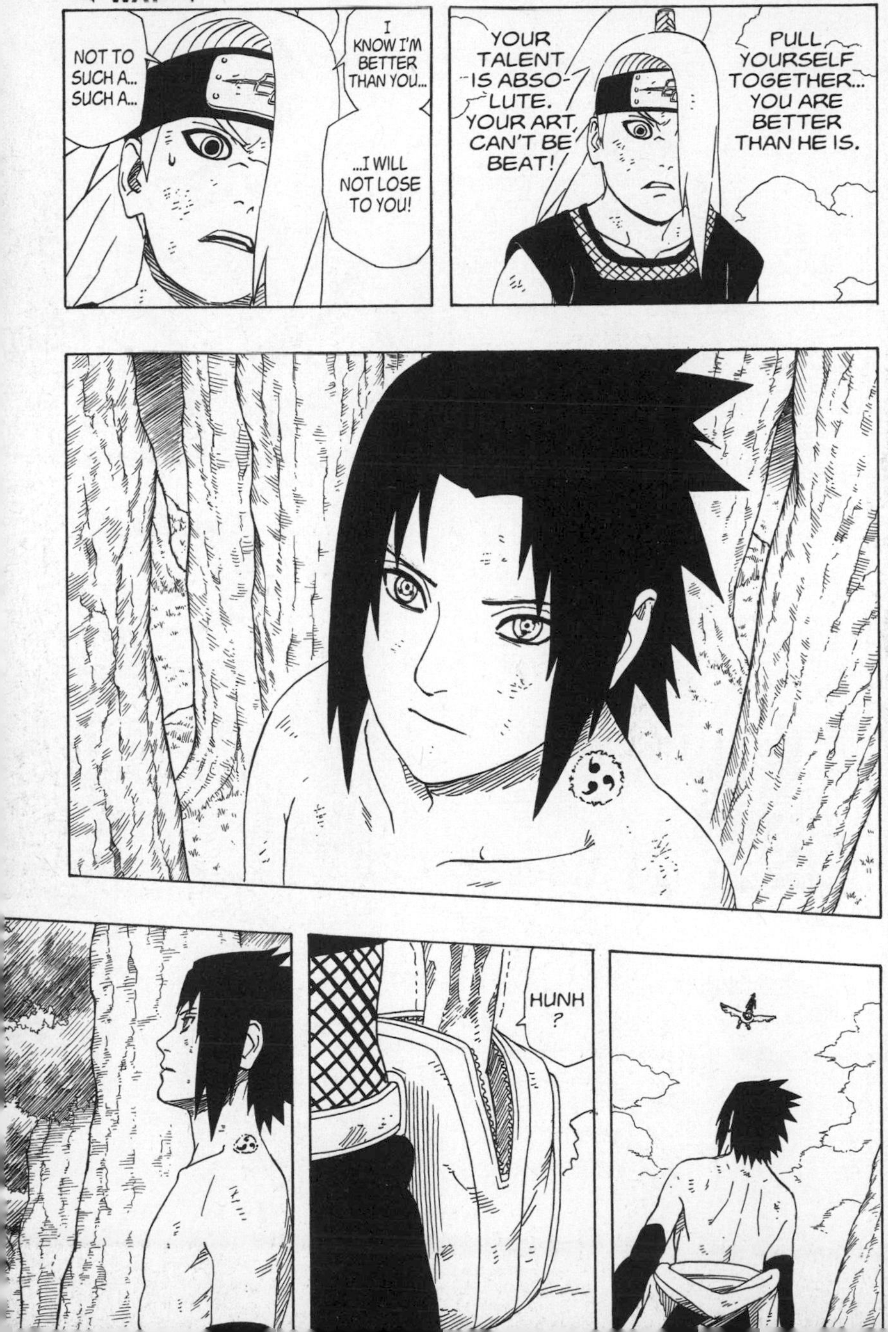
PULL YOURSELF TOGETHER... YOU ARE BETTER THAN HE IS.
YOUR TALENT IS ABSOLUTE. YOUR ART CAN'T BE BEAT!
I KNOW I'M BETTER THAN YOU...
...I WILL NOT LOSE TO YOU!
NOT TO SUCH A... SUCH A...
HUNH ?

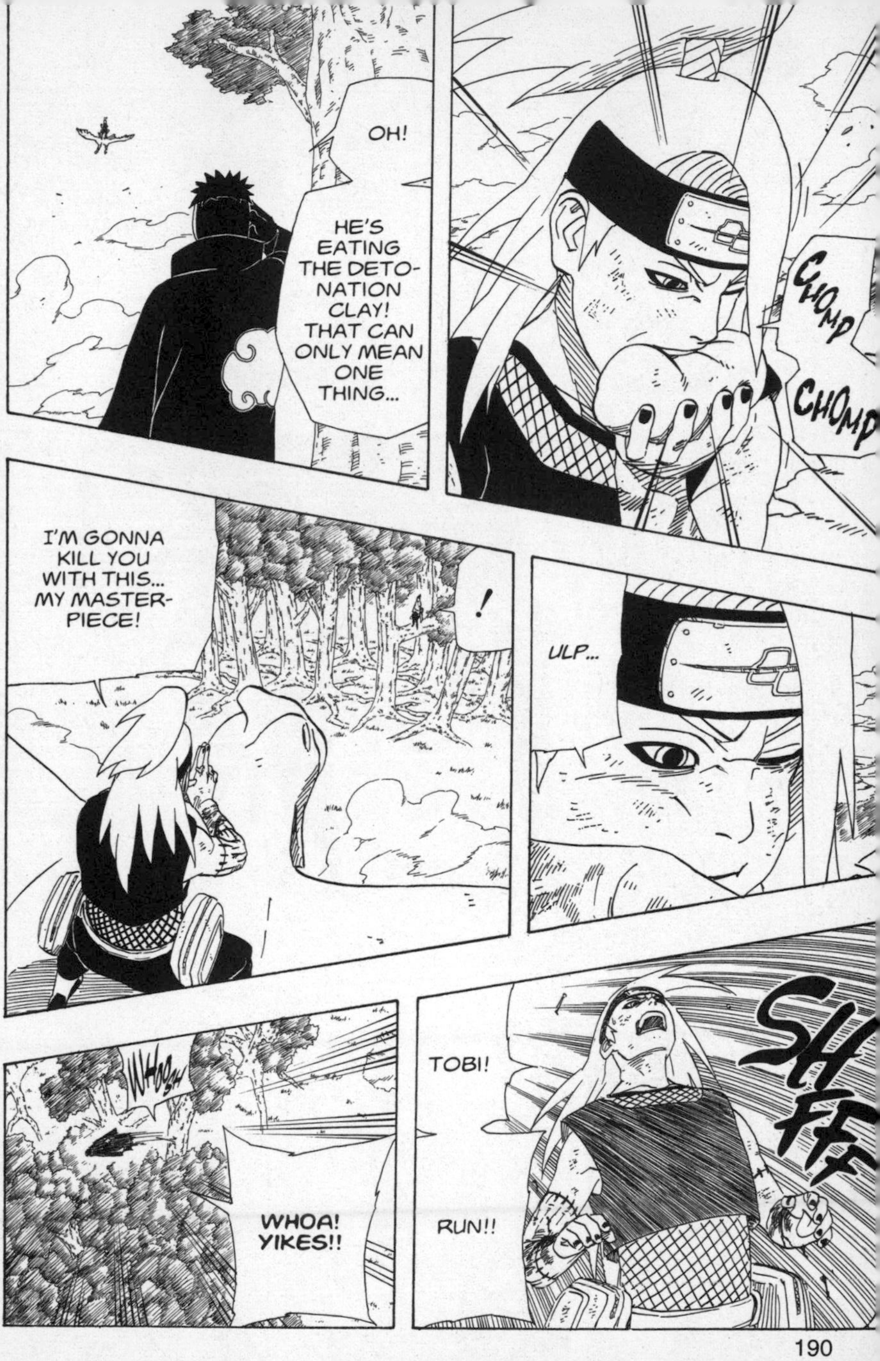
CHOMP
CHOMP
OH!
HE'S EATING THE DETO-NATION CLAY! THAT CAN ONLY MEAN ONE THING...
ULP...
I'M GONNA KILL YOU WITH THIS... MY MASTER-PIECE!
!
SHFFF
TOBI!
RUN!!
WHOOSH
WHOA! YIKES!!

READ THIS WAY

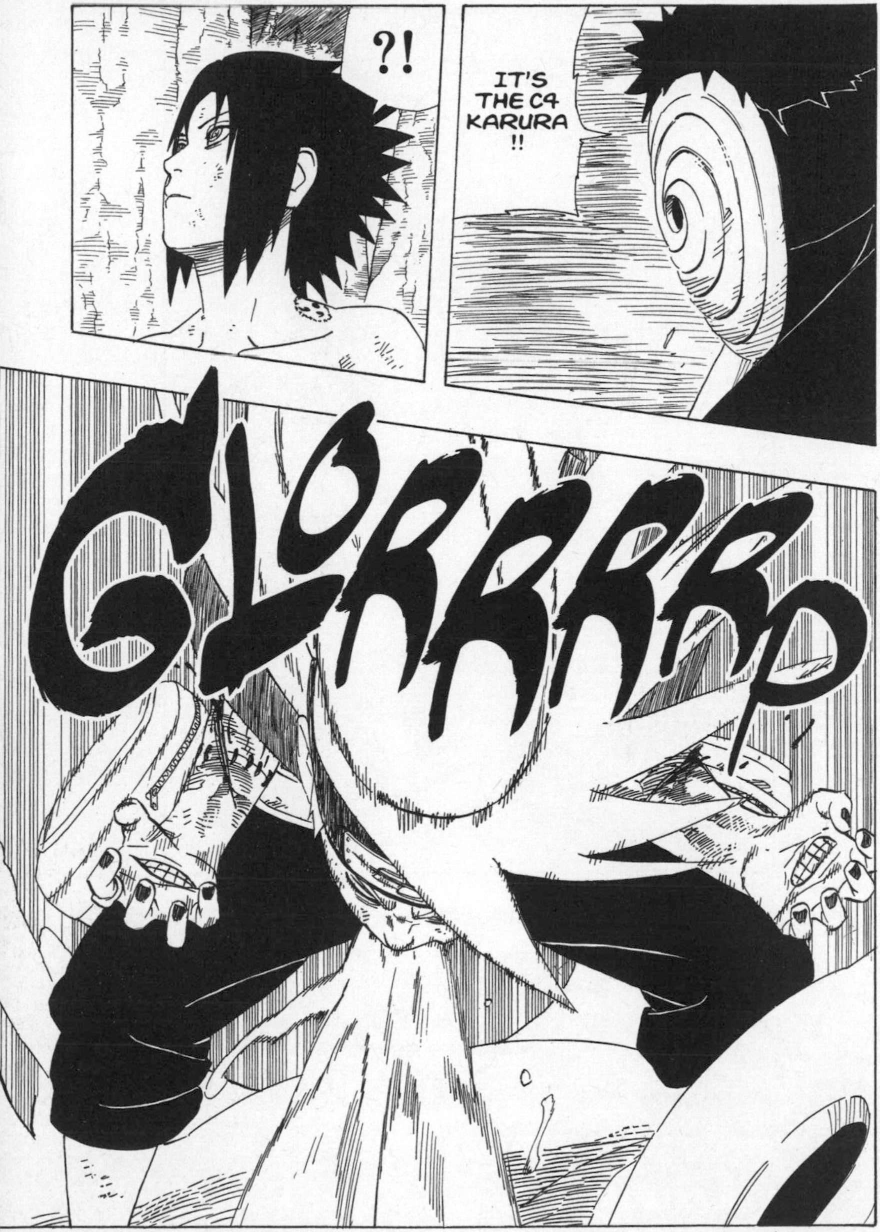
IT'S THE C4 KARURA !!
?!
GLORRRP

 TO BE CONTINUED IN *NARUTO* VOL. 40!

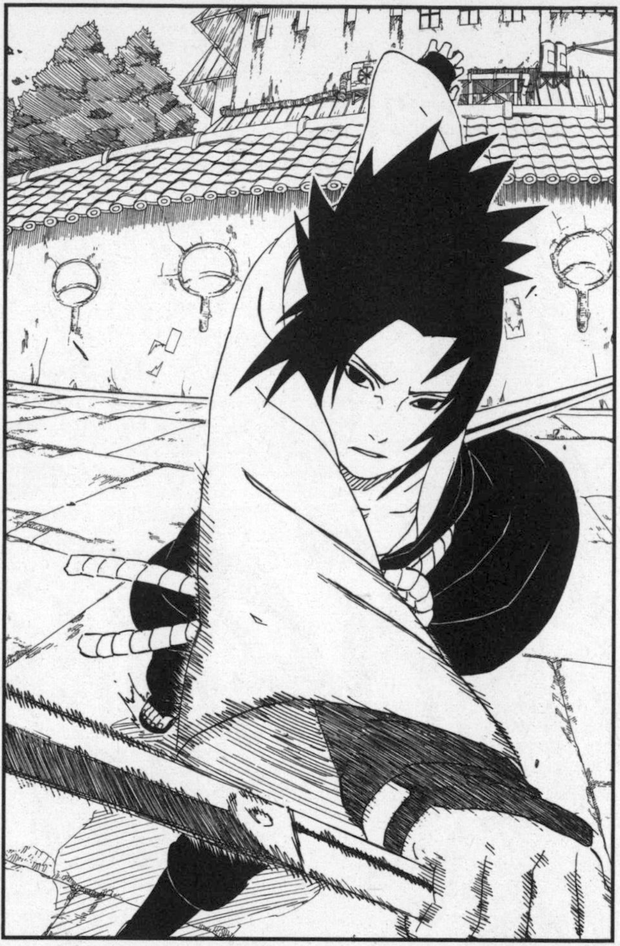

IN THE NEXT VOLUME...

THE ULTIMATE ART!!

It's Deidara vs. Sasuke! Is even Deidara's Ultimate Art no match for the all-powerful new Sasuke? Plus, deep inside the Land of Rain lies a secret of the Akatsuki that sheds doubt on the mysterious organization's true intentions as well as their bizarre leader, Pain

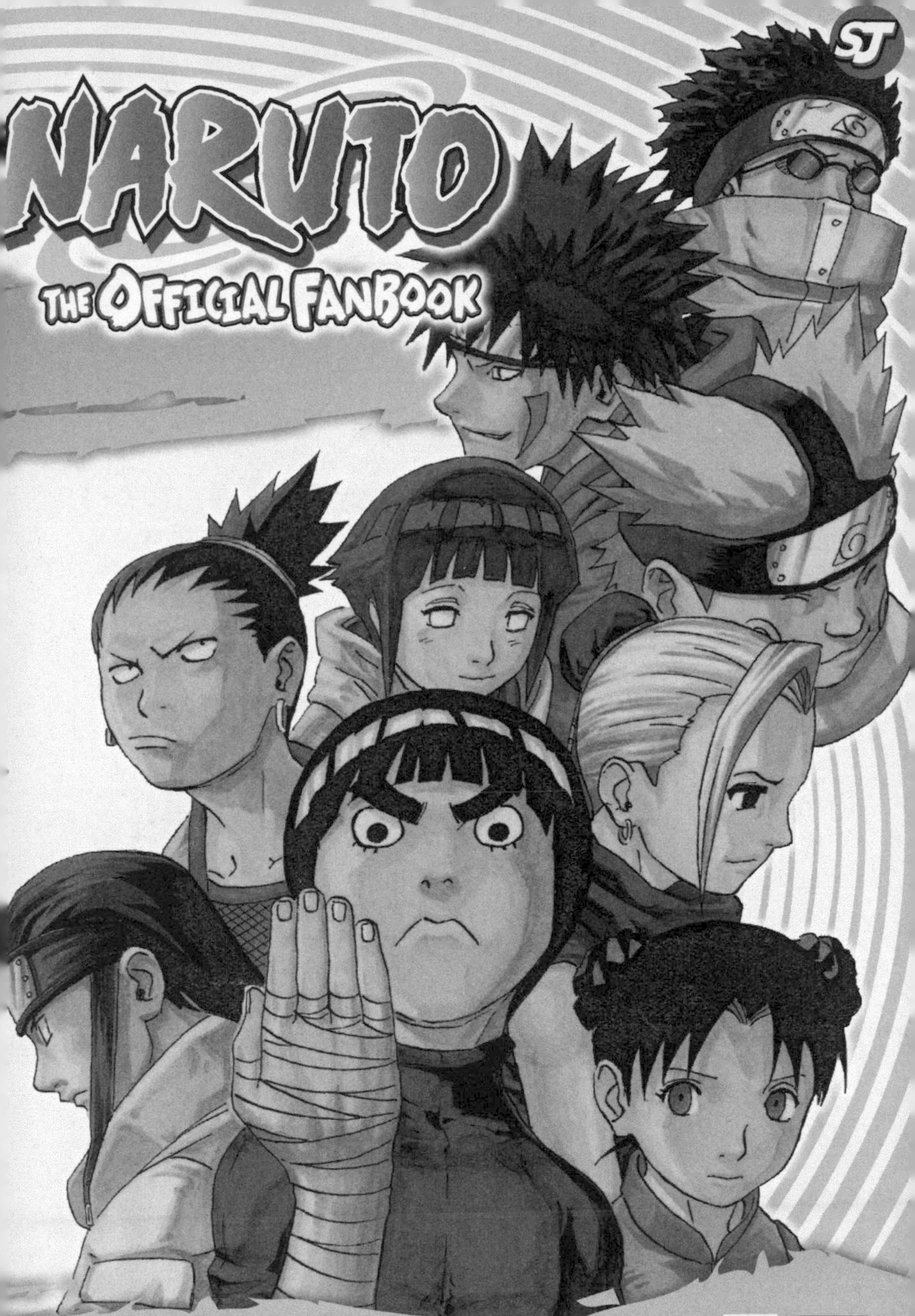
SJ
NARUTO
THE OFFICIAL FANBOOK

ANNUAL MEMBERSHIP*

- ⇢ **48** weekly digital issues
- ⇢ Simultaneous with Japan
- ⇢ **4** *Yu-Gi-Oh!* cards per year
- ⇢ Own all your issues
- ⇢ Special one-shot manga, digital gifts and more!
- ⇢ Available on the Web, iOS, Android and Kindle Fire

GET THE STARTER PACK
OVER **300** PAGES OF **FREE MANGA!**

WE'VE GONE **INTERNATIONAL**!

Monthly subscriptions and single issues now available in the **U.S.**,
Canada, **UK**, **Ireland**, **Australia**, **New Zealand** and **South Africa**
on iOS Newsstand and Android!